Dylan Remembered
Volume Two

For Seren Berry Hurst

Dylan Remembered

Volume Two 1935-1953

Edited by David N. Thomas

Interviews by Colin Edwards
Transcriptions by Joan Miller

seren
in association with
The National Library of Wales

Seren is the book imprint of
Poetry Wales Press Ltd
Nolton Street, Bridgend, Wales
www.seren-books.com

Interviews © The Interviewees and
the National Library of Wales
Editorial, Introduction, Chapters,
Appendix A © David N. Thomas, 2004

First published in 2004
ISBN 1-85411-362-3 hbk
ISBN 1-85411-363-1 pbk
A CIP record for this title is available
from the British Library

The publisher works with the financial
assistance of the Welsh Books Council

Cover image: Sketch by Oloff de Wet, 1951

Printed in Plantin by The Cromwell Press, Ltd, Trowbridge, Wiltshire.

Contents

Part Two Stories and Facts

Appendices

Photographs

Introduction

This is the second volume of *Dylan Remembered*, containing material from tape recorded interviews carried out, mostly in the 1960s, by the radio journalist Colin Edwards. The volume begins in January 1935 with the twenty-year old Dylan in London. He had no literary or other reputation but was determined to make his mark as a writer. Within just four years of his arrival, he had published three collections in Britain and one in America, and, by the outbreak of War, had become one of the best known figures in London's literary and artistic circles.

Several of Colin Edwards' interviewees comment on Dylan's remarkable achievement of so successfully making the transition from Kardomah boy to prince of the pubs and cafés of Fitzrovia. In the 1930s, London was a very long way from Swansea, both geographically and culturally and, in the economic and political circumstances of the time, Dylan's decision to go there may be considered 'heroic', on a par with those who today make the long journey to London from small villages in Pakistan or eastern Europe.

It is well to remember that Dylan had no day job, nor wanted one. He had no private income, nor parents who could afford to send him more than token amounts of money. There were no social security payments to keep him going, nor credit cards nor Arts Council bursaries. Dylan lived from hand-to-mouth by camping on people's floors, and learning how to take money from wealthy acquaintances who saw themselves as patrons of the up-and-going-places:

> When I lived in London a few years ago, in the bedsitting-room with the scribbled card on the door, cultivating a number of voices and obtaining at considerable cost the clap and the itch, first at the bottleparty and last to go, paying for the rent and the kippers on the gas fire with a pound a week from my parents, determined to get there, not knowing where 'there' was but having a very good idea.[1]

He also worked at the writing. Between 1935 and 1939, Dylan completed or revised many of his Notebook poems that were to appear in *Twenty-five Poems* and *The Map of Love*. He also wrote twenty-eight stories that were published in a variety of magazines and journals, and reviewed more than a hundred thrillers and novels, as well as collections of poetry. This was also the time when he made his first radio broadcasts, and started to attract more speaking invitations at clubs and colleges, preparation for which he took seriously:

> About poems: I don't know that I've got anything much good at the moment, but I probably will have by the time I see you. I'm working hard enough but so slowly, & a lot of my time for the last week or two has been spent in preparing a smug paper for the L.C.C. Institute of Education. [2]

During the War years, Dylan helped to make ten propaganda films, and also began in earnest his apprenticeship as a broadcaster at the BBC. From 1940 onwards, he made more than one hundred and fifty radio broadcasts, of which thirty were scripts he himself had written. This extensive programme of work for the BBC involved preparation and studio rehearsals. Those who worked with Dylan at the BBC – Philip Burton, Aneirin Talfan Davies, John Ormond and John Laurie – have commented in their interviews with Edwards on Dylan's reliability and professionalism – as John Arlott did in a *Radio Times* interview: "He was never late, he was never drunk, and he never did a bad job." Douglas Cleverdon said much the same: "In my own BBC experience he was industrious, sober and conscientious during rehearsals."[3]

More such testimonials can be found in the Edwards archive – time and again, his interviewees speak of Dylan's capacity for hard work. Alban Leyshon also told Edwards about Dylan's "enormous respect for work, whether it was his own or anybody else's." This is helpful, because Dylan's attitudes to work have often been obscured by the swirl of colourful stories about Dylan the bohemian, the good-time boy who roared his way through drink, women and life. Certainly, there were periods when he played hard but he was also able, for most of his life, to sustain a remarkable output of poems, stories, radio and film scripts, reviews and radio broadcasts. Dylan also travelled widely in the United Kingdom giving readings and lectures, and judging poetry competitions. There is no record of the number of these events, but *Collected Letters* is a useful source for identifying some of them.

New Quay and Oxfordshire

The four and a half years from September 1944 to May 1949, encompassing New Quay, Oxford and South Leigh, with some key months in between at Blaencwm, Carmarthenshire, were the most productive of Dylan's adult life: eleven poems completed, fifteen radio broadcasts scripted, most of the first half of *Under Milk Wood* drafted and fourteen film scripts hacked out in part or whole. All this was achieved alongside a demanding schedule of radio broadcasts, and the distractions of a four-month holiday in Italy. The major part of the poetic output was done in New Quay, during one of the coldest winters on record. Dylan and family lived in a small wood and asbestos bungalow, called Majoda, that had no water, electricity, indoor privy or privacy.

Paul Ferris wrote that "the bungalow deserves a plaque of its own" (it has one today) whilst FitzGibbon in his biography described the time there as "a second flowering, a period of fertility that recalls the earliest days." This productive period was interrupted, if not halted, when Dylan's friend, William Killick, fired four machine gun bullets into the bungalow. There is no basis for accounts that the bungalow was indiscriminately sprayed, raked or riddled with gunfire. Dylan's claim that Killick fired "many rounds" into the bungalow is an exaggeration. There is nothing in the arresting policeman's notes about bullets passing into Aeronwy's bedroom, or of any being found there – a full account of the incident is given in Thomas 2000 with further details of the policeman's notes in Thomas 2002.

In New Quay and South Leigh, Dylan displayed a remarkable capacity, as he did in Laugharne and Tilty Mill (see p341), to fit in and to get on with local people, adapting easily to the rhythms of village life. He enjoyed the company of locals and their everyday conversation, and took part in community activities. The Edwards interviews confirm the point made by many of his friends and colleagues – here was a naturally shy man, modest and unassuming with little or no sense of self-importance, many of whose happiest hours were spent sitting in country pubs talking with farm workers.

Laugharne and America

Dylan and family moved to the Boat House, Laugharne, in May 1949. The four and a half years to his death in November 1953 were relatively lean years: six poems completed (but they included some of his best), eight radio scripts, two short stories, two articles and thirty-four radio broadcasts. The period was dominated by four trips to America, where he worked extremely hard through an exhausting schedule of poetry readings and lectures that were topped and tailed by lunches, dinners, parties and receptions where he was expected to be "the great poet" and to entertain. Mervyn Levy, a life-long friend, has speculated on the effects of these tours:

> I think it's the misfortune of people who come to be legendary figures that they're turned into legends in their own time. And Dylan suddenly found himself in a legend and had to live up to that legend, particularly when he got to America. The idea of the tremendous, boisterous, wonderful, drunken poet, immaculately funny always, terribly brilliant and clever and amusing and witty and outrageous and daring. This was something that he suddenly found was expected of him; he had to live up to it. And I think this is part of the death of Dylan Thomas. I think in his having to live his legend in his own lifetime are the seeds of his ultimate death, of his doom.[4]

Dylan the Womaniser: More Legend than Leg-Over

In March 2003, the *Daily Mail* ran a story on Dylan describing him as "a sex-obsessed drunk". Such headlines about the "randy drunk" or the "alcoholic womaniser" have followed Dylan since his death and have become part of the public's perception of, and fascination with, the bard of Cwmdonkin Drive. It is helpful to reflect, however, that these descriptions are internally contradictory because, for men, a career of philandering is usually not compatible with a life of heavy drinking, unless libido is extremely strong – and in Dylan's case it apparently was not.

Dylan's reputation as a womaniser derives partly from his own embroidered stories of his American visits handed down, long after his death, from one bar stool to another. The substantial derivation, however, comes from John Malcolm Brinnin's account (1955), particularly of the first visit in 1950. But in his biography, Ferris has trawled through the evidence and concluded that Dylan's supposed lechery amounted to little more than obscene ditties, bum pinching, risqué remarks and lewd propositions, designed largely to enliven dull academic gatherings. This impatience with the ordinariness of social events goes back to Dylan's teenage days when he (and Wynford Vaughan

Thomas) brightened up the Little Theatre evenings with party games and stories – see the Thomas Taig and Ruby Graham interviews in Volume One.

Several other writers, including Tremlett (1993) have also cast doubt on the accuracy of Brinnin's reports, not least because he sometimes comments on events at which he was not present, or relies on Dylan's own stories. Curnow (1982) has described Brinnin's account of Dylan's Harvard engagements (at which Curnow was present but Brinnin was not) as "false" and his book as a whole as ill-balanced and ill-informed. As importantly, there are other testimonies in the Colin Edwards' archive that need to be taken into account to obtain a more rounded understanding of Dylan and women.

In Volume One, those who knew Dylan as a teenager confirm various kinds of boyhood sexual explorations, and then teenage friendships with girls including one, scandalously, with a Woolworth's shop assistant. FitzGibbon, like Robert Pocock, also notes in his interview (p85) that "Dylan had a lot of girls before he met Caitlin" and speculates there were extra-marital flings. Lycett presents a (very short) list of Dylan's wartime girlfriends, suggesting, implausibly, that the War had heightened his libido and made him promiscuous (pp210-211). FitzGibbon more wisely notes that "in the morality that was prevalent in that circle in the Thirties and Forties, physical fidelity was not prized particularly highly" (p85). The War had also brought a general relaxing of moral codes. Even so, Dylan's sexual exploits were insignificant compared with those of some of his friends and contemporaries. How strange, then, to single out the Welshman as a promiscuous deviant and a sexual profligate.

There is nothing in the Edwards interviews to suggest that Dylan was a sexual predator, or that he had a strong sexual appetite. On the contrary, he seems even to have lacked what might be considered a normal and healthy interest in girls. Friends such as Eileen Llewellyn Jones told Edwards that "I don't think there was anybody who was less interested in girls as girls... it never occurred to people to flirt with Dylan because he wasn't that type at all." Frances Morgan made several passes at the young Dylan and, with some difficulty, inveigled him into taking her out: "He wasn't the sort of fellow who wanted to maul you around or anything like that. I don't think he was terribly interested in girls."

The indifference to girls was confirmed by Gwen Bevan Courtney, Bert Trick and Eric Hughes in their interviews in Volume One, as it was by Trevor Hughes, who knew Dylan in both Swansea and London during the 1930s: "when Dylan was young, when I knew him first, he had not the remotest interest in girls." When Dylan first went to bed with Caitlin in 1936 she found him unskilled and shy.[5]

Several interviewees in Volume One thought that Dylan would have made a fine actor but for his physique. Mervyn Levy, something of an expert in these matters, considered physique also counted against Dylan as a lover:

> The idea of Dylan as a great woman man is a little bit ludicrous, because he was not a very attractive person sexually, I wouldn't have thought, and many other women confirmed this in those far off days... I can think of occasions when models didn't want to go to bed with him, and they did with me, let's say. Where they thought Dylan was just a little... you know, puny, asexual sort of person... Dylan would tumble into bed with a woman when he was an acknowledged poet if she'd give him twenty-five pounds the next day. And what she said afterwards about him or his prowess in bed was an entirely different thing, he didn't care about that at all. I think Dylan was very largely sexually incompetent... that it to say, he was not impotent but I don't think he was terribly interested in sex... and I don't know how many American women will jump forward and say "I'm sorry, this isn't true." ' Cause they may not tell you the truth, anyway.[6]

In her interview on page 154, Pamela Hansford Johnson also warns us to be very cautious about the legend of Dylan the womaniser. Edwards asked *Dad's Army* actor John Laurie about Dylan and his reputation as a ladies man. Laurie replied that "I would say that he wasn't very much good at that." By the 1950s, his libido had been lowered even further by alcohol, as he complained to Mervyn Levy: "Dylan used to tell me very often 'I couldn't do anything to anybody most of the time when I've had a lot to drink. What do they expect of me?'"

Oscar Williams has commented on Dylan's American trips that "Dylan never had either the capacity nor the interest to chase women... he was not a Don Juan in any sense of the word" (p219). David Hughes, the family's doctor in Laugharne, confirmed that Dylan was no womaniser, and also drew attention to Dylan's limited libido:

The impression you get from a play like *Under Milk Wood*, is that he might have the odd woman of the village tucked away – the odd mistress or two in the village. But there is no evidence of this at all. Never has been. And in his own environment, he was quite immune from any criticism of this sort... my summing up of Dylan is that he had no great masculinity to spare to go round as a *roué*. I think there's an awful lot in his poetry and in *Under Milk Wood*, which amounts to a sort of over-compensation... as a rule, a man who likes his pint of beer would more readily say "I prefer a pint than a woman."

In his interview with Edwards, Mably Owen also made the telling point that Dylan was very far from being a professional lecher because they "have to be the one thing of all things he wasn't, and that is *calculating*... the essential quality about him is that he was innocent."

Sources outside the Edwards archive offer further confirmation. Dylan's wartime lover, Pamela Glendower, commented that "It wasn't a passionate relationship. I wouldn't say that Dylan was all that highly sexed." Another girlfriend, Ann Meo, found that he was "a disappointing lover".[7]

Anthony Burgess' wife, Lynne, had the same experience, as Burgess himself has pointed out:

Dylan Thomas's sexual appetite was much exaggerated, especially in the United States. During my absence abroad, Lynne technically committed adultery with him a few times, but to go to bed with Dylan was to offer little more than maternal comfort. He was usually too soused to perform and, when not soused, he foresaw his morning guilt and was inhibited. All he really wanted was female warmth and a protective cuddle (1988, p289).

Several passages in Dylan's early letters were homophobic but in later life he dabbled in gay sex with fellow bohemians. As many interviewees make clear, Dylan preferred the company of men. His attitude to women was at best ambivalent – Gaston Berlemont of the French House pub told Edwards that Dylan deliberately insulted women because "his attitude was a love/hate attitude to women. I don't think he ever made up his mind whether he loved them or hated them through loving them."

Dylan's reputation for being offensive towards women was confirmed by Elizabeth Ruby Milton, a dancer with whom Dylan had a long-term "romance but not an affair… we had a completely pure, chaste relationship." She witnessed many of his verbal assaults:

> the women he used to attack were rather precious people, girls who would sit at bars with their knees tightly crossed and in suits, and little hats. He used to attack them. Go up and offer his stud services in the most… four-letter words… now that used to excite the men he was with. He was always with men… I'm not sure he didn't sometimes deliberately try to hurt people in order to break them down. Especially English people… very English people… and the women he insulted were sort of rather English lady types, and the sort of BBC types he was not in sympathy with, and he would provoke them… he was very rude to them in order to provoke them, to get past their guard… that used to amuse him… for a man who professed to hate violence… he was always provoking violence in women. Outraging them (Edwards interview).

Dylan was more of a pest than a predator, a play-acting Priapus whose interest in sex, and capacity for it, have been greatly exaggerated. Dylan's behaviour with *some* women in *some* circumstances was often juvenile and sometimes unpleasant but the Edwards interviews demonstrate that there was another Dylan – sensitive, kind, charming, attentive and gracious. There is a puzzle here that needs further thought.

The Drinking

It is not unusual in Wales to hear people remark that Dylan Thomas was "buried in Laugharne and crucified in Fleet Street". Within months of the funeral, his reputation was being shredded, and the caricature of Dylan the drunken, cadging buffoon was being defined. One of the achievements of Edwards' interviews is that they provide more than sufficient material to arrive at a more thoughtful judgement about Dylan's drinking.

Even when we discount for Edwards' own anti-Brinnin agenda, and for selective and partial recall by his interviewees, the clear and strong consensus is that Dylan's drinking was often more moderate, and more complex, than the legend would have us believe. It seems that the question of "the drinking" is best considered in four phases:

– *teenage experimentation*, sometimes of extremes that involved beer, gin and other spirits though, on the whole, lack of funds precluded much drinking. This experimentation was allied to a great curiosity about the people and life of Swansea's docklands, and the coalmining villages in its hinterland.

– *bohemian excess* in the period from 1934-37, when funds allowed it. Heavy drinking was an accepted part of literary and artistic life in London and for Dylan alcohol was a way of overcoming his natural shyness. Beer was still his main drink.

– *adult restraint* in the period between his marriage in 1937 and his first American trip in 1950, when the combined effects of a happy marriage, a blossoming literary career, long periods away from London and wartime restrictions substantially reduced his consumption of alcohol. As Ferris pithily put it about Dylan's time in South Leigh: "He was no village drunk".

– *sorrow drowning* in the last three years of his life, when increased alcohol consumption was associated with a crumbling marriage, worries about declining creative powers, money and tax problems, and the strains caused by the rigours of four American lecture tours. His consumption of spirits increased when he was in America and the strain of being constantly "on show" often resulted in boisterous, and sometimes outrageous, behaviour. This behaviour became both more newsworthy and prone to exaggeration because Dylan was by now a well-known public figure. Even in this period, interviewees report quiet phases of beer drinking in Laugharne, as well as periods of abstinence, particularly when he was working on a piece of writing. [8]

Binges and benders there certainly were. Dylan had been drinking since his teenage days, and there is no doubt that he often drank to excess – both his notes from St Stephen's hospital and his post-mortem report clearly reveal the effect on his body of a lifetime's drinking. But there is a consensus through the Edwards interviews that Dylan "was a drinker but not a drunkard". He was not seen as an alcoholic, as that word is commonly understood, because of his periods of abstinence, displays of moderation, and his preference for beer over wine and spirits.

If Dylan was addicted to anything, then it was to the atmosphere of pubs and company. He appreciated the taste of good beer, and he enjoyed being with 'ordinary' people – he was a public bar drinker who "wasn't very fond of the satins and silks". Many of the interviews in this volume show that what drew Dylan to pubs and to parties was the quest for good talk, as Oscar Williams describes on page 216:

> He rarely ate and never slept and, oddly enough, my opinion is he never really drank the way we understand it in America. He was not a drunkard. He drank beer, and drank it very slowly, and he drank it only to keep the conversation going. As long there was conversation there was beer, and as long as there was beer there was conversation.

The Edwards interviews also show that Dylan liked pubs where there was something out of the ordinary about the landlord: cosmopolitan and worldly-wise Gaston Berlement at the French House; Jack Patrick at the Black Lion in New Quay, extremely well-read and interested in the arts, as was Mrs Giles at the Singleton Hotel in Swansea; Thomas Vaughan at the Vale of Aeron, near Talsarn, a knowledgeable and accomplished conversationalist; Albert Hopkins at the Mason Arms, South Leigh, with a passion for cricket and a wife who ran a local drama group; and Sean Treacy at the King's Arms, Chelsea, a budding writer and later a novelist.[9]

Several of Edwards' interviewees attempt 'psychological' explanations of Dylan's drinking, including references to his shyness, his need for company, and his dislike of being alone. Gwen Watkins' wise words on this matter are echoed by many interviewees throughout the Edwards archive:

> The poet drank very little, and needed to drink not at all; writing, reading or talking about poetry, he could make do with a glass of water if nothing else was to hand. The child, on the other hand, needed constant oral gratification; sweets or pop would do as well as beer. If he was at ease in his company, liked and admired (not flattered), he rarely seemed to drink to excess, and certainly he never showed in these circumstances the uneasy urgency of the true alcoholic for more and stronger drink. I remember him spending a whole evening with Vernon and Alfred Janes, reading and discussing the first draft of his Bank Holiday script, on a single bottle of beer. But any pressure, any anxiety, any uncertainty – and respites from all of these were rare in Dylan's life – drove him to alcohol as a child turns to its mother's breast for comfort (1983).

Sponging on the Brain

The popular stories about Dylan the Drinker are inevitably bound up with the legends about Dylan the Cadger, as they were for Philip Toynbee in his *Observer* review of FitzGibbon's book on October 17 1965. It is quite clear that Dylan had no compunction in taking the money, and sometimes the possessions, of those he thought could afford it. But the evidence in the interviews – see the Index – from friends and colleagues was that money borrowed by Dylan from them was usually returned, though often late, and more than matched by his generosity when he was in funds. The interviews from Laugharne and South Leigh also tell of a Dylan who seldom cadged from local people and who endeavoured to settle his debts in the local shops – even returning to South Leigh in 1951 to pay his 1947-49 newspaper bills – see Note 40.

Other testimonies on these matters are also available, such as that of Laugharne JP and art collector, Phyllis Bowen, who lived in Castle House:

> I knew him for roughly six years… I never saw any signs of drunkenness or quarrelsomeness or cadging for money, and I found him to be extremely modest… He never caused any sort of row or disturbance that I heard of in Laugharne – he lived a very quiet life indeed (2002, pp153, 160).

Under Milk Wood

Some Edwards interviews in this later period contribute further information about *Under Milk Wood*. Several interviewees suggest the inspiration behind some of the names in the play. Jane Dark describes how she told Dylan about Rosie Probert, a resident of Horsepool Road, Laugharne, and explains how Duck Lane got its name.[10] Dosh Murray suggests, perhaps implausibly, that the name Probert came from Harry Proberts, a South Leigh cowman. Harry Locke claims he was the basis of Nogood Boyo, and that his wife, Cordelia, was Mrs Dai Bread Two. And Edna Morgan Dark reveals all about Little Willy Wee:

> One evening, Dylan came to our cottage… and this little cat came along and I said "Oh, Willy Wee, stop jumping on Dylan!" He said "What did you call her?" "Willy Wee," I said… he didn't say

anything more about it at the time, and he came again a few weeks later and he said "Where's Willy Wee, Edna?" And I said "Willy Wee's dead". And he said "Oh" and he brought out his little Woodbine packet and he wrote something down. So I didn't think anything more about it, until we heard *Under Milk Wood* – as everybody knows "Little Willy Wee is dead, dead, dead". And I said "Jackie, that's our Willy Wee!"

Not surprisingly, it is Captain Cat that attracts most of the interest of the Laugharne interviewees, though there is no agreement between them as to which Laugharne character, if any, was the inspiration for the blind sea captain. There is more on Captain Cat and *Under Milk Wood* in chapters 2 and 3.

Paraclete Days

Whilst volume two was in preparation, two new tapes were discovered in the Edwards archive. These were of an interview with Avril Fisher and Gwyneth Bell of Newton, Swansea, who were both childhood friends of Dylan and parishioners at Paraclete, the chapel of the Rev. David Rees, the husband of Dylan's aunt, Theodosia. The interview adds to the material about Rees, and Theodosia, that was presented in chapter three of Volume One. Fisher and Bell described Rees as a popular minister:

> He was a father figure, I would say, to all of us. He was rather on the short side dark, and a very cheerful face. Everybody loved David Rees... oh, he was a wonderful minister, he really was.

Not surprisingly, chapel services were "packed every Sunday" and on "anniversaries and special occasions we had to put forms down the aisles." Rees preached in English, and was particularly effective in using his botanical knowledge to make his sermons of interest to children: "He was a wonderful naturalist... he knew every weed and always wonderful children's sermons we'd have – everything was applicable either to fruit or flowers."

Fisher and Bell also describe Dylan's holidays with David and Theodosia Rees ("she had a lovely face and a lovely smile, and always very pleasant. She was an admirable minister's wife... she was always a perfect lady.") Dylan's boyhood contacts with the Reeses seem to have been more extensive than previously appreciated, and started from the age of four or five:

> He'd stay for perhaps three weeks or a month there... he'd stay
> here often, alone with them over there. And there wouldn't be his
> sister or mother or father. He'd often be there alone... I can always
> remember him sitting at the side with his aunt Dosie... the left-
> hand pew. Because they always sat up the top of the left-hand
> pew... he was always very mischievous, but I would say that he was
> very, very feeling, very sympathetic... he used to amuse me a lot.
> He was very, very witty... and when he spoke, there was just that
> little lisp... I know as a younger child, Mr Rees would love having
> him there and he'd relate to us the latest poem or whatever...

According to Pamela Glendower, Dylan "had a thing about aunts",
hardly surprising given the time he spent with them while he was a boy
and teenager. The material about Dylan's stays with David and
Theodosia Rees helps us better to understand the importance of his
mother's extended family in his upbringing. The young Dylan stayed
not just with the Reeses but also with his aunts and uncles on the
family farms in Llangain, as described in Volume One. These were
frequent and extended holidays, especially before Dylan had started
grammar school, and Dylan was often there without his parents. It is
highly likely, too, that Dylan would have spent time staying down in St
Thomas with his aunt Polly and uncle Bob before they moved to
Blaencwm – as Alban Leyshon indicates in his interview:

> Dylan, through having a fantastic memory, seemed to know as
> much about St Thomas as I ever did... he was able, with exquisite
> politeness, to talk to my mother endlessly about old ladies she
> knew. He could even describe the wallpaper from their living
> rooms and say how many pictures were in the passageways of their
> small houses.

Boy, Manse and Gentry

David Rees was not the only minister in Dylan's family. His maternal
uncle, Thomas, was also a minister, as was Dylan's great-uncle,
Gwilym Marles. Dylan's grandfather, George Williams, was a deacon
at Canaan chapel. There was even an Anglican priest in the family, and
a gent to boot. The Rev. Thomas (Mansel) Edward Gwyn (sometimes
Gwynn) was Dylan's maternal first cousin – he was the son of
Florence's half-sister, Anne.

In October 1891, Anne had married John Gwyn of Plas Cwrt Hir (Cwrthyr), the son of William Edward Bevan Gwyn ("Landed Proprietor") and his wife, Ann. Lying just south of Llangain, Cwrt Hir was a "delightfully situate" six-bedroomed gentleman's residence, though the whole estate – 70 acres – was comparatively small. It stood in "the midst of a Shrubbery and Pleasure Ground", with kitchen garden and tennis court.

Marrying John was a real catch for Anne because the Gwyns were proper gentry, an important family "of ancient lineage" in the county who had previously lived in Pilroath on the estuary. Yet the marriage is also another pointer to the standing of the Llangain Williamses – they were just ordinary farmers, not gentleman farmers like the Gwyns, but the Williamses and their relations worked sufficient acreage (almost a thousand acres) to be taken notice of.

There were probably many Williamses who were delighted to have gentry in the family, particularly Dylan's aunt Polly with her airs and graces and ambitions to live a genteel life as a country woman of independent means. There must have been even more joy at the arrival of John and Anne's first child, Thomas, born on May 7 1892, twenty-two years before his first cousin Dylan. But soon there was tragedy, for John Gwyn died a year later in June 1893. Anne remarried, this time to Robert Williams, and brought up Thomas at Rose Cottage, Llansteffan, along with the two children, Doris and William, she had with Robert Williams.

The young Thomas Gwyn was educated at Carmarthen Grammar School and St. David's University College, Lampeter. His calling to the ministry took him first to Shropshire and then to London where he was ordained in St Paul's Cathedral in June 1915. He became curate at St. Jude's, Bethnal Green, where he became known as "a very well read man and a wonderful preacher." His obituary also notes that "by sheer force of character he had become a powerful extempore preacher and an effective and convincing open-air speaker."

After a winter's hard work amongst the poor of Bethnal Green, Thomas became ill. He came home to Rose Cottage to be nursed by his mother but he died there of TB on April 14 1916. The social ambitions of the Williamses were now at an end as far as the Gwyns were concerned. Still, they turned out in force for the funeral, the report of which lists those who came from Maesgwyn, Llwyngwyn and Pentowyn, as well as Jim and Annie Jones from Fernhill. Thomas Gwyn's half sister was also there, the fourteen year old Doris who later married Randolph Fulleylove.

The following year, on August 3 1917, Doris' brother, William died in a bathing accident at, strangely, Gravel Gwyn, Llansteffan. His mother, Anne, was told about the tragedy as she was travelling back from the funeral in Llandyfaelog of her own mother, Amy, who had died on July 30. It was the pull of the current off Gravel Gwyn that had done for William, and it was the pull of the Gwyns that determined his funeral arrangements – he was buried alongside his half-brother Thomas in the Gwyn family graves in Llangain churchyard. Within just fifteen months, Anne had lost two sons and her mother, a scale of family bereavement that would be repeated some thirty-six years later when her half-sister, Florence, lost two children and her husband within months of each other.

It was literally the end of the line when the Rev. Thomas Gwyn died from TB in 1916, and Cwrt Hir was eventually put up for auction in June 1919, about the time that Dylan started holidaying at Rose Cottage with his aunt Anne and cousin Doris. When Anne died in May 1922, Doris and her father Robert Williams were content that Anne should also be buried in Llangain, next to her first husband, John Gwyn.[11]

Dylan's Religious Beliefs

Throughout his life, Dylan continued to enjoy friendships with men of the cloth. Not just Leon Atkin, but also the vicar at South Leigh (see p126) and the vicar at Laugharne, Canon S.B. Williams, whom Dylan appears to have consulted on spiritual matters. And the day before he left Carmarthenshire on his final trip to America, he and his mother took tea with the Rev. Hopkin Evans, at the manse in Llansteffan.[12]

Several interviewees discuss Dylan and the matter of religious belief. In his interview, Aneirin Talfan Davies comments "that, in some intuitive way, he arrived at the same place as, say, a Roman Catholic had arrived." Intriguingly, Nellie Jenkins, the district nurse in Laugharne, told Edwards that Dylan "wasn't a Catholic, but he was very inclined that way" and that an Irish priest had heard that Dylan had written "a lot of beautiful poems about Our Lady", which he travelled to Laugharne to see. Dylan's February 1933 letter to Trevor Hughes is interesting in this context:

(One day I may turn Catholic, but not yet)... you may think this philosophy – only, in fact, a very slight adaptation of the Roman Catholic religion – strange for me to believe in. I have always believed in it. My poems rarely contain any of it. That is why they are not satisfactory to me. Most of them are the outer poems.

Ivy Williams of Brown's Hotel, Laugharne, took a very different view on Dylan and religion: "He was very conventional. And all the children were christened and all the children went to church. He really and truly was a Welsh Baptist at heart." And Dylan himself gave his religion as "non-conformist" when he was admitted to St Stephen's hospital in 1946 – see chapter one.

A Birth, Two Marriages and a Pickle

In his *New Life* first published in hardback in 2003, Andrew Lycett writes well about Dylan's family background and provides some interesting pieces of new information. He tells us that 5, Cwmdonkin Drive had been named Glanrhyd after Glan-rhyd-y-gwiail, the farm of DJ's grandfather, providing a striking indication of the strength of DJ's feelings about his Brechfa family background.

I had not been able to find anything on D.J. Thomas' uncle, Thomas Thomas, but Lycett notes that Thomas became the manager of the National Provincial bank in Aldersgate, London. Whilst his *New Life* wrongly gives Thomas' birth as 1837, Lycett is now able to confirm that it was September 13 1851. Thomas Thomas lived in Finchley with his wife, Emily Jane. He was evidently a prosperous man – on his death, his estate was £9,453.[13]

Some readers may have been puzzled by the discrepancies between the family tree I presented in Volume One of *Dylan Remembered*, and that given by Lycett, who seems not to have checked the data he collected against birth certificates and other records. His account highlights the need to verify genealogical data found in the Edwards archive at the National Library of Wales. Since Lycett acknowledges his use of Edwards' material, it would be unfortunate if his failure to verify brought the archive itself into disrepute, or made readers hesitant about the reliability of family data in Volume One of *Dylan Remembered*.

I have discussed these matters with Lycett, and provided copies of some of the birth and marriage certificates I have gathered, so there is every chance that there will be corrections in future editions of his *New Life*, including the paperback. But there is always the possibility that many readers, especially those using libraries, will consult only the 2003 hardback. For this reason, I list below some inaccuracies that I have identified in Lycett's family data – I hope this will be of value both to my readers and his.

Lycett's material on Dylan's grandfather, George Williams, is largely incorrect. He gets George's date of birth wrong, as well as his parents, who were not, as Lycett portrays in his family tree, Benjamin and Elizabeth Williams. George's father was a farm labourer called George Williams, as George Junior's wedding certificate shows – see also Note 43 in Volume One of *Dylan Remembered*. Nor was George Junior working at Waunfwlchan farm when he met his future wife Anna – he was almost certainly a labourer at Pilroath, for the marriage certificate shows that he was living there.

On page 45 of his book, Lycett indicates he is aware of the story, as he puts it, that George Williams Junior had fathered a love child, Anne, by his wife's sister, Amy Williams of Waunfwlchan. But in his family tree he has a David Jones as Anne's father. Lycett writes that Amy and David had been having an affair and that they did not marry at the time of Anne's birth because David was already married. This is wrong on two counts. David Jones was only 12 at the time of Anne's birth; and when he married Amy in 1882 at the age of 28 he was a bachelor, as the wedding certificate shows.

Lycett also seems to have overlooked the testimony of Anne's daughter, Doris Fulleylove, for he does not mention it in his text or notes. In her interview with Colin Edwards, Doris said "Dylan was my cousin, mother and Dylan's mother Auntie Florrie being sisters." Off tape, she told Edwards that George Williams, Florence's father, was also the father of her mother, Anne. Edwards recorded this information in one of his notebooks that are in the archive in the National Library.

The facts about Amy's married life are relatively straightforward. Following the incident with George Williams, their daughter, Anne, was born in January 1866. Three years later, on February 16 1869, Amy married Herbert Jones from the parish of Llandyfaelog. The Edwards archive describes him a publican but at the time of the marriage he was a farmer. It was only after Herbert Jones' death that Amy married David Jones, a Ferryside master mariner, on May 7 1882.

Lycett is also wrong in his hardback about the birth date of Dylan's mother, Florence, as well as those of her siblings Polly and David George, her uncles Evan and William, and her nephew Idris Jones. I have the certificates for these births, except Evan's which I could not trace. However, he is shown, aged 3, in the 1841 census return for Waunfwlchan and could not have been born, as Lycett has it, in 1842. Lycett also makes other mistakes about the Thomas and Williams families which are detailed in the following Note.[14]

Once Below an Oversight

Reviewing my research notes for this book, I saw that in preparing Volume One I had overlooked some useful details about George and Anna Williams' keen ambition to improve their lot after leaving Llangain. The first child to be born in Swansea to George and Anna was Polly, in February 1867. Her birth certificate shows the family living in Fullers Terrace, Swansea (no number given), and that George was a porter on the railways. But by the time of Theodosia's birth in 1869, the family had moved to Lucknow Street, St Thomas, and George was now a railway guard. At the 1871 census, the family were at 29, Delhi Street and George was still a guard, as he was at the time of Sarah Jane's birth the following year. But when David was born in April 1874, George had already been promoted to railway foreman. He was still a foreman at William's birth in 1877, but by the time of the 1881 census he was an Inspector with the GWR.

Sometime after 1884, George succeeded W.H. Mabbett as Shipping Inspector at the South Dock. By 1901, he was Shipping Inspector of both South Dock and Prince of Wales Dock (Kelly's Directories), and by the time of his retirement in 1905 he had attained the post of Chief Shipping Inspector.

In Volume One, I omitted the full birth details of Florence's brother, David George. They were April 11 1874.

Carreghollt, the home of D.J. Thomas' sister, Jane Ann, was in Llanon, a few miles south of Cross Hands. A newly-found Edwards notebook gives the address of her daughters, Minnie and Dilys, as 37, Severn Road, Weston-super-Mare.

Brinley Edwards was mistaken that Marjorie Owen was either the mother or grandmother of Ken Owen of Port Talbot. She was certainly a relative of either Florence or DJ (as funeral reports show) and may have been Ken Owen's aunt. The relationship between Florence and

D.J. Thomas and Ken and Hettie Owen appears to have been very close. Not only did the Owens stay for part of the 1939-45 war at Blaencwm, but Florence also stayed with the Owens in Port Talbot for some period during her last years. Letters from Florence to Hettie also convey a close and affectionate family relationship – Florence's letters greet Hettie as "My Darling" and she signs them as "Mam" or "Mummie".[15]

The "unknown couple" standing between Arthur Thomas and Florence Thomas in the Poplars family photograph is Arthur and DJ's brother, William Thomas with his wife.[16]

Some readers of Volume One have kindly pointed out that the "unknown woman" on the right of the photograph on page 218 may be Sarah Evans of Maesgwyn, another photograph of whom appears on page 205.

Transcriptions

Joan Miller's transcriptions of Colin Edwards' interviews have only now (2004) been placed in the National Library of Wales. The transcriptions have not previously been available to researchers and biographers, who have had to manage as best they could by listening to the tapes, a mammoth task not completed by any biographer to date. Hard copy transcriptions will now make investigation a good deal easier.

David Thomas
Ciliau Aeron

Dylan Remembered Volume One 1914-1934 was published by Seren in November 2003. It includes a brief biography of Colin Edwards, as well as a list of those he interviewed. The first volume also contains material on Dylan's family tree, together with accounts of life at Blaencwm, the Fernhill hangman and Dylan's acting career.

Part One: The Memories

1935-1945
"Slightly drunk, slightly dirty, slightly wicked, slightly crazed."

Dylan, Fred Janes and Mervyn Levy "ring the bells of London and paint it like a tart." Dylan networks with the great, the artistic and the literary. His poems and stories appear in more than twenty literary magazines and papers, and he publishes *Twenty-five Poems*. He holidays in Derbyshire and Ireland, marries Caitlin Macnamara in Cornwall, and Llewelyn is born in Hampshire. "Money and property I should like," he tells Henry Treece, "but my life's set now towards not getting them." War breaks out. *The World I Breathe* is published in America, and *The Map of Love* and *Portrait of the Artist as a Young Dog* in London. He writes *Adventures in the Skin Trade* and co-authors the satirical novel, *The Death of the King's Canary*, but the poems largely dry up after 1941. He escapes military service, joins the Ministry of Information and lives in Laugharne, Blashford, Marshfield, Bosham, Hedgerley Dean, Bishopston and Talsarn, at several addresses in London, and in many pubs, hotels and guest houses as he travels the country making propaganda films. As German bombs fall, Swansea is flattened, Aeronwy is born and his parents evacuate to Blaencwm in Carmarthenshire. In 1944-45, he stays in Blaencwm and New Quay – living conditions are difficult but the Muse returns in both places, especially at New Quay where *Under Milk Wood* is begun.

Fred Janes

I remember distinctly meeting Dylan for the first time in the house of Dan Jones. This would have been somewhere round about 1931. I was already a student at the Royal Academy Schools in London, and spent a great deal of my time when home on holiday in Swansea with Dylan, who had a very great interest in painting and, of course, in poetry, as well as in music. Dan's house was quite a kind of centre for several of us who were interested in the same sort of things... I do know that Dylan and Dan worked together a lot in the very early days, probably before I'd met them, on writing poems jointly, line for line, and so on.

... we all used to play together, instruments of various kinds... we used to call these efforts 'Percys', playing Percy, where we would all play various instruments together, may all be playing on the piano together or with the violin, or even the coal scuttle, something like that, a sort of timpani effect...

... I [came] to London with three others who went to the Royal College of Art – Kenneth Hancock, who is now the Principal of Swansea College of Art, and Ifor Thomas and there's

1. Fred Janes and Florence Thomas

Mervyn Levy... one interesting aspect of this London period was some little time later, when we moved to Coleherne Road, William Scott, the painter, was living upstairs with another friend of ours, Robin Pierce. Both Robin and Scott were old friends of mine; we were at the Academy Schools together....

... when Dylan left Swansea, he came up with me... my parents drove us up, and he came and joined me in a room in Redcliffe Street in South Kensington... we lived very, very cheaply. We didn't have an awful lot to spend, any of us, and the room that I speak of now was an unfurnished room, and it's very interesting that the furniture that we eventually accumulated was largely lent us by Pamela Hanford-Johnson and her family. They were very kind in this way... [According to her diary, Hansford-Johnson helped Janes and Dylan move in on November 13, 1934]

... we used to do our own cooking. I largely did the cooking... Nancy used to visit us, too, and bring along various things to eat... she'd often turn up on a Monday morning, if I remember rightly...

32

Was Dylan any good as a cook?
No, not interested – not terribly interested in eating either, or he ate
very irregularly... I was very much tied to the place, painting away day
after day... this would be in contrast to Dylan's comings and goings –
I mean, he might disappear for a week, even a fortnight and then turn
up again, stay a few weeks...

... Dylan was tremendously good company. Wonderful storyteller...
as well as being extremely profound about his own work. In serious
conversation, it was an enormous experience to be with him in this
way... Dylan's humour as far as I remember it, was the kind of humour
which I like very much myself, which is not joke-telling... it was as a
result of his being able to see the funny side of an actual situation and
to put things in an extremely funny way, in quite a creative sense... his
humour certainly wasn't remembering long strings of jokes and so
forth...

What about Dylan's working methods when he was writing his poetry?
... this one period... where he wrote out the whole poem in a geometric
form, obviously was linked with the poem as a visual experience, as
well as having significance from the structure of the poem point of
view, and it's interesting to recall that at this time Dylan liked very
much to write out the whole poem on the back of a cardboard box or
something. I remember one period particularly, he liked to use the
laundry packages and write out his entire poems on these, and actually
hang them on the wall and, and enjoy them as a visual experience. I'm
referring now to poems like 'Vision and Prayer' and that period.

... when Dylan was writing, he always worked extremely hard. He was
an absolutely and deliberate and conscientious worker, to a fantastic
degree. I think that this fact isn't sufficiently appreciated about him...

*And when he was getting down to some serious writing he cut out any
drinking completely, didn't he?*
As far as I remember – completely. Completely. One has to remember
that at this time we didn't have very much money. There was very little
drinking done. At all. What happened to Dylan when he wasn't
forming an active part of this establishment, I can't say. But one needs
a lot of money to drink, and we just didn't have it.

... it is interesting to recall that, at this particular period, Dan's
whole family had moved to London, where they lived in Harrow-on-
the-Hill; we would go there at weekends from time to time, Dylan and
I, and spend the entire day with the Joneses. Go up in the morning,

have lunch, tea there, the lot, and supper, come back late at night, and we resumed exactly where we left off in Swansea with exactly the same kind of activities and interests.

... the Jones family were very sort of non-conformist people; very liberal-minded but the question of drink wouldn't enter into it at all. We might occasionally go along to a pub and have a pint of beer or something in the evening, from Dan's place... Dylan could enjoy whole days or a weekend with people who weren't drinking, and where there wasn't a drink in sight.

... it didn't seem to be important to Dylan intrinsically at any time. To him, as far as I could see, it was part of a social set-up. If people with whom he liked to spend his time wanted to drink, he would drink with them. If they didn't want to drink, then he was perfectly prepared not to drink... it was the people who interested him, and being with them, discussing things, being funny with them, laughing with them, crying with them and so forth. I think he was fundamentally interested in people...

... I think that the most interesting times that I spent with Dylan were after this period, in Swansea. I had come back and was working there, painting away, and Dylan was still moving around a great deal, spending part of his time in London, then coming home and living with his parents in Cwmdonkin Drive. It was at this period that I think I saw most of him on the kind of regular basis where we really had some of the most interesting conversations. Some of these conversations took place at Bert Trick's house, where we went fairly regularly on a Sunday evening. And we would just talk, and talk and talk and talk, and do crossword puzzles. Lots of these word games. Talk about politics... talk about poetry and music; play records. Lots of these conversations took place then at Dylan's... there was certainly no drinking done in Dylan's house at all. His mother was *extremely* hospitable, both parents were very hospitable; although his father, as is well known, was an extremely shy and retiring person. He wouldn't appear very much at these little gatherings, but Dylan's mother couldn't do enough for us in the way of feeding us sandwiches, huge tables of sandwiches...

... I don't think that Dylan was theoretically political in any way, any more than he was theologically religious in this sense. Dylan was an intensely *human* human. Intensely so – to a fantastic degree. What human beings did interested him; every aspect of their behaviour. I don't think that he could have possibly thought in terms of narrowing

34

down his sympathies or his activities to a single attitude of mind. This was why I think that, certainly from an orthodox point of view, he was not a religious poet in this sense, any more than he was a tremendously active member of any political party. All of these things were included in the world: Buddhism, Christianity, Communism... Dylan was interested in every aspect of life. One feels enormous sympathy with him in this way. This dividing of things up into categories, and one category excluding another category, appeared to him to be complete nonsense.

The absolute unity of life... appealed to him as a whole. I don't think he was ever interested in excluding any part of it. I think that he would have felt tremendously antagonistically towards people who did want to exclude parts of it. It was kind of an inclusive philosophy – a general kind of love of human beings and he could even feel tremendous sympathy with people who were completely opposite in point of view... he had this universal outlook...

... I think that if Dylan had ever affiliated himself in any close way with the Communist Party – I don't recall his having done this, or knowing about it – I'm absolutely certain that this would have been in line with what I've just said in that he was anti-fascist, anti-fascist most certainly in the sense that fascists were exclusive people... they wanted to narrow things down – they were dogmatic and so forth... to me fascism is completely anti-human, and Dylan would have been anti-fascist on these grounds. And that if Bert Trick had had this interest in socialism and communism, I think it would have been for the same reason. They were intensely human people... and they would have been prepared to fight against this other sort of totalitarian frame of mind, which is so tremendously against the arts, against the liberal outlook.

I wonder if you recalled the anti-semitic element of fascism repelling Dylan particularly at that time?
Only in so far as anti anything human would have repelled him. Certainly anti-semitism would have repelled him utterly. But this would have applied to any other category of human beings who would have been dealt with in this way.

... poetry was his interest in life and everything else was very subsidiary... these other things were on the periphery of his life. This went for him, it went for all of us who were actively engaged. I think one can't come back to this point often enough – that Dylan was a poet turning out at this time some of his best work, some of his most concentrated and involved work, and that these other aspects of his life were peripheral.

... it's this intense regard and sympathy for life itself, for things that are living and the dilemma of living creatures, living human beings, animals, being alive... the pain and joy of being conscious. This comes out constantly in his personality, his tremendous sympathy with other people. He could say the most devastating things about people but behind these things was always an understanding of his relationship to them as human beings.

... Dylan's deal was being alive. Dylan was intensely, as near a hundred per cent alive as a human being could be, and as I say, death to him was the opposite of this. The calamity.

What did Wales mean to Dylan?
I don't really feel that Dylan was chauvinistic or nationalistic or patriotic in that particular sense... but I think that he was grateful for being Welsh, and for the obvious volatility of his nature, for the power to express that he had. I think that he was grateful, for instance, for what he was able to take from Welsh preachers – from the *hwyl*... from the warmth of feeling and the ability to pour himself out, for not being restricted in this sense... there was something in this Celtic spirit which helped him to be a poet, which helped him to be uninhibited and fully expressive, to exaggerate the emotional content of his life. A rather vague idea, but quite obviously if a race is known to be expressive and volatile, and you are engaged in work which needs these qualities, you're grateful for your roots. His roots were in an expressive race... in an emotional soil... he was grateful for the richness of the emotional background which it gave him.

Mervyn Levy [17]

Life with Dylan in London was very exciting [but] he wasn't with us all the time. Neither did he have a room of his own. The arrangement quite simply was that Dylan was there when he wanted to be, and this meant that he used the place to sleep in, to be in, to eat in, to drink in from time to time, as and when it suited him. And what happened when he wanted to go to sleep was that he suddenly arrived, and whoever had a free space in his room allowed Dylan to put down his mattress.

Dylan didn't really enjoy a normal breakfast as other people do... he didn't really want to sit down to bacon and eggs or toast and marmalade and coffee. His breakfast consisted of beer and an apple or a piece of cake... Dylan would usually pull a bottle of beer out of the bed. Because he went to bed in his clothes most of the time. He would get into his bed in his overcoat, a great big heavy coat which made him look much bigger and tougher than he really was. One of the things he wanted to do, incidentally, was to try and make it appear that he was tough, that he was a chap to be reckoned with. He wasn't. Out of that great big coat he was quite a thin, weedy little bloke...

... we liked weaving fantasies, right from the first moments of a new consciousness, as it were. When Dylan woke up it was a new world, a new age, a new time, a new beginning for him as it was for me and the other of his friends who lived with him in those days. And we liked to start weaving fantasies straight away. I would walk in on Dylan, and he would pull out his beer and start nibbling his cake or his apple, and then say "Hello, Mervy. I wonder what it would be like if one wanted to pull the Glasgow to Euston train all the way from Scotland down to London using only mice? Could we do it?"

And I'd say "It's a question of how many mice." He'd say "Could you do it with five million mice?" And we would try to work out whether that would seem enough. And then we would say "No, it wouldn't. It's obviously very heavy. There'd be a lot of overnight passengers, they'd all be sleeping. It'd be a terrific weight. I think you'd need twelve million mice." Then what would you do? You couldn't run the thing on the normal sort of railway track. Well, you have to tear up all the track, obviously, and build mouse tracks for twelve million mice to drag the Glasgow to Euston down to London. And he'd say "Yes, that's a marvellous idea, a little track, millions of mice all hurrying along like they're putting in eighteen miles an hour. How would you keep them in the mouse track?"

And then I might say (I remember on one occasion we discussed this point at some length) "We could have cats to frighten them, all the way down the line. Or we'd have men with whips, perhaps midgets." Dylan was very fond of midgets – "get back, get back, all of you get back! All you mice." And eventually we get to London. It seemed quite a reasonable thing, if you had enough mice, if you had enough cats, or enough midgets with whips, you could – it wasn't beyond the bounds of possibility – get an express train from Scotland to London.

Dylan's choice of company, apart from his close friends, was very odd. He liked anybody who was gregarious or liked drinking, who liked pubbing. And he wasn't particular at all about the kind of person that he became friendly with. I know that on occasions he would arrive back at our place with perhaps a couple of boxers or a drunken down-and-out struck-off solicitor or some suspect doctor or a couple of jockeys. I really mean this. Provided people were prepared to drink and laugh and listen to him and be happy – because he liked to be happy in those days – they were friends of his. And he had this wonderful knack of making anybody feel that they had known him all their lives. And this is one of the treacheries of many people who think that they know Dylan or that they knew him. They didn't. He made them feel, in a very short time, that they were old buddies, but, of course, they weren't – they were just people to fill in the evening.

... Dylan was happy in any pub, provided he could find people to drink with, provided he could find people who preferred drinking to eating, people who liked staying out rather than going home. Because the most curious thing about Dylan was that he was always adrift, he never really wanted to be settled anywhere. He didn't like being at home, wherever the home was, unless he was asleep. He had to be out in a pub mixing with people, losing himself in people.

... Dylan didn't really drink as much as people like to think he did or as much as he likes you to think he did... I have known Dylan to go for long periods without drinking at all... he drank at first because it increased his sociability, not that, Heaven knows, he really needed that, 'cause he was a very sociable person. Then he began to drink 'cause other people pressed him to drink. And the idea gradually grew that he was a drinking man. And I think that had people not inveigled him as often as they did into drinking, his friends, who didn't drink much, could have kept him away from the bottle... we could have kept him under control.

... Dylan was terribly fascinated in all these curious obsessions with dirt, with excrement and urine and nose picking and so on. I remember one extraordinary application of his addiction to nose picking when he visited some people in the country – this was during the War years. For some reason or other he didn't like the people, who wanted to meet him very much. A distinguished English writer, and his wife were mad to meet Dylan – many people were. And when we took him along he didn't like them. And they went out to get something from the local pub. It was a nice little cottage in the countryside, a very nice, beautiful, freshly decorated cottage. And Dylan suddenly looked at the kitchen door, which was painted in a beautiful, shiny white. And he said "Bloody swine." And he put his hand over his nose and he pulled out a great string of snot and wiped it across the door and said "Hee, hee." He defiled something that was beautiful and fresh and new to them because he just didn't like them. And this was his way of showing his antagonism to law and order and balance and security and discipline and method and friendliness. He didn't like these things, they hurt him.

Mably Owen

I'd been in college with his great friend Daniel Jones... and Dylan called one day... it was immediately after the publication of *18 Poems* [December 18 1934]... I was overcome, like the rest of mankind, with the enchantment of his address. He was an extraordinarily fascinating character. One thing that struck me was his extraordinary physical grace – at that time, at any rate. His nimble, light movements and his rather angelic appearance in those days, a bush of tawny hair, pink cheeks and enormous eyes...

... he talked about surrealism and did the sort of thing he was very good at doing – made up samples of surrealistic verse *ad lib*. I remember one: "'Where is the spinach, Uncle Harry?' 'I threw it at the moon.'" And talked about his life in London. He'd gone to London with Fred Janes and Mervyn Levy. They seemed to be living in the utmost squalor in a single room, which had three horizontal beds for sleeping on, and one vertical bed which was a sort of wardrobe, and an accumulating pyramid of rubbish in front of the fireplace, on which little friendly mice played – so Dylan said.

... Dylan did dramatise himself a lot. He did act a lot, but was never, of course, taken in by his own act and would very frequently de-bunk it, but he did sometimes take it upon himself to play the role of a doomed young poet, and talked about galloping consumption and coughed ostentatiously, smoked very heavily. I remember one time he'd got hold of some filthy Mexican cigarettes wrapped in brown paper, which he smoked with glee saying "These do you an enormous amount of harm, you know."

... I remember Dan and he in the back bar of the Café Royal drinking iced lager of all things. Seeing who could drink the most quickly. But beer was what he drank mostly... even enjoyed appalling pubs, you know. He'd say "Now I'll take you to the worst pub in Swansea." He had a nose for them and we'd go to a foul place. I remember his comment on the sort of rather frowsty lounge of one of these places "It smells of mouse's armpits." And he delighted in all sorts of pubs and all sorts of people, too. He might well be found, and especially on a bright, sunny day, when everybody else was out was on the beach, in the very back and darkest bar of the Duke playing cards – and drinking and smoking... I remember going to the Duke very often. And a bar we all went to was Mundays' Wine Shop... opposite the Post Office... a little bar where you sit surrounded by enormous barrels, vast quantities of bottles, completely cut off from the world outside, where time seems to stop... you could sit for hours, without being conscious of being part of the world, and surrounded by all the atmosphere and apparatus of drink.

... I think that when he was working seriously, he didn't drink at all during the day. I remember staying in Laugharne once, and for the whole day he was immured in his little wooden shed, and sometimes he'd pop out and ask someone to give him some cigarettes, but he didn't drink at all, and didn't emerge until the evening, when he'd done as much work as he wanted to do... I never thought he was an alcoholic because I can't imagine that he would sit down and drink anything if there wasn't somebody there to drink with, and to talk to. And he preferred to drink in pubs where there were people. He didn't very much mind what sort of people as long as there were people and a pub atmosphere and the unexpected happening, moving from one pub to another.

... he got drunk fairly quickly... but he seemed to be able to go on in that state without getting very much worse... he drank out of exuberance, he was a social drinker... I don't say that he didn't romanticise drinking... it was part of the bohemian attitude which he again assumed, but again assumed without any self-deception... always as long as I knew him he had this salutary ability to de-bunk himself. He'd say things like, looking at his bohemian corduroys, "I feel just like a poet in these trousers."

... he always had an interest of a kind in clothes. I remember one thing he said about clothes was that his ideal was "a combination of the country gentleman and the Soho Jew". Which sometimes I think he achieved quite successfully. He did these things largely out of an enormous sense of fun.

... one of the things about Dylan is that, although he loved talking and talked marvellously and endlessly, he also liked listening, and was very ready to listen to anybody and everybody, and delighted very much in their company. I remember in Brown's in Laugharne once, there was a man there, telling stories and reciting poems, mainly in Welsh, which I had to translate for Dylan's benefit, and he was very much delighted with the man and his company, and his stories. So he wasn't one who monopolised conversations by any means.

What about Dylan's feelings abut Wales? Because from some people you get the impression that he grew to hate Wales.

No, I never had that impression. I think that his character was entirely Welsh. I remember him saying once "Here I am, a little fat pub armchair anarchist, full of the Welsh guilt." I never heard him say anything against Wales; he liked living in Wales, he seemed especially to like the Welsh people. One of the things he loved doing was going on the sort of boozing trip that you read about in... *The Outing...* he seemed to delight in the Welsh character and Welsh wit, the whole background of Wales.

2. Dylan as a young man

How would you describe Dylan's humour?

This is another thing in which he is Welsh, which you get in other writers like Gwyn Thomas, who might be called the pauper's Dylan Thomas... [Dylan] wasn't what you might call a professional wit, seeking opportunities for the brilliant bit of repartee; he was a creative and an imaginative talker. I think everything about him springs from this central gift of the gab, which is both a national thing and particularly remarkable in his case. But it wasn't that he said intellectually clever things, but that anything would start him off on a great saga, embroidered with grotesque and exuberant fancy, and with extraordinary verbal invention, which just went on and on – but which sprang out whatever was being talked about. They were not prepared set pieces. There is a story about Oscar Wilde talking to a woman at a dinner party, and holding a very brilliant conversation, and at the end he says "I'm afraid I haven't prepared another conversation; would you like to have that one over again?" [Dylan] wasn't like that at all – it was all impromptu, exuberant, imaginative, spontaneous and quite extraordinarily funny.

...he was not very efficient about practical things of any kind at all. I never remember his doing anything at all, for example, about the house, like chopping sticks or putting coal on the fire, or anything like that. In such matters he appeared to be perfectly helpless... I remember him slicing some French beans very inefficiently. That's the only domestic task I can actually remember that he did.

... he wasn't particularly, as far as I know, interested in food. In fact there was a time when he had the same attitude to food as temperance fanatics have towards drink; it was a thing he deeply deplored and had as rarely as possible. There is a story – probably exaggerated – about he and another who had been drinking for a long time, and the friend weakly put up a little plea for food, and Dylan turned to him with great indignation and said "Good God man, we had a sandwich three weeks ago!"

... he was quite innocent about money. A very serious thing to be innocent about, but he was – and tended to categorise it as "some", "none" or "a lot". In those days, nobody had much money anyway... there's been a lot of nonsense talked about his borrowing money and so on, but the point is, as far as I knew Dylan, if you had money, he expected you to share it with him. But he was even more ready to share whatever he had with you... it was a thing which he was indifferent to, he just didn't care about and when he had it, he spent it – exuberantly.

... Caitlin had the same attitude, too. Caitlin had no regard for money as such, and spent it as freely as he did when they had it, and went without as willingly as he did when they didn't have it. I think they both thought that money was just beneath contempt; not a thing that one really ought to have to bother about at all. There's an interview in *Horizon* where Dylan is one of those who answer the questions, and he says that the necessary things of life should be provided – house and shelter and food and the basic necessities – and that one should work to gain the necessary luxuries or the luxurious necessities.

... he had an enormous compassion for people. One of the things that affected him most, of course, was the War – and the suffering. And especially the extermination of the Jews and the horrors and cruelties. He really was shocked and horrified by that. I think the War made a tremendously deep impression on him, but his politics were an expression of his immense and enormous and all-embracing compassion for mankind.

... he hated the War, of course. Our generation could see this coming. It was a thing that one talked about, and that seemed to be inevitable, it seemed to be looming, and getting ever nearer. There seemed to be no way of escaping it. Everybody worried about it and everybody worried about what they would do, and theoretically most people felt that they would object... of course, many of Dylan's friends did – I for one... I think Dylan himself, too, felt that killing people was an impossible thing, a thing one couldn't do, and a situation into which one could not enter. I don't think at all it had anything in the least to do with protecting himself. I think he was quite prepared to share the fate of mankind, the fate of his fellows. What he couldn't imagine himself doing was killing anybody else.

... it wasn't any sort of self-protection, because, as I want to emphasise more than anything, the one thing that he was not was calculating in any way at all. And this sort of looking after his own interests was a thing that he'd never done, he never did look after his own interests... it was out of character. Even if he did know the right people, he certainly didn't say the right things. He was never tactful for the wrong reasons. He never promoted his interests by intrigue or any form of calculation.

... he talked a lot about the sufferings of the Jews, which seemed to have entered very, very deeply indeed into his feelings and into his imagination. He told lots of stories about them. About one family, I think in Holland, where the father had said – the Jews were being rounded up and although he was not a Jew, he and his family went out wearing the Star of David. He talked about a schoolteacher, I think in Germany – I think she was an English teacher – who had gone to the gas ovens with her charges, saying quite simply that that was her job, to be with those she looked after. He had a tremendous admiration for that sort of courage in the face of all this horror.

Dylan had a great feeling for his father, D.J. Thomas, didn't he?
Yes. This was never apparent in their personal relationships. His father was a rather remote man; I think also possibly a slightly disappointed man... and was, in any case, rather cynical and disbelieving about most things, and he had a personal remoteness and dignity, possibly partly professional, which I never saw break down at all. The apparent relations between them were always a kind of rather distant politeness. They used to talk quite freely about literature and such things, but there was no obvious warmth in the relationship that I could see.

There is a, possibly apocryphal, story of Dylan coming in one night, very drunk, and his father saying "Now, look here Dylan. I'm a rational man, but you're nothing but a little sot." And Dylan would say "No – not a sot." And his father would say "I use the word 'sot' advisedly. It is from the Anglo-Saxon so-and-so." And Dylan would say "S'not

from Anglo-Saxon, s'from French." And the whole thing would degenerate into a sort of argument about etymology. I don't know whether
that's true, but it's quite characteristic, anyway.

... I think his [D.J.'s] professional status meant a lot, you know. He'd
climbed into this middle-class and was determined to preserve its digni-
ties. He had all the detachment and the irony – cynicism – of the
scholar; he was a real academic. A most charming, polite and likeable
man of whom I was very fond indeed. But never one who would display
emotion. I think he'd schooled himself not to do so. I think he'd formed
himself into a certain pattern which he felt appropriate to his station.

... I talked Welsh, of course, to Dylan's father and to his mother,
quite a lot – especially to her – and I don't know why he didn't teach
Dylan Welsh. Of course, Welsh was rather suspect socially in those
days... the only sort of convincing middle-class pose you could assume
was an English one, there being no technique of snobbery in Welsh!
Not that it was really snobbery. I think it was simply that he carried out
the conventions of the middle-class, as he saw them... Dylan always
regretted that he couldn't speak Welsh; but, on the other hand, he
would not have exerted himself to learn it.

... I think there are certainly things, fundamental things, about
Dylan which are completely Welsh – his temperament, his feeling, his
delight in words, his volatile nature and so on, but his cultural
background, of course, was English entirely... there was no obvious
Welsh cultural counter to this fact that his upbringing was entirely
English in that sense.

*Now you're one of his few really Welsh-cultured friends. Did he try to pump
you for some things, of an understanding of Welsh?*
Oh, very much, yes. He loved hearing Welsh poetry and having it translated. He liked asking about the words of Welsh songs and having them
translated. Jokes in Welsh, translated into English. In London, he often
used to ask me to say some Welsh poetry – to people like John
Davenport, and translate it. He was tremendously interested in it, and
greatly regretted, I think, that he didn't read it direct.

... I think the main thing is that Dylan was not the sort of man who
had made the successful and, in many cases, perhaps necessary
compromise with life as it is. He hadn't the qualities of compromise
and duplicity and falseness and intrigue that most people have to
develop as a sort of protective shell... he was terribly vulnerable to the
pressures and assaults of our society and of our time.

... I've said more than once he was extremely intelligent and perceptive – he was talking about himself and two or three other people. And he said "So-and-so's fault is that he intellectualises every-thing. So-and-so's fault is that he commercialises himself. My fault is excess." And that sort of excess, I think, did rule his life. He wouldn't accept compromise and he wouldn't accept limitations, either. "My symbols have out-elbowed space" is a sort of typical declaration. And he'd developed this sort of tempo of life, and I don't think he could have lived in any other way.

Glyn Jones

It was in 1934 that I first saw some poems over the name of Dylan Thomas in the magazine called the *Adelphi*... I thought they were strange, beautiful, wonderful. In fact, I was so moved by them I wrote to the editor expressing my great admiration for them. I had no idea then who or what Dylan Thomas was... presently I had a letter from Dylan himself... eventually a meeting was fixed up and I went down to Swansea to see him. He was then a man of about eighteen years of age... he wasn't known nationally – certainly was not known interna-tionally. He was quite an obscure writer, in more senses than one.

What was his reaction to your letter?
I think that he must have welcomed it, because, I suppose, I was one of the first people outside his own very small circle in Swansea to take any notice of him. I was almost certainly the first person in Wales to take any notice of his work, and I think he was very pleased really. His parents, too, seemed very pleased that at last he'd got one fan, as it were.

... I think that he did value my opinion, especially on short stories, because he gave me quite a bundle of short stories and asked me if I would read them and say what I thought about them. I happened to be writing for the *Adelphi* myself at the time, so I think that we had a bond there, in both being Welsh and both contributing to the same magazine. And in some ways our literary ideas were similar.

... his short stories in the early days were tremendously important to him. I should say when I met him first that short stories were almost as important to him as his poetry... those stories obviously come out of the same world as the early poems; and he also did some coloured drawings at that time which are fantastic and might be illustrations for some of the stories.

... as a person, the great thing about him, and the thing that you'd

notice first, was his receptive-
ness and sensitivity. When you
were speaking to Dylan, no
nuance or shade of difference
or a difference of direction in
the conversation was lost on
him... he knew every change
and that was a great thing,
because it made him so very
easy to get on with. Dylan was
never the man to drop a brick;
not unintentionally. If he
dropped a brick, it was a
purposely-dropped brick... he
was very warm-hearted, and

3. Glyn Jones

he was able to establish a flow between himself and all sorts of people.
I think that was one of the sweetest things about him, this sense of flow
that you experienced when you were in his company... you felt that he
was friendly; and there was a sort of loving atmosphere between him
and his friends. Many people have noticed that about him.

... he was inclined to take very much the atmosphere of the
company that he was in. I've heard him myself condemn opinions or
actions in one group of people, and then when he goes into another
group, whose atmosphere is different, he would then not condemn, but
perhaps praise this... which I found at first very trying indeed. I know
we must all exercise a certain amount of accommodation. We can't
voice our opinions all the time; we must use common sense. But it did
shake me at first to hear Dylan express different – radically different –
opinions for the purpose of accommodating himself to different
groups. Especially was this so, I think, in his early days when he was
young and feeling insecure...

... it was the time between the Wars and the popular poetry (if
poetry can ever be described as popular) was the poetry of Auden,
Day-Lewis, Spender and so on, which was Communist poetry, indus-
trial poetry as it were, very modern, the vocabulary was modern, it
brought in pylons and machinery and all that sort of thing. For poetry
of this sort, a person of my temperament could not feel very much love
and admiration, but when I read Dylan Thomas' poetry, this poetry
appealed to something below the level of one's intellect, as it were,
appealed to the diaphragm and the midriff... I think that the appeal of

poetry, is fundamentally emotional and not intellectual – for me, anyway. And that is what appealed to me in the poetry of Dylan Thomas; it bypassed, as it were, the intellect and landed a blow right in the midriff.

… there is one point there that I'd like to mention about Dylan reading his own poetry. People tell me that once they hear Dylan reading his own poems, that it all becomes clear. Well, that's far from being my experience. I don't think that most of the poems are any clearer at all. I don't say that they're worse or they're not as good when Dylan reads them; they're just as thrilling. But they're certainly not any clearer.

… his poems are full of words with double meanings. I don't know that he invented very many words. He used double-barrelled words, which was a thing that the old Welsh poets used to do, of course, and I think he probably got that idea from Hopkins, but he's not a great inventor of words. I think his puzzles, the puzzles of his poetry, are other than that. They don't derive from the difficulties of the words themselves. My feeling about Dylan's poetry is that often I can understand all the words but I can't understand the poem!

… there is an element of playing a game in all his poetry. I don't mean playing a game in the deceptive sense, but that poetry has an element of play in it, this changing of words and alterations and so on. There is, for the poet, an element of play in that; poetry is not all dead serious and in dead earnest… there must be a certain – what does Yeats say – a certain amount of song and chance in the poem. There must be the lighter side, even when the poet is writing a serious poem… and I think it's quite strong in Dylan's poetry.

… it's very obvious that he loved Wales, and that he felt very much at home in Wales. I think that Welsh society, if we may call it that, the Welsh mode of life, is one that suited him very much. He was very much at home in this lax, easy-going atmosphere that we've got here, where there are very few class distinctions and so on. That sort of society Dylan liked very much. With all the world to live in, after all, he came back to live in Wales, didn't he? He could have lived anywhere in the world… and he chose to live in that little village which was, like himself, Welsh but English-speaking… of course, in some ways he was very ignorant of Wales… he knew more about what was going on in literary London than he knew what was going on in literary Wales, for example, or in Wales in general.

… Dylan, of course, could not have been influenced by Welsh poetry because he knew nothing about Welsh poetry… the only Welsh poet I ever heard him mention was Crwys-Williams, the former archdruid, and he mentioned him because they lived near him in Swansea and not because of any knowledge of his poetry. But, of course, Dylan was influenced by Gerard Manley Hopkins, and Hopkins was a Welsh speaker... he was a student of the *Cynganeddion*, the rules of Welsh bardic poetry and he was quite a scholar in that field... Dylan was influenced by Hopkins, and that is the way it seems to me in which he is influenced by Welsh poetry. At one remove, as it were.

... I do think it's a pity that Dylan hadn't been a Welsh speaker and that he hadn't had a knowledge of the *Cynganeddion*, because he would have been a superb *Cynghyneddwr* had he had the chance. If he had known about the rules of Welsh prosody he could have used these in English, it would have been to a great advantage to his poetry... it's obvious that he felt the need for some sort of discipline to his verse. I think that the diamond shapes that appear in *Death and Entrances*, and the wineglass shapes, into which he squeezed his poetry... I think that those indicate a desire for some sort of discipline... also the fantastic rhyming scheme in 'Prologue'... well, it seems to me that that's technique running to seed – it's purposeless... but if this great concern with technique had been channelled into work on the *Cynganeddion*, it would have resulted in something very great, I think.

... he had great admiration for Joyce. He used to read, I believe, *transition* in the old days you know, when Joyce used to write for *transition*. Dylan somehow or another got hold of it in quite early days, when most people in Wales had never heard of *transition*. He was, as a young man, very much on the ball, he knew what was happening. Although he was living in Swansea, in a provincial town, he knew what was going on in literary circles in London. Long before he went there... no, I never heard him mention Blake.

... I'm afraid I don't accept that Dylan is a religious poet. I think that he wrote one or two religious poems, but not enough for me to regard him as a fundamentally religious poet because he doesn't deal with the great questions of a religious poet – forgiveness, atonement, separation from God and so on. These things do not appear in Dylan's poetry... he writes, as it were, a paean to Nature, to God in Nature and so on, but I don't think that his religious poetry goes beyond that. To see how little of a religious poet he is one only has to compare him with Hopkins, who is a profoundly religious poet, in everything that he wrote.

... yes, he uses these symbols and images of the Christian faith to a very large extent but this was I think merely because he was familiar with these in his childhood, and anything that you are familiar with in your childhood is always potent for you, even at a subconscious level. And then when you write the poetry these are the things that surge forward, as it were, and he does use those. But the use of these images does not, for me anyway, make a man a religious poet... I'd be inclined to say, rather than a religious poet, that he was the poet of childhood.

... I think that the one unfortunate thing about Dylan was that he had too narrow a conception of what the poet was, or rather an unhealthy conception of what the poet was. I think that if he'd had a healthier idea of the function of the poet, that he might have been happier... might have lived, perhaps, a longer and happier life. I feel that he thought the poet was a man set aside from all other men, and that he's distinguished from other people only by this gift – of being a poet. Well, there's an older Welsh conception of the poet as the man who lives in the community, who is a part of the community, and not a man who was set aside at all. I think that if Dylan had had a less romantic idea of what the poet was, and what his function in society was, that he might possibly have been happier. If he could have taken his place naturally in the community and not regarded himself as a man cut off.

... you get the *bardd gwlad*, who writes his poems. What is he? He's a garage hand, or a farmer, or a local postman, or the minister – and he writes his poems, he's accepted. It's no more strange for him to be a poet than for a man to be a county councillor... Dylan never had any job, and I don't think that was perhaps a good idea... he saw himself as a poet pure and simple... if he had not himself been cut off, he might have – he's a great writer as it is – he might have been an even greater one.

In the last few years of his life, people have pointed out that his production of poems was quite limited – his genius seemed to be burning out.
I think it was burning out. I think that as a poet he was more or less finished. Because it seems to me that he had the type of gift which we can perhaps best describe as "morning glory". It afflicts many writers. They write their best when they are young; as they get older they get – Wordsworth is a fine example of it – they get more prosaic. Dylan didn't get more prosaic; he just didn't write at all. And I think his was the type of gift which blooms in a great outburst of creative energy and then gradually trails off. I think myself that the poetry he wrote in his early days was, without question, the best...

He was turning to other forms of expression in his later years, wasn't he? He was planning a stage play with Philip Burton. Do you think that he then would have flowered in another direction, in another medium?

Well, unless some radical change took place in Dylan, I don't see how this could happen. I know that many people say that he was going to write large-scale works for the stage and so on, but the evidence of Dylan's own life is against it. He took about ten years, I should think, to write *Under Milk Wood* – which is quite a small thing... he wrote the novel *Adventures in the Skin Trade*. He took many years to write that and never finished it. So from the evidence of his own life and work, the suggestion that he would one day write large-scale stage works seems quite out of the question...

... his genius was essentially lyrical. He was a poet of the short flight. Even in *Under Milk Wood,* all the flights are short. There is no grand conception in the thing at all. You get a series of quite short episodes and these are strung together but there's no development of any sort, and there's no climax. There's no reason why it should finish when it does, or why it shouldn't go on for another half hour or another hour. It just finishes there, an arbitrary end. There's no external shape. So I can't see Dylan developing into a man who could conceive of something on a great architectural scale, as it were. I think that he was essentially a poet of lyrical gifts and of the short flight... I don't think that he could ever master a play, or a novel even, which had form and shape.

Dylan grew up in Wales in a period when there were hard conditions in Swansea and South Wales, but he didn't deal with these conditions.

I think that one reason is that the hadn't the sense of guilt which the Communist English poets had, like Spender and Auden and so on. They came from the English upper crust, as it were, and they have a sense of guilt about the conditions in the country... but Dylan, having been brought up in Swansea and his background was lower middle-class, he wouldn't feel this guilt, naturally, and I don't think that these conditions burnt into his consciousness as they did into the consciousness of these Communist poets – as they've been called – to anything like the same extent...

... he told me that he was going to join the Young Communists, but I think that their limiting age was eighteen and he was already over eighteen, so he couldn't join... I met him once or twice in London when he was wearing a violently red tie, the reddest tie I've ever seen anywhere I think... obviously Dylan would not stay long in the Communist Party. That was evident to everyone, because they would want him to write propaganda poems, wouldn't they? I think he would be quite incapable of writing propaganda poems.

... I'd be inclined to think it was more a personal revolt than a sense of something ought to be done. I don't think Dylan was a great doer, but he would feel that he would like to be on the left, at the most extreme limit of whatever sort of revolt was in the air at the time, Dylan liked to be there, and at the time it was the Communist Party ... if the Communists had achieved power, he'd probably become a Quaker or something like that.

... I think he was a shy man at heart. Durrell talks about him being too shy to come to one of his parties. He phones from outside – Dylan was too shy to come in. But, of course, he became tougher than that later on and he met all sorts of people. He was lionised, and being lionised is a certain way of overcoming shyness, I think. But he certainly did start off as a shy man in London, and I think that's perfectly understandable. After all, he was very young going to London, and he moved in a literary society which was, on whole, from a class which was better off than the class Dylan came from. I think English literary society is more class-conscious than anything in Wales, and Dylan was shy, from what Grigson says about him... the early outrageous behaviour was partly like the little boy showing off at the party... he was perhaps a little bit of an outsider, and yet he was conscious all the time, must have been, of these great gifts that he had. Because he was a much better poet than almost anyone that he was meeting there.

... it was one of the great things about him that while one sees people with not half his talent who had many times his self-importance, he was not self-important about his work. His work was tremendously important to him but he didn't become, because of that, a self-important person. He never was that; he was always friendly and approachable. I don't think he forgot any of his friends; it was just against his nature to do anything like that.

... in the early days, I think he was a happy man. But I don't think his life later on was happy. How could he be? I think the last time I saw him, there was an air of desperation about him which I found very, very sad.

Was he doing things with you and for you at the BBC?
I did a series of interviews with authors, and I asked Dylan if he'd take part in this. The title of the series was *How I Write*. And I sent him about six or ten questions that I proposed to ask him in the radio interview, and then I went down to Laugharne, where he was living then, so

that we could rough out the interview between us. When I got there, Dylan had written enough material to answer the first question to last the whole interview. It was brilliant stuff, but in my opinion not at all suitable for radio because it was much too thickly clotted, and I suggested that possibly if I could insert the other questions at reasonable intervals in this first answer, that we'd have a first-rate interview, and if he wrote a little more just to fill up for the half-hour.

... he said he would do this. Well, the date of the interview got rapidly nearer and nearer and not a word from Dylan, and then the telegrams began to arrive. The telegrams arrive but no Dylan. On the night of the interview, Dylan didn't turn up. His own explanation – you needn't put this on the tape – he said "I'm terribly sorry about that, but I had trouble with my rib." Now, there's a biblical meaning to rib and I think that he meant the biblical meaning. Because she... she didn't... when we were there she said "What are you giving this interview for?" (Don't put this down will you, eh?) "What are you giving this interview for? What are you giving all your secrets away for?" she said. She wasn't willing, you see. And I think she probably told him "You're not to do it."

Benjamin Morse [18]

I first met him at the bookshop of Ralph Wishart in Swansea. It was a hot, sultry summer afternoon... at the far end of this cool bookshop, I saw a young man with a fresh complexion – young, in those days, of course, he was not yet stout – and browsing among the books. When I got nearer to him, he looked at me shyly and I thought rather humbly, and he said "I think you're Ben Morse, aren't you?" And I said "Yes, I am. How did you know?" "Oh, I was told that you call here... shall we go and have a drink?" To which I replied "No, it's rather late and I don't usually drink in the afternoon." "Oh, that's all right," he said, "we can talk. Let's go and have a coffee." And we did.

... there's one famous occasion when he came to lecture – he came twice, actually – in Cardiff. On the first occasion, he was lecturing at the University College. He brought a suitcase which he couldn't open, he fumbled about with it. He said "My wife packs that for me. I can't open it." So it was opened for him. Then we discovered that inside he had one clean shirt, which he wanted to put on, so as to appear respectably dressed in front of the students whom he was going to address. After his lecture – his series of readings – we adjourned to the

Park Hotel, where he was staying at the moment. And the students were told that they could ask him questions if they wanted to, and some did. Some very foolish questions, some very enlightening ones, but they were all answered with as much humility as if the great poet had been a poetaster who knew nothing at all about poetry. And I distinctly remember his putting one student in his place, who maintained that poetry was a matter of inspiration. To which he replied "No – that is not true! It is a matter of technique, not of inspiration."

... on that evening, Glyn Jones was present and as he left... Dylan told me that "He is the best poet, the best of all the Anglo-Welsh writers living today." That was his considered verdict, and he said it with his brassy voice full of admiration and a great deal of respect.

... I think I am the person responsible for the first German translation of a poem by Dylan Thomas. I translated his famous prize poem, the one that obtained the *Sunday Referee* prize... when I gave him a copy I thought he might be somewhat shocked to find that it had been rhymed, since he had written it as unrhymed and free verse, of course. But he just said "You did that for me? Good Heavens! What admiration – it's wonderful! Thanks very much."

... I have not read, in any book, references to the great humility, the deep humility of the man, and the shyness, the way he used to look at people, almost like a young girl looking at someone whom she admired very, very greatly, beyond the power of words, so to speak. Or his great devotion to the technicalities of his writing. That, I think, is something that is inviolate and untouchable.

W.T. Pennar Davies

I remember seeing Dylan before I actually met him. I went to some plays that were being performed here in Swansea... I remember seeing Vernon Watkins there, of course, and also Keidrych Rhys, and also Peter Hellings, who was a new discovery of Dylan's and Keidrych's, so I gather. I remember that Keidrych was saying that this was a real discovery, this pimply youth who was going to become famous as a poet.

... I was in the United States, on a Commonwealth Fund Fellowship, from 1936 to 1938, and during that time the magazine *Wales* began to be published and when I returned to Wales I found that a new and notable Anglo-Welsh school of writing had appeared. My own interest has been writing through the medium of Welsh, but I felt that it was very important that some kind of co-operative relationship should be established between writers who used the Welsh language, and this exciting new group, who were using the English language as their medium. And so I got in touch with Keidrych Rhys, who I think was editing the magazine *Wales* at the time, with Dylan Thomas, and I soon got to know Keidrych very well and I went down to stay with him and his wife at that time, Lynette Roberts, in their cottage at Llanybri. And while I was there, we had a visit from Dylan. Those were the circumstances in which I got to know him. Perhaps I ought to say that I believe it was after this that Keidrych Rhys and I thought of establishing a kind of permanent literary society in which Welsh writers using either language could come together and exchange views, and perhaps do something to foster the culture of the land to which they all belonged.

... I wrote to Dylan about it, and he sent a very courteous reply, which showed that he was interested, but at the same time it seemed fairly clear from his letter that he did not think that this idea was going to help very much. He didn't think that Welsh literary artists would profit very much by getting together, and I got the impression that his outlook on the writer's craft was somewhat individualistic.

... he seemed to be disinclined to commit himself to anything of this sort... he seemed to be moved by what I had written – I tried to write as persuasively as possible – and he seemed to think that he owed Wales something; I got the feeling that he did belong to Wales, and that that meant something very great to him. But he did not want to commit himself to any kind of association with Welsh language writers, or indeed with English language writers, except in the way of friendship and possible collaboration.

How did Dylan appear when you first met him?
He turned up I think in a fairly cheerful mood, chatting to Lynette Roberts, who had not long been married to Keidrych. He seemed to be quite happy. I believe that they had quite recently got hold of a record of James Joyce reading some of his prose and this record was put on, and Dylan was delighted with it. This, he thought, was magnificent.

Later on the same day, we had to go out to meet Ernest Rhys, and this was a rather interesting encounter. Ernest Rhys, of course, belonged to the old school of Anglo-Welsh writing, a rather tenuous tradition in those days... it might be regarded as a very tiny shoot of the stem of the Celtic twilight literature, which was a part of the phenomenon of the 'Naughty Nineties'.

... he greatly cherished his Welsh connections and, in his poems and his prose, belonged to a very different age, of course, from that of Dylan Thomas. He did seek to remind the English-speaking world of Wales' existence, and as a Welshman of that kind, he was keenly interested in meeting Dylan. And they met in a public house, not very far away from Llanybri.

Ernest Rhys and Dylan sat together at the bar, and conversed... it was interesting to see the way in which this old man, who had lived in the world of literature for so long, and who was deeply interested in Wales and had a sentimental loyalty to Wales, how he was obviously fascinated by the conversation of Dylan... I would say Dylan seemed to be quite polite, but at the same time a little cagey. He obviously felt that Ernest Rhys belonged to a different age and was writing poetry in a very different manner.

Did Dylan know Ernest Rhys' poetry very well?
I think not, probably not. Although I believe that he did know a great deal about the poetry of that period.

Did Dylan ever express regret that he had been cut off from Welsh culture by not being able to speak Welsh?
I never heard him say anything like that, but I have heard Aneirin Talfan Davies say that he'd expressed himself very strongly to him in those terms, and spoke very censoriously of his parents for not having brought him up to speak Welsh.

... I don't think that any direct influence of Welsh literature can be traced in Dylan Thomas' poetry, although some have tried to trace it. I do think that the very fact that Dylan had heard the Welsh language spoken and preached in the old Welsh style, could have given him a feel for the glory of language as such, and I think that this may have affected his whole approach to literature. I believe that, even as a schoolboy, he was entranced by the rich eloquence of the more gorgeous pieces in Shakespeare, and he loved to recite them, without really caring very much about their meaning. He was obviously charmed by the beauty of sounds, and I think that this particular approach to literature may have been greatly furthered in his growth by the fact that he had heard so much eloquent Welsh spoken without really understanding what it was all about.

... one thing that has always puzzled me about Dylan is that he did very little to make use of traditional Welsh fables and romances and myths... there he had a great mine of mythological symbolism, readily available in translation, but as far as I know he made little or no attempt to make use of it... he missed the great riches of Welsh literature, and that I think is a great loss in his poetry. I think his whole poetic outlook could have been greatly enriched if he'd had a grounding in the literature of his own country.

Dylan was essentially an English poet who happened to have Welsh parents and grew up in a Welsh town. This is what it amounts to, isn't it?
I think that very true, but at the same time I think he had a genuine Welsh consciousness and I think perhaps, in common with others, he had a lively appreciation of the fact that the Welsh background could be used to make a school of Welsh poets writing in English something quite distinctive in the English literary scene.

... I would say that the quite genuine attachment to some kind of Wales that Dylan had must have been an element in the whole complex of conflict that was going on inside him.

Vernon Watkins

It was in the spring of '35... his first book, *18 Poems*, had come out on the last day of 1934... I called at his house... and found that he was away in London, but I left a message, and when he returned he rang me up and came out to Pennard, where I was living, and we walked out on the cliffs... my first impressions of him were that he was younger than I expected. He was in fact twenty, and looked about seventeen, slight and eager and slightly flushed in expression, and very innocent and cherub-like in appearance, but as soon as one discussed anything with him, one realised that he was extremely keen and mature in his intelligence, even then...

You had already started publishing your own poetry at that time?
Only in one or two anthologies and magazines, and that was a good time before. I had not printed anything for six years when I met Dylan, and I was extremely opposed to printing any verse I wrote. It was Dylan who persuaded me to print poems, and I think I persuaded him to use titles to his poems. He was opposed to the idea of titles. He said that musicians didn't use them, so why should poets? They were a little label to simplify the work, and he said they were quite unnecessary and rather insulting, but I said that as he wrote more and more it would be difficult to refer to particular works by numbers and, although it took

him a long time, I think the poem for his aunt, 'After the funeral', was the first poem he titled, and then he reverted to the first line when it was collected in *Collected Poems*.

4. Vernon Watkins

... when I was very young, I realised that poetry would be my entire concern, whereas I think with Dylan, although poetry was the dominant thing, he was interested in language and all the manifestations of language – that was the thing he had to quarry. And of course, he was writing stories *and* poems when I first met him... with poetry as the dominant thing, but a thing which couldn't be hurried, and a most intense thing, so that one had to have something slightly more relaxing to counterbalance it. In my case, there wasn't a prose counterpart to what I was doing in verse; so, of course, I worked in an office, because poetry is not a thing you can make real by itself. If you begin to do that, you put yourself in a very wrong position.

... I always felt that if I did anything literary for a career, it would put me in a compromising position, where I might be obliged to write what I didn't want write, and the great advantage of working in an office was that I could write only what I wanted to write, and was never to be put in that false position. It was difficult at first; it took me a few years to get used to it, but I think the contrast was helpful to me.

Is it a really demanding thing to find the effort, the time to write poetry?
I think poetry writes itself in its own time, and you've got to give it time and I don't think it can be in any way hurried. I should have hated to be in a position where I had to finish a poem in a month, or two months, rather than be able to give it two or three years if I needed to. And I've always been in the position of being able to give a poem time, because I've made my living in another way.

... to devote yourself full time to poetry is to devote yourself full time also to other things. The tension which creates poetry is linked with all kinds of things, with all kinds of manifestations, from which you don't want to cut yourself off... if you were writing a long prose work containing a great number of facts, the question is to have enough time to get these down. Lyric poetry is not like that; it's a mediumistic thing, it's instantaneous and all you want is patience, to wait for what is unforgettable.

Dylan was a Welsh writer and poet, but not in the Welsh language.
He's an extremely Welsh poet. He's very much more Welsh than many people who write in Welsh, and also in his reading. I think the bardic Welsh rhythmic, incantatory way of reading, is a considerable influence in his reading, just as I also think that his father's magnificent reading of Shakespeare was an influence... I think he was acquainted with the Welsh tradition but the dominant influence was Hopkins, in relation to Welsh, because the influence of Welsh on Hopkins' diction influenced Dylan a certain amount, in certain poems. But I felt also that he was very close to Keats in his way of composition, late Keats, because they were both fascinated by extremely subtle musical elements in language and adjacent sounds and the substitution of words. And Joyce, of course, was a considerable influence on Dylan... he regarded Yeats as the greatest poet of the century, but I think Hardy was his favourite, because he used to say that he liked bad Hardy almost better than good. He felt personally drawn to Hardy, and he liked every poem he wrote.

It's been said by some of Dylan's critics that he concerned himself more with sound than with meaning.
Well, I think that is nonsense, because sound *is* meaning in good poetry.

He worked very hard to find sounds that conveyed the meaning. And he even invented a great number of new words, or combination words, didn't he?
Yes, I think he did break ground in language, a thing which I've never been so much tempted to do myself. I've always felt that Dylan was doing all kinds of things I could not do, just as I had to concentrate on totally different things, so that I always felt that our work was complementary. Although we influenced each other a lot and had great affinity of belief in our approach to poetry, too.

... I don't think he invented words in the way Joyce did. Joyce took roots from all kinds of languages and produced European words, very mysterious compounds. Dylan showed great brilliance in unexpected adjectives which were exactly right. I should say he was very close to the late Dickens in his late broadcast scripts. I don't know any writer since Dickens who was so close to that late style as Dylan is in the late broadcast scripts of *Quite Early One Morning*. I think that is quite extraordinary – but I wouldn't say that there are many sort of brand-new minted words in those things.

... the language is mainly traditional, it's just that he produced compounds of word roots which aren't used normally together. I think he did this thing with great genius... he hated the clever, or even the ingenious, in poetry. It's rather difficult in that the whole question is so subtle. What Dylan wanted was the right word for what he was saying – however simple. The elaborate word was not at all what he wanted. I can think of a line of Yeats, where Yeats had used "child hid in the womb" in one of his later poems, and I remember Dylan saying that all kinds of poets today would think of all kinds of words for this... but, of course, the best of all words is "hid". And I think Dylan really wanted to simplify his language to the utmost, to give it the utmost clarity and force.

Did he find difficulty in getting down to the task of writing?
I should say after about 1935, he didn't sit down to write verse, ever, without already having in his imagination a line or beginning. In some way his imagination had been stirred. He might find the beginning of a poem in any kind of place. He found the beginning of one poem in Rilke, of all people, a poet so different from himself; and in another case, he found a germ of a poem in an extremely bad thriller. He would read a lot of thrillers, and he said this one was a particularly bad one but he came across a most wonderful sentence in it, which he quoted.

Did Dylan regard himself as a religious poet?
I believe him to be a religious poet. I don't know that Dylan would attach any label to his poetry of any kind, but I do know that almost his favourite lyric poet was George Herbert. And he loved Vaughan also, certainly... he was a great admirer of Blake; in his selections of poetry that he made, there were very generous quotations from Blake, always.

... Blake had an extraordinary vision so that no poet really can be compared in any way with Blake. And in the same way I feel Dylan was a unique phenomenon, but, of course, he hadn't got Blake's visual imagination. Blake had this extraordinary faculty of seeing visions everywhere and Dylan certainly believed in visions, but I don't think he saw them all the time as Blake certainly must have done.

There was a group called the Apocalypse Group that sometimes Dylan is lumped with – they claimed him, but did he claim to be a part of that group?
No, I think 'apocalyptic' was a word that Dylan disliked very much, and when I showed him *The White Horseman*, which had a lot of poems of mine, he was very much out of sympathy with the kind of trend and

criticism of the book; completely out of sympathy with it... there are many apocalyptic elements in Dylan's work, but as a movement he hated that, really.

Spender has been compared to Dylan as a romantic poet, but Spender was more intellectual.

I know Dylan would have hated to be called an intellectual, but I think that Dylan, intellectually, was more mature than Spender – a good deal. Because I think that Spender's feelings in his work are more significant and more important than his intellectual ideas. I think the value of the poetry comes from the perceptions of feeling more than from the perceptions of intellect. I should have said that there was more logical intellect in Dylan's compositions...

... he was not a political poet, of course. Not really a sociological poet at all... a very odd brand of Communism cropped up in his conversation... Dylan didn't like possessions, and he didn't like the divided classes of society. He really believed in the classless society... these elements of the Communist Party appealed to him very much... he used to quote me things like "Property is theft" and these things got hold of his imagination a bit – but they never really affected his writing very much.

... Dylan affirmed. He said how easy it would be to write poems of defeat and despair, but what he wanted to do was to write poems of joy, and that's, of course, what he set out to do in the last poems. And, because it's more difficult, it's really more true.

People have remarked that Dylan was a little scared of academic people, or the high literary types.

I think Dylan always had a dread of intellectual and academic conversation, and that kind of atmosphere, anything high-falutin', was obnoxious to Dylan, because he had a very literal mind. When I first met him, he described the work of revision he did on his poems as very like plumbing – getting things in the right position so that they functioned properly. It was all to do with technique, but he simplified it as much as that.

... he was more at home when people were relaxed and the pretentious was what Dylan dreaded, and although he met a great many very intelligent people in America and here, and got on splendidly with them, he was always afraid before meeting these people that he might encounter this thing.

Artificiality was the thing that he hated most probably?

Yes, I think so. The inhuman aspect of academic life, the sort of clichés of academic writing and critical writing were nothing to him... I don't think he wanted to present himself to anybody as a highbrow. I think he wanted to emphasise the opposite in company, and to appear more disreputable than he was. That is a kind of mask he put on with a lot of people, and strangers were totally deceived by this mask. His intimate friends, of course, were not taken in at all. He never changed really; I never knew him to behave badly – I met him such hundreds of times – but I saw him act in a very strange way, many times.

Dylan was gradually becoming recognised, and yet he didn't take his fame seriously?
I don't think the recognition influenced him at all. The poetry was the simple thing; he worked terribly hard at it and the older and the surer he became, the harder he worked.

Did he find the fame a difficult thing to deal with?
He must have found it a bit embarrassing, but perhaps it hindered his work a little. That's to say, he wouldn't touch verse while people were messing about and hanging on his words and that sort of thing. That would be a time of suspense between poems, because he never did things carelessly in verse... I'm quite sure Dylan would be the last to believe that you could work while you're drunk or affected by drink. At the same time, I think getting drunk and that kind of experience probably impressed itself on the retina of his mind and came out in some of his stories, but the writing itself was always a cold and deliberate thing.
    ... when I used to go round pubs with Dylan, I always felt that he drank rather less than he was reputed to drink, or to have drunk. We were with people who drank, sometimes, so very much more. Because Dylan on the whole went to a pub to talk, and he would put down his pint and he would take a long time to drink it, and certainly he would have more pints, but I never thought of him as a really very heavy drinker – and really he liked beer but, of course, spirits were rather poison to him...

What about Dylan's influence on you and your work?
Oh, it was very great indeed, because he showed me how very stuffy and derivative a lot of my work was, because I'd written certainly more than a thousand poems before I met Dylan, and when I showed him three or four, he said "Are there any more?" and I brought out a trunk which was full of work, because I'd been writing ever since I was a child... he helped me a great deal to show me what really belonged to

my work rather than belonged to the work of other poets.

Would you like to say something about what you observed of Dylan's relationship with his parents?

He was quite devoted to his parents and looked after them very well. When his mother had an accident, he would take her out every day in the wheelchair and certainly he was one of the most devoted sons I've ever met. He loved his parents tremendously... he [DJ] was much more misanthropic than Dylan; Dylan was extremely sociable by nature, and his father more withdrawn and misanthropic, but Dylan revelled in his father's darker sayings... I should say he was a deep influence on Dylan, certainly.

I think it's his father who's been rather misrepresented in America, as a sort of marginal figure, who never encouraged his son or something of the kind, whereas he was a great support to Dylan, at the beginning, and there was nothing he wanted more than Dylan's developing art as a poet. I remember the very first time I heard Dylan broadcast; that evening I returned to his father's house and his father was at the gate. And he said "I have never enjoyed anything on radio so much."

What about Dylan's great-uncle [Gwilym Marles]? He was a minister, and a poet.

I've seen his book... I remember Dylan showing me his book.

What were Dylan's feelings about Wales?

Well, he loved Wales, and he loved living in Wales. One thing he particularly asked for was if he could have certain wishes – I think there were three as far as I remember – one of them was to be able to live in Wales – that was the thing that he wanted to do more than anything else. His poetry was in the tradition of English poetry, but Welsh was in his blood. He would call himself surely a Welsh poet writing English poetry, because Welsh was in his blood. I always feel that Anglo-Welsh is a slightly uncomfortable term, and suggests more a child of English and Welsh parentage, rather than a Welsh person writing in English. You can be wholly Welsh, and write only English poetry. And that's what Dylan did.

... both my parents are Welsh, entirely, and I'm certainly entirely Welsh – writing English poetry, yes. I don't like being called Anglo-Welsh. I think of myself as a Welsh poet, but all the influences on my poetry came primarily from English poets... I have laboriously read the very early Welsh poetry, which is quite wonderful – the oldest poetry in Britain, quite unlike anything else, and it makes me regret very much that I don't know the language enough to know the original and to be able to read it aloud in the original tongue, but my father used to do this while I watched the translation – this was when I was about twenty-six or twenty-seven, and later. We would go over certain poems line by line, and certainly feel those poems, and even in translation the force and splendour of the poetry comes through.

Was your father a writer or a poet?
He did translate a certain number of Welsh poems into English, but he was a bank manager.

He was a speaker of Welsh – and your mother is?
Yes, both Welsh-speaking.

But you didn't learn Welsh?
No, I only got a smattering of it. I hardly knew more than Dylan; perhaps I know a few hundred words.

Rayner Heppenstall [19]

Our first meeting was in December 1934. I was living in Chelsea and Dylan came round to see me... he'd been given my address by Sir Richard Rees, editor of the *Adelphi*, a paper both Dylan and I had been published in. I had already seen Dylan's poems and liked them and I suppose Rees told him that, and he came round with a signed copy of *18 Poems*, which had just appeared... we got fairly thick and drank around the place a great deal together for some weeks to come.

... because Dylan didn't have much formal education and wasn't abstract-minded, he's always rather presented as though he was some sort of inspired zombie – but I always thought him extraordinarily intelligent... I felt that his mind was quicker in every way than my own... I was also very much impressed by how quickly responsive he was to other people and to social situations which, in view of the kind of bad social situations he tended to find himself in and possibly to create, is also a little anomalous.

... the amount we talked about poetry could very easily be exaggerated. We were much more inclined to talk about girls and pubs and comic people. We didn't sit down and have solemn discussions much about poetry... it's certainly the case that, while I heard Dylan talk about all kinds of other poets and poetry (and indeed other arts too), I never once heard him speak of a Welsh poet, except possibly personally some contemporary he knew... I formed the impression that he knew nothing of the tradition of Welsh poetry; not that I was in much of a position to judge at the time, though it's a subject I rather 'got up' later.

... at the time at which I first met him, one poet he talked very happily and favourably about was Thomas Lovell Beddoes. He talked a great deal about *Death's Jestbook*... he was also very keen on the novels of Caradoc Evans... another matter, not poetry, but a music that I also remember him being very keen on in those early days... was *Wozzeck*... the opera [by Alban Berg].

... in contradistinction from lots of things I heard him say about other writers, about whom he could be extraordinarily vicious, he was being very pleasant about a fellow Welsh writer, a novelist, Gwyn Thomas. It so happened I'd been reading for the first time something of his and was very taken by it, and asked Dylan if he knew Gwyn Thomas' works and what he thought about them. He said he had certainly read them and he liked them, and in fact he said he thought they were great. Giving the word I suppose some kind of full force. But then Dylan was not a simple fellow or one to accept any word at it's face value, so then he immediately started adopting somebody else's tones and saying "Although I am chary of using words like great" and then giggled and said "And words like chary!" [20]

... I never heard him mention Rimbaud. I don't think he ever read anything in French. It might be relevant here to mention Norman Cameron, who later translated a great deal of Rimbaud and must be regarded as an authority on him, and it's quite conceivable that Cameron talked about Rimbaud to him... Cameron would also, of course, be quite likely to put the notion into Dylan's head that he was another boy Rimbaud. [21]

... I would say he wasn't a religious poet at all in the usually accepted sense of the word. If he had a religion, it would be some sort of pantheism, very concerned with some dark life force, driving energy through plants and human beings and so on... the only signs I ever saw of a religious poet were quite harshly satirical and at moments rather obscene. I recall that he was composing a gospel story in the form of limericks... I remember, too, at about the same time he'd composed a long song called "The Rape at the YMCA". And that's really about all that I know about Dylan as a religious poet.

Did he talk about politics?
Not in those days. The odd thing was that Chelsea was at that very

moment – the King's Road at any rate – still full of young men in black shirts with buckled belts, broad buckled belts and so on, so that there was plenty of sign of it in the neighbourhood. Indeed, I remember on one occasion on which Dylan and I both met George Orwell together. We were very drunk, I'm afraid, and we ended up in a very good little basement restaurant in the King's Road which was rather a fascist headquarters. Not of the Blackshirts but of comparatively intellectual supporters, and despite that background I never heard Dylan actually talk about fascism at all... apart from this thing against war, I was never aware of him expressing himself politically at all until some years after the War, and I suppose it would have been after this visit to Prague...

... I simply remember him coming into to the Stag's Head, a pub near the BBC, late one evening... and he was absolutely livid at some American there who'd been inveighing against Russia. I don't know that he was particularly anxious to crack up Russia, but he certainly took that view that it wasn't up to Americans to say anything politically against anyone, so that at the very least he had a 'plague on both your houses' attitude, which I may say was my own at the time. But I had a feeling that he was being more fellow-travelling than I would have been prepared to be at the time, and it surprised me and, you know, it stuck.

What about Dylan's drinking, which is a big part of his legend?
Oh, I've got a slightly special attitude to that... during the weeks after I first met him I drank far more than I'd ever drunk before... though two or three years younger than me, he had done a great deal more drinking than I had and was able to carry it better than I was... so that when we got horribly drunk and misbehaved and the one who was misbehaving was usually me rather than Dylan. I soon saw that I had to give it up. Certainly in those days, financially apart from anything else, nobody ever drank anything much but beer, though I know he was rather addicted to the rather strong very good cider that was on sale in those days in Henekey's pubs. Once I remember we drank too much... the evening that he and I went to Bertorelli's and had been invited there by Sir Richard Rees, who was with George Orwell – an occasion when both of us first met George Orwell – that had started on the Henekey's cider in Holborn and really ended up quite disgracefully.

... but even in those days, my impression was that Dylan was mainly drinking beer... I have the impression that he was never a compulsive spirit drinker. His drinking was entirely social. I can't imagine him, though I have no direct evidence on the matter, having the bottle of whisky in the cupboard and putting it down quietly by himself at home. I'm sure that he was just not that kind of drinker at all, and I'm sure that kind of drinking is far more damaging than the sort of extrovertive, social, convivial drinking, which was the only kind I ever saw him going in for, and the only kind I imagine he ever did go in for.

... I also was given the impression from his conversation that he was also more successfully and assiduously promiscuous. He used to tell all kinds of little stories about girls in Swansea, for instance. One I remember being called Little Billie, always referred to herself as Little Billie, and I accepted this. I don't know how true it was... but then this is only his conversation and, after all, I suppose that almost everyone is a bit of a liar about two things – sex and money.

Robert Pocock

I first met Dylan in that pub well-known in Charlotte Street called the Fitzroy... early in 1936. I was introduced to him by our mutual great friend, Nina Hamnett, the artist; and the immediate impression in those days was of Harpo Marx. He had this mass of very fair, curly hair and this pair of gooseberry-coloured eyes, which looked as meretricious as Welsh eyes can be, and he put out a tiny hand rather like a fin – and there again one thought of Harpo Marx – it was rather as though you expected on gripping it to have a motor horn give a squeak... and I must say, he lived up to that. I can say he was halfway between Harpo and Rimbaud. And we got on well from the start.

... he was staying then at Norman Cameron's house down in Hammersmith. One used to go down there and occasionally doss down for the night there because in those days, being very much younger, people slept rough in other people's houses and on their floors.

... I don't think there was anybody who influenced Dylan very strongly in London. Norman Cameron was, on Dylan's own admission, his father-confessor and he used to show all his verse to Norman. And in those days, as always, he used to work very closely, he would never drink while he was working. I have been on occasions in the room next to him, and I have heard him chanting out words, putting words against each other, and that more usually early in the morning. I can say he wasn't as slothful as some people seem to imply. I've even shared the same bed with him and he'd suddenly bounce out of bed at eight o'clock and get right on to work, of whatever kind it might be. And that went on, certainly, when first I knew him, and again after the war in the late Forties, when I came back from the East.

... the great myth about Dylan is that he was a hard drinker. He was a hard drinker in the fact that he could swill beer – he was very fond of beer – it was necessary to him in some way. I've often thought that the way in which he used to pass out after drinking a certain amount, suggested that he might be a diabetic, or eventually become one. Rather like Constant Lambert. But unlike Constant Lambert, he was not a hard tack drinker. He liked to drink beer; I remember being with him once down in Wales with him, Dan Jones and Fred Janes, and we went into a pub after a car drive with Dan and his wife Irene, the four of us, and we were served some unspeakable beer, and you have to go to Wales to get bad beer and we all said "What vile beer this is." And Dylan said "Yes, isn't it?" and swiped all our pints.

Elizabeth Ruby Milton

It was before the War, about 1937... he sort of rescued me from these sophisticated film people, when I made that awful *faux pas* about thinking a lesbian was an omelette... it was in a film studio; I'd been made overtures to by a little chorus boy with sort of crinkly hair, an absolutely beautiful creature, and I was dressed in sort of country clothes. I'd just come down from Scotland, it was my first job and it was during the rehearsal, and he said he'd never had a lesbian before, and I asked him if he did his own cooking. Dylan overheard this, and I think he felt sorry for me and took me under his wing. Which really meant he introduced me to Bohemia.

I was a dancer, and I came down from Scotland... and I thought I was going to be a great film star, and did in actual fact work for Jack Buchanan...

... when I first knew Dylan, I had this little chaste room, white bed and a cross on the wall. He and this other man, Wilfred Huysent, used to escort me, both of them, firmly back to this room I was living in and leave me, very chastely, and I'd go upstairs to my little room. I honestly don't know where he lived at the time. He was just a sort of a romantic character that happened... I used to meet him at Chinese restaurants and pubs and clubs and cafés. It was very exciting for a girl who had come from the back streets of Glasgow, suddenly to meet the one young man who was the most exciting young man of the generation...

... Dylan was quite different to the chorus boys and young film actors, his approach and his idiom was quite different, his clothes were different... he had sort of rough tweeds on, purpley tweeds, a sort of leather jacket... his clothes were always shaggy and his ties were lovely colours. His colours were always lovely... like his speech... these wonderful tones he used. We used to walk down the streets, he used to be talking, it didn't matter what he was saying; half the things I didn't understand then what he was saying. Just lovely to listen to...

5. Elizabeth Ruby Milton

... I saw him quite a lot... we had a sort of romance, not an affair. We used to go, he and Wilfred Huysent, we used to all go together, used to meet and go round all the places together and end up in a restaurant run by a girl called Sacha who was a Russian, and she had this little tiny restaurant behind the Fitzroy, and we used to end up there in the evening... there was another café in Soho called Colombus, where people used to play guitars... there was a lot of boys and girls who went to the Spanish War about that time.

Did Dylan ever make any comment to you about the Spanish Civil War or any other international issue?

Yes. He used to argue with each person, and he was much more concerned with the human side of it, not the political side. There was one young man, Oxford boy, who was going over there and he spent his entire time running away from his girlfriend who was pregnant... he was full of this, what he was fighting for and why he was fighting, and he had a lot of equipment that he was rushing around buying, and this poor little girl was running around from café to pub trying to find him. Dylan was very upset by this. He said: "This wretched girl's having a baby and there is this wretched boy going over to fight."

... I've seen him absolutely in tears, rather whisky tears, but tears. At girls pregnant, not being married – he used to be horribly upset and hurt by any sort of suffering. He was terribly good to Nina Hamnett, that poor girl.

... Nina was a very good painter... by the time that I met up with her she had been drinking a great deal... every time Dylan came into Bohemia – Soho, Bloomsbury, Chelsea – he always used to see Nina, give her some money... when she was very ill once, he brought her some blankets from his own home in Chelsea, and bought her meals, gave her money and encouraged her to paint... he used to giggle with her, and treat her with kindness and gentleness and love – he loved her, you know. Loved her... she must have been well over fifty and not a romantic person... there was no question of an affair or anything like that, he just loved her as an artist and as a person and as somebody who'd gone to seed, that was what he liked in her... sort of disappointed, he pitied the waste. I suppose that was his great thing – he hated waste.

... it's extraordinary he did hate waste so much and he sort of destroyed himself... Nina lost a great friend in Dylan, and a practical friend not just a sympathiser. Somebody who showed his love by practical, hard half-crowns, which was very important to her.

... then there was dear little Napper [Brian Dean Paul], who's now got his title but he had no money for twenty years, and no home... Dylan was terribly good to Napper... whose grandfather is Wieniawski the musician... used to find him in all-night cafés because he'd no home, and Dylan would take him around and give him some money and meals... Napper for nearly twenty years was more or less homeless... he lived a sort of strange life. His father denounced him... he has now succeeded to the property and the title, and he in his turn helps painters...

... the people are called Beatniks now... except they don't create. The Bohemians did... at the very least their idleness was creative... in conversation and wit... but this very conversation and idleness helped to destroy Dylan. Because he had this great genius for words... there he was, this Welsh, articulate, brilliant young man among a lot of people who weren't creative – or weren't positively creative – so that they got excited by him and in turn excited him, and excited him to drink, excited him to behave in this sort of extravagant way. It was they who laughed when he accosted a strange woman, wanted to seduce her... they thought this was a great joke...

... he had a great sympathy with tarts, prostitutes... he liked victims... he felt sorry for victims... he was obsessed by victimisation, and perhaps he offered himself as a victim and it may be he was a sort of saint.

... as far as I'm concerned, we had a completely pure, chaste relationship, although we got into tremendous scrapes, and I had to listen to some really crazy conversations and language... I was very grateful to Dylan because I learnt more with him about life and art and people and humanity than at anytime, anybody... it's such a hackneyed word to say he was sort of a saint, but I suppose you could say he's a sort of martyr... I've never known him to be violent but then, he provoked violence, so that's equally destructive, isn't it?

... he picked up a little girl at a railway station, and he was seen around with her quite a lot, and one day he came in again, sort of in a weepy state and said "Do you know what she said to me when I went to bed with her?" And we all said "No." And he said in a sort of very North Country accent this girl had "I hope you don't stuff me." And he was terribly moved by her idiom – you know, the coarseness of it, and that moved him terribly. She didn't want to become pregnant, she didn't know how to express herself. People who weren't articulate hurt him terribly.

... he was obsessed by death. And creation. Which is sort of contradiction; but creation always made him very sad. He used to cry when women were pregnant. Any re-creation scene or situation... really affected him tremendously... he was also obsessed by death and all his jokes evolved round death... what was known loosely as his dirty jokes, his obscene jokes. Coprophilia – one of the first jokes I ever heard him telling was on this theme, which I rather spoilt for him because after the end of the joke when everybody sort of guffawed and thought it was a great joke I asked "What does that mean? - what does coprophilia mean?" And he explained to me what it meant and that was a sort of instance of our relationship – he sort of educated me.

What would he be talking about?
Poetry, society, never himself... no, not his own poetry. He would recite. He wouldn't discuss his own social problems or emotional problems... we'd discuss events. Spanish War, Nazism – Jewish thing, you know – cruelty.

... at the beginning, nobody knew, nobody would believe these things were happening... we used to discuss if it really was happening. And one or two Jewish people were coming in... artists, sculptors... into London, coming away from persecution... and there were a lot of German artists in London, and some of them doing quite good work, so there was this conflict. You had to either believe German artists or have sympathy with the Jews.

And the German artists didn't want to believe what was happening in Germany.

No, they didn't want to believe... nobody would believe, nobody wanted to believe. Especially somebody as emotional as Dylan. It was too much to believe... then during the War and after the War, by that time he'd become rather cynical, and he used to say that the Jews were willing victims. I remember he and another man called Kafka, the cousin of the writer, were having a discussion about Jews and I remember Dylan jumping up and saying "The Jews went singing to their graves!" And he marched up and down the sort of room singing a sort of Jewish chant. And then he fell apart... didn't weep, you know, but had almost a sort of breakdown. He didn't want to know that people were suffering. Couldn't bear it.

... of course, he had a lot of Jewish friends... British people who had Jewish friends, people they loved, there was this conflict... I know this Jew, I love this Jew, this Jewish woman, this Jewish man, this Jewish child. Because artists can love, they can love people without being ashamed of using the word love... they're not just neighbours, you know, they love this person. Now what if Nazis came here and you had to denounce a Jew? This question was always being put to one, during the War. If you had to denounce a Jew, would you do so? Would you give a Jew food? Would you shelter a Jew? This was all being discussed at studio parties and things like that... this question came up again and again and again.

And what was Dylan's comment on this question?
He was a bit ribald. But then that was defensive, wasn't it? I should imagine half his vulgarity was really defensive, in a way.

... he was rather inclined to react against the British propaganda during the War. As a Welshman, I suppose. And he was always seen around with sort of Irish, IRA people, people like that... one of his best friends was an IRA man who had been in prison a very long time for IRA activities and had come out and written a book about it... He's written lots of books on tramps, and he's written this book about his imprisonment for IRA activities... Jim Phelan.[22]

... Dylan used to sometimes berate the British government for not letting him fight, sometimes he was relieved, and then sometimes he would say that the Welsh would send over their own regiment to fight for Germany. And when France fell, that upset him terribly. That was another time that I think he cried. If he didn't cry, he went through the motions of crying... he was always having emotional breakdowns at that particular period. Anything would make him cry. Put his head down on the counter and cry if the barman gave him the wrong change, because it wasn't a question of being given the wrong change, but what was behind the barman giving him the wrong change. He used to think "Oh, the barman must have a wife and twenty starving children, so therefore he is obliged to work at this dreadful job, and short-change the people." And that would make him weep.

... when I first knew him, he was a beautiful young man and terribly healthy – little peasant, little pony, you know. Wonderfully healthy. But when I met him in the War he was already dying... he came back to me when I was living in Charlotte Street, took him home with me, and I sat up all night with him. He was vomiting into a little basin, this horrible mucus... it was disease... all the time he was vomiting, poor man, he really suffered all night long... and he was resigned! He just went on suffering, sitting up and vomiting and lying down again, sitting up and vomiting and lying down.

... I've never, never, never known Dylan at ease – really. I've never known him relax... even when he was watching the Westerns and movies, he was pre-occupied.

... although Dylan was a very, very vivid person, most of my memories of him are tender and in shadow... when we used to walk down the Embankment together and the leaves would be silhouetted on the pavements... and we used to see those tramps and he used to give them money...

... he appeared to be very sophisticated [but] in a way he was very simple, primitive and elementary. He was like the air and the sea and water. He loved water. He used to spend a lot of time looking at the Thames... maybe he loved that in Caitlin – sort of mermaid quality. Still, I would never think of her as a mermaid... I only met her the twice and both times she was eating and one time she was about to give birth. I was scared of her...

... I think knowing Dylan had made me more of an artist than I would ever have been... if I ever did write or paint or perform it would be more valuable because I'd known him and listened to him and seen him suffering and the terrible, terrible sadness and tragedy and destruction, self-destruction – sort of an offering, almost an offering. And I think that it should have value – his offering that he himself has made, some value should come out of it.

... we used to walk down the Tottenham Court Road sort of avoiding the incendiary bombs. We didn't take any notice of those – we just sort of skipped them, and got on with our conversation, which was much more important, because we had a lot to say, all the time.

... there was that awful night when his two friends were killed... it was in Old Compton Street and we were all in the Swiss House and these two people, a boy called Onions – young man, rich young man, he had a flat in Chelsea, he was always putting people up, people who had no money, no homes, he'd put them up – and he put this girl up. She was a woman soldier of some kind, and he married her and we last saw him in the French House and we went to the Swiss House, which was a few yards away and a bomb fell in between this period and apparently they'd been walking to join us all at the Swiss House when this bomb fell and nothing was found of them except shreds of their raincoat on the door of the Swiss House... that was the end of Oliver and that upset Dylan very much. Actually, he prayed. That made him pray – he prayed at that one point.[23]

Did you know Dylan to go to church or chapel at all?
No. Never, never, never, never, never, never. But he gave the impression, when I first knew him, that he might easily have sang in a choir... he had that innocence with him, even when he was telling the most vile story, he had this look of innocence, and his hair was like a sort of halo – and he had this way of moving his hands, which were almost holy... he'd come to a climax of a story with a sort of papal expression – like a blessing.

... he sang Welsh songs and he'd speak Welsh. Little bits of Welsh he would intone, but he used to speak Welsh to you and you weren't sure whether he was cursing you or making love to you, so that was very disturbing because he might be speaking Welsh and saying the most diabolical things.

... when I first knew Dylan he was finding himself... and then when I caught up with him again he was in a sort of vice. Vice of life and living – his wife, his children, the necessity to meet a deadline... and he'd lost the spontaneous speech... he was depressed and depressive. And sad...

Richard and Frances Hughes

RH: The first time that I can actually remember meeting him is when Augustus John came to stay with us in Laugharne. Using our house there as a kind of base camp, from which to go and see his old father in Tenby. He brought Caitlin with him, and he asked me if I knew Dylan, and I said that Dylan was over at Llansteffan, so he asked Dylan over to lunch with us, and as far as I remember Dylan stayed four or five days...

FH: I just remember Dylan coming into the dining room at Laugharne, and thinking this was one of the most vivid and alive young men I'd seen in years. He was quite thin then, with very brilliant eyes and curly hair, and looked rather ethereal.

RH: It was all a little like a French farce. Augustus took Caitlin and Dylan the next morning in his vast car for a drive around the countryside, and came back with Caitlin only, having heaved Dylan out.

6. Richard Hughes

And from then on, somehow, whenever Augustus went out, Dylan wandered into the house. And he, quite fortuitously, seemed to wander out of the house just before Augustus came back.

FH: There were a lot of different doors, and the garden was divided into various parts, with shrubberies, which was very convenient.

RH: Of course, Laugharne was a peculiar place, and although it's by no means typically Welsh, it was Welsh in one thing of its respect for a poet. The town was very glad to have them there when they arrived. The small tradesmen didn't particularly expect to get their bills paid, but that was all part of one's debt to poetry. There was even an occasional cabbage left on their doorstep, anonymously.

... it was very un-Welsh in that it was the church which was all-powerful in Laugharne. And the chapel was very much the underdog. And whereas in most Welsh villages, there are at least six places of worship open, perhaps one pub, in Laugharne there were six pubs and about one-and-a-half places of worship.

How did the thought of writing Under Milk Wood *start?*

RH: Well, back in 1939, shortly after the outbreak of war, there was an amateur play got up... which Dylan produced in the Memorial Hall at Laugharne and my wife played a leading part, the local butcher played a part, I came back the night before, and was hurriedly pushed into a small part. It was pretty good rubbish, as a play, but when we were talking it over in the small hours afterwards – still in our makeup and still half-dressed in the comic clothes – Dylan was very much impressed with the natural ability for acting of these people, and he said "Of course, what Laugharne really needs is a play written about Laugharne characters. And get them all to play their own parts." I said "Surely, you'd never get them to do that." He said "Yes, they would. They're so convinced that they're absolutely sane, normal people, and that what they're doing is the only possible thing, they behave in the only possible way anybody can behave. I think they'd be only too delighted to have a chance of proving how right they are on the stage." And I think that that was the very first germ of the *Under Milk Wood* idea. Although, when he came to write *Under Milk Wood*, he didn't use actual Laugharne characters. But all the characters in *Under Milk Wood* are people who *should* have lived at Laugharne.

... that was partly what he liked about it was this burning sincerity with which they carried out all their eccentricities, as if they were the most normal way of behaving.

FH: Dylan was describing having been to Llansteffan to see cousins, and said that in the villages on that side there were so many people who were batty that there was a bus to the lunatic asylum once a week. And I said "Are they wild mad, or just melancholy?" and he said "Oh, just more or less sad. Just that everything everybody said of them, they think it's true."

... people who were very closed in and never talked to anybody else at all, would talk to Dylan.

It's said that he had a great deal of mysticism in his spirit, and this comes out in some of his early stories. Sort of dark, gloomy, morbid stories... Laugharne was infused with something of this sort of superstitious character.

RH: No, Laugharne wasn't, there was nothing dark and gloomy and morbid about Laugharne. Unless you consider lack of any sense of the passage of time dark and gloomy and morbid. We ourselves had the feeling that if we lived there much longer we'd suddenly wake up at our own funerals.

What about the people in Laugharne who became particular friends of Dylan? He had a feeling for the ordinary bloke, didn't he?

RH: Yes, except the ordinary bloke was never ordinary to Dylan. When he met an ordinary bloke and then came back and described them, it was somebody absolutely extraordinary.

Do you recall some of the occasions in which Dylan participated in some of the activities of the town?

RH: Dylan was very fond of going out in boats. I don't think he actually took part in the regatta. He more often went off in Billy Williams' motor boat, which had a usual crew of a deaf and dumb barber and a deaf and dumb other chap. And Dylan would go off with them over to Ferryside or Llansteffan, on some wild marauding expedition.

What about Dylan's drinking?
RH: Well, certainly at the time we knew him, he was drinking only beer, and not an awful lot of it. I think he did it for two reasons: one was his extreme sociability, always meeting these marvellous ordinary chaps, slowly drinking two or three pints. The other is that any poet gets himself to a state of nervous tension which has either to come out as a poem, or he's got to find some other means of short-circuiting it, and releasing the charge. And it can't always come out as a poem, and I do think that makes a poet particularly glad of the odd pint, because he's got to run that charge down quickly somehow.

But he certainly didn't drink in order to work. I think he drank occasionally as an alternative to work; a psychological alternative to work. But I don't remember his ever getting really tight, then.

… he worked very hard… if he was writing, he wouldn't want a drink… in the pre-War period, I don't remember his drinking spirits unless he was with a spirit-drinking friend, then he might.
FH: I never saw him a nuisance with it, but I think after he'd been out with Augustus John he probably slept late and wasn't happy the next day, because I know I thought it was a pity.

One of the major problems in Dylan's life was always money.
RH: He managed it very well, in the sense of managing to get rid of it at once. He'd never got any money. Occasionally he'd get a publisher's advance…
FH: I've got something to say on that. After they'd been for a certain amount of time in Laugharne and had a few bills, they had an advance, and they went to the shops and said "We wish to settle up – because we have some money." And the tradesmen had laughed before at the idea of friends of ours not having money to settle bills, and most of them didn't even bother to produce the bill when Dylan and Caitlin asked for it. So then, within a week, there wasn't the money to pay it. Which seemed to me a bit unfair, as they were young, married people.

… I imagine when his ship came home, which it did from time to time, he treated his friends in the pub, but as regards ourselves, as soon as they were established in Seaview, they were terribly generous asking us to meals, and particularly at times when it was very acceptable; such as they asked Diccon the night after my fourth child was born. And so on – oh yes, and when I came down from North Wales to see to the house and had really not opened my own house, then they would ask me to meals. Really, in that way they were exceedingly generous at just the right time. Towards us – they were very generous.

What about family relations?
FH: They were certainly very much in love all the time we saw them. Caitlin never believed in the husband helping very much in the house. She always said it made it much, much more complicated, and in fact I remember her mocking when Diccon was, one day, cooking one course of the dinner, or maybe the whole dinner. Once she was ill with a poisoned finger – in Seaview – which was a very inconvenient house. She was in bed on the first floor, and the kitchen was in the basement and Dylan was anxious to do something for her, and she said she would like a cup of tea, and she told him how to do it. So he went down to the basement and he was there quite a long time, and he boiled a kettle, or nearly boiled it, and put the tea leaves in the teapot and then he poured the water on, but he couldn't find a cover to put on, and he knew that there should be something over it, so he took a half a pound of cheese and put it on top, but he took the paper off the cheese first. And another time in the same illness, I remember her saying that she'd asked him to get her some hot water, and he hurried away to get it, but he came back without it, and he said "Well I did hurry to get it – you can't expect everything."

... when they first had a child, they hadn't got into the way of very regular meals and times, but Caitlin did make tremendous efforts that the child should have a regular upbringing and all the right food. Which was very difficult for her, as they'd been accustomed to stay up very late at night and, if they wanted to, sleep on in the morning. But she was very keen on Llewelyn getting as good a start as possible.

... they always had more or less *pot au feu* or stew of some kind, which was practically necessary, as they had such very limited cooking arrangements, but it was always palatable, and there always seemed enough food in her house, however difficult it was to get it.

In the book that Brinnin wrote, he recounts a visit to Laugharne, and the turbulent atmosphere in the home, at that period at least. Would you say that this characterized the atmosphere in the Dylan household?
FH: No, I certainly wouldn't. Caitlin, in the early days, used to get a bit

fed up sometimes when so many young people came from Swansea to see Dylan, and in the end stayed to three and four meals, and perhaps stayed the night, because it was difficult for her to cope with all the cooking and washing up and looking after her child. And that was the only thing that I remember that used to make her annoyed from time to time, and that was perfectly understandable.

... I remember one occasion when I went to call on them in the afternoon, and they were all in bed and the baby, too, just reading novels and eating sweets, and I thought that was very beautifully happy and relaxed.

RH: He certainly borrowed a lot of our books. When they left Laugharne, we went round and collected one wheelbarrowful and one blanketful of books.

FH: While Dylan was a neighbour in Laugharne, or he was living in our house, we never saw any signs of him being in love with anybody but Caitlin. Such squabbles as they had were absolutely short-lived and of a very, very minor nature. Certainly I think there would have been opportunities for Dylan to meet attractive young women, and he never seemed to want to take them.

RH: Yes, I think one had a feeling that they were outstanding example of monogamy, with all its advantages and disadvantages.

What would you say were Dylan's main qualities? One thinks of his generosity of spirit and so forth, his boisterousness...

RH: It may have become that later on, but I should have called it more a vividness than a boisterousness, when we knew them. He had this very rare power of seeing everything and everybody in, if you like, a slightly distorting light, but a light that was so clear and bright, that it made them more real, as he described them, than they'd been to themselves walking down the street... it's a little like the prep school boy. When your boy comes back from school, and starts describing the masters – whatever school it is, and whatever boy it is – they're always the oddest set of individuals that ever walked this earth. And to that extent, I suppose it was a childlike quality in him.

What do you feel about the image of Dylan that has grown up, since his death, through the book that has been written by Brinnin?

FH: Absolutely terrible. It was rather mesmerising, and one wanted to go on, and yet I'd have been very happy to throw it in the fire, and I had to before the end.

... I think not quite enough is said about Dylan's extraordinary humanity. It was because he saw people so absolutely clearly, as it were in the nude, divested from all their dressing up, that he could tell the real from the false, in everyone, when he saw them, even for a short time. He used to come back from the pub, and sometimes he'd seen someone from a distance, like I remember a very, very silent young captain in the army, whom Dylan only had got talking for the first time, and they talked half the night. And then, another time, with Caitlin, they'd stayed with some millionaires, and he described to us the sadness, the terrible sadness, of life there, and how they had to have the same lunch and the same dinner every single midday and every single evening. I remember all this, and I suppose he taught me more about humanity in very, very many other people... he could see so clearly what was the real and what wasn't. And what wasn't real was boring to him.

Jack Wallis

The first time I met Dylan was in the Ship [Mousehole, Cornwall], and I was introduced by Wyn Henderson... she kept the Lobster Pot... a little hotel, boarding house... everybody in the village loved her. She would do good for anybody. She was a kind of person, if somebody was down and out, she would look after them.

... the most vivid remembrance I got of him was when he got married to Caitlin. I was at sea that day in a small boat – what we called a longshore boat. I were working over on me own... I were fishing then, going to the Longships – that's a spot where the pollocks used to run. And mackerel.

And when I got home in the evening I said to my wife "I'm going down to the Lobster Pot, because they're throwing a party for Dylan and Caitlin." My friend, Joe Maddern, who was harbourmaster and engineer of the lifeboat at the time, he went to the wedding and the afternoon do. There was all in the afternoon and all in the evening, a proper do. A proper party.

Wyn's two sons, Ian and Nigel, and Dylan and myself, we were four of us and, I can tell you, it was who now can make the most mischief and who could get into the most fun and games.

... the Ship Inn, Mousehole, was the pub we used to go into there, because a lot of fishermen used to use it... when we went into the Ship to have a drink we used to go down to the lounge – there was several people that all knew one another. There was Betty John – that's a relation to Casper John, the artist... then there was Mary Humphreys and her brother Kenneth, Joe Maddern, and Ben Jeffery. A reporter of *The Cornishman*, Trevor Waters, was a great friend of Wyn's and Dylan's and us – so we were quite a little party, and we used to have fun and games. In they days, you had to make your own fun, there wasn't no television nor nothing then, not like it is now.

... they would all go to the Ship and have a bit of sing-song. We had songs like *Maggie May* and *A-Mining We Shall Go*, and *A Merry Place you may Believe was Mousehole on Tom Ballcock's Eve* – we used to sing all them... he would sing, yes, he would join in. Oh yes, it used to be lovely singing in the Ship Inn in those days.

... I was working a small boat, and there was plenty of bad times that we would be in the pub – you'd go there and gather around and have a yarn and crack a joke... and then the British Legion Club was open then, and we used to go up there dancing, four of us used to go up there, and we would try over and over who could dance more dances... Dylan, Nigel, Ian and myself.

You think Dylan liked the company of fishermen and other ordinary people?
Oh, he mixed. He was a good feller; he used to mix up with us all right. But he had two sides to him, which we used to laugh about sometimes – if somebody'd come in a little bit high up, as we called, he would be just as good as them.

... one of his favourite places, if he was writing or doing work, he would go down on the box by the harbour mouth and sit there, and one could see him writing then... .no, he wouldn't say very much about his work or himself in the pub. He's only in there, as the saying goes, only in there for the beer.

... he've asked me once or twice "What do that mean, Jack? That's similar to a word in Welsh". A Cornish term we use, like "gwine" or "brem"... he would make a note of that...

... I knew at the time he must have been writing... because sometimes Dylan had plenty money, or seemed to have plenty of money, and other times he wadn't very flush, but as soon as Dylan got any money it was "Come on, let's go in and have a drink." He would treat us, you know, the people who was good to him.

... I've never seen him cadge anything, he never had chance to cadge, because if he was down in his luck a bit, if he didn't have a load of money, we would – as he would treat us – so we would treat him. And you didn't have to cadge because Wyn Henderson had a heart as big as the world.

... when we go sea in these little boats, long-lining, longshoring, we go away with what we call our bag – that's our eats – and we're out all day to six, seven o'clock in the evening... Dylan has been out in her once or twice, and Wyn. She'd say "Jack, get us out the boat." A twelve-horse power motor, Kelvin. She was a very nice little boat, called the *Silver Spray*... they would book the boat then, and we'd go across and down to Porthleven. That's the village right across the bay. And we'd get there right about the time the pubs open – little pub that's called the Wheat.

... I remember one instance, we had a few beers and the boat was down by the pier. He said "Jack, warn't be going out to have a trip now, by this lovely moonlight." So we went down the pier and got aboard the boat, and when we got outside I said "Where do you want to go?" He said "Steer straight for the moon." And this went on for quite a while; we was all there, making fun of him and one thing and another, and I said to myself, if I don't turn around and go back we shan't be able to get in the harbour. Unknown to them, I turned her around, and we got back, everything okay, to Mousehole.

Brigit Marnier

I'm with Mrs Brigit Marnier, Caitlin's sister. What is your recollection of the first time that Dylan came into the life of your family?
He was like a cherub – beautiful. Round face, quite thin – and rather helpless, with his little hands, little thin hands, and my sister opening his boiled eggs for him in the morning... he stayed with us [Blashford, Ringwood]. And he wrote in one of our rooms – there was a horrid oil stove in what used to be the woodshed, and we called the big room, and he had a little table there... we had thirteen rooms – it was a big house... a very rough house, but a lot of room in it... about three or four acres, yes, which I looked after.

... we used to go every day to the pubs, and play bar billiards. We all played that. But he was a very cosy person – very cosy to talk to round the table. And we all loved him. Mother loved him, I did. Very nice... he always made you feel that you were interesting. He had this wonderful gift, that *you* were entertaining, didn't matter what you said. Very *sympathique*... and with great kindliness – kindly man. I remember him during the War in a pub, and a Jew came in, and Dylan, a bit drunk, dashed up to him, "A Jew, a lovely Jew" and hugged him, and kissed him, and had him for the whole evening. There was real warmth.

Dylan's children must have enjoyed coming down here.
Oh, they loved it. And Llewelyn's a real country boy now. Loves the country. Bird-nesting and suchlike... Llewelyn spent about seven years there, until they suddenly took him away – it nearly broke Mother's heart... Colm came when he was a little boy, because he went to school with mine, I had him for quite a long time, when he was about four or five... Edward, my younger one, is the same age as Colm... they're very good friends now. In fact, Colm always leads Edward astray. Last time they were in London, Edward finished up in jail, or something.

We used bicycles at Blashford – we hadn't got cars in those days. We used to set off on bicycles. And buses. And we had a horse and cart for a bit... we were mad bird-nesters, and I know my sister would take him [Dylan] out... we used to have this passion for swimming, but he didn't like that much... you'd put the bath water in the bath and put Dylan in and he'd just sit there. Wouldn't wash, wouldn't get wet all over. Caitlin used to very often splash him about and wash him... didn't like water much.

... I remember Dylan in Italy, when we went to Elba – all these Italians, these huge men showing off what they could do, throwing stones across these old mines... Dylan was tiny next to them, picking up a stone and throwing it miles further than them... but his health was not very good, already by then, in Italy... but he was very much a fighter, you know, would not give in to it. Not a hypochondriac at all.

Did Dylan talk much about Wales, and Welsh life or culture?
No – never spoke about things like that. He hated culture being upheld, rather hated the Italian thing. He was always down-to-earth, day-to-day things. That's why he was so cosy to be with. Most unpretentious.

What about Caitlin's attitude to Dylan's poetry? Did she become a friendly and useful critic to him?
Well, in Italy I remember her – she was very good, she was very strict about what he wrote and would criticize quite firmly – don't do this or don't do that. Whether she was right or wrong, I don't know, but she was for keeping the standards up always, Caitlin – very high standards.

Constantine FitzGibbon

It was either late '36 or more probably early 1937. There were pubs in and around Charlotte Street which were then frequented by painters and writers and so on. I was very young – it was before I went up to Oxford

– and having lived in Paris, and moved in such society, I quite naturally gravitated to that area of London while I was waiting to go up to Oxford, after having won my scholarship. I think I first met Dylan in the Wheatsheaf. He was a little over four years older than me. In our little society he was already famous. Both *18 Poems* and *Twenty-five Poems* had then been published and he was regarded as a great character.

Who were the people he was meeting at this time that might have had an influence on him?

I think by this time he was getting beyond the stage of being influenced... it was in the earlier years, '33, '34, when he first went to London that one could perhaps talk about influence, although even then I think the word is one that, so far as his writing goes, is very suspect and very dangerous. He was very much his own inspirer, as it were. He was parthenogenetic almost as a poet. Of course, he was very widely read in poetry, but, as for direct influence, I think such as there was had occurred in Swansea before ever he came to London.

... how was he supporting himself? I really have no idea. But how were any of us supporting ourselves? Some of us had tiny private incomes. There were some rich people floating about who would occasionally buy a bottle of champagne or something of that sort, but in general we were all living very much from hand to mouth. It was a small society of painters and writers and Dylan was not an exceptional figure. There is a sort of legend that Dylan was always quite different from everybody else. Well, in this group of people he wasn't. We all drank about the same amount, we all flirted with the girls in the same sort of way and Dylan was only different from the rest of us in that he was, first of all, much the most amusing person I've ever met in my life, much the wittiest person I've ever met, and secondly, he was perhaps a genius.

... we none of us had any money and we'd borrow half a crown from each another, or a quid if we could. But we'd always pay it back when we could. There were one or two notorious spongers about, and they didn't get the half a crown and the quid after a little while. Dylan was not one of those. At least not among his friends he wasn't. But he certainly adopted a different attitude towards the rich. He was quite happy to take the largest possible sums he could get off those who could afford it.

... I remember on one occasion, one of the rudest things I've ever heard a man say to another... there was a rich young man who had taken up Dylan, and Dylan had got quite a bit of money out of him and this young man was irritating Dylan and Dylan said to him "If you weren't rich, we wouldn't even talk to you." I don't think he borrowed any more money from him after that.

So he could hurt people? Really rather savagely.
Yes, he could. I don't think he did so very often, and I'm sure he didn't like doing so. After all, why should he? He was a gentle creature.

... Peter Watson was extremely good to him – the man who financed *Horizon*. He was usually good for a hundred pounds when the worst came to the worst. It should be stated here how extremely good his publishers were to him – Dents. They could almost always be relied on for something or other at the last moment. Largely owing to the very, very careful attention to Dylan's needs that David Higham his agent gave. Who really did an enormous amount for Dylan, which has not been recognised. In every way. Even to the extent of meeting the train, and taking his children off the train. Not the sort of thing one expects one's literary agent to do.

... he was extremely generous and I can tell a story about that which I think is characteristic. A friend of mine called Francis Butterfield, a painter whom Dylan knew only slightly, through me. I don't think he particularly liked him; they certainly weren't close friends. When Dylan was down in New Quay, he still had Wentworth Studios, and Francis had nowhere to live at all. My wife suggested that he move into Dylan's studio, which was empty. So we sent Dylan a telegram and Dylan said "Certainly, by all means. The key is with the landlady", who was the proprietress of the Cadogan Arms, a pub in the King's Road. And so we went along there, and she said she had no objection to Francis moving in, but the rent must be paid first that Dylan owed her. It was something like eight pounds. So we cabled this to Dylan and he sent the money at once, and that eight pounds must have been hard for him to find at that time, but he sent it at once rather than think of Francis having nowhere to go. I think that is an example of his generosity, and thoughtfulness, and kindness. [24]

... when I was seeing him, he was mostly in film work. He wasn't really in the BBC then, or not much. And he regarded his film work as a dead bore. Simply money-making. He had no interest in it whatsoever. Except one or two little films he liked, but in general it was an office job which he reluctantly went to in his attempt to support his wife and family. You see, there's all this talk about Dylan being such a bohemian and so on, but a real bohemian would have said "To hell with my wife and family," but that was not Dylan's attitude.

... I would say, in the first place, that Dylan in the Thirties didn't drink any more than the rest of us. In fact, rather less than quite a number of people with whom I was knocking about with at that time, and whom he was seeing. He always had a very weak head. He would get tight on a couple of glasses of beer, if he was in the mood. Later on again, I would say, when I was seeing him in Chelsea at the end of the War, that he was perfectly normal. We all drank rather heavily, you must understand that, but he was not exceptional in that. What he was exceptional about was the sort of *joie de vivre* that he brought to it all...

... Dylan was accustomed to drinking beer, we all were, for two reasons. First of all, before the War he couldn't afford spirits, and secondly, during the War spirits were extremely hard to come by. Beer was certainly his steady drink. But he was only too delighted to drink a bottle of whisky if there was one going.

... Dylan had a lot of girls before he met Caitlin. A lot. There was no question about it. And he made no attempt to disguise the fact. Why should he? As for his extra-marital affairs – I would say that when Dylan was away from Caitlin he had not the slightest hesitancy in going to bed with any girl who was willing to go to bed with him. But when he was with Caitlin it was a different story. That is to say, I can't imagine Dylan carrying out a hole-in-the-corner affair with somebody, in secret and so on, there was none of that... but in Dylan's morality, in the morality that was prevalent in that circle in the Thirties and Forties, physical fidelity was not prized particularly highly. But emotionally he was faithful to Caitlin, pretty well all through.

Their relationship was rather turbulent at times. Do you think this became a strain on him?
I think it became a great strain on him. I think the real basis of the strain was Dylan's endless money troubles. I know that Dylan felt it was bad and wrong of him that he couldn't support his wife and children in a proper way. That Caitlin was constantly kept short of money and so on. She went for him about this, as I think most women unfortunately do do, and I think that was the real basis of the strains and tensions that built up between them.

There was another basis of conflict, too, because of the attention that Dylan got in company. This bothered Caitlin because she liked being the focus of attention, didn't she?
Well, it's not quite as simple as that. There were some times when Caitlin would be in the best of spirits and be in a very good mood when

Dylan was being amusing and talking a lot. At other times this would obviously irritate her and then she would tend to go for Dylan and put up a sort of rival show of her own. Or sometimes just walk out. But she didn't like it if she thought Dylan was getting all the attention. I think that is undoubtedly true.

… Caitlin could be entertaining. She could be sullenly silent sometimes when she was in a poor mood. Just absolutely nothing for hours on end and sort of scowl at people. And at times she could be absolutely bloody but in general she was all right. She was good company in general. She was never amusing in the way that Dylan was, but she was all right.

… I remember Dylan staying with me in London, on more than one occasion, and Caitlin was coming up and Dylan was very pleased that she was coming. "Cait's coming up tomorrow and we must – I must – keep sober this evening and be in good shape when Cait comes up." And "I must have a clean shirt" and "Isn't it fine Cait's coming up tomorrow" and so on. There was no indifference there, as far as I saw… but on the other hand he would wander off sometimes, and so would she. Dylan prized his freedom very highly, you see.

Some people try to pin the blame principally on her for Dylan's descent into excessive drinking towards the end.

I don't think that's a fair charge really… the strain to which I alluded… there might have been women so angelic in temperament that they could have avoided that strain. Caitlin did not have such a temperament. I doubt if I've ever met a woman who did. The point was that Dylan loved her. Had she had any other sort of a temperament he might not have loved her as much as he did. It's a chicken and egg question this.

What about Dylan's feelings for his children, and what they meant to him?

I don't know very much about that. You see, I never stayed with Dylan in Laugharne, unfortunately. I wish I had. I don't remember his talking a great deal about his children, but I remember his attitude being more or less a normal one towards his children. I know that when they were living in one room in Wentworth Studios that Dylan used to come round and work in my tiny little house because Aeronwy made such a din that he couldn't do his work at home, but that doesn't imply any sort of irritation. I think it's quite a natural thing. I'd have done the same under the circumstances.

What about his feelings for his parents?

I never met Dylan's mother. I met Dylan once with his father, in London. His father had come up – this was again at the end of the War – and Dylan was very, very much on his best behaviour with his father. I remember that the first evening he was there – Dylan told me this – that he wanted to, not exactly impress his father, but show his father that he had some decent friends in London, and he introduced him to, I think, Augustus. And the next evening he introduced his father to Matthew Smith. On the third day his father said "Haven't you got any friends your own age, Dai?" and so I was taken along and I remember their attitude towards one another was characterised by the word 'respect'. They seemed to respect one another very greatly. Mr Thomas was obviously very proud of Dylan and Dylan was very anxious not to say anything that could offend or hurt his father. I mean he was very careful in his choice of language. He wasn't averse to rather strong language at normal times, but not then, not with his father. He was very much on his best behaviour. It was touching to see them together.

T. S. Eliot figured in Dylan's life didn't he?

He regarded Eliot with enormous awe – as we all did. He wasn't a friend of Eliot's. Eliot had turned down his poems, you see. But I never came across any resentment... he used to drop in and borrow a fiver from Eliot from time to time... Eliot has told me. And, of course, Eliot published him in *The Criterion* magazine early on but there was no friendship, he wasn't a friend. He was far too remote a figure for Dylan. I mean, Mr Eliot is not a man to sit around in public houses.

How would you characterise Dylan's sense of humour?

What I remember chiefly of his conversation is this piling up of imagery on imagery. A positive wedding cake of words would be produced. And it would go on and you would think this must be the end, and there'd still be some more, and there'd still be some more. That is what I remember. The tremendous richness of humour, of imagery, and of language.

... when he was drunk he was occasionally a bit aggressive. On the whole, I would say not. Dylan was a very timid man in many ways. Somebody has said of his putting out these – I think it was Aneirin Talfan Davies – of putting out all these prickles and spikes to keep people away from him. Well, that was one aspect of it. But the other aspect of this sort of timidity was that Dylan's idea of earthly bliss was a snug little corner of an unpretentious bar with two or three close friends and some beer and a nice warm fire and fun and jokes and laughter, tucked away in this little corner. That's what he liked, that's what he was looking for an awful lot. He was frightened in big, noisy, brassy, smart places. He was physically frightened of them.

What were Dylan's forms of relaxation, when he wasn't writing and drinking?

He was very fond of watching cricket. I went to Lords once or twice and I think he found it extremely relaxing and pleasant. It is very pleasant after all. One sits there, it's a pretty spectacle, it makes a nice noise... I don't remember his being very interested in the techniques of the batsmen and the bowlers. No, I think it was the general atmosphere and the spectacle that he liked, and this feeling of freedom when one is watching cricket. After all, one can get up, one can walk away, one can go to the tavern and have a beer. One can walk out of the thing altogether whenever one likes. One isn't tied down. Unlike going to the theatre or something, when one is tied to one's seat.

I did go to the music hall with him occasionally. At least once, and I think twice, we went to the Chelsea Palace. But there again, one has the feeling that one could get up whenever one wanted to and go out and come back whenever one wanted to and so on. I know from Dylan's letters that at least in his early life he occasionally went to the theatre. But I don't believe he ever went to the theatre after about 1937. I'd be surprised if he ever did. Unless it was to see something special – something very special. But I can't imagine his ever going along to Shaftesbury Avenue and just going into a theatre because he wanted to spend an evening in a theatre.

What was his response to the music hall?

He absolutely loved it, and the simpler the humour, the coarser, the better. That's what he liked... as a boy, he was a great cinema-goer, yes. Oh yes, a great cinema-goer. And I remember going to a Marx Brothers film with him once and he adored that. We went to see some film once. I can't remember what it was. It was a very sentimental thing. I think it was about a dog – why we went to it I don't know – about Lassie or something, and Dylan blubbed like anything. He was very easily moved to tears by any sort of sentimental thing like that.

... he liked jazz, yes. He wasn't an aficionado, but he liked the words of these songs. I think he was particularly fond of a song about a paper dolly – "I want a paper dolly all my own" – which he thought were wonderful words... he didn't think it was a great poem or anything, but wonderful that anybody could write such things down, on paper. [25]

... I remember his saying to me that he simply could not understand how any man could write a symphony. How any man could carry so much music in his head at once. He could understand how anybody could paint, or sculpt, or write anything, but the idea of writing a symphony was to him incomprehensible. The complexity of it.

I believe that Dylan was best man at your wedding?

My second marriage, in 1944. I asked Dylan to be best man, and he was very pleased and flattered at this. It was the sort of compliment that he appreciated very much, which is part of his charm. And he was down in Wales at that time and he came up especially and – he was late. It was a very simple Registry Office ceremony. And then we had some drinks at the Ritz afterwards, had lunch at the Ritz. And one of those enormous footmen there came in and said "There's a person at the bar who says he's a member of your party." This was about two o'clock, half-past two in the afternoon – it was quite empty. Except for Dylan... he seemed to have two overcoats on and looking rather like a taxi-driver and quite out of place at the Ritz, and he was extremely upset that his train had been delayed. It wasn't his fault at all.

... anyhow, we went off and had some drinks, and then he came back to our little house and we went down to the pub and I remember we picked up an old tramp in the street who had a guitar, and Dylan said "Oh, aren't you lucky. Troubadours at your wedding. Caitlin and I never had any troubadours." And then we went back to the house – still with this tramp and his guitar – and went to bed and Dylan and the tramp slept downstairs in the drawing room. There was a terrible air raid that night and Dylan had expressed to us his great fear of air raids. Next morning, we heard the tramp going off, still strumming on his guitar, and I went downstairs and there was Dylan and he said "It was terrible. I was sound asleep and it was the first time I had ever been able to sleep through an air raid and that beastly old man woke me up and said "You needn't be frightened, Dai – I'm here to look after you.""

I noticed that the term 'Dai' was used. That's the second time it's cropped up now. Was he called Dai by his friends in London?

He was sometimes called Dai. Usually called Dylan.

Was he ever called Taffy?

Never, to my knowledge.

Just Dai?

Yes.

Bert Trick

Swansea was full of omens about the disaster which was to come. Although I think there were very few people in 1938 [who] thought that Swansea would be virtually destroyed... but there was this background of dread and doom which was creeping over us, and it certainly affected Dylan very much indeed. Give you another example: I remember being up in his house – Fred Janes and Tom Warner were with us... we switched on the radio for the news, and they announced the fall of Madrid. Well, we'd followed the civil war in Spain with a great deal of interest. This was nothing academic, because there were Swansea boys who were known to us, who had gone and died in Spain, in the belief that they were going to stem the tide of fascism... I remember organising a memorial service in Fforest Fach Institute... in memory of the boys in Swansea who had died in the International Brigade. So these things, they came right into our own homes.

... and on this particular night they announced the fall of Madrid, and I remember my own personal feeling was one of profound dismay, and I know that Dylan shared it, because he had been asking from time to time what I thought was happening... of course, Dylan wasn't quite as remote from these things as you might think, because there were a number of poets who died in the International Brigade.

... Swansea and Spain you know, there'd been a very close tie for many years because the old potato boats used to come into Swansea – in fact there was a character in Swansea at that time known as Potato Jones, who defied Eden's blockade... if I remember rightly, it was *HMS Hood* that was stationed outside the Basque country, supposedly to stop fascist penetration from the outside, but it was equally effective in stopping the refugees getting away from the inside. But Potato Jones is a local famous character... he defied *HMS Hood* and he just carried on and plied his trade and snooted his finger at the majesty of the British Navy at that time. There was too, a big Spanish colony in Swansea – that again is traditional, so that it wasn't surprising that we people in Swansea offered sanctuary to eighty odd young Basque children that came over.

... Dylan was down on one of his home visits from London, and it was the time that the local authority had taken over Sketty Hall for the children. And as usual, of course, I was in the throes of that. I was on the reception committee. And Dylan found out about this, and he came to see me and he said "Look, I've got Caitlin and her sisters staying here, and we'd like very much to visit the Basque children's home at Sketty. Could you arrange it?" I had a few misgivings about taking them, because I had no idea how they would get along with these eighty children there...

I always used to take little bags of sweets and trinkets and that sort of thing when I went visiting, so as soon as they saw me coming there were shrieks of delight and the kids came tumbling down this slope, down towards the entrance gates. Meantime, I don't know if it was Caitlin's sister or who it was, it was all very confused, but she opened the boot of the car and inside was the biggest stock of sweetmeats I've ever

7. Bert Trick

seen. Liquorice allsorts, peppermint rock, jelly babies, the lot! They just handed these out to these children, and they were received in great style. So I took them along, with the children all trailing behind us, up to the house to the matron, who was a Swansea-born Spanish person... I think it was one of the relatives of Caitlin – she spoke Spanish to this matron, and, of course, immediately they were made most welcome. They were guests of honour. It was a royal visit, one which I had had misgivings about, turned out to be an absolute winner.

Eventually they decided to take their farewells, much to the children's grief because they were having a whale of a time, but they said they were going to motor to St David's, in Pembrokeshire.[26] So they got the car and started piling in, but they couldn't find Dylan. So then a real hunt started... eventually we located him. He'd been down in a field where these children had been making an air raid shelter, a ground shelter. They'd dug a turret through a mound of the ground, with a sort of exit. And, of course, Dylan had gone into this air raid shelter with the kids, and couldn't get out through the exit – he was stuck. So we had to lie down and crawl in and catch hold of his ankles and pull him out backwards, very dishevelled! That's one little incident which I always remember with great joy...

... I remember Dylan calling with Caitlin; he was visiting his people who were then, I think, living at Bishopston... in the evening, after we'd had a meal, we went up to the lounge... and I showed him some of the letters I'd received – which I still have – from the ordinary persons, the average resident in Swansea, who wanted to be provided with air raid shelters, because the raids had already started on Swansea. And I remember showing these to Dylan, and he really had tears in his eyes... just to give you an example of the sort of thing I'm talking about. It was from two old ladies... asking if I could do anything to provide them with an air raid shelter. I was in charge of that, as you know. And it said "We are both over seventy years of age, and when the bombs start dropping we get very frightened and we scramble over the wall into the field next to the house and we put two galvanized sheets on top of us, but we get very cold. Please could you let us have a shelter in the garden?" Now that's one of the sort of letters I showed Dylan that night.

And this brought tears to his eyes, you say?
Really, tears to his eyes. He was really emotionally upset. He had a tremendous feeling for people in distress, or people who were very old. It was all part of his make-up.[27]

... the Swansea Blitz [February 1941] was the most devastating... I remember going down to my office – we had taken a building right opposite the Market, on the corner of Union Street, I think it is, and Oxford Street. It had been previously been R.E. Jones' place, downstairs... we'd requisitioned this for the Air Raid Shelter Department, and I was going to the office. I had to walk all the way, there was no transport, of course... as I stood on the corner facing where the office had been the night before, there was nothing but a heaving mass of smouldering buildings. Oxford Street and the Market – all that had been flattened, and there were firemen's hoses snaking all over the mounds. And when I stood there who should come around the corner, but Dylan and Caitlin. And as far as I can remember, that's the last time that I physically met them... now you're talking about the compassion of Dylan, I remember standing there with Caitlin. I was there with a Warden's helmet on, incidentally, and he said "Bert, our Swansea has died. Our Swansea has died." And by God, he was right. The Swansea that we knew, the pubs, the places, were gone, and gone for all time. And that's the last time that I remember talking to Dylan, because within the next year I came up to Wrexham... Hitler's bombs not only blew Swansea apart, they blew Dylan and I apart.[28]

Gwynfor Evans

It was very early in the War. I was then the honorary secretary of the Welsh Pacifist Movement, which was quite a substantial movement – we had about twelve thousand members. I had a letter from Dylan asking me if I could help him to keep out of the forces. He wasn't in any sense a pacifist, and he didn't claim to have any conscientious objection to war, but he didn't want to go into the forces. He asked me, as the secretary of this movement, whether I could do something for him. Whether by enrolling him as a conscientious objector and seeing him through the tribunals, or by finding him some kind of job which would keep him outside. Well, I didn't find this a very attractive proposition, and I didn't respond to it in a very kindly way. I thought he was taking the easy line, far too easy a line, and I didn't have a great deal of respect for it, and I just told him that I couldn't do anything to help him, and that was the end of the matter.

... no, he didn't explain this at all, but I can understand why he didn't want to serve in the armed forces. He felt that he was a poet, in the first place, and that he ought to be exempt in order to do the work that he was most able to do. And, of course, he was a good poet and he should have been free in order to do that work, but the way he went about it wasn't the right way.

Some people claim that he attempted to join Plaid Cymru during the War, perhaps to evade military service.

No one could evade military service by joining Plaid Cymru. Nobody was released from military service on nationalist grounds. I haven't any record of his trying to join Plaid Cymru. Maybe he did... political grounds weren't recognised as being sufficient, and people, as I said, weren't released for political reasons at all. But if a man was able to establish that he had a sufficient Christian conscientious objection to war, then he would be usually released to do other work... like work on the land, or work in hospitals, or work underground. Only some two per cent of the conscientious objectors were given unconditional exemption.

Could, for instance, an agnostic object on humanitarian grounds to bearing arms?

Well, he could, of course, but that wasn't usually accepted because it would be very hard for him to prove, to show sufficient proof, of his conscientious objection to war. A Christian could show that his membership of a church, his activity in a church, was an indication of the honesty of his beliefs. It is very hard for an agnostic to produce evidence of that kind.

Actually, Dylan did write scripts for propaganda films during the War, so this was his War service, I suppose.

That showed, didn't it, that he had no conscientious objection to the thing at all. I don't think he'd mind at all that he was releasing somebody else to do military service, by taking a job.

Gwen Watkins

What I came to think about Dylan was that he had developed the poetic side of his character to immense maturity. The other side was very childish, like a child – unless somebody changed his clothes and bathed him and washed his hair, he didn't bother; it was just a nuisance to him. I think he needed somebody to look after him, physically, always.

I think he thought so, too. You remember his script on his American experiences; the appalling difficulty he had in finding clean shirts, or drip-drying them, or anything like that. You were talking earlier about the early stages of the creative gift, what caused it, and I certainly think that in Vernon and Dylan this was true – both of them found ordinary, practical life terribly difficult to cope with, and in a sense they wanted to remain, chose to remain, or had to remain, immature. Words were things they could always cope with, both of them, cope with magnificently, and be better than other people and do it with no difficulty. And in a sense, both of them turned to that world where they were so much at ease, so mature and found easy, away from the very difficult, practical world of money and bus tickets and taxes and clean clothes.

… I used to say to Vernon that he only got married to have somebody to do all this, and I think Dylan always seemed to find somebody on his tours who would do all the finances, the arranging, the laundry, the train tickets, and I've always thought part of the creativity, did come from the fact that they found words easy and everything else difficult.

Vernon always felt that the War made a terrific chasm in Dylan's life. That before that Dylan found life good and interesting, and after that life had a kind of horror about it that he could never get across. He looked back across the chasm; he could write great poems about childhood, but he couldn't go forward to an adult world in which such horrors could exist. He used to, before the War, enjoy symbols and surrealism and after [the War] Vernon thought these weren't ways for him of dealing with reality. He couldn't go forward at all. His letters to Vernon during those years show that the War was a recurring nightmare to him, but not because he himself was a coward. One night in the blitz, in Manresa Road, he and Vernon were sheltering under a table while the bombs were dropping round, and Dylan trembled so much that the table shook. Vernon attempted to calm him by saying that, if they were killed, it wouldn't be the end of life, he believed. Dylan made the very memorable statement "It's not my own immortality I care about, it's the deaths of others."

Laurence Gilliam

I met Dylan in the Stag's Head and he was drinking half a pint of bitter, as usual with a cigarette jutting out of his mouth. "Hello, boy." he said to me. "I got an idea for the radio. It's all about a village that was mad. You hear people talking in their sleep, and dreaming. Is it worth fifty quid advance?" I said "Yes." He said "Now?" and I said "Yes." So I took him over to the copyright department and got him fifty quid... several years later, and several fifty quid advances later, there was still no manuscript because Dylan had got stuck with *Under Milk Wood* and hadn't finished it. And I was rather surprised to see it published in... *Botteghe Oscure*.

... I met Dylan one day, and I taxed him with his treachery. "Oh sorry, boy, I was broke. The Princess offered me five hundred dollars for anything I had, and that was the only thing I had to offer her. I hope you don't mind." So nothing was said about that, although it was BBC property.

... I remember giving Dylan and Caitlin lunch in the French Club in Cavendish Square, near the BBC, one Saturday afternoon, just after the War, and I'd ordered a magnum of Chateau Margaux to sweeten the flow of talk and Dylan said "I'm terribly worried about money, you know. Caitlin's terribly worried about money. How about giving me a contract?" "Oh," I said. "I don't suppose there's any contract you would keep. Except perhaps one you wrote yourself." And I pushed the menu across to him: "Write your own contract, and I'll see if the BBC can back it." "Alright," he said. And this is what he wrote:

Clause 1. £10 a week to be paid direct to Caitlin for the groceries.

Clause 2. Must live in Wales.

Clause 3. Must come to London two days a month for a piss-up.

Clause 4. Don't pay me anything 'til I've written it.

He said "That's one I'll keep." And I believe he would have, but I could never persuade the BBC to take it seriously.

... he was never really fit and he used to have blackouts. I remember him in the pub, with MacNeice and myself and Hedley MacNeice, and occasionally he'd put his head on her shoulder and say "I can't last, you know. I don't know what it is." But he had blackouts.

... I never thought of him as a really heavy drinker, because he was a beer drinker. I think what killed him really was the hard stuff in the States, the whiskies and the martinis, because he wasn't used to that. He was a social drinker, and a beer drinker. I wouldn't say he'd refuse anything, but his normal pattern of drinking was English beer-drinking, which is not a heavy routine on a seasoned stomach, on a seasoned nervous system... he certainly wasn't an alcoholic, and he was what we would call a social drinker...

Edward Evans

With me at the Castle Hotel in Lampeter, Mr Edward Evans, a great friend of Dylan, at one time. This was during the War years, was it?
That's right, yes, it was. The first occasion I met Dylan was on one of his visits to his wife, who had come down here to a friend of hers [Vera Killick], due to the bombing at Swansea, who had rented a house [Gelli, Talsarn] in the vicinity of Lampeter. And Dylan used to come down to visit her.

How often did you see him?
Well, every opportunity he had of coming down, and every time things were serious in London, you see. If there was tiredness and things like that, he'd come down to the country and have a little retreat and find peace here to continue his work.

Dylan used to stay here, and he ate here a lot?
Oh, yes, yes. When he had the time. And if his appetite was sharp enough, which wasn't often.

Where did Dylan usually drink?
He drank in the common bar. He wasn't very fond of the satins and silks. And the *crachach*.

What was Dylan doing at this time? He was writing film scripts, was he?
He was right in the middle of his scripts. Yes, of his writings. Very busy.

Always said that he was busy... he never discussed much of it, and we never encouraged him to discuss it with us. Being such a genius, of course, it would be folly to have any conversation with him on the issue, actually.

What do you recall of Dylan as a person, and the way he made his friendships here?

A very liked man here. And full of what we thought was method. You see, he'd do his reading, he never overdid any mph, excitement, excitable things; he'd never overdo it. He'd sit down there reading and he'd naturally have his earthenware pint, which without he wouldn't be the character he is. But I never saw him overdoing it in the company of others. He'd do it privately with me. He'd never mix with a lot of people in, say, a drunken orgy, or a party or something like to that to celebrate a victory that had happened that day or something. No, we would never find him like that.

Did he usually stick to beer?

Oh yes – very severely. Very severely. He had one little thing, which he taught me. He'd have a little gin and tonic in the morning, and he called it an "eye-opener", and I've always stuck to it.

I know that Dylan didn't speak Welsh, but a lot of Welshmen who don't speak Welsh know Welsh songs, and I've not heard from anyone else about Dylan singing Welsh songs. Do you recall this?

Yes, I do; and more incidents than one. Now here, it's quite a little singing place, being a rugby headquarters, and he used to enjoy to hear them, and on more than one occasion I met him in London. And we used to go places where we'd meet Welsh singers... nothing pleased him more than to join in an afternoon's singing with, say, a famous Welsh singer, who we'd meet, invariably, around the West End... a singer that had seen better times; well known, but not quite up to the standard of an opera singer.

... he'd love hymns. Indeed, it was amazing the knowledge he had of Welsh hymns... he liked bass singing, for some particular reason. He loved the thunderous voice, you know... *Dafydd y Garreg Wen* – he was very fond of. David of the White Rock. Sung by the famous Trevor Jones, the Welsh singer. He was frightfully fond of a very famous Welshman, I doubt if he's alive now, Watkin Watkins.

What was Dylan's pronunciation like of the Welsh words in those songs?

Well, he was very Welshy in his normal conversation. Oh yes. Swansea Valley drawl, if I could put it that way. Which we in Cardiganshire are very proud of that we don't use!

What do you recall of Caitlin?
Very clever; very, very intelligent. Very amusing. I don't think she'd make a Kay Kendall, you know. Or a Mrs Beeton, but apart from that, very amusing and a very good customer; a very, very good social customer. Interesting to everybody. Lackadaisical in dress. A slip to her would be as good as an Elizabethan crinoline.

Did you ever hear him talk about politics here?
Never in my life. Only the oratory of King's Road, Chelsea. Those were the only politicians he ever associated with in his life. He'd simply glance at the headlines of a newspaper which was left on a settee, but he'd never catch hold of one. No.

It's said that Dylan made friends among all types of people.
Oh yes, yes, yes. Anybody that was interesting. A wireless man [Dewi Ianthe] he was very interested in while he was staying in New Quay. He was very, very keen on recordings and that kind of thing – the way he did it. Then, garage proprietors; I don't know how much of a motorist he was, I never saw him drive a car in my life. But he was very friendly, because I suppose they were local people which I'd met with him.

Did Dylan ever discuss any religion with you at all?
No! I've no recollection of religion at all with him. Justice, yes! He felt that somebody was having a wrong deal, he was an aggressor to justice. To the administrators.

Was he aggressive ever, or was he more shy?
I think he had a temper you could arouse with aggravation, and maybe due to a little environment of, say, a stimulant – yes. I wouldn't like to remain in his company when he was merry and bright. I wouldn't like to argue with him, for instance. Because he was too great a man, you see, his command would be too great for anybody. And the thing was not to take part in it, which we've learnt over the years in this business, of course.

Dylan had problems throughout most of his life in supporting himself.
I don't think he was ever embarrassed, in my opinion. He looked prosperous to me always – at least, comfortable. In any case, he never complained. So I took it for granted that his project brought him in whatever he demanded. This being an agricultural place, he'd love to pay for everybody's and get their conversation, as if he was trying to captivate something from them, not by paying for drinks or anything like that, but he enjoyed the company of a different kind all the time.

He used to ask me sometimes "Who is that gentleman there now, he looks a very interesting type?" Well, he'd make way towards him then, as if he was trying to get knowledge from something and elongate his smoke-room knowledge. Always on the probe.

He visited Lampeter College?

Yes, he was very fond of going round the grounds, too. He was very fond of the characteristic architecture of Lampeter College. He thought it quite unique. And he took a great interest in the College, for some reason; whether he knew a lot of the clergy, a lot of his clergy friends that had been to the College or not, but he was very fond of taking walks there.

When news of Dylan's death came, how did you receive the news?

Oh – terrific shock. Terrific shock, until this very bad report came from America that he was more or less alcoholically poisoned. Because nothing would be less from our minds in this country, I can assure you.

In other words, this was not the Dylan you knew?

No, far from it.

John Patrick Evans

Dylan Thomas arrived in New Quay [1944-45] with his wife and two little children and he was looking for some accommodation, and he rented a charming little bungalow on our bay… he spent a lot of his spare time with me… he came down for some quietude… he seemed to do his best writing among us local people – he was always with a pad on his knee during convivial hours. Always busy, making notes of any local characters who came in.

Did you later see some of these characters in his plays or in his other writings, poems and so forth? For instance, in Under Milk Wood*? Did he work on* Under Milk Wood *while he was here?*

He'd started at the time. But some of the characters were in one of his smaller publications, called *Quite Early One Morning*.

Was there great exaggeration, or was it a fairly true picture of some of the local characters?

No exaggeration at all…

What did people here think about it when it came out? Did they see themselves in it? Did they resent it, or did they take it in good humour?

No. I don't think they noticed, because they never heard about it for quite a long time afterwards… as the local landlord [of the Black Lion], most of the characters of the locality frequented my house. He was so interesting that he had one little corner of my house where we used to gather. He was so interesting that... it seemed to develop into a little Welsh village, a Johnsonian society – it's the only way I can describe it.

... he was interested in the characters, the people themselves... just interested in people, any character at all, and listening to them and busy with his notes at all times.

... I've never seen him drunk... he never showed any signs of inebriation. He was more interested in conversation and people – with his pad on his knee... always busy with his notes... he always seemed more interested in people, making notes on people at all times.

So this little community was a great source of material for him?
Yes.

What about Dylan's physical condition?
He had a very, very tough physique... I broke down and we were caught in a blizzard - we had five miles to walk home one winter's night... over a mountain road... Dylan's recuperation was a few pints of cold beer. He refused to go to bed – all he wanted was the settee and a few blankets, and as fresh as a daisy in the morning.

... they lived in a bohemian way, but they were very happy... while he was here he was a happy family man leading a convivial life... in our little Welsh community... I enjoyed his company... our regret is that we did not appreciate him in those days. We enjoyed his company, but little thought we had a world celebrity in our midst – we just treated him as one of ourselves... no, he never gave an inkling of his connection with all the world-famous people of letters that he knew intimately... he just mixed with us all... it was just a matter of being with us, understanding us.

Olive Jones [29]

I first met Dylan, I suppose, having a drink somewhere, and, well, I didn't think much of him at all. I knew he was writing a bit of poetry but that's as far as it went. But he was always very charming, kind, a gentle personality, unassuming and I liked Dylan very much.

... it was an extraordinary married life, hectic and bohemian, very bohemian – they lived very roughly [at Majoda]... it was all very rough and ready, dirty dishes piled up everywhere – a sink full of them, and she washed a couple of cups and we had a cup of beer each. Then we went in to see old Dylan who was lying in bed writing by candlelight, no sheets on the bed, no pillow-slips. Perfectly happy – just a couple of blankets thrown over him. I think they sat on the floor most of the time, as far as I could gather, on cushions. So, all very higgledy-piggledy – but that was their way of living, and they just washed up things as they wanted them.

What was your reaction to the book, Dylan Thomas in America, *by Brinnin?*
I was horrified, actually. I hadn't seen that side of Dylan at all... I never saw Dylan any the worse for drink. And I never saw him drink anything but beer... I was completely horrified. I thought it was an absolute scandal.

... I never heard him read his poems or short stories to anyone... he was a very unassuming person. We had no idea he would become so famous... he kept it so quiet.

... I did like Dylan, yes... and several people have said to me since "Oh, I wish I'd shaken hands with Dylan Thomas." We didn't realise in those days what a famous man he was going to become. Lots have people have said that to me here.

... I don't know why he left. But he was crazy about Laugharne and always wanted to go back to Laugharne to live. He used to say "It's the only place – ooh, you don't know Laugharne, you don't know it – it's a wonderful place!" I know he wanted to go back there very badly.

... I thought him a very nice man and a very gentle type, really. Always very charming when you met him... he was sweet. Very sympathetic... I never saw him very boisterous.

Much missed?
I would say, yes.

Mrs Warfield Darling [30]

Now with me, at the Dolau Inn, New Quay, April 21st 1964, is Mrs Warfield Darling, who knew Dylan when he was in New Quay. How did you first meet Dylan?
I met Dylan in the Black Lion, and his wife, one Saturday evening, and then after one or two drinks, we came out to my cottage, 2 Belle Vue, on the New Quay road. We talked, and I said how much I'd enjoyed his poems – I'd read several of them, and I thought they were extremely good. There was something very much of the human touch about his

poems. And then we met several times afterwards.

What impression did you have of their married life?
I don't think that they were very happy together, but there were times when they were most affectionate... I think she rather bored him... she was very fierce at times, and he'd be very Platonic-like, and then they would probably have a row, and things would go right again in a day or so. She usually brought the children down to the Black Lion, and used to say to Dora, the girl there, "Have you got an empty room? Pop these two into bed, will you?" And they were charming little children – a boy and a girl – and then she'd collect them. She'd go off, nobody knew where she went, leave Dylan at the Black Lion, and she'd come back for them some time between eleven and twelve... but they were a charming couple to meet, socially. I enjoyed it very much.

... I think Caitlin and he were very happy when they were at Laugharne, at the beginning when they were married. But it all dwindled, and I felt very sorry for them. I was really terribly sorry when I saw the account of his death in the papers. It was a loss, a great loss.

He told me all about his home at Laugharne... he said that he'd go out at Laugharne – of which he loved every stone – and he'd stay up all night, under the twinkling stars, and he'd get something from that, and he'd come back, and he'd go on writing, and he'd stay at his writing all day, and not go out for a pint or anything... he went out for walks and never knew when he was coming back, and didn't come back some nights at all. But there was always some meaning for it, and it usually resulted in his poems.

... he drank a colossal amount of beer, which I didn't think was hurtful to him, not at that time, but it was when he didn't have his food and kept drinking... he liked to talk to ordinary people, and he'd sort them out, you know. And that, I think, was one of his great successes in life... there were some very wonderful characters there then in New Quay.

... he was a simple man at heart. And you can hardly realise what came out of that man was so wonderful... he was a charming man when he was sober – and in drink he was charming, but there was times when he went on for weeks at it and he got rather on the slovenly side... I never saw him pick a quarrel with anyone... he was rather retiring from people that he didn't know. But I should say that he liked people. A good mixer.

The image that has been left of Dylan by the book by Brinnin has been that of a great poet but also a man who was a great drunkard and a lecher.
Oh, no. No, I wouldn't say that. No, I don't think that's right. He certainly loved his beer, but he was not either...

He wasn't a woman-chaser here?
No, no – not a bit of it. Not a bit of it... I shouldn't think he was either a womaniser or a lecher. Definitely not.

1946-1949
"My basic melancholy; sullen glooms and black studies."

Dylan lives in A.J.P Taylor's summerhouse in Oxford. He becomes a public figure, as he devotes more of his time to radio programmes, but writes only one poem in the next three and a half years. *Deaths and Entrances* is published, as well as *Selected Writings* in America. *Return Journey* is written and broadcast, together with the five other radio scripts recognised as milestones in the making of *Under Milk Wood*. In March 1947, the Society of Authors awards him a travelling scholarship and he and the family go to Italy for four months, staying in Tuscany, where he writes 'In Country Sleep', and Elba, where he works on *Under Milk Wood*. By September 1947, Dylan is living in South Leigh, Oxfordshire, where he continues working on the first half of *Under Milk Wood* and churns out film scripts for Gainsborough productions. He visits Prague in March 1949 to attend a conference of the Czechoslovak Writers' Union and narrates extracts from *Under Milk Wood*.

Mario Luzi[31]

My meeting with Dylan Thomas happened in a typical Florentine restaurant, one of those that are called 'buche', holes, in Florence, which are basement restaurants... the Buca di San Giovanni, near the Baptistery. I remember when I went to the restaurant I found Dylan Thomas but not alone: Spender was there, too, and it was quite a strange evening. Naturally, the contrast between Spender and Dylan Thomas struck one straightaway. Spender was a man who was already officially recognised; Spender was also of a generation that had believed more in the public office of poetry and in some way behaved according to this idea of being an intellectual representative of his country, whereas Dylan Thomas' attitude was more peculiar, more individualistic and you might also say more indifferent. He was very taciturn and he seemed to pay almost ironic attention to what Spender said.

Anyway, while Spender was just passing through and only stayed here for a very short time, Dylan Thomas stayed on for a few months, and during his stay we had many occasions to meet. He didn't have a house yet, he did not have the villa, he was in a hostel in Via dei Calzaioli – a hostel but I can't remember its name – Albergo

8. Mario Luzi

Patria, perhaps, yes – and sometimes I'd go and visit him there.

Thomas obviously sought the company of local poets and literati of this area, to share his love of life and his worship of poetry. But there were some very serious obstacles, to tell the truth, to mutual conversation. The first was the language difficulty, because Thomas didn't speak any language apart from English, not even French. The second was his – how can I say this – his constant predilection for drinking, for alcohol. At that time at least, Thomas was often not in command of his senses due to the large amount of alcohol that he drank. I remember he used to start in the morning with some beer, then in the afternoon he continued with whisky and other spirits, and he was often drunk, not unpleasantly so, but in a state of somewhat euphoric absence. And I particularly remember certain long silences which, however, revealed a kind of ecstasy in him, a kind of trance, which demanded respect, which actually made one sense some great concentration.

All in all, I don't think those were happy years for Dylan Thomas; in particular, those months spent in Italy can't have been months of great creative satisfaction. He seemed intent on reconnecting or retying the threads of his poetry which had been interrupted during the War. There was clearly some kind of internal struggle going on, some unspent tension that kept him in that state of friendly, sociable availability, but at the same time in a state of isolation. One might say that although Thomas willingly surrounded himself with friends and admirers, he was still a man alone, a lonely man who had problems that nobody else can solve for him. This took nothing away from the man's friendliness. He exuded his cordiality, his need for friendship and also his offer of friendship, but at the same time there was this distance which in some way was imposed by the internal problems that Thomas seemed to have to solve at the time.

After the months spent in Florence, I know he went to Elba with Luigi Berti, and I seem to remember that it was actually in Elba that he started writing again, after in fact several years of barrenness or at least creative difficulty. On the island of Elba, he managed to get started again, to break his silence, resuming the typical lilt of his poetry but at the same time renewing it. I think it was actually in Elba that he wrote *Under Milk Wood*, if I'm not mistaken. I think that's the composition that he at least started in Elba. I didn't see him again after that, but Luigi Berti, who remained in contact with him even after he left Italy, said that he had, in fact, had a good creative season. And so his stay in Italy was clearly not just a distraction or a waste of time or merely a rest. Clearly, it was this gathering of his concentration that allowed Thomas to continue his work.

Thomas appeared in those years, I mean in those months he spent in Florence, to be in almost exuberant health, except that at times, perhaps, he showed some little signs of alcoholism, you know, some trembling of the hands, unexpectedly dozing off, the somnolence of the alcoholic. But there was nothing to make you suspect that his constitution was as threatened, as unfortunately the following years were to show.

Thomas might perhaps have wanted to talk about important subjects, let's say, topical subjects, but he came up against the language communication barrier and also his state of internal tension. Even so, on certain more uninhibited evenings, Thomas used to talk about poetry and especially English classical poetry, at least that part of English classical poetry that he preferred. He gave some readings in some friends' houses... as a reciter of poetry he was truly exceptional, although not all of us knew English well enough to appreciate his diction, so to speak, but the emotional content and especially the musical richness of the text recited by Thomas, came across to the audience like magic. Those evenings, even though they were unpretentious and just easy-going gatherings, turned into poetry evenings that have stayed in the memory of everyone there, acquaintances and friends.

As I said, I didn't get any direct news of Thomas after that, and I think his friends, apart from Luigi Berti, rather lost touch with him as well. Of his friends, I'd like to remember Ottone Rosai, the great painter, and, of course, the poet Montale, who lived in Florence at the time, and Bigongiari, Parronchi and Luigi Berti... and it was quite a surprise, a kind of bolt out of the blue, when we learnt of Dylan Thomas' sudden death in 1953. No one could foresee that such a rich, exuberant figure, in the physiological sense too, might be struck down so suddenly. Besides, we also had the impression that his poetry was still developing, he hadn't finished what he wanted to say, and so the news of his death... was first and foremost a surprise, a surprise even before it was sad, and it was very sad especially because in the meantime Thomas' poetry had become well established in Italy too, through translations but also directly through people acquiring a knowledge of English, and Thomas was now considered one of the greatest contemporary poets.

Therefore, the figure of Thomas passed through Florence, let's say, in a rather special, rather meteoric light, and you might also see one side of him as a *poète maudit*, in that solitary figure who loved company but in some way concentrated especially on his dreams, dreams he seemed not to... I can't find the word. Sometimes Thomas' gaze actually had that intensity of far-off concentration on areas that words can't always describe. This poet, so often made brutish, let's say, by alcohol, we might see as the origin of a myth of a *poète maudit*, but let me say straight away that Florence was quite used to these careers of *poètes maudits* – it had them in ancient times and also more recently, and so it is not a city that can reject or scandalise a destiny that perhaps in a bitter phase may include such, let's say, unpleasant situations on the part of the poet. And basically, even though he only passed through fleetingly, he has remained in the memory not only of the people most closely linked to him, but among the city's cultural myths.

It has been said, especially by British witnesses or correspondents, that there was a basic incompatibility with the intellectual atmosphere of Florence or of Italy in general, but I think it has been greatly exaggerated. Thomas certainly didn't love or couldn't appreciate a certain, perhaps rather official, order that some intellectuals had in some way gathered. Figures who were somewhat established, such as Montale, who used to live according to a sort of strict order, who were apparently perhaps even bourgeois, and so lacked that madness that seems to be a necessary ingredient in Thomas' talent. I think that, when viewed from outside like this, there was a kind of rejection by Thomas to certain rather over-orthodox figures in our literary society. But essentially, his friends, the ones who kept him company most, the ones he would most willingly be with, were still young. In general they were people of the same generation as him, indeed the same age. For instance, I myself, Bigongiari and Parronchi were all born in 1914, like Dylan Thomas. None of us had that demeanour of a man who had made it, of a man – let's say – who was part of the establishment, and so there seemed to be empathy on all levels, even though, I repeat, communication was limited because of those language difficulties and that particular state of internal tension that Dylan Thomas found himself in.

No, I don't think Thomas can be considered an intellectual. I would say that about Spender, for example, and in fact right at the beginning I stressed the contrast that could be seen between Spender and Thomas right from first impressions. If by intellectual you mean a man who feels culturally responsible for his times and also feels like one who has to point the way and guide people, then Thomas seems to me to have been quite free from all these imaginary or necessary obligations that an intellectual, on the other hand, feels he has. Dylan Thomas just looked like someone who was outside all that, or even opposed to all that. There is clearly a break between the generation of intellectuals like Spender and his own. There was a basic repudiation of the intellectual poet. And in Thomas everything revealed precisely the vital poet instead, the poet who insists on existential and vital order rather than just intellectual responsibility. There was already a clearly *maudit* – or 'beat', as one would say today – vein in Thomas. There was, then, that feeling of repulsion towards a literary society, but not just a literary one, a traditional order, which clearly no longer had any reason to exist in him. So I would say that there was in Thomas' attitude a conscious opposition to the dominant intellectualism of European and also Italian and, at least in some respects, Florentine literature, and certain disagreements or certain idiosyncrasies may have arisen precisely from that; it also came out, of course, in his social behaviour.

I don't think he knew Italian literature, apart from some Dante, perhaps, but very vaguely; that is, he had clearly heard of Dante, perhaps partly through English or English-language poets like Pound or Eliot, and perhaps also through some rather detached reading, but basically he had no knowledge of Italian literature; he simply knew a few names who for him were clearly just literary myths rather than acquired knowledge.

I think when he arrived Thomas knew of Montale, certainly, at least by reputation, but I don't think he had any direct knowledge of his

poetry, partly because in those days Montale's poetry hadn't been translated into English; in fact, no contemporary Italian author had been
translated into English... I don't think Thomas was able to really appreciate or give his opinion on the works of contemporary Italian poets.

At that time, some of Thomas' poems had been translated, some I
think certainly by Montale, then also by Luigi Berti and perhaps by
others, too, whom I don't remember now, but in magazines, never
collected into volumes, so they were sporadic, fragmentary encounters
that we had with his work, but these few poems were enough to arouse
considerable interest in Thomas' work. A few texts had been translated,
but in pretty good or even sometimes excellent translations, like those
by Montale, which gave a glimpse of the complexity and richness of
Thomas's original poems, and so even though their circulation was
small, it was enough to arouse great interest in his person.

Did Dylan's poetry influence any Italian poets, young poets for instance?
I wouldn't say so, at least, I can't see any influence of Thomas, partly
because I think Thomas' poetic language is so unique that, although it
holds a great fascination, I don't feel it can provide any elements for
other poets, at least poets of another language. I don't know whether in
Britain Thomas had any real influence. Great prestige, certainly, but
while you can talk of obvious influences of other English poets, I
wouldn't say that Thomas' work had had effects of this kind, although
it is present but basically almost as a myth: there's more a practical
mythology of Thomas in Italy rather than his literary presence,
although there's a highly favourable opinion of his work here. But it's
precisely the fact that his language can't be reproduced that in some
way cuts him off from having any literary heirs among us here. Except
for deliberate and critical works, I don't think there are any poets, or at
least any significant poets, who have felt the influence of Thomas, the
real influence of his poetry.

I had said that no direct influence of Thomas can be seen on recent
Italian poetry. I would have great difficulty if I had to demonstrate that,
but I'd say something about the basic common feeling between
Thomas's poetry and that of writers of my generation. A basic
common feeling deriving principally from the way of understanding
the function of poetic language, freed from the tight constraint of rational definition that the preceding generation had imposed on it.
Basically there was a reawakening of the power of intuition and imagination, as in Thomas' poetry and the Italian poetry that was
contemporary with Thomas', simultaneous with Thomas'. Especially

that part of Italian poetry that goes under the name of *Ermetismo* (Hermeticism). And especially the *Ermetismo* of the years around 1940, the war years, *Ermetismo* in which the creative power of the word was, so to speak, heightened to its greatest tension and in which the power of analogy was also exaggerated. Therefore, Italian readers that were involved in the climate of *Ermetismo* found common ground in the great freedom and density of Thomas' language; they also obviously found encouragement for their own trend, their own doctrine.

So I'd say there already was a basic empathy, you know, which was fully confirmed through reading the poems, through reading some poems translated into Italian, or even reading them in English, with some difficulty, of course. Whether we then had discussions together on the nature of poetry and Thomas' poetry in particular, I don't remember, but I think it's rather unlikely given the basic difficulty we had in talking to each other, precisely for almost material, linguistic reasons. Anyway, I understood very well what interested him, that is to say, basically which poetic vein in modern literature might interest him, and evidently I found that I agreed; in fact, we had a kind of under-standing about that. Because he too preferred highly synthetic poetry: imaginative, vivid expression, let's say, not rationally argued; you might call it anti-intellectual poetry, not the poetry of a Valéry or an Eliot, a poetry that had all the resources, all the imagination that you find in adventure, poetry as adventure, as discovery and adventure. In that respect, I believe we understood each other beyond what we could actually express in words. And I remember what he found annoying and irritating, and on the other hand what really attracted him, what attracted him in modern poetry, in the European poetry of the century in fact. And they were in a way the same things that attracted me and friends of mine.

Did Dylan speak of political problems?
He informed himself about Italy's problems and naturally he saw that people were disgusted with certain situations that were still, especially in the immediate post-war period, quite serious and in some cases even distressing. He informed himself about this, so there was some inter-est, but as for his specific relations, let's say, with men who could in some way inflame these problems, even politically, I don't know, I wouldn't know. I don't think he would have had much contact, though.

I do think he felt a kind of intolerance for a type of society; that did show through. For a bourgeois society, which was expressed through a certain type of politics; but whether he had a political doctrine, or had at least accepted a formal political doctrine, that I don't believe. Yes, he was bothered by seeing the external aspects of a kind of bourgeois society, and I remember the scandal he caused at Montale's, for instance, because Montale at the time lived a bourgeois life, as in fact he has always done and still does today. He lived quite comfortably, or at least decently, and this bothered especially that kind of bohemian poet that Thomas liked to be. So I remember that he went round to Montale's and got really drunk, drunk enough to cause this kind of little scandal, to break the sort of mould that he thought Montale was stuck in, you see. Even though he liked him a lot. But clearly, he didn't think the poet should live like that, though. I remember that. Then I realised from things that have been published, from letters published posthumously, that basically all that very elementary, very quiet arrangement of Italian literary life bored him, it all seemed a little too ordinary, in fact. I think I read in a letter that there are poets in Italy that live with their mothers, and even go back regularly to eat and sleep at home; that, then, seemed to him to be really ridiculous, highly contemptible.

But essentially I'm saying that basically the literati, the Italian writers of those days tried basically not to show any external, apparent sign of their profession. Instead, they always tried to disguise their exceptional nature as ordinariness. And this was anything but provincial, as it might have seemed to Thomas; it was, instead, a sign of maturity or even of criticism towards an earlier time, a Futurist time, in which writers rather took centre stage. Well, he came across an environment just like that, an environment that might appear set in a bourgeois mould but which was instead an arrangement, a very neutral arrangement in essence, very neutral, far from set in bourgeois ways. All of this annoyed him. I could see this then and later I saw it better in some posthumous letters that were published, which were not very kind, I might say, towards the intellectual, literary and cultural life of Italy, and Florence in particular. But regardless of this, on an individual level, then, a certain empathy had developed and it was a deep-felt empathy, that perhaps went beyond actual communication. It was precisely because we felt basically that he was somebody who expressed something that was also at the root of the aspirations that we, too, had.

Did he discuss religion at all?

Well, I don't remember whether we talked about religion, but he was interested in the profound aspects that we had in certain expressions of religious art here in Florence. Of course, he had been annoyed, on the other hand, by all the traditional Catholic religious customs. But I remember some of his comments on pictures or churches or religious monuments, in which there was not just aesthetic appreciation but also a sense of creative admiration even, for the power of religious feeling. There was that.

Did he talk about Wales, his country, at all?
Ah, yes, Wales. This is a subject that was very dear to him. I heard him talk about Wales but mostly because of the human landscape and also the natural landscape of Wales, and the Welsh language, that richness of images of the Welsh language. I remember hearing him make these comments, but then he was loathe to talk about social issues in Wales, workers' conditions in Wales.

He spoke little about England and a lot about Wales, little about London and a lot about Wales, that I do remember. I mean, he never missed an opportunity, I'd say, to recall something about Wales or episodes from his personal life or traditions, customs, in which we could see a kind of similarity to or distance from our own. Anyway, I had the impression that Wales for him was truly a country of the spirit much more than just his country of birth. He talked about it with great tenderness, that I remember. About the miners, and then certain songs, too, Welsh folk songs. And then something else that made me think a lot about this business of Wales is the fact that when he had to mention some major English-language poet he would mention Yeats and he would mention Hopkins, I don't know if he is Welsh, though, Hopkins. I realised that Wales for him was truly a very organic world, not just an environment but also a way of thinking, of imagining, a way of speaking, of using language, of using the imagination, which was relevant to him and necessary to him. Yes, I remember that quite clearly.

What impression did you have of Caitlin and Dylan?
I didn't get the impression that there was any friction between them. I remember that his wife was here with her sister, and they had lots of children and there seemed to be altogether quite a festive atmosphere. Maybe they didn't give the impression, however, that there was a deep understanding between husband and wife, though they are just impressions, of course. It all seemed very friendly, cordial and rather festive; I think it was perhaps due to the children, especially, and Thomas seemed very affectionate towards them. But there were no signs of disagreement or incompatibility; they were basically quite a

noisy family, rather rowdy I thought, but also happy and festive. That's the impression I had.

It seemed that he left home very willingly, wandering around a while by himself, yes. But he also talked about his children with great affection and tenderness, though perhaps not in the same way about his wife. Not that there were exactly any obvious quarrels, but you could see that what tied him to home, what linked him to home, were his children. The main tie of affection seemed to be the children, certainly. On his part. Anyway, they looked rather like a gypsy troop... dominated by a sort of taste for life, I thought, or at least for adventure.

I think he led an existence that was rather isolated and at most he liked the company, the band of friends he could go drinking with, but I don't think he had any, let's say, risqué curiosity, and anyway he wouldn't have been able to satisfy it in Florence because Florence is a pretty chaste city. It's a city where life goes on very quietly. Maybe that even bored him, but, anyway, I say it's an experience that he certainly couldn't find in Florence.

Piero Bigongiari (with Sergio Baldi as interpreter)[32]

Professor Bigongiari said that he met Dylan Thomas in June or July 1947. Signor Luigi Berti introduced Bigongiari to Dylan Thomas, and from that time on they became friendly. Bigongiari and Berti helped Dylan Thomas to find a home. And finally they found it at the Villa dell' Beccaro near Scandicci, but for several days Dylan remained in Florence, waiting for his wife and his sister-in-law and his children.

They didn't talk much because Dylan had no Italian and the English of Bigongiari and the other poets was very scanty – I mean their spoken English. But anyhow they tried to get in touch, especially with gestures and things like that. They had long walks, and they informed Dylan about modern Italian poetry, of which he knew very little or nothing. They tried to translate literally what the Italian poets were doing, and Dylan tried to explain to Bigongiari and other people his own poems. So Bigongiari translated into Italian a few poems by Dylan, being helped by Dylan himself. Dylan used to come here, to this same house [in the Piazza Cavalleggeri, Florence], and the house of Professor Parronchi.

... sometimes it was like a pantomime, because they practically had no language, but they liked each other, and sometimes Dylan, when he was in this flat, used to read not only his own poems, but poems by

9. Professor and Mrs Bigongiari and Sergio Baldi

Milton and passages from Shakespeare. It was until the early morning, until two o'clock in the morning. It was euphoric and very lively but suddenly Dylan went to sleep, even on that same sofa where you are sitting now.

Some of the biographers have given the impression that he was very unhappy, but I get from Professor Bigongiari's comments that there were moments when he was very much in tune with the people here.

Professor Bigongiari says that the impression you get from books that he was unhappy here is certainly wrong. He thinks that Dylan was really in touch with the other people – at least, with the literati of café Giubbe Rosse, and the climate there was congenial to him.[33] Of course, Professor Bigongiari adds, you must remember that those were the years just after the Second World War, and Florence was still half-destroyed by the War. There were terrible times, and he says it was a kind of tragical happiness. That the atmosphere of tragical happiness was not only Dylan Thomas'... the Italian literati realised that in the beginning he was unhappy because he was not able to write. But at the end of his staying here, they thought they he had begun to write again.

... once Dylan, his wife and Piero Bigongiari and two girlfriends of his went to see the Capella de Pazzi, and so they had an appointment in Piazza Santa Croce. But before they entered the church of Santa Croce, Dylan said, "Why shan't we celebrate this marvellous Florentine morning?" And so they went to a small bar near Via Verdi, and Dylan ordered a flask of chianti, much to the wonder of the waiter who wasn't accustomed to such orders so early in the morning; it was ten o'clock in the morning. In the end they did not go into la Capella de Pazzi, they started touring round the town

Did drinking really dominate his life here, or was it just one aspect of it?
Professor Bigongiari says that Dylan certainly drank. But he was not dominated by his drinking. Certainly, this drinking in a way influenced him. He was merry, and he was half-drunk – but his being half-drunk made him more understand what he saw. And certainly, various people, I mean those Italian people, got very well in touch with him, and he was in this state of – well, may I add personally – of forgetting his complexes!

... once Bigongiari, Dylan's wife and those two girlfriends of Bigongiari, went to Fiesole, and Dylan was not with them. They had a date at eight o'clock in the evening [with him], because Dylan and his wife had to go to dinner at Montale's flat. So they arrived at the hotel and Dylan was very, very happy, and a bit tired maybe, and he started performing sketches, as a comedian, and then he took a flask of wine from his night table and started pouring wine for everybody, and asked for information on Montale and wanted to celebrate his visit to that great Italian poet. At half past eight, Signor Berti came, but as soon as Dylan heard Berti knocking at the door, he went and hid in a big cupboard where he remained in hiding. When Berti entered, he found no Dylan Thomas there. And Dylan suddenly came out of the cupboard with a big straw hat on his head, and a poncho and just went on performing sketches and did not want to go, until about ten o'clock they were able to take him to Montale.

He also hid in a cupboard in Montale's.
Bigongiari suspects so.

There have been many accounts of Dylan alienating people by his behaviour.
That's absolutely untrue. Professor Bigongiari strongly denies it. We Italians liked Dylan, probably because we believed that his love for drinking and for enjoying life was very Welsh and very Italian, too, at the same time. And he adds that Dylan used to see almost every evening the great Italian painter Rosai. Bigongiari and the other friends had told Rosai that Dylan was a very great poet, and when Dylan was in financial need, Rosai went as far as giving Dylan fifty thousand lira, which was a round sum at the time. That's just to show that we liked him and trusted him... the help given by Rosai was important, because it helped Thomas to go back to England, otherwise he wouldn't have had money to pay for his ticket.

It's absolutely untrue that he become rough when he had drunk, and when he was with the Italian literati. On the contrary, it seems that the alcohol made him become very lucid, and he tried to explain images of his poetry... he was very lucid and very, very agreeable and Professor Bigongiari still goes on denying that Dylan became rough.

Did Dylan demonstrate any interest in hearing Italian poetry?
Not much for classical Italian poetry, but a very lively interest for the contemporary poets – for the poetry of the people that were living around him. They were more or less of the same age, they all had just passed the experience of the War, and Bigongiari finds that in Thomas there was a human interest for poetry. He asked several times to hear the Italian poets recite their own poems, and he was much interested in the vocality of Italian poetry. He was interested in poetry as language.

What about his health while he was here?
Bigongiari says that Dylan was in very good health and really Dylan's vitality tried the vitality and the very poor health of the Italian literati! And he said that once Dylan spent a whole night under the stars in July, and in the morning he was perfectly all right, while all those Italians were just broken down!

Did Dylan ever have a blackout here?
No, he never remembers. He remembers, he thinks that he was quite all right. It was a wonderful summer, a wonderful season, he says literally. He says that in certain moments Dylan was completely absent from the environ, but, Bigongiari adds, that it often happens with poets. If I may add, they could not distinguish the origin of this absentness for a moment, but from what I can say, personally, I don't think that there was anything pathological in it.

Dylan used to describe himself as very interested in films. Was he interested in the Italian films, the neo-realist films, of that period?
Yes, he was very much interested in the realist film, and he went into technicalities, and it was quite clear that he belonged to the film world. And they went and saw some pictures of Rossellini's and he used to talk about it to them, and he was very much interested in it.

Did he express a desire to meet some of the directors?
It can't be done here in Florence – there was nobody. It was impossible to met anybody connected with the film industry here because it was entirely in Rome... Dylan was here as a private citizen, and he didn't like to meet VIPs. He used to say that the more important people were of the least interest to him.

... it seems that when the children arrived here, the familial situation was rather heavy; there was confusion and it seems that the children limited in a way the freedom of Dylan Thomas. He was less free when the children were here; it was a difficult situation, a family living abroad... he thinks that Dylan regretted not being able to live in Florence. He lived in the villa at Scandicci, and Bigongiari thinks that the idea of Dylan's melancholic was born out of this situation – Dylan regretted not to be able to be here – to be alone and to be free with friends. Well, the idea of Professor Bigongiari seems to me that the family was an encumbrance for him.

Did he express a feeling that he would like to settle down and live permanently in Italy?

He may have said so, but Bigongiari doesn't remember. He doesn't remember that he ever had expressed any idea of settling permanently anywhere. The main themes of their talking was about the technique, the technical problems of the line itself, and the differences between Italian and English and Welsh. I mean, the difference in the structure of the languages and the difference in the structure of the line. It seems that the technical problems of composition were the main themes of Dylan's and of Bigongiari's conversation.

He says that we must find a deeper reason for their meeting. Why did they meet? They met because there was something in common; they belonged to the same generation, the generation 10-18 – that is from 1910 to 1918. And they were looking for something – Dylan Thomas and the Italian poets were looking for something that was alike – the image that generates another image and the second image generates a third and so on, this multiplous (*sic*) generation of images.

... Bigongiari says that the passage of Dylan Thomas to Italy was not useless. Meaning, that he certainly exerts a certain influence on the Italian poets, that were getting together at Giubbe Rosse. Just on account, perhaps, of the technicalities they discussed, and the exchange of lines...

... in 1947, just after the War, there was a kind of a season of expectation. We lived in a world that had completely fallen all around us, and we all agreed that we should build a new society on purer lines. We might disagree on the lines themselves, but we all agreed on the fact that those lines should have been purer. So there was a kind of a climate of expectation, a kind of eternal spring, because we did believe in a better summer.

Alessandro Parronchi[34]

Even though it was many years ago, my impression is still as vivid as on the first day I saw Dylan. He was with Spender, and we saw him in the evening after dinner at the Giubbe Rosse café. Dylan had a very childlike, calm expression, and impenetrable, too, because you couldn't really tell what was going through his mind while he was smiling. He spoke very little; he only spoke English, and so it was difficult to know what he was thinking, but even so he managed to communicate with those of us who were around him. Spender left a few days later; Thomas, however, stayed on for a long time, he spent a whole summer with us. Not that we saw him very often, because he stayed at home a lot. He had rented a villa near Florence, and he stayed there a lot and worked. But every now and then we would see him. Anyway, the impression he gave was always very vivacious, because in the end when you were with him you could really catch hold of that well-being, that kind of poetic joy, which he now and then managed to communicate through an expression or a look.

Well, at that time we really didn't know his poetry – we got to know it as soon as he went back to Britain. The first we heard was that he was a poet along the lines of Imagism, or people talked about him in connection with Apocalyptic poetry, but when he was told this, Dylan violently rejected any kind of definition. What he loved was that his poetry and he himself should be considered outside any preconceived lines. And, of course, in his poems, even though we didn't understand English very well, we saw a great difference between those three or four very famous ones, e.g. 'The conversation of prayers', which managed to come across with an absolutely shattering, new, unexpected force; and others, on the other hand, which were poems that made themselves noted straight away for their complexity and difficulty. Well, certainly over time even those became comprehensible, as far as a translated poem can.

The first news we had of Dylan we got from Spender himself, who told us that this was a very important young poet. On the other hand, Dylan's attitude towards Spender was, how should I say it, a bit jaunty. Not that any conversations happened between them at all, but I mean you could see straight away that these were two diametrically opposite temperaments; and if there was actually something new in Dylan that was attractive it was that kind of freshness of impressions, that sense of an eye looking out from somewhere but you were not sure where, but with a cynical look at reality without any prejudice, without any preconceived ideas. Quite the opposite, in fact.

I remember one evening he had come with some friends to my house; I read a poem by Leopardi and straight after that he recited an excerpt from Milton's *Paradise Lost*, and that recital by Dylan struck us greatly because Dylan was transformed when he recited, he became a kind of actor in full command of his resources, his powers: he bellowed, he writhed, and so we were not surprised to hear that once he had gone back to Britain he had made some broadcasts which were enormously successful.

In Rome, he visited Mario Praz, the author of The Romantic Agony. *In Florence, he talked with Gino Magnani Rocca, the composer. Did he tell you about them?*

No, I never heard him talk about that. He certainly met Eugenio Montale, he was close to him and then others of those who used to go to the café, that is to say, Luzi, Rosai, Landolfi and others.[35] Poets were particularly close to him, and then during his stay here in Florence he met André Frenaud; he got on well with him, they spent two days together, and then Frenaud left. He became a great friend of Dylan's... it may be that Frenaud had seen him before. The fact is that as they happened to be here in Florence, unbeknown to each other, they were very happy to have met and so spent two days together at the villa where Thomas lived.[36]

Was he writing much in Florence, in the villa?

I have the impression that Thomas spent his days writing, composing verse and particularly the poem that he wrote during his stay ['In Country Sleep']. This composition occupied more or less his whole stay here... he was always busy, working at his verse every day... we never saw him except occasionally in the afternoon, when he'd come down to the city and spend a few hours in the café. He spent all the rest of the time working.

I have the impression that he wrote in the villa itself, which was a large, empty, very peaceful villa, so perhaps he didn't need to leave it to find the ideal atmosphere. There were woods all around, and in the evenings the song of the nightingale, the moon... it was utterly peaceful, so I think that basically even the title of that poem somehow reflects the environment in which it was written.

Was his drinking a problem for him?

While he was in Florence, you might say he did drink beer all the time, but he didn't look like an alcoholic at all because he didn't speak like one, he wasn't red in the face, he was very calm, and you could see that from all this drinking mainly beer he was already sort of – not fat – but he wasn't thin either, he was a bit plump, a bit like someone who drinks a good deal but this was not reflected at all either in his external appearance or, I believe, in his writing activities. Even in his gaze, a crystal-clear gaze, a gaze like a child's.

... I think everything went very well in Elba, and you could hear him talk about those long swims with Luigi Berti, but not much else is known about his stay there. When he came back from Elba... he found himself in great difficulties and was helped by a friend of ours, the painter Ottone Rosai, who had become good friends with him. From the start the situation was really terrible for Thomas, who had to stay here with his wife, sister-in-law and two children with hardly any money. But then things were sorted out thanks, in fact, to Rosai's help, for which he truly showed extreme gratitude, and then Rosai never had occasion to see him again.

Rosai is the greatest artist Florence has had this century, in the first half of the century. He is an artist who has come up from the people, he was brought up before the First World War, he took part in Futurism but after the War he started his kind of Realism, his direct take on reality, and he also started on his definition of the reality of the people, absolutely devoid of any rhetoric, full of very intense colour and substance. He is an artist who has counted a lot for Florence; it has been noted that he is an artist who is difficult to understand outside his environment, but as soon as you get to know a little about the workings of the city, you can see Rosai's greatness and strength straight away. Rosai stands out even in the context of Italian painting precisely because he is an artist deeply attached to an environment who actually reflects the reality of this environment. Naturally, then, Rosai got on very well with Thomas; they may not even have exchanged a word together other than perhaps a few gestures or a joke, but they were certainly made to get on well with each other because they were very authentic people, both of them. I remember he said this to Rosai: "The time when I am back in Wales, in my field, I'll dig until I find some gold coins to send you as a present, in thanks."

I had the impression that Thomas' only occupation really was poetry. He was a man with whom it was impossible to think about anything else other than poetry. Perhaps the same could also be said about us in those days, but anyway what was clear was that whatever came into conversation always came via that direct road that leads from poetry to things. It was a time when one didn't feel any need to talk about anything else because the War was still too close, too present not to weigh heavily. A tragedy that rather overshadowed everything. Life had still not got back to normal, some roads were still cut, queues were long, economic life hadn't restarted at all. The economic miracle hadn't begun happily and so one then felt the need not to talk about matters that were too worrying.

To tell the truth, with Thomas we expressed ourselves in monosyllables, we expressed ourselves by looking each other in the eyes more than actually having long talks, partly because of the actual difficulty we had in communicating... you could perhaps ask for his opinion on a poet or something and get a bellow for an answer, or on the other hand some great 'ohs' of admiration, but talking didn't get very far beyond that.

I made a distinction at the beginning between certain poems that are universal, like the poetry of Shakespeare or Hopkins, which come across directly. Other poems, on the other hand, are much more complex. The same can be said of Mallarmé; in Mallarmé, too, there are basically certain poems which come across directly to all readers, and there is the complex part of his work which presents an indecipherable side, a side of an encouraging obscurity, an obscurity that entices one to penetrate it. The same can be said of Thomas, though, of course, he's not Mallarmé, he's not the same thing, he's something completely different. All the more because in Thomas you feel caught up in this kind of power which breaks through the obscurity, lighting up the darkness; it's really fascinating. Thomas' poetry is certainly endowed with great, shattering power, and you might say it smashes the romantic concept of poetry to give a true, imminent meaning to things. And, of course, it is poetry that emerges during the Second World War, it is that poetry that has the tragedy of what was happening in the world at that time. It rejects what could be the natural side of things because an inhuman violence has been unleashed on nature, and Thomas's poetry tries to capture that violence.

Eugenio Montale [37]

I think it was in Florence. Dylan came to me accompanied by his wife, and by Luigi Berti, his translator. But they refused to see me, and I found him hidden in a cupboard. I opened the cupboard and he was half-drunk... he came to see me but when he was in my house he decided that he couldn't see me and I found him hidden in this cupboard.

I told him "You are Mr Dylan Thomas?" "Yes." "Very glad to meet you" and there was no explication about the fact he was hidden.

How long did he stay with you that day?
A few minutes. Then Luigi Berti left my house with him and his wife... I met him again in Oxford, in a sort of a café. And I exchanged a few words with him. He was drunk, also. He was a very nice man.

Did he discuss poetry with you? Did he talk about anything serious with you?
No, not serious questions. We exchanged a few words but not about poetry.

What was he talking about?
Oh, the time, the food, the sky, the clouds, the beauty of the flowers and so on. Not important things.

Augusto Livi[38]

I'm now with Augusto Livi who knew Dylan in Elba.
Yes, in July 1947. I was on honeymoon. I met Dylan, his wife, his son and his daughter and we lived very, very freely in the little town, Rio Marina. It was a town of miners, the nature was wonderful, the earth was blue, green, yellow because there were fragments of iron and sulphurous material and Dylan admired these colours and this nature... I think that he saw in the landscape, the naked landscape, a souvenir of the Galles, of Wales. Without grass practically. Without trees. Certainly there are trees but along the coast was a stripe of mine earth, very variously coloured. He loved this, I think, and certainly the Mediterranean vegetation.

... he worked all day, in a relatively little room in the hotel where we lived and generally walked in the afternoon... a very little hotel with a restaurant... I don't remember exactly but five rooms, no more. Not expensive, a very cheap hotel.

Did he like Italian food?
Yes. Practically, yes... I remember a curious particular. In Italy, we eat the octopus, and for an Englishman it's horrible. When I proposed we eat the octopus, I remember that Caitlin told: "Oh, it's repellent, it's repellent."

He drinked not too much, he drinked the very fine wine of Elba, but little, little. Several times he drank strong, but I remember that he drank very little and that he was thirsty, and he drinked water. Water, when he was thirsty. Without alcohol... practically, I never saw him drunk. I don't remember, I didn't see him. Without hypocrisy, no I didn't.

... he was a very interesting man, he spoke very rarely, he contemplated the landscape, and he was a little distracted in his thoughts. A very, very correct man. It's strange, a very reserved man. And very alone, very alone.

We walked with him. Along the coast of Elba, one hour, two hours. Two times. I remember one of these promenades. They were practically a completely silent walk. Caitlin spoke but Dylan very, very little. He was [preoccupied] by poetical activity, I think.

He had very intense conversations with his wife, which lasted half an hour even. They were sitting apart from us at a table and talking together, without letting anyone else in on their secret, not even their children or his sister-in-law... my impression was that he was very united with his wife.

He was very kind, a little strange. I am an intellectual and it is strange that I speak so. I understand the strangeness of Dylan, that was an interior strangeness, not a comical strangeness. But always when I think of Dylan, I remember this character of aloneness, strangeness, the melancholy of this man.

... a painter of Florence, Ottone Rosai, thought that he is like a little Bacchus, a little Bacchus of Caravaggio. His appearance with the curls, red face. Cherubic. The strange impression that I had was that he was a passenger, a man who passes on earth. And I don't say this because I know he is dead, he died early and young. I had the impression of someone who was passing through this world, a definitely dramatic figure, a dramatic witness to our times, a man destined to pass among men but not to stay until he was old. It's not just an impression, as we say in Italian 'del senno di poi', in hindsight, but it was a lyrical, spiritual impression of a man who wouldn't last long... a major romantic poet, a physical romantic poet. Even childlike, boylike in his innocence, in that strangeness of his which wasn't the strangeness of the beat generation, no, no, it was the strangeness of a poet.

Had Dylan's poetry or prose been translated in Italy? Did you know his poetry before you met him?

No, no. after... I knew only the man, not the poet. I had not a preconceived image of him. No, no, I met with a man, with a man [who was] strange and poetical, a sweet man.

Dylan was not an intellectual...

He never spoke of Italian literature or French literature, no.

Did he ever recite any of his poetry?

One time, very indiscreetly, I saw in his room a little paper. I was invited in his room and I looked... he smiled and said: "Yes, it's poetry. I have written it this afternoon." It's all. I was very embarrassed of this.

... in Elba he spoke, with fishermen, with simple people of the little town... we were in 1947, two years after the War, and it was not a society of consumers, like it was in Italy in the Thirties, Twenties... the Mayor of the municipality was Communist and I remember very well. He was a friend of us and he drank with us, very interesting. I remember his name: Mariannini. He was a very kind fellow... speech evolved with Italian gestures, with fragments of French, of Italian, of English... there was a man who had been in America, like an immigrant, who spoke English, but very badly, and he remembered his past in America and he sang the songs of the Twenties, and Caitlin, too, sang. A curious episode.

He thought Rio was a very tough place, the men were very tough and likely to fight each other, when they were drunk.

You see, they were fishermen, very strong men, there was political competition more than personal. Between Democratic-Christians and the Communists and government Socialists... provincial, very kind atmosphere. Very kind and human atmosphere. Dylan loved this atmosphere.

Did Dylan talk much about politics?

He knew that we were people of the Left. All of us were on the Left, I am on the Left, but I don't remember... he did not speak of religion, no. He spoke of Wales my country, my 'patria'. With nostalgia.

Bill Green

I remember when he first came to the village [South Leigh, Oxfordshire, 1947-49], with his old caravan. He came down to my grandfather and asked him if he could park it in his land down the road – which he did. And from that period we met him every night... he was a grand man. And used to write a lot of poetry. He used to recite a lot in the bar of the local...

Who was running the Mason Arms in those days?[39]

Mr and Mrs Albert Hopkins... my mother and father – which was Herbert Green – kept the post office... after coming out of the public bar, [Dylan] used to come back to them for supper and another drink. I used to go where I lived, next door. I used to go in and play the piano for him and his wife. Play all the Welsh hymns and songs, and really have a good beano there. And he usually finished up we had to put him in the car and take him to his caravan, the worse for what he drank... under the influence he was a very difficult man, but a very good-natured man. Never caused any trouble. We used to undress him and put him into bed, until the next morning.

... he used to, like everyone after worse for drink, to argue some, 'bout something. But I never saw him in any fights, or really any great arguments. I took him about in the car all over the place in Oxfordshire, different public houses, different hotels; and I never see him cause any trouble whatsoever when I been with him. But now and again, when he'd had a few – when he was on his beers, he was all right. But when he went onto his spirits, then you'd got to watch him. And I used to put my hand down and say "Well, look, that's enough for tonight. Have another beer, we'll go." And that used to be the end of it.

The time he came to South Leigh, did they move straight into the Manor House?
No, no. When he first came to South Leigh, I suppose he was in this caravan for about three months... just the wife. The children weren't here... it was one of these old-fashioned gypsy caravans, all painted different colours, golden-brown and... wheels painted brown and yellow, and the iron round the wheels. It had a small bed in there, each side, for two, which was folded up, two single ones each side... then he'd got his table in the front. He used to push open the rear and sit looking out, into the sky. With his knees under the table, and writing away. In the front they had an old primus stove with a kettle and an old paraffin convector heater thing, very old-fashioned one. They lived in it nearly three months.

What did they do for cooking, and washing up?
Oh, they just used to have everything from tins and soups. Come up to my father's for dinner and suppers... no water supply, but a little tap on the edge of the lane.

Where did they get it?
It came, I think, by truck to Witney and they hired a horse... one of Mr Parsel's horses and fetched it from Witney.

... then they had this house, the Manor, which is across the fields and when he moved all his goods and papers, I went down with the car and helped them move it all down to the Manor House. And on this occasion he gave me a lot of papers that hadn't been published... he put it all into a box and say "Here you are Bill, you can have this." Of course, I brought it home and it was in the shed for a very, very long time, and I thought, well, this is just a lot of rubbish, so I took it up the garden and just put a match to it. Much to my resentment now, when I hear about Dylan Thomas.

Was it Margaret Taylor who owned it?
That owned it, yes, they became very great friends. Used to come down here nights.

She was devoted to Dylan – to his work, yes?
Oh yes, she used to get all his papers out, you know, unpublished papers and read them all through... but I never saw anything between them at all, or any...

... the Manor House lays right back in the fields. And in the winter, when we had a lot of rain, it was absolutely impossible to get there for water, floods. And he used to put on a pair of thigh boots, and I used to meet him at the gate on the road, and take him where he wanted to go, which pub he wanted to go to. Or come up to see my father. Or take him up to see the clergyman, whichever it was, very often.

The clergyman – the vicar?
The vicar, yes. Used to go up...

Church of England?
Yes, Church of England, yes... and sit up and have a talk with him and after waiting for him some time he used to go and say "Look, I'm ready to go." And he'd come out and bring back to father's house, stay there and have a few drinks and tell a few yarns. Most of them dirty, but still – that's beside the point. And he would go around and say "Well, I've got to put my knees under the table," he'd say, "and do some writing."

What was his routine?
He used to come up here and have his pint first. In the morning. He'd go straight down and get his knees under the table... just have his eleven o'clock drink in the morning... just a light beer which then used to be from Burford. It was Garn's beer then.

And then he'd go back home?
Ten thirty, eleven o'clock. He used to say, "Get my knees under the table." That was always his expression.

When would you see him next?
In the evening he would have a walk up, just as far as Dad's, sit out talking, have a drop of home made wine. He'd then go along to the public house at about half-past nine. Come back to Dad's again, sometimes till about twelve.

... then he just wrote for days and days without drinking. And then he came up again. He said "I'm getting tired of this, Herbert." He said "I'm gonna have a drink."

You said Dylan sang Welsh hymns, but Dylan didn't speak any Welsh.
Well, he used to break – well, an abrupt Welsh he used to sing... oh yes, he used to recite and all in Welsh, I'm sure he did.

I think he was fooling you!
... but I'm sure some of the poems he wrote, he used to recite some of them in Welsh, anyway. I'm ruddy sure of that.

... he [Bill McAlpine] was an Irish man and Dylan was a Welsh man – well, that meant two periods of drink: St Patrick's Day and –

You mean he celebrated St David's Day?
Oh yes, he most certainly did! I remember once it came on a Thursday... I took them all in to Witney, the pub down Corn Street – the Angel. And that's where they stopped. They drank theirselves drunk and they drank theirselves sober. They came back here, in this room we got, we're sitting now – they brought the whisky and beers with them – they just sat here and drunk 'til about two o'clock in the morning. You couldn't make them drunk any more 'cause they just got past it. I got the car out and I took Bill McAlpine home first, and I took Dylan down to the Manor after.

What was his health like in this period?
I think his health wasn't all that good. He used to smoke a terrible lot... took him to the doctor in Hensham and he gave him some pills and it sort of brought him back more, return like, back of all the drinking.

Oh, he did give up the drinking for a while?
Yes, I think that's why he packed up. He had to.

What do you remember of Caitlin, and what about their relationship?
Some time they were real husband and wife, next time they were foreigners to one another. But on the whole I think she kept him in hand... and I think she was an ex-Windmill girl, according to her dancing – because she could really dance... I used to play the piano to them.

At your father's house, in the post office?

Father's house, yes, yes – she used to do all the dancing there…

… and another thing – he used to come up here and just sit on the side of the bank out here and get his pen out – that's when he thought of something coming up that what he should write down. And he just sat out on the road and used to write… made notes all the time, yes. And even when he was taking to a pub, before he'd have enough to drink, if he had a dialect of someone, he used to put them in his purse or something else, and make a note of that.

You mentioned that you took him on little trips. What was the purpose of the trips? Was it just a pub crawl or what?
It was a pub crawl, but he just wanted to learn the people who got in there and see what information he could get from going into this pub… on a tour, used to go up and stay in about half an hour in one. Perhaps if he got interested in there, he'd stay for an hour. Or if he didn't like it, he'd just have one drink and away… within a twelve-mile radius I should think, actually. Stanlake. Abingdon. I been to some in Oxford, but not many – he didn't like Oxford pubs at all. He couldn't get on with Oxford – he said too crowded and too snob-nosed there.

Did Dylan go up to London?
Oh, he used to stay up in London perhaps for four or five days at a time. Writing his scripts at the BBC. And he used to come down here and run through them with some of the staff and what have you, and he would go up there again and I suppose they would make a recording of it… the train ran right the way through to Oxford… used to have three to five trains a day to Oxford.

… he was a genuine friend, there's no doubt about that.

Bill Mitchell

I was in charge of the railway station here [South Leigh]. He was very sociable. Nice to talk to. And he had a bit of an impediment in his speech. He used to sort of stutter now and again. Then when he went and started talking, it come out fluently. He'd got this little impediment in his speech, but that prevented him from mixing in with the upper crust, like… but when he went to the phone or anything like that, he was as clear as a bell. Or when he was saying anything like a bit of poetry or a line of anything it was as clear as anything.

What do you remember of Caitlin?
Oh, she was a lovely girl. She used to dance up in the pub, up on the

tables in there... oh yes, lovely dancer – do the handstand, cartwheel on the table – yes... he encouraged it... Caitlin was quite an enjoyable person to be with... oh, she was a peach of a girl.

... I wouldn't say he worked every day with special hours. He used to do his bit of work in the caravan and the next thing you'd know, he'd be up the road, him and Bill [McAlpine], they're off to Witney... the only time I went out with Dylan on drinks was when we used to go with darts, down at the different villages, down at Glanfield and Alvescot. Used to have night trips from the village in a coach.

... I've never known him drink spirits... oh, he was a good drinker. I wouldn't say very much, no... I've never known him boisterous. Of course, he wasn't going to put up with anybody's cheek or anything like that – well, nor would anybody... he was very good tempered.

... very seldom had anything to eat, I don't think. I can't remember him eating anything. Not in the way of bun, or anything.

So at lunchtime he was drinking his lunch, was he?
I should think so, yes. Working man's lunch that, isn't? He was a bit tight for money very often, because I used to have to wait for my paper money for a long, long time.

Did he borrow a lot of money from people?
Never borrowed any off me. But his paper bills, he was a long time paying them, you see. [40]

So he didn't have a reputation in South Leigh for sponging off people?
Oh no, no, no. He never borrowed any money off me, anyhow. Nor never borrow any off anybody else...

What about his attitude to women? Because in America people said that he was chasing women.
Never known anything to do with women while he was here. 'Cause we all used to go together, and my wife used to come, and then we used to go down to these other places for darts and one thing and another in the coach.

Did Caitlin come back here later?
Oh, she came back here two or three times.

To visit friends here?
Well, Mrs Green that used to be at the shop, where the post office is now. Just to see the people in the village, see people she knew... she never brought the children with her, I don't think. I don't remember seeing the kiddies after they went away.

Lionel Drinkwater

I was cowman up at the Church Farm... and that was 'bout 1948, I s'pose. I lived along the bottom of the village here then, just along the bottom row. We used to see him go by... every head was out of the window to see him come along when he was going to the pub, 'cause they know they was out for a good night!

Do you know why Margaret Taylor chose this village? Did she have a previous connection with it?
I don't think so. The Manor was for sale, wasn't it, and she came and bought it. And put Dylan and his wife in... Mrs Taylor used to come down here, just for breakaways from Oxford, I s'pose, because she was an Oxford don's wife, wasn't she?

Yes. Did she live in the Manor with Dylan and Caitlin, or did she have a separate place?
I think they all lived together. They'd got their own bedrooms, separate bedrooms and whatnot. They all lived together when I was there, when I ever went there.

... Dylan was here before Margaret bought that... 'cause he lived along in the caravan... he was on his own, and then about three – maybe six – months after Margaret bought that and... I'm not sure that she didn't lodge here before they went to the Manor.

When was the first time you saw Dylan?
I think I was along at the local and he came in and he was a very good-natured bloke, and I was told "Keep the right side of him, you'll have a pint."

He was generous?
When he'd got it, he was very generous.

He had a reputation amongst some people of being a sponger on his friends. Was that true?
Well – yes and no. He knew where he could and where he couldn't, if you understand the meaning! The people that he was in with, outside the village, that used to come, they used to get out of him what they could... he didn't seem to have the valuation on money as such – he'd let it go whilst he'd got it. Then, if he hadn't got the money, he'd tell the landlord straight "I'm not paying for this." 'Course, they all knew him, and he was trusted.

... when he come down the pub he was always just ordinary. You know, open shirt, everything. And I don't think he was a feller as found the cold much. I think he'd got a very good constitution. He seemed always amiable that way.

... she was highly excitable, you know. If you went out on a bus, it was nothing for her to do a cartwheel down the middle of the bus. That's plus dancing on the table... she'd get up there and do the Spanish dance as nice as pie... she was as much a boozer as him. She could put it back, but she could carry it... Dylan was one of those fellers then you could not judge. He might be putting it on for the benefit of other people, to see what other people's reactions would be to him, try to think he hadn't got his wits about him.

He liked telling stories about things that had happened to him – that was his form of humour, wasn't it?
Oh yes, yes. It was always, "it happened to me" – always. He'd never tell a story about, you know, like anybody getting up, like telling stories about an Irishman. It was always him. Always him, in his younger days, when he was a child. He'd tell you his history... oh, very interesting. I was interested in the man; I liked being in his company.

Mr Mitchell has told me of outings they'd take, some regulars at the Mason Arms would go on outings.
Oh yes, we used to have the coach out from Witney, and oh, they'd all muck in and come with us. They were good company. We'd go to Bampton – always the New Inn which has just been renamed the Morris Man... Ampleforth, I think, up Eddington. Then come back to the Bannock Gate, the Britannia. We always finished up at Ban at the Brit.

Did Dylan ever read his poetry or any of his writings in the pubs?
No. No – he'd never divulge none of it.

It's said that Dylan preferred the company of ordinary people, rather than the academics and the intellectuals.
Well, he was very much like that. He was more with the poorer class in this village than he was with the upper class of it... he was a very good judge of, he could tell you what a person was... whether he was any good.

Did you get anything from him about his attitude to women?
He never seemed a woman's man to me – unless there was anything between him and Mrs Taylor, I wouldn't know... he was never what I'd term a ladies' man... he was men's company more than a woman's... he was more at home with a man's company, in my opinion... in that day, when they were here, there was no nothing, no neck in the women... it's more so recent years... that they've had open and showed their bosoms, boobs or whatever they call them. But he was

never like that. I don't think he – well, he may have despised women, I don't know, but I don't think so, but as I say, he preferred a man's company here.

Ethel Ann Gunn

... on Thursdays, my sister and I used to catch the ten o'clock train into Witney, and Dylan came in, and shared our railway compartment, and that's how we first met. And he often did that... we went in for shopping but I really didn't inquire what he did... he'd usually come back again on the midday train.

... Dylan came here several times... he'd come and have a chatter, you know, and then go. We used to talk about everyday things... he scarcely ever spoke of his work in any way. Not to me... perhaps we didn't give him the chance... he'd just hop in and out again, just when he felt inclined.

... we used to have a small dramatic society and Dylan always came for the dress rehearsals, and just passed his opinion on the characters... he'd tell us if he liked our costumes or if he didn't, and if we'd done well in the parts... oh, we used to look forward to his coming... he didn't take part in it but Mrs McAlpine, of course, entered into the characters with us... Mrs Hopkins at the pub... she was the producer.

He made a lot of friends in the village?
Ooh, yes – he was very popular... he was never disagreeable – slightly moody sometimes, but never disagreeable. Always trying to look on the bright side of things.

... he was typically Welsh... he was always proud of being Welsh, wasn't he? That he'd always speak well of anything Welsh.

He didn't get a reputation for drunkenness here? Because that's been talked about a lot.
Yes. I know it is, but I actually never met that... I had the BBC people down here several times... and they particularly said about the drunkenness, so I said "I never met it." And I said "I think if there was anything, your people were worse than he was."

Dorothy 'Dosh' Murray (née Worley)

Mrs Hopkins [landlady of the Mason Arms, South Leigh] was my aunt... when I was eighteen, she asked me if I'd like to come and live with her. I've always loved the country, so I came... have lived here ever since… almost like her daughter, you know. They had no family.

Tell us about the Hopkinses.

My uncle farmed the land, about three hundred acres… uncle was really quite the John Bull type, thick-set and stout. And he mostly wore plus-fours, and very jolly, nice outlook on life… he was a great cricket fan… I think my uncle spent part of his life in Wales… my aunt was a complete hostess, she was very social, she liked social life and did a lot of good here, really. They were ardent churchgoers… they never opened on Sundays.

When Dylan came here you were… ?

I was married, living here, but I used to go frequently to my aunt's… Dylan was a very nice little man – I met him on many occasions.

When would he come down to the Mason Arms?

Mornings, when they were out for a cycle ride – when he and Caitlin were out. They used to go for bicycle rides round the country… and they would drop in – well, I don't know whether I should divulge this, but there was something wrong with their plumbing. She used to come to my aunt's to have a bath… that used to bring her along, and if my aunt was baking cakes in the kitchen, he'd love to go and sit in there with her and have a little cake out of the oven… and, of course, my uncle sold coal, and so he ordered coal from him… he [Dylan] just used to call… nothing regular about it, just when he felt he wanted to drift in and talk – he used to like to talk about the country… he would have a little half-pint… and drink some of that with a cake.

How would you describe him?

Very likeable, very unassuming, quiet and yet happy… very friendly with everyone… you'd have just thought he was, apart from his accent, just one of the village people… I think, perhaps, you could say he was rather nervy. Nervy, would you call it? Yes, I think perhaps you could say that.

… he used to talk to my aunt – he wrote us our Christmas play… but unfortunately, when my aunt moved house… her two sisters came, and they must have burnt it on a bonfire… it would have been priceless, wouldn't it?

Your aunt, Mrs Hopkins, was very active in local dramatic work?

Yes, she produced plays… we had what they call a Mothers' Union, which wasn't at all stuffy, as people think Mothers' Unions are, and we used to do a Christmas Nativity play. We started during the War, to make some entertainment, and then we did Passion plays and we thoroughly enjoyed it.

Some people have accused Dylan of being a sponger...
His dealings with uncle were scrupulously honest and businesslike, you know. He would sometimes order a crate of beer, little orders he had – but coal chiefly and logs, and it was always – as I remember – nothing dubious about it, or long paying.

10. Dosh Murray

He never left your uncle with a big bill unpaid?
Ooh no – no, no, no. Quite honest about all of it.

Did Dylan ever talk about politics at all when he was here?
Not to me – I don't know whether he did to my uncle or not. He was rather more of a man's man, I think – he enjoyed men's company rather than female company.

In America the people say that he was after the women...
Yes, that's what I can't believe, that's what I cannot understand. I cannot accept that, really – unless he changed drastically. I don't know if anything happened to him, whether he became ill... mentally ill. That wasn't the Dylan we knew...

Of course, here he was drinking beer.
I've never seen him what I call drink too much... I should think, perhaps, when he went there they overwhelmed him with... and that got hold, I don't know... to me that's unbelievable – the picture they made of him. So sad – I thought it was dreadful.

What is the most striking memory you have of Dylan?
Well, just a very nice, unassuming, happy little man, who was interested in all country things and just a very normal person... I often think about them.

Harry and Joan Locke

HL: We first met in 1946 at a party. I told Dylan a story and it made him laugh so much he had to go out of the room and be sick! It was in London at Bill and Helen McAlpine's flat and we took to each other straight away... I didn't know a thing about his poetry.

Was he living in South Leigh then?

HL: Yes, at the Manor... a beautiful, old rambling house with about two, three acres in which they grew grass. They grew grass until it was about seven feet tall and Caitlin would be out there with an enormous scythe, hacking away at this grass and she said "I hope to God none of the children are in here!"

... South Leigh was lovely, and everybody in South Leigh loved Dylan. They absolutely adored him. Of course, he was a shove ha'penny champion at the local pub... oh God, he was absolutely superb at shove ha'penny... at the Turf in Oxford where they've got a board that nobody's touched except the very experts for about a hundred years, Dylan was the only man who was allowed to play on it... when I used to try he'd say "You've got to see the patterns, Harry – you've got to see where they're going, otherwise you'll never play at all." And he was superb.

JL: Margaret Taylor had an uncanny instinct about Dylan, didn't she?

HL: He'd come round early in the evening, and he'd say "Come on Harry, let's go out. Because I've got a feeling Margaret's coming round. Let's go to a pub where we've never been before." And we'd go right the other side of London... and we'd be sitting there, happily having a couple of pints of bitter and sure enough, the door would open and in would come Margaret. And she'd say "Hello, boys. I thought I'd find you here." And Dylan would say "How does she do it? How does she know?" Poor Margaret; she was so much in love with him – but she knew by a sort of witchcraft...

What about Dylan's drinking in those days?

HL: He just loved his beer. That's all.

JL: Did he get drunk?

HL: Oh, often... I tell you something more than that – that he often pretended to be drunk.

This was Dylan. He pretended to be drunk, but I knew he wasn't, because I'd been with him all day. And the night before. And I knew exactly how much he'd drunk and he wasn't drunk... if anyone offered him a whisky, he would say "No, I don't like it". He liked pints and pints and pints of beer.

... one day he got up early, when he was staying at my house, 260, King Street, Hammersmith. The night before, Caitlin had sewn all the buttons on his suit and he said "I've got the most important job I've ever had. I've got to go and see J. Arthur Rank. How do I look" I said, you're fine, you're fine. He ordered a taxi and I said "I'll come with you. What are you going to see him about?" And he said "The most wonderful job, the job I've wanted to do all of my life. Rank wants me to do a screenplay of *Ulysses*." And a button went pyoick – and hit the ceiling of the taxi! And he said "Oh Gawd, oh gee" he said. "*Ulysses* – I love *Ulysses*. I know it inside out, I know every paragraph of *Ulysses*." And pyingeeck! Another button came off! So I left him in Piccadilly and off he went to see J. Arthur Rank, and when he came back in the afternoon I said "How'd you get on?" He said "Oh, my God. Oh dear." I said "Didn't you get the job?" And he worked for a fortnight on doing a screen treatment of *Ulysses*, and he said "I went into Rank's office, I put it on his desk and he read the first page and he said "Thomas – you're a bloody fool. I meant Homer!" [41]

JL: He'd written a great deal of *Under Milk Wood* at that time, hadn't he?

HL: Oh yes, he worked on *Under Milk Wood* for about six years but he finished it off at 260… he finished most of it in the pub. In the Ravenscourt Arms.

Did he tell you about the origins of the idea for this?

HL: No. It was simply about Laugharne and everybody in Laugharne that he knew.

JL: Go on – tell him about coming down in the morning and finding Dylan there with the beer bottles on the table.

HL: I'd come down to get my son's breakfast and there would be Dylan, still with the light on, possibly half asleep with the kitchen table covered in papers and beer bottles, and he'd say "Harry! Listen to this." And he'd read something that he's written that was absolutely outrageous and I said "Dylan, the BBC are never going to accept this." He said "I know, boy – but it's bloody funny, isn't it?"

Had you worked at all professionally with Dylan or been connected in anyway with him in the theatre or in the films?

HL: No, except that he was instrumental in getting me my first job. In *No Room at the Inn*.

Dylan wrote a part specifically for you, didn't he?

HL: Yes. Part of the tobacconist. As well as Nogood Boyo… Cordelia's in *Under Milk Wood* in no uncertain terms. She's there – Mrs Dai Bread Two.

JL: She's the Spanish gypsy wife.

HL: Who sits on the doorstep and drinks wine and eats nuts! That's Cordy!

... I only ever knew Dylan to be unkind once and that's when we were in a pub, and there was a little old man who'd got a withered hand, and he knew that Dylan was a good shove ha'penny player and he came up to Dylan with his little withered arm and his withered hand, and said "How about a game of shove ha'penny, Mr Thomas?" And Dylan copied exactly this little man's withered arm and said "No, I don't think we'll play tonight." And the next night we went into the pub the landlady said "Oh, Mr Thomas you upset poor little Pete last night." He said "What did I do?" She said "Well you imitated him. You imitated his withered hand." And he said "Oh, I didn't. Did I?" And she said "Yes. He's very upset." And Dylan said "Oh, God. I must put this right." He said "What does Pete drink?" She said "Well, he likes a drop of whisky" So Dylan turned to me and, as usual, you know, he'd got no money, and he said "Harry, lend me a couple of pounds, will you. Mrs Richards – could I have a bottle of whisky? And keep it for Pete"

... Lord knows why we were up in Covent Garden at half-past ten in the morning but we were, and Dylan as usual, feeling dreadful, said "Let's go and have a beer." So we went into a pub and he ordered a couple of Worthingtons, but his hand was so shaky, before he'd even picked the glass up, he knocked it over the counter and he said "Oh well, that's that, isn't it. Oh, that's the fastest Worthington I've ever had." And he was laughing his nut off, but then he saw that the barmaid had tried to catch the glass and she cut her hand, and it was bleeding badly and he said "Just stay where you are Harry, will you? Just stay where you are." And he went out into Covent Garden, and he came back with the biggest bunch of flowers you've ever seen. A marvellous bunch of flowers. And he said "Miss – I'm sorry. Very, very sorry" And she said "Ooh sir, you needn't have done that." And he said "Do you like them?" and she said "Oh, they're lovely." He said "Right – now I'll have my Worthington."

JL: Everyone took Dylan so seriously... everyone worshipped him as a poet and what Harry brought out of him, and what I've seen of Dylan in his work since I've re-met Harry, is this lovely gift of looking and seeing people. And when I listen to *Under Milk Wood*, and especially when I hear Nogood Boyo, I think oh, you wicked man – you know! It's exactly Harry. He saw too much, he saw much too much...

Did Dylan talk to you about his feeling about Wales and about the fact that he couldn't speak Welsh?
HL: No, no; I don't think he ever did.

Did he ever talk to you about politics?

HL: Ooh, yes. Ooh, yes. He had a fierce political conscience, about the peace of the world and about the atom bomb and so on. I introduced him once to a South African multi-millionaire gold miner, and we went for a Sunday morning walk round the park. Dylan had got this thing about parks. Think that's why he loved my house... my house was right inside the park, and Dylan had got this strange nostalgic thing about old park seats and wet, soggy trees and wet grass, and he loved it. If it was misty or foggy, he loved to walk round Ravenscourt Park. And we walked round this park – can you imagine three stranger people; me, Dylan and a multi-millionaire from South Africa, Larry Jacobson. And they had this fierce argument about politics and colour and Larry said "Well, Dylan, where d'you get your money from?" And Dylan said "Every word I write down on paper means a pound to me. Where do you get yours from?" He said "I bend down and pick it up out of the earth!" And Dylan said "You call yourself a Christian?"

JL: There were many occasions in 260 when he did sweat.

HL: Oh yes, oh yes. He worked like mad. He locked himself in. We used to go up and bang on the door and leave some food on the tray outside, but he was locked in... he never touched anything. When he was writing, he was writing. He wasn't drinking. When he finished, alright – out to the pub.

... we were in the Gluepot [the George] one day and it got to closing and Dylan was supposed to be at this reading of his poetry in Broadcasting House and I kept saying as one always said to Dylan "Look, the time's getting on. You must go." And he'd say "Oh no, no, no. There's no hurry, there's no hurry." And I said "Well look, it's three o'clock. We've got to leave here, the pub's closing." And he said "I'll tell you what we'll do. We'll go down the road here, just down Great Portland Street, there's a beautiful sweet shop, we'll buy a bag of sweets and we'll go and see *Mighty Joe Young*." The film about the big monkey – you know, sort of King Kong. And Dylan went and bought about a pound of sweets – assorted toffees and humbugs and goodness knows – I said "Dylan, you can't!" He said "I can, boy – you watch me." He said "Come on, I'll pay." And we went to the Marble Arch Pavilion and went and saw *Mighty Joe Young*, which is a load of rubbish! But Dylan all the time, stuffing sweets into his mouth and – "Have another sweet, boy, go on." Thoroughly enjoying every moment of this appalling nonsense.

... Ray Bradbury used to send him the first editions of every one of his science fiction books. He must have met Ray Bradbury in America and Dylan used to watch the post and suddenly, plonk, there would come an envelope through. And he would say "Ah – Ray Bradbury's sent me another book. Oh boy, oh look at this. Woar!" And he used to hop around like a kid, you know, saying "I'm not gonna get up tomorrow morning, boy, I'm gonna read this!" He loved it.

JL: Tell about Dylan and Prince Philip.

HL: We had an evening at the Savage Club and Prince Philip came along, and there was Dylan leaning up against the bar, next to him, elbow to elbow, and Dylan was saying to me "Who's this? I know his face."

Emrys Morris, Llwyngwyn

What do you remember of Dylan?
Down for a walk down Llansteffan, looking at the seaside and thinking of something... he didn't talk a lot, but he was always thinking of something... they walked down from living in Laugharne for a long time, and then walking up on the riverside... good voice on him. He had a good voice – singing sometimes! Oh, he could sing anthems... English language he was, Thomas.

Did he speak any Welsh at all to you?
Sometimes!

What did he say? Bore da and that sort of thing?
Bore da, ay.

Not much, though?
Not much, no.

When was the last time you saw Dylan?
I think we were up in London we saw him last. I was up there... Idris and me and Mr Hobbs went up there... we went out with him... Pictures in the night there. Pictures and everything. I was younger then... we had a few drinks.

Some people say Dylan was a drunkard.
Oh, no. No. Wasn't a drunkard, no.

John Ormond

I first met him in London in 1946 when he was recording a verse reading for Patrick Dickinson in a series called *Time for Verse*. He was sick man that night, with a simple cold and colic – I don't think any ordinary performer would have turned up in the studio. He was certainly very sober, at that time, so it wasn't drink that was making him as he felt, but he was a professional, doing a job. I rushed home to listen to the broadcast, having been in the studio, and nothing betrayed the fact that he was at all ill, which he certainly was then.

... I had written to him sending, as a young poet will, poems to a man who has got a name and whose work is exciting and is affecting the younger man. I had sent him poems when I was still a student and had got very kind replies, encouraging me, breathing on whatever talent he thought he saw or said he saw, rightly or wrongly, and he was kindliness itself. We met later and, because we had been at the same school, although at different times – I was younger than he was – we got on straight away, on an ordinary conversational basis at which certainly poetry was never discussed, but we discussed Swansea and we discussed west Wales. And generally got on with the drinking.

... if the reputation for drunkenness, or the image that Thomas has in America, depends on the Brinnin book, then it's pretty far removed from the kind of man I saw and knew. It may well be that in his last weeks of his life in the States that he behaved as Brinnin described – I can't deny this – but it certainly isn't the complete picture of the man... I also distrust anybody who can annotate in a diary the number of drinks a man had, minute by minute, hour by hour. If he's got this kind of mind, to be able to go back to his room and keep kind of a tally on what was drunk, then maybe he was missing other things in observing that kind of detail.

... I don't know about the early short stories but I'm certain that one particular passage in *The Meditations of Thomas Trehearne* – the passage that begins "The corn with orient and immortal wheat which never should be reaped nor was never sown" and which ends "But with much ado we are corrupted and made to learn the dirty devices of this world" – I am certain that this particular passage of Trehearne, the seventeenth century metaphysical poet, had an enormous effect. It's almost a keystone in Thomas' thinking and I think it's affected his imagery, and it's affected his poet's innocence, and what innocence sprang into the poems. Certainly a religious poet in this sense.

... when his *Collected Poems* first appeared, I was then working on the *Evening Post* in Swansea... I reviewed this book and pointed out this passage from Trehearne and the importance I thought it had in Thomas' work and his thinking. That day, the Saturday the paper came out, I walked two hundred yards down the street for my usual Saturday pint in the Metropole Hotel and there, not by previous arrangement, was Dylan at the bar. We talked for an hour and, knowing full well how embarrassed he could be from time to time by pub discussions of his work, we talked about God knows what at the time. But when I was leaving an hour later to go back to the office I said "I've reviewed your poems today." He'd already read the review and hadn't mentioned it but would I meet him in another bar when the pubs opened again at five-thirty and when I'd be available?

... it was then that he said that nobody had said that this passage of Trehearne was terribly important. He admitted the importance, and if you go back and check it, you can see the whole golden heyday of innocence in the poems coming out and the whole vocabulary is almost key to this passage. Recently, re-reading *The Doctor and the Devils*, I find this critical phrase "with much ado we are taught, we are made to learn the dirty devices of this world." This very phrase is put into the mouth of the anatomist – Knox originally, Rock in the finally published script of *The Doctor and the Devils* – it's put into the mouth of this character. I first heard Thomas read this passage from Trehearne on the radio in some anthology or other, I think for Patrick Dickinson, in the mid nineteen-forties but here it comes up in *The Doctor and the Devils*, as a critical phrase in a piece of dialogue, and I think this lends some support to my belief that this affected his whole way of thinking. That it should have outcropped in many directions – it was a key thing in his work.

Philip Burton

It was in London in the BBC... I was a member of the Features Department and he came looking for a job... I knew his work, but I'd never met him and it was a very memorable meeting. He sat diffidently on the edge of a chair, trying to size me up, to see if I was good for a contract and I'd been warned that this is what he was after. But I was after something else. I wanted a work from him. Anyway, the result of that first interview was *Return Journey*, which I think was one of the best things he ever did for radio.

... we went down to Swansea together... February 1947... what was left of Swansea was under the snow... it was a very, very bleak visit but a very, very exciting one and I remember his first problem. How can I talk about myself? How can I go looking for myself? So we decided he was looking for a stranger called Young Thomas, and once he had that little peg to hang it on, all went well. We met his friends, and we reminisced and talked to Dan Jones for hours and Fred Janes and so on, and I think the result was an extraordinarily exciting programme. Most revealing one.

... there's a rather funny story about it. He told me it was going to be forty-five minutes long, and this I doubted *very* much, so I gave him a contract for thirty minutes. And when the script came, it was twenty-two. So then he came down to stay with me... incidentally, when he was working it seemed to me that this story about the old drunk didn't work at all. At that time, he was drinking Guinness, and I laid in a whole supply of Guinness for him and he never touched a bottle within the whole time we worked, which was about a week or ten days.

... I told him that he had to write more. Twenty-two minutes wasn't enough. And he said "Oh, he couldn't work like that; it was just impossible". So I said "Well, you must. I can't put this on as a thirty-minute show; what are we going to do – put records on for ten minutes, or whatever?" And I said "There are two things missing in this autobiographical search. One is your first experience of girls; and the other is your first experience of books." So he said, assuming that I wouldn't take up the challenge "Alright. You do one, I'll do the other!" I said "Fine. Make a choice." "Girls," he said. "Okay – I'll do books." So I did a little pastiche of Dylan in a bookshop. *The Spectator* came out with a review of the programme and most of it was devoted to this scene in the bookstore. Of course, when the thing was published, we couldn't publish it because it would have been strange at best.[42]

Anyway, that was a most happy association – he really was marvellous to work with. He was so different when he was alone, you know. He was the poet. You had to see him alone to see the poet. Because there was this frightful conflict in him between the poet and the performer. And if a third person walked into the room, the poet was pushed into a corner and the performer stepped forward. And this is one of the things that destroyed him. It was an incredible conflict... I must be absolutely honest, I rather avoided Dylan the performer. Because to me it was not the important man.

... incidentally, I think he would have made a magnificent actor. The instincts, the performing instincts, were extraordinarily strong in him. But on his own, there were moments of rare intimacy where you saw the greatness in the man. The humility of the man. I really think that there is true greatness in Dylan, but most of it's on the printed page.

... what is marvellous about Dylan is that he is definitely by his very nature not a man merely of his time. What preoccupied Dylan is what has preoccupied Man from the birth of civilisation – birth, death, the life after death. Even though he wasn't a religious man in the orthodox sense, he was a truly religious man in that he saw this life in the context of Eternity. He was always concerned with the ultimates, with the absolutes. And this to me is religion.

... no, I don't ever remember talking politics. We always discussed literature, and the theatre. Those were our two great subjects.

... we talked a good deal about his process of writing, and it was unlike that of any poet I know. Suddenly a metaphor would occur to him and it would be stowed away in his memory, and then another one. It may be six months later, maybe six minutes later, and then when it became necessary in him to express something that was burning to be expressed about life, death, children or whatever, out of this grab-bag of his memory he would take these metaphors which would work like seeds and grow and the result was the fantastic poems that he wrote. But then came, if I may continue to use the metaphor of the garden, the most important process in him – the weeding and the pruning. He was the most ruthless critic of his own work and he wouldn't let anything get by... he worried and worried and worried about a word... it really was a sullen art for him. Creation was an agony.

... we talked a lot about Gerard Manley Hopkins, of course; but I don't think he got his Welsh feeling from him, but he did get his feeling for what I call true poetry from him. He had an enormous under-standing of the essence of poetry from Hopkins. Poetry isn't something that you read and get, it's something that you live with and get, and great poetry will grow and grow inside you as you grow. I get much more from Dylan Thomas now than when I read him first. And so I do from Hopkins. There was the other point too, of course. That the performer in Dylan loved Hopkins, because he only comes alive when you read him aloud.

There's this fantastic combination in one man with Dylan – the great poet, and the almost unsurpassable reader of poetry.
Well, there was something like it, of course, in Charles Dickens, the great novelist and the great reader of stories, and the problem of both men was something the same. The performer did much to destroy both men.

What was he like to work with?
I was told that he would be difficult. I never found it to be so... he was wonderful to work with. Most receptive, never late...

What about Dylan's family life?
He spoke about his children quite a bit, and had a sense of guilt that he didn't provide for them as a provider should, that he didn't spend time with them as he should, but he had great love for them and therefore was obsessed by this sense of guilt... he talked about his marriage a good deal but I think there was no doubt about it, he really loved the woman with all his being. Caitlin was difficult too, of course, for all kinds of very obvious reasons. He was not a good provider, and he was a womaniser and, furthermore, she had artistic ambitions herself, as a dancer, which she felt that her marriage had interrupted. There are all kinds of good reasons why she behaved in the strange way she did, but I think the fundamental thing was they were both terribly – and I use the word advisedly – terribly in love with each other... and this gave them an incredible power to hurt each other... they were like two very bright flames.

Aneirin Talfan Davies

My first professional contact with him was over the first recording he made of *Reminiscences of Childhood*. This was the first creative talk that he had made, and I think I remember the moment I suggested that he should write about his childhood days. It was on the train going up to London from Swansea, standing about in the corridor and then in the restaurant car, drinking, and I remember trying to persuade him to write a talk and broadcast it... many months, if not a year later, after a lot of badgering, he turned this one out...

... I remember quite well that when I sent the first script of *Reminiscences of Childhood* to London it was sent back to me. I was a cub producer at the time... they sent it back and said "Ask him to rewrite it. This man can't handle these sentences, just get him to rewrite." Of course, this was the last thing I would do, and in the end I sent up the recording to them and then gradually it circulated around the departments... I'll never forget the way, the condescending way, in which they dismissed this first talk, not having heard the man read it.

... then somewhere about a year or two later, he turns in another one, *Quite Early One Morning*. This is because I happened at that time to be down in Carmarthen with a studio... he was in New Quay, not very far away, and again this idea of a talk, and this time about New Quay, which turned out to be this fantastic talk which was in some respects the germ of *Under Milk Wood*... I remember giving him a title – *Portrait of a Seaside Town*.

What kind of person was he like to work with?
I found him very amenable. I never dared, of course, alter anything that he wrote... I accepted everything that he wrote, I respected it, and I wouldn't dare to try and produce him. He was unproduce-able in that sense. All you did was give him the freedom of the microphone... the only thing I could do was to keep on badgering him and get the stuff out of him. I thought that was about as much as I could do. Once I got it, I saw to it that it was put on the air.

... in all the time that I had any dealings with him, he turned up on time with the manuscript and I can't remember a single occasion on which he didn't turn up to the studio at the requested time and in the requested place... as far as I'm concerned, he turned up to every appointment that I made with him... as far as his professional work was concerned he acted as a professional and respected all the contracts that were given him.

... I think he was a religious poet, and I think every poet is a religious poet in one sense. I think that Dylan faced some of the challenges of Christianity very early in life and what surprises me is that you find this religious element right from the beginning. It isn't something which has been injected at a late date or something that has been shoved in in order to make an impression. It's there right in his very first poems. He's facing the fundamental things. That's why he's religious. He's facing the fundamental things about humanity, about Man's place in the Creation, about God, about all those relationships between Man and Man, and between Man and God which is the basis of any religion. I think he faces these problems very early in life and you can see this right through his poetry, right to the end.

... I think you have to remember one thing about Dylan is that he wasn't brought up in a religious atmosphere. In the atmosphere of Wales, certainly. I think his main reactions, religious reactions, were to what he considered to be the hypocrisy of Nonconformity. Now I don't think myself that it was genuinely felt. It was merely something that was in the air... I feel that a lot of this stuff came from Caradoc Evans... Dylan was reacting at second-hand in that sense, but in a deeper sense he was facing far more religious themes than merely whether a man should drink or whether deacons were hypocrites or whatever. He was facing deep-down; for instance, you will remember the lines

You who bow down at cross and altar,
Remember me and pity Him
Who took my flesh and bone for armour
And double-crossed my mother's womb.

[from 'Before I knocked', 1933]

... now there was a chap who was facing a challenge. He doesn't accept the Christian religion in that verse. It's a kind of ambiguous statement, an ambivalent statement. And there he is, the fact is that the challenge he is facing is the cross and the altar. And later on in life you'll find this cross and this altar still with him, all the time. And when you say that he doesn't tackle the normal themes – he does, you know... he's always hiding, he's always hiding. When he talks about religion he always hides things deep down. For instance, take 'Over Sir John's hill'. Now in that you get the sense of sin, in the birds. What does he call them? The "the led-astray birds."

... I'm not saying he ever came to a point where you could say, here is a man who accepted the Christian religion in the way that, say, a good Roman Catholic or a good Anglican or a good Nonconformist accepts it. It wasn't that kind of acceptance, of a dogmatic religion. I think that, in some intuitive way, he arrived at the same place as, say, a Roman Catholic had arrived. Minus the many things which he objected to in Roman Catholicism. Why, for instance, does he, as he gets on toward the end of his life, more and more accept Catholic imagery? You just can't say we accept it because it was there. But it wasn't there in an obvious sense. He was brought up in the Nonconformist, Protestant community, where all these things were objectionable. They were not things which could be accepted by any decent man. They were objectionable, but they come in, they creep in.[43]

... I rather remember Dylan as a friendly chap whom one loved, rather than remember all this business about his drinking and womanizing and all the rest of it. I'd prefer to remember the man who was full of love for his fellow-man, for his neighbour, which is the essence of religion again.

... I'd sent him up to the house one morning when we were sitting down doing these anthologies, reading through books and sitting on the floor of my office, and sent him up to fetch a volume from home... my wife said that she asked him in and he sat down, and my wife said how humble a man he was – she'd never met him before – and she very gently said "Would you take a cup of coffee?" and he said "No, I never drink coffee but I will drink one with you." And he drank a cup of coffee, and my wife said then she thought he must have hated every drop of it but he drank it, humbly, and the impression that she was left with, the only time she met him, was of a very, very humble, kind man.

... but I know that there was another side to him. He could be very, very vicious when his integrity was attacked, or when his privacy was encroached upon. He could be very vicious and say some very nasty things. I don't think they meant a great deal, except that here was a man who was throwing out all the prickles and all the spikes that he could in order to safeguard something within himself. Some kind of integrity and the loneliness of the artist – he hedged it around with all kinds of blasphemy and scurrilous kind of talk that he flung at people. Strangers, especially. You know, merely to frighten them away. I've seen this done by very respectable men – men who were littérateurs in Wales. I remember one example of a very great littérateur of Wales who did exactly the same thing, and he was exactly the same as Dylan, he was very shy. Very, very shy.

Did you say that Dylan had a distinctly Welsh style of speaking; that he was greatly influenced in developing this by what he may have heard from Welsh preachers, Nonconformist preachers?

I think it's true to say that this kind of reading of poems, and of talks, which we've had from Dylan is incomprehensible to most English people. When it hit the English audience, they were amazed at this kind of uninhibited performance, whereas in Wales we take to this thing like ducks to water. The background of the Welsh pulpit, or the oratory of men like Lloyd George and Aneurin Bevan is part of the very makeup of the Welshman's background. I don't think that he thought that he was doing anything unusual when he orated these poems and these talks. I think that he was being as Welsh as he was, in fact. It wasn't an act, it was just being what every Welshman is. I don't think you'd get this kind of reading of poems in England. Certainly, when he read T.S. Eliot on the air, for instance, he had great difficulty in finding the right way to do it.

... mind you, I think that on the other hand he was a far more delicate reader of poetry than many people give him credit for. The fact is that some people think that he is a kind of Welsh bard with a white gown and flowing hair, and he just mouthed poetry, but he was a very delicate reader of poetry. His poem, 'In my craft or sullen art', isn't mouthed, it's said in a very quiet, intimate way which is appropriate to the poem itself. There is a great variety of skills in the readings made by Dylan during his lifetime. Varying skills in interpretation. As far as his own poetry is concerned, I think that one of the magical things about his reading is that he has made people believe that they understand his poetry. He has insinuated the meaning into the reading and he has made people think and believe that they understand.

... it's surprising that his poetry has sold in such vast numbers... people must have bought these volumes because they heard him read the poetry and they thought that they understood what he has read... I am sure many of them have been disillusioned when they have read the poetry. But this insinuation of meaning by reading, he was a past master at. Another thing about Dylan's reading is that he himself as he grew older realised that in reading poetry that you must have an obvious meaning, if you like, on the first reading. That at the first reading of the poem there must be sufficient meaning there for the person who is listening to be able to understand and to accept... I think that this did have a great effect upon him as a poet, because as he grew older I think he became far more lucid and far simpler because of the very fact that he used the microphone and the public audience as his main audience for his poems. And I think that this public reading did lead him to a far simpler style of poetry. His later poems it seems to me are far easier to understand, although not as easy as all that, but they are far easier to understand than his earlier poems, which sometimes reek of the midnight oil.

... I think it was quite natural for him to do things in this way, because this was the background of his life. He was used to sitting in the pew and listening to the orator in the pulpit, you know going into the *hwyl*... the spoken word is our life, in fact. I think poetry in Wales has always been an art of public utterance. The great poets have always been read in public. Welsh poetry has always been a poetry of public utterance.

Richard Bell Williams

With me is Mr Richard Bell Williams, who knew Dylan when Mr Williams was licensee of the Mermaid Hotel in Mumbles. At what period exactly was it?
From 1947... when I first went there... I didn't know he was a sort of a poet or anything like that, or a literary fellow. I thought he was a nice, quiet little chap, really. And he was. He drank his pints of bitter and enjoyed them... one or two, or three perhaps...

How would you describe the Mermaid?
... I remember it vaguely before the War... it was a small place then, quite popular on weekends and things. It had a little square for dancing. In the lounge bar. And you could have sort of a shuffle around there. Large enough for about six couples, no more. A little Panitrope [?] thing playing in the corner. And then they had this one bar, the hotel bar. And there was also a bar there which was never used. It was closed – I can't remember what it was called. Well, when I went there in 1947, we had a few alterations made and eventually the two back bars and that dancing place were knocked into one.

... I never did see him drink spirits as a matter of fact, not in the Mermaid anyway. I did see him drink spirits at parties, but I never in the Mermaid, or, as a matter of fact, in other pubs where I've met him.

... he couldn't drink an awful lot before getting tight, you see. He'd get drunk very quickly... on beer, oh yes, it was on beer. And he used to get tight very quickly on it, and after that, of course, he'd just go very quietly into a chair and that's it.

... I never saw him nasty, no... he'd tend to sort of rather flop down in a chair and be more inclined to go to sleep than anything else... sometimes he might say something that annoyed someone. I've never seen him in a brawl; he might have been in one, but I certainly haven't seen him, and if there had been any trouble I'd have soon stopped it.

Did you see Dylan suffering any of these blackouts that he was supposed to have had?
Yes, I did. A couple of times, as a matter of fact, and I thought at the time, he couldn't possibly have collapsed with the few pints of beer that he had.

What happened exactly?
He just sat down and he just went more or less unconscious. I took him upstairs one day – in the Mermaid, again. Took him upstairs, and just laid him out. And eventually he came to... he just said "Sorry about that."

... first of all I thought he'd drunk too much, but I realised the fellow was sober when he came in, and after about four pints of bitter, he just passed out... he just gone slump and my wife and I took him upstairs and laid him out on the bed there... and then, it happened twice. And on both occasions, he hadn't had a lot to drink.

John Laurie [44]

It must have been soon after the War. We were doing a very ambitious broadcast on the Third Programme of *Paradise Lost* [October-November 1947]. I think it still remains one of the most adventurous things even the BBC did. It lasted over twelve Sundays... we rehearsed at the Grafton, at the top of Tottenham Court Road. Dylan then wasn't drinking a great deal, but as we rehearsed in the morning and had an hour's break before we began doing the show itself, it was necessary that Dylan didn't drink hardly at all, because he was playing Satan, which is no easy role. In fact, it's the toughest of all the parts... I was the only one he really got on with in the cast. A cast of squares, naturally, doing *Paradise Lost*. Dylan was rather an exotic flower in that *galère*.

I used to go with Dylan to the local pub, just he and I together, and for that hour we talked and drank a couple of pints, and went back to rehearsal. I liked the man enormously and, gradually, over the twelve Sundays, our mutual affection grew quite a bit, and I got very fond of him... I like to remember those days because he had a sweet mind in the middle of the day. If you could catch Dylan just at the right moment... I think he was one of the loveliest men I've ever known.

... he used to talk about his poetry and I used to ask him "Dylan, some of those early ones, in the first little volume, some of them, I don't quite understand." And I remember he used to say "Well, John – candidly, I don't either... because I was very young when I was writing them and I look back and I read them and I recognise that they're good, but what the hell they're all about, one or two of them, I really do not know."

... he must have been a remarkable boy... I think he himself was not quite aware of what was happening. I believe he was in a way as vision-ary as, say, Blake... some of his later poems, of course, are indeed lovely, but I feel that there was a period when Dylan was alone with himself and God, and he was writing greater than he knew.

... I always thought of Dylan as a fine Elizabethan speaker, thinking of Elizabethan as the rolling Marlowe line rather than Shakespeare's finest poetry. He was a rhetorical speaker and, again, it seems sad that there was nobody that could keep him just dead right, because the potential was there of possibly the finest verse speaker of our day, but to my ear it was sometimes overloaded, both emotionally, rhythmically and vocally. The whole thing was just too rich a fruit cake.

... he took direction admirably. He was very humble. There was nothing about Dylan that made you feel that he couldn't have taken guidance and sometimes, as I say, the sad thing is, he didn't seem to get the right kind at the right time... I suppose he'd be alive today if he had.

... I'm terribly glad that I did meet Dylan. I'm terribly glad that I had these twelve Sundays, when Dylan was on his best behaviour, and was mentally alert and was one of the most delightful men I've ever spent these hours with.

... the next time I met him was during a rather grand poetry recital in the Wigmore Hall [May 14 1946], with all the modern poets who were alive then, reading their own favourite poems and two or three of us professionals who had specialised in verse speaking were there to back 'em up. I remember dear old Walter de la Mare was there, John Masefield was there – all of them. Eliot? Yes, he was there, too. And Dylan. Well, Dylan arrived very late. The Queen – well, Queen Elizabeth the Queen Mother – and her two young daughters were sitting in the front row. Very grand it all was, and we were well into the concert before Dylan arrived. The rest of us had dressed up in our Sunday best, but here Dylan rolled in, just a wee bit high, with his wife, and he was dressed in a fisherman's jersey with baggy bags, looking really rather awful I thought... he was both unshaven and unwashed, and it was a great pity.

... he suddenly realised he was on a difficult assignment and he got just a wee bit frightened and he pulled me aside and said "John – hear my poem." It was Blake's 'Tyger', and indeed he wasn't doing it very well, down in the corner with me, and I gave him what advice I could, and he got through it.[45]

... Dylan even at his best was somewhat hammy. He did labour it rather, ladle it out – sometimes with enormously great effect, but when you're in the company of very fine verse speakers and very reticent poets, he would have stuck out rather like a sore thumb, and it might have been just a wee bit embarrassing. So I got him just to tone it down a bit, and go just a little bit faster, and so he did. And it was all right. I'm a great admirer of Dylan's verse speaking, but I think sometimes he could have done with just a little bit of good advice, which I don't think there was anybody there to give him, really.

... he always seemed a little boy among them, and I doubt if he would have had the courage to go up to Masefield and speak to him... I think he was a respecter of reputation. He was very little of the revolutionary, as far as I knew. He was a great conformist, except in the one particular that he did drink too much. And then he was a different man entirely. And then he should never be judged. And people often judge the midnight Dylan as being the real Dylan. It wasn't. I didn't like him at all when he was drunk. I disliked him and would certainly have avoided his company.

… I never felt that Dylan was really a happy man… he seemed to want something stable to hold on to. Every time I met Dylan, he brought out in you a feeling that you wanted to protect him, to guide him; like I did over the poem. It was an impertinence, really, but you felt that he needed something, he needed someone just to hold on to… because his night life was really very sad, that a man had to keep that kind of company, night after night. It wasn't good for him – a lot of toadies and worthless people, who would say they were great friends of his, and really they were his greatest enemies in some ways, many of them.

What about his relationship with his wife? There were difficulties already, by that stage, between them.
Well, I don't like to say anything. She was a fine-looking girl, really was, and most attractive at that time, but it's just possible she became over-possessive in her attempts to keep him away from what were, in her sight and in mine, looking back now, malign influences. It's just possible that she had every excuse for her possessiveness.

Now, with regard to his attitude to women, because he had this tremendous reputation, which I think he rather enjoyed exaggerating in people's minds.
This I'm quite certain about. I'm quite certain it was a defence mechanism. Because if I was to make a wild guess, I would say that he wasn't very much good at that, on that particular side.

Do you remember any occasions when he was aggressive in this direction.
No – certainly his aggression, if it did ever come out, was a defence mechanism… very much a front.

Did he ever speak about Wales at all?
Not a great deal. No. Strangely not. I wish I could remember what we talked about. I only know that there was great talk, and I think I did talk about his poems quite a bit, but he was reticent about them and about his life and that sort of thing, and his friends… he kept off his private life… he was always interested in what I was doing. He was interested in the fact that I had played all the big parts in Shakespeare and that kind of thing, and he obviously would like himself, unquestionably, he'd have loved to have been an actor… but he was the wrong shape;

the wrong face, and all that. And this he knew. This he knew fine. But I'm quite certain that if he'd been born with a different face, he'd have been sorely tempted to have gone on the stage. Our first real poet-dramatist since Shakespeare.

... his talk was always bubbling – the strange thing is I've lost the content of it, but the feel of it, the quality of it, remains. And he had a great sense of humour... a sense of fun, more perhaps than wit... he was a fine talker, and of course it was a beautiful kind of Elizabethan accent he'd adopted. This rather grand voice... you'd never have guessed that he came from a wee Welsh village... he never lapsed into Welsh – he wasn't as Welsh as you are.

... he hadn't any great general culture. But this you would never guess. Whether it was because he'd steer the conversation his way, or not, I wouldn't know... I never was aware he hadn't read Dante or didn't know much about French literature, or the Germans or anything like that. One would never guess that.

... I hope I've not said anything that would blemish Dylan's reputation because, as I say, the Dylan I knew was a darling man.

Pamela Hansford Johnson [46]

The last time I saw Dylan, that was very curious indeed. It was in 1948 and I was walking along the King's Road and somebody walked past me. They looked vaguely familiar, no more. A fat man. And when he'd gone by I thought – Good God, that's Dylan. I've never seen such a physical change take place in anybody in my life. I had known him as this rather peculiarly fragile-looking young man, very slender, very small, with really a very delicate top part to the face, and very delicate in his limbs, or giving that appearance. And suddenly, here is an almost unrecognisable man who's put on tremendous weight... and by that time I was too far on to go back, and I didn't turn back.

... there wasn't much wrong with Dylan's health when I first knew him, but he had some curious romantic ideas. And he had three. He said that a poet should be tubercular, drunk, and eventually fat. But he did not achieve being tubercular... he did drink very much for effect at that time. He was very strange. I remember that he would fake it. I had been sitting with him, and we had something very modest like a pint apiece during the whole evening. Then gone out into the street, met some of his friends, and Dylan would immediately play drunk. It was somehow a romantic thing to be.

... I've always wondered about Dylan and the legend. I don't think it's very fair of me to say very much about it. There's just an aspect that I can't quite see, and that is the idea that grew up that Dylan was an absolute remorseless womaniser. This I've never really believed... I know he was always flattered and delighted by the attentions of women. I know he liked women; there was no question of his liking anything else, either. But when I knew him, and for a long time, he was just about as monogamous as a swan with a hen. I mean, there was one hen at a time, and it just wasn't his thing. And whether this developed as part of the act, part of the romance later, I don't know. But it's always something that's said about him which I view with very great suspicion indeed.

Anything else to do with the legend?
Of course, he wove his own exactly like weaving a cocoon around himself, till he got very much trapped in the legend. Now it's very hard to try to untrap him when he was quite young because you could see that this was going to happen, that he was going to build this, and that it would trap him. In the end it did.

Aloys Skoumal, 1965 [47]

I was partly responsible for Dylan Thomas' visit to Prague in March 1949... he accepted my invitation to attend the founding of the Writers' Union there. Before Dylan left for Prague, he came to my place in Willesden – 32 Chatsworth Road – where he spent an evening with my wife and me. We talked about various topics; also about Wales. To my remark on Welsh National Eisteddfods – I had attended one in Colwyn Bay in 1947 – he reacted in a tone which was not exactly hostile, but certainly rather sarcastic. Then I showed him some translations of his poems into Czech made during the War. He asked me to read a few stanzas of these, and in return he offered to read to us a couple of his poems.

When Dylan was speaking to you, he was not exactly enthusiastic about Welsh cultural institutions – I mean the 'Welsh' Welsh.
Well, no. This, of course, was something I couldn't know at that time. I only learned about his feelings when I read, many years afterwards, *Under Milk Wood*. There I think his mixed feelings about Welsh nationalism and the various forms it adopts are expressed succinctly and sometimes rather strongly.

... I liked Dylan Thomas' poetry, and I thought that he will find many friends in Prague who knew him from the various translations published in '46 and '47. In this, I think I wasn't disappointed, nor was Dylan... I approached him through the Jack Lindsay couple; the late Mrs Lindsay was Welsh. Her name was Ann Davies. I think it was she, together with her husband, who helped me to approach Dylan and persuaded him to accept the invitation.

... he was accepted – I mean his poetry – as something which was new and, on the whole, not unacceptable. The criticisms as far as they appeared were favourable, and, as far as I can judge, the influence of Dylan Thomas' poetry on Czech poetry has been, on the whole, beneficial.

... Dylan was the only English delegate at the Congress... [he made] a short address given on March 5 1949. Unfortunately, only a literal translation of this address in Czech is extant.[48] I invited Louis MacNeice but he never answered my letter. At that time, there was a cultural agreement between my country and Great Britain. On the basis of this agreement, a number of other authors went to visit Prague, among them Elizabeth Bowen, Rex Warner, Stephen Spender, Herbert Read and a number of musicians and scientists and scholars.

Some people have maintained that Dylan was a Communist Party member and so forth. Was he considered to be a Party member?
I don't think so. He certainly wasn't invited as a Party member, and I never described him as a Party member to the Prague authorities when I was sending him to Prague. He was simply invited as a poet, as a great poet.

He said he felt he was the only non-Communist at the Congress. Was he correct in that?
I think he was absolutely correct in that, but it wasn't his fault. It was the fault of those who were invited but did not accept invitations.

... I learnt about his stay in Prague from what I heard from my friends, when I returned to Prague in 1950, especially from Jan Drda, at that time Chairman of the Writers' Union, who gave a charming description of Dylan Thomas at the Dobříš Castle: "There was still plenty of snow when they took Dylan Thomas for a walk in the park of the Castle. Properly speaking, Dylan Thomas did not seem to walk at all. He frisked and gambolled, he made the impression of a bear floating in the air."

Jiří Mucha, 1968

I knew Dylan during the War, because I was in London, in the Air Force. In my spare time, I was part of the group round the magazine *New Writing*, edited by John Lehmann. This group consisted of well-known names like Stephen Spender and Cecil Day-Lewis and Louis MacNeice and so on. And also Dylan, and that's where I met him.

... when I went back to Czechoslovakia, I got one day a letter from him saying that he's coming to Prague and that he hopes that I'm here because I think that naturally he had very few friends in this country, except probably for Miss Jiřina Hauková, the poet. I don't know really how they met, how they got together, where the sort of connection started, but we had been really old friends, and so he came to me to pilot him round.

... and so we went together to the first day of the Writers' Congress. That was 1949, and the whole thing was very much going the Stalinist way, and so we stuck it about an hour... Dylan said "Look here, this is rather boring, don't you think?" and I said "I think it's awful." He said "It's ghastly – let's go away." At that time, I owned a vineyard and produced my own wine and so we went back and we were just sitting and drinking steadily this white wine of mine and talking and having a good time.

... we were sitting, the two of us, the whole day, doing nothing but talking and discussing every topic... not here in this house, it was in my father's house, in his studio. My father was art nouveau painter, Alphonse Mucha.

When Dylan first heard about a Writers' Union he is said to have exclaimed "What a marvellous thing for writers to have a union to stand up for them." So obviously he had some disillusionment.

Oh, I think it was the quickest sobering up that he did in his life... the Writers' Union, which was created after the War, was formed in a country which was perfectly normal and on democratic principles. But after 1948, it became suddenly, firmly, a part of Stalin's empire... it was not standing up for the writer, but really it was a way of putting the writer properly in line with Party requirements. It took Dylan five minutes – he couldn't understand a word of what was being said on the platform, but he knew exactly what was happening in the polling. When you see voting going on when everybody lifts his hand, there's always something fishy. And he smelt the rat...

... he saw that the writers themselves were sort of falling into line –

in 1949 nobody yet forced them to…
Dylan saw that suddenly people were
falling into line. I was there only an
hour, then we went away, but there
was something being voted and I
thought "This is nonsense. Why
should I vote for it?" I didn't, and I
looked round and we watched the
people and suddenly we saw the sort
of hesitating movement of a hand
being lifted, and then another, and
then we saw that everybody gradually, after giving a good think,
thought "I might rather lift my hand.
Who knows whether somebody
won't have it against me in a few
months, that I didn't vote for…" One
after another gave in to his inner

11. Jiří Mucha

objections and voted, and this was what made me fed up and what
Dylan immediately realised.

… I must say one thing – and I knew him quite a lot in London, I saw
a lot of him as well – I was extremely surprised after I read all the things
about him and so on, that I never really experienced him as an alcoholic.
Never. With me, whenever he was with me, he was always sober and
when he was with me at my house and we were drinking, there was
Dylan, a sort of historical alcoholic, and he was perfectly sober the whole
time… it's the drunks who get together with drunks, but Dylan, with
somebody who didn't drink, didn't go on his great sort of drinking bout.

… Professor Taylor told me about having him at his garden house,
because I knew Professor Taylor quite well, and he came to see me, I
think, in Prague as well. Anyway, I went to see him in Oxford quite a
lot, and when he told me about Dylan and the way he lived there, I sort
of winced – I didn't quite get it, you see. I thought, well, Taylor was
probably a bit of a prig, because for me, Dylan wasn't a drunk.

*Did you come to think of him often as a man who turned his thought often
to religious questions?*
No, no I didn't, no. I think that sometimes he liked to talk about things
which just simply were a nice way of saying things and had a poetic
content, for instance, religion but I never saw him as a person who
would be religious.

He used religious symbols and images in his poetry...
I think that they are an excellent vehicle for expressing certain... either feelings, thoughts or counterpoint, which is very quickly legible to anyone. Religious symbols being what they are – being understood so clearly and being part of one's education – are a very easy way of conveying a poetic sort of counterpoint. But I don't think that in his case they were an expression of his sort of belief... if somebody would come to my house and look round and think that I am a deeply religious person because I have a lot of religious objects – because they are works of art so I've got them because I like them, or they're folk art – but certainly not because they represent Christ or the Trinity, or anything like that. I think in Dylan, the use of the religious symbols is the same as I, for instance, use them for my decoration. That is aesthetic value and not ethic value.

... I definitely was always vividly aware of the fact that he was Welsh....definitely. Not only the way he spoke but I think that he did somehow to me make a point of being very Welsh.

What about politics?
I found that he was always the sort of an intellectual left-winger you find very rampant in England. That is, somebody who is left-wing by feeling, that this is the right thing, that it is cricket. It's not cricket to be right-wing. But when it comes to realities, I think that they are fairly muddled. I always had this feeling whenever I spoke either to Dylan or any of the people who had the same attitude to the Left, as when Mr C. comes home and finds his wife in bed with his best friend Mr G. So he stops in the doorway, stares at G. with his wife in bed, and then says "But G. you don't *have* to." This is always what I've felt. Why the hell do they brandish the Red Flag with such fervour? They don't have to. We have to – that's understandable – but why the hell do they? And this is what I felt about Dylan as well. It was an attitude since the mid-Thirties. Yes, since the Spanish War. It became unthinkable for an artist who wanted to be on the right side of the ethics to be anything but left-wing. I think that it was something so ingrained that finally I think that most of the people who were like that never, never really thought deeply about the implications.

Dylan had in my opinion, not really delved very deeply into political theory anyway – he would have found it too boring.
Boring, yes. And that's why when he came to this Congress, I was terribly surprised that he came. I said "What the hell are you doing

here?" He said, very proudly "I've been invited." I couldn't figure out why he was invited – it just escaped my understanding. So he said "I was invited" He explained it in the sense "Well, I'm left-wing and so on, they invited me." But then he said to me "I think they made a mistake and they don't know it."

Did he have any knowledge of Czech poetry – even in translation?
Well, he knew some – at least, he knew that which I had published in London during the War. I remember he had some knowledge of Czech poetry, things which I got into *New Writing* during the War. There were translations done jointly with Stephen Spender and Norman Cameron. The poetry of Nezval – we just loved Nezval – and of Seifert. There were two long poems and these Dylan knew definitely. I remember he asked me how actually we did it, because I did the literal translation and then read it a number of times to Stephen or to Norman and then they got the knack of it, and then did an excellent re-write of the thing in English – and this he knew. This we were discussing, and he wanted to know how it was done.

Jiřina Hauková, 1965 [49]

I had translated his poetry, some two or three poems, and so I wanted to see him and to speak with him about the poetry, and about the translating of the poetry – it was 'Fern Hill' and 'October wind'. I tried to read them to him, but he didn't understand – only the sound. And he told me it seemed good... it was very useful for me. Especially when we talked about the sound and some complicated pictures. He tried to explain me his pictures – sorry, his imagery... he read us some of his poems at the castle of Czech writers... it was just a private, small meeting. The Union of Czech Writers took him there by car.

Did Dylan go to any theatres here?
I think he saw some films here. And one theatre piece – I don't know what it was – I don't remember. [50]

... I and my friends, we met Dylan quite privately and we spoke with him openly... his poetry had many readers here, and became very popular... we had a very good impression of Thomas in Prague, as a very sincere, quite open and very honest man... he remembered his wife here, and he wanted to buy something for her, so he liked a blouse, with a folk embroidery, and so I bought one for him.

Did he talk about Wales at all, or did he tell you any words of Welsh?

Yes, he told us Welsh, but we didn't understand anything!

Oh! He didn't speak Welsh.

But he spoke some!

But he only knew a few words.

Yeah, but he taught us. Maybe some short sentences.

[Colin Edwards' interview with Jiřina Hauková was probably one of the least productive he had ever carried out. It was done in 1965, and Hauková may have thought it unwise to speak openly with a foreign journalist. Or perhaps it was

12. Jiřina Hauková

just a matter of chemistry, something that often affects, for good or ill, the outcome of an interview. Her letter to FitzGibbon, which is partly reproduced in his biography, was more forthcoming but still relatively guarded. But Jiřina Hauková has given a more honest and authentic account of Dylan's time in Prague in her own memoirs (1996), and this is reproduced below in a translation prepared for this book by Dr Jonathan Bolton, assistant professor in the Department of Slavic Languages and Literatures at Harvard University. The italicised passages are in English in the original.]

"He was sent on behalf of English writers to the congress of Czechoslovak writers... At that time I was at the English-American division of the Ministry of Information and they assigned me to take him around Prague. I looked for him in the Hotel Flora, based on his photograph. I recognised him only from his hair. He had become much fatter. I told him, out of politeness, *You are bigger now*, and he replied: *I am fat.* So we recognised each other and laughed. I suggested he might want to take a ride through Prague to look around. He was very much in favour and I smelled alcohol coming from him. His cigarette fell out of his mouth. So then I knew what the situation was. He was really glad that it was snowing. That's how he had imagined Prague. He wanted to know if we were going to get a beer somewhere. I promised we would go to the Old Town for some Pilsner. On Wenceslas Square he asked how far it was. The next stop, I said. He was relieved. I asked him how it was possible that he was sent to the writers' congress now, in 1949. Why not, he says, *I am left.* He was excited about the art nouveau buildings on Old Town Square. He recognised the first pub immediately, by smell. We went inside and he ordered *a big one*, gesturing with his hand, and the waiter understood him. Then he had another beer. I told him they had instructed me to translate his poem, but did he have something more comprehensible – they wouldn't print an incomprehensible one. He said he didn't. I asked him if he was still writing the same type of poetry as before. He nodded. I showed him the translation of his poem in the anthology. He said: It has the same form as in English. I told him that I was no longer a member of the Syndicate of Writers, just a candidate. He said that he had spoken with Mucha the day before and Mucha said the same thing. He had gone to his place for lunch; they knew each other from England. I asked him what he would do if he were in a situation like ours and couldn't publish his poetry, since only socialist realism can be done. He said that he would never do socialist realism, that he would have some job, maybe he would do film as he was doing now, or write small articles for the newspapers, and he would write what he wanted for himself. A poet, if he is a true poet, must withstand everything, he can't be concerned with whether he is publishing or not. Then we went outside and said we would go to another pub in the Little Quarter. I confided in him that he shouldn't repeat what I told him anywhere, or they might throw me out of my job. He said: *It is terrible.* Apparently Mucha told him the same thing: *Don't say it to anybody.*

It was the beginning of February, it was snowing heavily outside, he had bought a short coat with a hood especially for the plane trip to Prague, he called it a "*flying coat,*" everyone turned to look at him on the street. His shoes were hob-nailed, he kept slipping and falling, the freshly fallen snow stuck to him, so that he looked like a snowman. He recognised the tower on Charles Bridge from its photograph. He liked the view of the Vltava and of the castle best of all, he asked where Mánes was, he had been there yesterday. I forced him to go up the stairs to the castle, he was wheezing, out of breath, and I thought he would get angry, but he withstood it and made it to Vikárka. He didn't even want to look at Saint Vitus's Cathedral, he said he had seen it yesterday in a short film and it was a very badly made film. Once we sat down at Vikárka and he had a Pilsner and slivovitz in front of him, he was happy again. He said that the poet MacNeice was his friend in England, otherwise he didn't see anybody, he valued Eliot, his first poems, but not the last ones, he didn't resent Eliot for converting to Catholicism, that happens with poets, he valued Edith Sitwell, but he didn't much like Kathleen Raine. We bought a bottle of slivovitz and said we would go to Holan's, but the next stop came already at the Dalibor, where we had another beer. We walked down from the castle and it was still snowing. It was one of my happiest days. Thomas stopped down below, by Kampa, stretched out his arms and said: *Your snow, your snow, I should catch all your snow into my bag and take it with me.* We stopped at Holan's, but he wasn't home. We walked through the snow across Kampa to the National Theatre. Dylan kept slipping and falling, to the point where people turned and looked at him. With great effort we made it to my apartment. He fell onto the couch, I took off his shoes and gave him slippers.

He waved his legs in the air like a small child. It was hard to talk with him. I showed him the translation of Eliot's English poetry and my book. He kept saying: the lines, the lines, I don't understand it. Then I showed him Muir's poem 'Good Town'. He liked the poem, but he didn't like the poet's one-sidedness. It begins: *It was a good town once.* Nothing is ever just good or bad. I asked him if he liked Blake. He said he was the greatest poet. Then I took him to a taxi and left him to fate.

The next day, I found out from Václav Navrátil that he had sat down on the sidewalk in front of the Flora and there the driver picked him up and took him to the theatre. Dr. Navrátil didn't want to let him in, afraid that he would make a scene, and Thomas said he wanted to go to a pub. He took him to the Parliament and then wanted to take him to his hotel, but Thomas proclaimed that he had to go to the reception (I had told him to do that, he didn't reveal where he had been). So they took him along. There, in front of the government minister, he did a Cossack dance. I called him early on Tuesday morning, he said he would stay until Thursday, and I arranged a meeting with Grossman for him that evening. The poet Vladimír Holan also came. The evening was, for all of us, unforgettable. Dylan didn't know Czech and Holan didn't know English, but they understood each other and showed with their hands how great various poets were. Dylan loved Blake most of all, and he knew him by heart. He was an excellent reciter of poetry, which he read on English radio and on his trips to the United States. He said that he was a *screenwriter*, that he wrote *love stories* from the Pacific Islands, that he invented the names of flowers and trees, and that once they found him out. We confided in him about what had happened to Holan, that they had expelled him from the Writers' Union for his provocative speeches. Holan reproached him for what he had said at the congress: how wonderful it is that poets here can earn a living from their poetry and the state will pay for them. Thomas denied he said that, it was a bad translation and the translators told him what he was supposed to say. He said he wasn't sorry for being drunk and dancing in front of the ministers, he is never sorry for what he does, but he reproaches himself for being a liar. (When he spoke of the Pacific Islands, he said that he was dishonest.) He declared that he would consider it his responsibility to stay here with us. About Holan, he kept asking whether what he was saying was poetry. We told Thomas some facts about Russia and Czechoslovakia and Holan said: "Is that worth a human soul?" Holan reproached himself for confusing human souls in his poetry. Then Thomas narrated the first version of his radio play *Under Milk Wood*. The town was declared crazy and its citizens protested. So a meeting of all the inhabitants was called and someone came from the government with a long document. He said that the document, which had proofs of their insanity, was too voluminous, so he would only read some of the proofs at random. "In this community they play the organ for goats and sheep." The citizens were angered by this and called on the organist. He says: "One evening I went to church to play the organ, I left the gate open and the goats and sheep came into the church and I played for them." "In your city there is also a baker who has two wives." The people protested again. But two women at the assembly stood up and said: "Yes, we both live with the baker and we all like each other," etc. Finally the assembly acknowledged that they were crazy, and even agreed that the town would have a fence put around it and would be separated from the rest of the world. He then entirely reworked this theme into the form that came out as a book.

The whole time he was crumpling a piece of paper in his hand, until he gained enough courage and pulled it out. It was a poem about the Dobříš castle, about the lords who have a good time, they have wives and beds and for the others there are shackles. Immediately afterwards he tore up the paper, saying he couldn't take it across the border. He didn't want to leave it with us. Then he wrote into Grossman's guest book: "We spoke of lords and slaves, but the people I spoke with here were neither lords or slaves, but my friends." Holan told him that they should hold on to the little bit of freedom they had in England. When they parted he told him to say hello to all the English poets, living and dead. Before Thomas's departure, I went to his hotel to help him pack. He had his books in a big travelling bag and his clothes outside. So we unpacked it and did it the other way round. He gave me the books he didn't need. He remembered Holan and said: *I am terribly glad.* He stroked my hand and added: *I shall take you into my bag.* We went to lunch, to the car, to the airport. We said goodbye with a kiss. Thomas left and I was sad. I went to the airport to watch people leave, and I had to go back. To this day I remember Thomas's sad eyes as he departed.

Zdeněk Urbánek, 1968

I think the Congress lasted for three or four days and on the third day... there was a kind of reception arranged by the foreign minister for the writers assembled for the Congress. We were standing in the big room of an old Prague palace where the Ministry now is. The Czernin Palace. It was built in the seventeenth century by a family of the Czech aristocracy. One of the nicest buildings in Prague, such a big hall inside... there were chandeliers and such old pictures from baroque times – baroque was quite late in our country. I remember Dylan Thomas entering just at the moment when all the participators of the reception were eating and were assembled at the tables with some food and drink and all the hall was empty and Dylan entered the door and looked around and went across the big empty space of the room. I was standing with two or three friends of mine and he was just a few steps from us when another man intervened who was – I am not going to name him. Not because I don't like him but because it's better not to remember him. He was one of the worst people, as it showed out later, during the Stalinist era in our country. He asked Dylan – I'm not sure if I'm exact in my memory, but I think it was a question – "Where did you get so drunk?" – or something like that. And Dylan didn't look at him and turned round and went away again... what I was told afterwards was that he was drinking with the drivers of the Ministry downstairs in the basement... so my memory on Dylan Thomas is connected with unpleasant things which happened in our country at the time. But he is a bright spot in my memories of these times.

How many people were there?
It could be four hundred, five perhaps, because the membership of the Writers' Union in Czechoslovakia is quite surprising! About six hundred people now. Well, not all of them are poets, or good poets, I must admit.

Who were among the people who met Dylan?
Jan Grossman, Josef Nezsadba and Jiří Mucha, a Czech writer who afterwards was in prison for some time. For three years he was in prison. They accused him for some espionage or something. It was absolutely framed.

How many others of you were imprisoned?
Well, there were about fifty thousand Czechs in prison during the Stalinist era. Quite a lot of writers.

Did any of these meet Dylan beside Jirí Mucha?
Yes. One of the best Czech poets, Jirí Kolár, who was imprisoned in '53 for some absolutely dark reasons – no one knows. After seven months, he was let go again fortunately. No, there was no trial. They didn't even apologise to him. Never explained to him why they arrested him. [51]

How widely were Dylan Thomas' poems known here?
Whoever was interested in poetry knew about Dylan Thomas. The interest of those who knew him was intense. They wanted to know more. He was represented in the anthology of English poetry which was published very soon after the War. It was called *Between Two Wars* or *Between Two Flames*, I think. He had a large representation in this – the largest of all the poets of the time. Who translated it? Partly it was Miss Jiřina Hauková at the time already, but perhaps it was even was some other Czech poet who translated it. One must say that it's very hard work to translate, you know, Thomas' poetry. One who knows his poetry in the original must understand the problems at once.

How was Dylan's poetry regarded? Was he seen by Czechs as typical of the general feel of English poetry, or was he seen to have a particular Celtic quality?
I think he was esteemed mostly on the personal merits of his poetry, not as an expression of any typically national character. I think it was felt as a kind of universal poetry – perhaps the translation made it to sound like this... after the War, there was such a positive reaction against any kind of pointed nationalism so whenever one could find a poet who didn't use such typically nationalist themes, he was much more liked than other poets who were singing about the glories of their nations. We had enough of it from the Germans. By this I don't want to say that being Celtic in one's expression is something bad. It forms a part of the personal character, after all.

In the period following his visit here, there wasn't much published of Dylan Thomas' poetry. Was it banned?
No, not exactly banned, but the editors of the magazines did not accept it... everything changed after '48, slowly, then about 1950 all the editors of magazines, of newspapers and of the publishing houses were people who knew in advance what censorship would stop, so they didn't even try to get involved in some controversy with the censorship

so they were representative of the censorship themselves... the first wave of change came after '56, there came again a cold wave after 1960 and it lasted almost till the spring or January '68.

And Dylan's work became published here at what period again?
I think it was about '58 or '59.

About five years after his death then? This is Jiřina Hauková's translations?
Yes. It was very liked, very much liked, very much looked for by young people who came to know the name of Dylan Thomas for the first time. Everybody liked him at once. Only the other day I had here the visit of two young students who asked me about something about my translations of Shakespeare and we had such a talk about American and English poetry in our country, about translations of it, and they remembered Dylan Thomas as one of their most loved experience in poetry.

Jan Grossman, 1968

With me at his modern experimental theatre in Prague, the Theatre on the Ramp, is Jan Grossman, the theatre director. Would you tell us about first meeting with Dylan?
I met him in my flat where he was invited, and it was a party with Mrs Jiřina Hauková and Mr Chalupecký and Mr Nesvadba whom you probably would know; his stories now are translated also in English. And also Vladimír Holan, who is one of the best, the most prominent, Czech poets today. [52]

And it was a really marvellous meeting. I can remember the special conversation between those two big poets. Holan spoke Czech because he doesn't speak English. Dylan Thomas spoke, of course, English. They didn't understand each other but they understood each other very well... it was something important for us because that year, 1949, was actually the year when the tragic isolation of our literature from other literatures, and the political and cultural isolation, began. I felt something like a hope for the future when I saw those two poets speaking very different languages, not understanding the words of these languages, and yet poets who understood each other very well.

... it was a party... I don't know if it was beer or slivovitza we drank. It began with interpreting, but after one or two hours it was quite unnecessary to interpret... they were also reciting poetry.

How would you describe Holan's poetry?

Reflective poetry. It's something different from Dylan Thomas. It has not the sort of free imagination, or free association. It's more a metaphysical poetry... I remember that Dylan Thomas spoke about Blake and Holan likes Blake very much and, if I'm not mistaken, they also translated some poems by Blake. And it began with drinking and now I remember one sentence by Dylan Thomas. Dylan told us that drinking is not the method or the way to get out of things, but how to get into the things... he meant that it's not the way to escape the world, but how to get into the middle of the world...

Dylan didn't bring a book with him from which he read? He was just quoting from memory, I take it?
Yes, I can say quite truthfully that he had no book. No book with him, because otherwise I would probably have tried to get it from him.

... the visit in this country was a sort of eye-opener for Dylan Thomas. I think that from a certain point of view that is correct because it was also an eye-opener for us because, as Dylan said, he was a Leftist. We, the people who met him, were also Leftist, although nobody from us is a member of the Party, but we were Leftist who believed and tried to make this Socialist culture, but who from the beginning disagreed with all the so-called Stalinist reformations.

Did he get into long political discussions?
No, I don't remember; there were some political discussions...

Did Dylan at all say anything to you about the theatre, and his interest in the theatre?
I remember that he spoke about *Milk Wood* – which is the radio play – and that he quoted some parts of it, but there was no special discussion about theatre.

Dylan has had a reputation as a big drinker.
Yes. I think he drank a lot.

Beer or slivovitz?
I think it was combined, because I remember that he liked the beer very much, and we tried to get as much beer as it was possible. If he drank something else, that's probably possible. I think that he drank very slowly and, therefore, I recall this sentence that drinking is the way to get into it, not out of it...

Dylan has been given a reputation for misbehaving badly, especially with women. Did he misbehave that evening, with the women?
No, he didn't. He didn't.

Did he talk about Wales at all?
I think that he spoke about the Welsh language, but there was no discussion about social or political problems.

Viola Zinková and Josef Nesvadba, 1968 [53]

VZ: I didn't know his poems before he came here. He impressed me by his personality only... it wasn't because he would be jovial, but I had such a feeling that I know him, I knew him all the time. Maybe it was because they are sitting all night. And they were talking about everything, and they were discussing all matters in our Republic, and poetry everywhere, so I have such a feeling that I know him a very, very long time... he looked like a teddy bear. He was a bit fatty... he looked really very healthy. He had very nice colour in his face.

Dylan had a reputation. When he saw a beautiful woman...
In that evening, he was very correct, behaving very correctly, and he was very pleasant, and very nice all night.

Would you like to read what he wrote in the book?
"I came to a house at the end of Prague, where people told me bosses and slaves were the two kinds of people allowed to be. How can I agree, when the people I met weren't slaves or bosses, but my friends? Dylan Thomas."

Now, with me in the home of Viola Zinková in southern Prague, is Dr Josef Nesvadba. And you were present on that great occasion.
I was quite young at the time, twenty-four, twenty-five and I played a sort of interpreter role. I just remembered that it was Edwin Muir, or Vera Muir, who called me in my flat and said that there is going to be an evening and I am going to come along and then there was Dylan. And he had such a funny coat on him, which was very unusual for Prague after the War. It was a very short coat, very yellowish – woolly, and it did not have any [button-holes] just wooden...

A duffel coat.
And it was a sort of great excitement in Prague when he went around in this. And we had an interesting talk – we have been all obsessed with this political topics on that time... I could understand him mostly, with Grossman, who also had an English grammar school in Prague, so we both understood him – and he was a little bit unhappy because the day before that meeting he visited the Czech Writers' Union castle... he even read me a poem, or something which he has written, and it was

about the conditions here. We have been all very distressed at that time, because everything moved very rapidly to the totalitarian conditions: "If there is a factory where the people have work, it should be very clean and very co-operative", and so on. And then made such graduations and the last words were "But if there is a house where people should create, it is a house which is, as if it should have, look like a cage." And I asked him "Well, are you going to publish this?" And he said "Never, never." And he tore it up before me and said "I don't want to be misused by the capitalist press in attacking Socialism."

And we had quite a chat. He was, we all have been, pessimistic about the situation here at that time, and he was very unhappy. Because I understand he came with certain ideas and ideals which he sort of has been correcting here... he was losing a sort of faith which he had had.

... I think that he was a little bit leftist, and to justice, and the situation, which he felt here more than he understood, a sort of depression of the intellectuals, touched him very, very greatly, and I think this little poem was such an illustration of it. Then we had a walk around Prague with Edwin Muir and his wife – he was working with the British Council here... then there was one evening in some pub which I don't recall exactly, and then there was the great occasion in this flat with Holan, which was very rare to get him out of his flat, he is such an introverted man who makes friends with people in a very difficult way. He's a genial poet, but in his connections to people he's very shy. And this was an exceptional thing, that he really came here, and the remarkable thing was they contacted and they understood each other in a way which is not to be described in words... so this was a remarkable experience because of this art of communication, which was almost like something mystical I would say. Telepathy, yes – something as a mystical communication – and, of course, this mystic alcohol was a big help.

He was very, very happy, I would say, on that evening. We had a talk in the morning, and I asked him about his moments when he is very happy. And he told me – which impressed me very much – that he is taking part, I don't think it is very regularly, in a ceremony which is being held in Ireland on a peninsula which is going to the Atlantic Ocean. I think it's gypsies who are doing this ceremony and where you have a goat which is being killed in such a ritual way. And he told me about this experience which he is enjoying very, very much.

Did Dylan read any of his poetry that evening?
He recited some, I think. I don't know if it was *Under Milk Wood* or if it was from somewhere else, or if he just told us the content... he just

told us he is trying to write that. And he was telling me that he is going to write a play for radio, but I don't think I got the idea very clearly about that...

About a town that had gone mad?
Yeah, yeah, about the Voices he has been speaking.

Did Holan recite any of his verses to Dylan?
Yes, Holan recited a very short poem; it was something that one day he awakes in his bath and he looks through the window and he sees there are two moons in the sky, so he goes to the window and says "Now this is going to be the end of the world – there are two moons." And in that moment, the other part of the window which has been mirroring the moon shuts, and he sees that there is one moon again, and he goes to his bed and says "No, the end of the world isn't going to come yet." In such a very unusual way. It is a metaphysical poem of his. I have told it to you in a rather cynical way, but it was full of feeling.

... we all discussed a lot of poetics, but a lot about the contemporary situation in Europe. But he wasn't very precise on this; he just listened to us and to our grievances. I think I met him first with Edwin Muir. I knew about him but, of course, we didn't know very much about him until it has been told by Edwin Muir and we have been told by Skoumal. In those days, certain people have been still very ignorant about the sort of literature which had been written in the War in England and America, but it slowly emerged.

His reputation had spread here?
It was also his personality... you somehow didn't need to use words in contact with him and so I think that is why so many people have been impressed by him.

Did Dylan use religious references very much, or discuss religious ideas?
No, no. He discussed mostly the socialism, mostly the present situation of Eastern Europe.

Now when I talk to people and they use 'socialism', they use it with a different meaning from we in Britain. We talk about socialism as something distinct from communism, meaning, parliamentary socialism, and Dylan would have used, I think, socialism in the same way, wouldn't he?
No, in that case, in this sense of reference, I would say he discussed communism in that matter. That means, in this country, you talk about communism as a part of the socialist movement. But what he was so apprehensive about was the situation in Eastern Europe at that time. And the realisation of the ideas here. That must have been for him a

big experience. I don't think it was an exhilarating moment.

Did he refer at all to Wales, and any of the conditions in Wales?
Yes. Well, he just mentioned about the situation. Everybody knows that there is a Welsh minority and so on and so on, but we didn't know about the constitution of the new Welsh national image, or the new Welsh national feeling. In my presence, he only just touched this. He said it is beginning to re-emerge somehow. I had the same question, as I put to you, with him, about the Basques and so on but I don't know nowadays what he answers to me.

Did he make any references to the pre-War period, and the elements of fascism in Britain and the move against it. Did he try to explain this?
I think we discussed – in the presence of Muir – the whole situation amongst the poets at that time. There was Spender, Comfort and all this, and Cecil Day-Lewis and so on. But I don't think he liked this very much. He just was touching the ideas that there has been. But I personally worked with Edwin Muir and with a friend of Muir who is now in America, on a book about these poets who have been fighting in Spain, so we just asked him. There has been one of them who was dead – I think it was Alex Comfort? I mentioned this name, because the book was just going to be published and so we asked him, but I don't think that he was very keen on this.

I don't know if we all drank so much, but I cannot say that it was somehow apparent that he would be an addict, or that he would be a chronic alcoholic, as we call it in my medical profession. He just seemed to me what we call social drinker. For instance, I can recollect that on this walk we had with Muir, he didn't drink, and it was a long walk, two or three hours.

Where did you walk exactly?
On the Wenceslas Square, and then over the Charles Bridge, then we went with a taxi back to the Embassy. In these people who are real addicts... you have the situation that they cannot be without alcohol such a long time.

What was he drinking when he was with you?
I think it was hard liquor... I think he preferred to have beer, yes. My first idea was to give the answer he was drinking beer, you know. But then I am not quite sure about this... I could see that he is a very heavy smoker, and we discussed this. Yes, he was coughing a lot, and he was smoking one cigarette after another and, in a joking way I just mentioned the hazards of smoking and so he said he can't be without

it, that he had to work only with this, and so on.

... it was very funny, because with me, I had the idea of a healthy being, you know. And he didn't complain to me, although he knew that I have been taking my doctorship in possibly two months after our meeting. So he does know that I am in the branch, but he never mentions this.

Did he make any reference to having gone down to drink with the drivers in the basement below the palace?

No, no, no – he didn't say that, but he said that he is contacting privately people he meets on the street, and they have been very much helping, because you know at that time there had been a cult of foreigners, because the people hadn't seen any.

1949-1953
"Treadmilling small nightmares all the waking nights."

The Thomases move to the Boat House, Laugharne, in May 1949 and Colm is born in July. Dylan celebrates his return to Wales by writing 'Over Sir John's hill'. He goes to Iran in 1951 to make a film for the Anglo-Iranian Oil Company and on his return completes three major poems, including 'Do not go gentle into that good night'. *Collected Poems* is published. He tours America four times, falling in love in New York and visiting Hollywood, where he charms Stravinsky, Shelley Winters and Marilyn Monroe and dines with Charlie Chaplin. He writes most of the second half of *Under Milk Wood* in Boston and New York for its first cast performance on May 14, 1953. Back home, Dylan makes his television debut, his father and sister die, his tax bills mount, his marriage disintegrates and the Muse all but deserts him.

Alban Leyshon

I knew Dylan slightly at school. He was on the Arts side, the snobbish side as related to our modern side, where we took disgusting things like Chemistry, Physics and German. Obviously the people who took Latin and Greek were hardly likely to do other than nod, in a condescending way, at such people. I saw very little of Dylan when he was a reporter for the *Evening Post*.

When was the next period that you met up with him?
In the last few years of his life, when he was spending a great deal of time at Laugharne [1949-1953] and would make forays and excursions into Swansea in search of convivial company... I was at that time running a small manufacturing jewellery business in Swansea, and I used to meet Dylan either at the shop that I had, or in one of the local pubs. Where he was, of course very popular with anybody and everybody, and frequently had to be defended against invasions of people

that were invading his privacy. And that was frequently my job – to fend off the unwelcome guest.

What drew you together?
It's not poetry; it's a love of words as such. If one was lucky enough to say anything that scanned well, sounded good, Dylan would seize on it, repeat it, roll it around his tongue and enjoy it, and grin with pleasure. And he was equally delighted if one was appreciative of what he said, because his conversa-

13. Alban Leyshon

tion, his normal spontaneous remarks, had true literary merit – and he liked it to be appreciated. And it was in the plain, simple love of words as things, just as a man may like tools rather than the work he does. I think my affection for English is for the tools of the trade rather than the actual use of them, because I can't write myself, but I enjoy the words...

... Dylan had what one can only describe as a fear and a horror of the educated man. His own education wasn't formal; it finished at the Grammar School and I think that he felt to some extent at a disadvantage with the university-trained people; and he was a very modest man, a thing which seems to have escaped most people.

One of the things I like about Dylan's work are his short stories. They're so strong in what is essentially Welsh humour – the situation, the characters
It's paradoxical that Dylan was terribly Welsh – he didn't sound Welsh, he didn't have a very Welsh background, his father spoke without a trace of accent; he himself had no Welsh accent and he had no knowledge of the Welsh language whatsoever, but he was steeped in Welshness and he did indeed enjoy the ordinary humour of everyday Welsh life which, perhaps I'm prejudiced, but I think that humour plays a far bigger part, just as singing and noise, in Welsh life than in an English one.

Dylan was a great raconteur.
Oh, the stories he told could be anything from strictly factual to the wildest of imaginings; and I think that he was desperately keen on other

people's wild imaginings. He liked nothing better than the exceedingly exaggerated claims of large workmen to do prodigious feats. I think that he believed very greatly in these supermen... a glorious one of an Irishman who claimed to have swung a hammer weighing 56lbs for five hours on end. I think Dylan was quite annoyed when I told him that the man was a liar, because I burst the bubble of this lovely faith that he built up in his mind.

We've heard some people talk about Dylan's ultra-sensitivity to the suffering of other people. Do you recall any instances where this came out?
Well, I remember Dylan getting very emotionally hot and bothered about such things – his positive adulation for a Dutchman who said he was a Jew in order that he could be shot with Jews. There were many things like this, either near or remote, that would move Dylan enormously emotionally, for no doubt he was a sentimentalist at heart... he had an enormous sympathy for the underdog always, throughout his life.

Dylan made a few trips abroad. Did he talk to you about any of these visits he made, and his impressions?
No, I am conscious of the absurdity of the question. It seems to imply a rather courtly, quiet, dignified poet expounding on his travels. This sort of thing never happened... he might accidentally say something, but never did it start "I remember" or "A strange thing happened to me on the way to Laugharne tonight." There was nothing like that about it at all. It was all very spontaneous.

... I think if you had been lucky enough to meet him coming off the boat or coming off the train, you would probably have heard these, but so much happened in Dylan's life you would only hear what had happened in the three or four days previously. You'd hear that in a very amusing way indeed; but the thought of him locking away in a pigeon-hole in his mind something which happened in Prague in order to tell you about it at Laugharne three weeks later, strikes me even now as utterly absurd. It just couldn't happen. He wasn't that type of person at all.

Did you hear anything about his visit to Persia?
Yes, immediately after he came back... he was very amused at the idea of his having been sent to Persia to report on the marvellous things that were being done for the people of Persia in the way of schools, hospitals and so forth by the oil company who were responsible for it, and at the same time horrified at the condition under which the Persian

people were living. The revolting condition of beggars mutilating their own children to make them more appealing, from the viewpoint of getting alms. He came back writhing with indignation; but this, of course, only lasted until he was indignant about something else, or delighted about something else. As I said before, so much was happening in his life all the time that something that would be a major factor in somebody else's life was a mere incident in his.

And Dylan's feelings for his children? People think artists and so forth don't have much sense of responsibility to family…
Dylan's children were extremely well fed and extremely well clothed, and they were brought up in a – not a prosaic manner, but a very normal manner. They were very little affected by any wild bohemian scenes. The ordinary domestic side of life went on smoothly. Children were bathed, they were put to bed clean, warm and dry in comfortable beds. They got up in the morning and they were dressed well and adequately, and in that way, indeed, it was a very prosaic, ordinary, middle-class household.

How many people would be down there as a rule when you went down?
Oh, frequently nobody at all. There'd be a general air of delight to see you… life was quiet and domestic and on other occasions there would be perhaps two people. The McAlpines stayed there, I think, for five months on end on one occasion when they were in the process of changing homes in London. The odd bodies of ambitious poets would hoist themselves on to Dylan for weeks on end and neither Dylan nor Caitlin ever told them directly to go away. Hospitality was quite unlimited, and I think that probably Dylan said to other people many times as he said to me once when we met by chance in Carmarthen "Come down stay with us – six months!" With the air of one who's giving you a sentence from the magistrate's bench.

… he was generous when he had no money! And this is, indeed, a very great thing. Instead of most generous people who are generous when they've got money and moan furiously when they haven't, but Dylan would share whatever he'd got without any bemoaning of the fact that it was a little. I don't suggest that he never grumbled… but he was never rude enough to grumble to anybody who'd just arrived, or to grumble about anybody who was staying too long. I don't think he ever worked out the cost of what it cost him to entertain his friends. His credit was always good, too… if one had no money or he had no money, one always ate and one always drank.

... Dylan had an enormous respect for work, whether it was his own or anybody else's. His attitude towards it was that of any other workman. When we speak of his "art or sullen craft", it was very near the truth. It was a quiet, dogged, completely sober, enormous effort, and if he called on one when one was obviously preoccupied and busy he would immediately retreat swiftly and say "You've got work to do." I had work sometimes, too, and he would wait until one was free, and there was no question of his being the boisterous companion who would drag you away from your work. On the contrary, he had an enormous respect for work as such... I had a small jewellery shop. He arrived, poked his head round the door with a very large grin, which was quickly wiped off, and said "Right – I'll see you later." An immediate appreciation of the situation.

There's one bit I didn't mention when I was talking about his drinking habits, and that is in many ways he was almost a mediaeval drinker in that it wasn't unknown for him to have beer with breakfast – which was not immediately followed up by lots of other drinks – but to drink it as a beverage, with bacon and egg, or one occasion I remember, kippers, eaten frequently on the balcony of his house and overlooking the estuary. Very, very civilised and no different from a cup of tea or anything else. And I think it was towards the end of life that he began to rely on the food value of drink, and that was probably more serious than anything else; that he didn't eat a lot, but having drunk a fair amount felt no need for food. A thing with which I can sympathise because indeed I found it so myself.

I was conscious as a friend, toward the end of his life there was a great move on his part towards clarification, simplification of vocabulary and a genuine desire on his part to make himself conversant to a larger number of people. Not to get a bigger audience, because that sounds like somebody who is looking for an audience, but to make his thoughts clearer to more people. That is perhaps the best way of putting it.

... Ralph in the bookshop will tell you that Dylan was a very keen collector of old bound copies of the *Boys' Own* paper and work of that type, and I believe he sincerely liked it for the simplicity of the prose and read it with great enjoyment. Not as a means of escapism or any other high falutin' reason for reading such stuff.

... my best memories of Dylan are purely domestic, of the early rising, completely sober Dylan, with no trace of a hangover. The angelic expression of one who spends his life well, walking down from the Boat House to Laugharne with me, with a can to fetch milk. And talking very little, quietly, rationally, until you'd come to the converted garage in which he worked, and we had one repeated joke: we'd always look, one after the other, through the keyhole, and then lament the fact that the bread-earner was not earning bread – lazy blighter. "How does he keep his wife and family? Never working, never see him working. Disgusting. This generation." And then we'd walk on, and fetch the milk. But I remember one morning, Dylan, after walking two or three minutes in complete silence, said "How many friends have you got?" I said "Three, or possibly four. That's including you." There was another long silence, and he said "That's a hell of a lot of friends." I often think of this when I hear of the enormous number of people who claim his very close friendship.

Jane Dark, Laugharne

I'd never had very much chance to talk to him at all, but I did find that if you were on a bus or something... one particular journey, we came round a very sharp corner, and he was fast asleep, and he jerked himself awake and then he said "Oh, Mrs Dark, I didn't see you there." Well, do you know, he leaned over the back of my seat and he chatted – anyway, Laugharne seemed to come just like that, he was so interesting.

... I can't say exactly what he talked about... but I really did know that he was something different – I'm not very good, I don't recollect my speech perfectly, but it flowed beautifully from you, too, because he made *you* so easy... and that's quite a big item on the programme, really, for a person like me – he always gave you his full attention.

... by the way, it was through me that he found his Rosie Probert name... I came out of the greengrocers and he was coming in, and he bumped into me. And he said "Whoops!" And I said "Are you ever stuck for work, Mr Thomas?" He said "I'm stuck at the moment." "Well," I said, "shall I tell you something that happened here?" We have a road called Horsepool, and it has a queer trick of light. While you are on the top of the road, the sun shines beautifully, but the road itself is almost in darkness, and then if the doors are opened on the left-hand side, the sun streams out into this dark street. One day some visitors came who had a little girl, and she was eating an apple and she walked into this street, and looking down through this shaft of sunlight, she saw ducks, baby ducks, in the gardens below, so she asked "Could I come and see the ducks?" Well, she was so thrilled with these ducklings that she put her apple down, and she picked up the ducklings, and she was so thrilled "Can I go and tell my mummy?" We don't know what happened, but she didn't come back... she tried to get round to find these ducklings again, following the water which runs at the bottom, and she was drowned. And the house that I was talking about, that this old lady lived in, had been two houses, so it had an extra-wide passage and, of course, an extra-wide shaft of sunlight, and

14. Jane Dark

this old lady was telling me afterwards that she couldn't remove the apple, it was still there. I told Mr Dylan Thomas that it had been the only place where coloured people had lived, and the girl that lived in the other half of this converted house, her name was so lovely, I used to love it – Rosie Probert. And he called, of course, his character, Rosie Probert and he called it Duck Lane.

And Mog Edwards?
He's a mixture of two people, which was the straw-hatted man, who was the draper here, and he was a character, too. He was a drinking man, and, of course, Dylan knew him well. And he was a rather dramatic "I love you" sort of person, you know. In drink he loved his wife Maggie so much when he was tight, and, of course, she was such a refined sort of person.

... Captain Cat, yes. We can quite find him. He was a very, very old, blind man who spent most of his time in the Cross House, and he was full of tales of the sea... he and Dylan were inseparable companions for quite a time. I think he outlived Dylan, too. He was a wonderful old man... he's nicknamed Cat, yes.

... my husband admired Caitlin terrifically, as it was obvious later, because to him she turned at the end, after Dylan's death, he was the one that backed her up, he helped her right through her time, she tried to commit and all that rest of it – he was one of the men that really did help her.

... I also saw her kindness to children – in all fairness... they always welcomed children, and the children were always fed if they came there. She was noted for always giving gifts to children, and sometimes the parents used to be rather annoyed... she'd bought a lovely costume for a little girl and this man returned it. He said "We can afford to dress our own kids – we know

15. Dylan at Pendine for the filming of *Pandora and The Flying Dutchman*

your circumstances, and we won't accept it." But her heart was terribly good, you know.

... he'd have days like everybody else, the Muse wouldn't work... he wasn't always able to work. I've seen him tight, coming along in the street in the bright sunshine, sort of carrying the weight of beer – and, by the way, he was a beer drinker. There's one thing I would like to correct – he did *not* drink spirits.

... he certainly drank beer, which the local lads found funny, because they could drink twice the quantity that he did, but he looked so portly in drink, he loved taking people to the back of the Boat House to talk, parties too. He liked a good political argument. He liked winning at darts; not that he minded playing if he lost, he just liked to win... he accompanied the boys – dart players, that is – to places as far off as Treorchy.

... it was very hot one day, the workmen were telling me, and he passed them going over, and when he came back, he had a bottle of beer and a cigarette for them, and they said they appreciated it on such a hot day. And I find so many little kindnesses that he's been doing for people. A lady who's collecting here for several things, the blind or something like that, and if they asked him he always put his hand in his pocket – half a crown. Never gave pennies or anything like that.

It was Nancy found The Boat House for Dylan, wasn't it?
Yes, it was Nancy I knew first... oh, she was a sweetie. She and I got

on like a house on fire, you know how people click together – she got the best out of me.

... I don't think people realise how much influence his father had on him, because I think he and Dylan must have been strong, their minds must have been akin, because it seemed to me as though Dylan started from where his father left off... mind, the mother was a fine woman. And somebody offended her very badly by saying to her "I wonder where he got his brains from?" It really did offend her, which was stupid, because she was charming.

... I have a friend who was the sister of Alfred Janes, the artist... [he] had done a portrait of Dylan, and he said "What do you think of the portrait?" So I said "There's only one thing," I said. "Being that I cut his hair, I knew that he hated the tips of his ears in sight." So the next time I saw the portrait in Laugharne Castle, it had been painted; he'd painted hair over the tips of his ears.[54]

... I find Dylan's real friends are capable of being as shy as Dylan would have them be, as he himself was a shy man.

... I know that they did do the other kind of life, too, because they dressed for dinner, and I know they went to Tenby... *Pandora and the Flying Dutchman*, scenes were shot in Pendine, Dylan taking part in the crowd scenes, by the way. And when it was released, he dined at Tenby with Mr Lewin, I know that.[55]

... and they liked fishing, and they went out with the wade net when they were on honeymoon. They accompanied the fisher folk in the boats, fishing from boats. They cockled – which is taking cockles out of the sand... they certainly took a part in the fishermen's type of life and liked it very much.

... they were very fond of the countryside. They did a lot of picnicking – ever such a lot of picnicking. They used to go in the boat across the river estuary and picnic on the other side... he liked to relax and be a simple man. I think it must have been good, it helped him to clear his brain, probably. Of course, what do we know about him, really – not a great deal, you see.

John Morgan Dark

With me now is John Morgan Dark, gunsmith, and purveyor of fishing tackle and sports gear in Carmarthen.[56]
To me, Dylan was an actor; he acted practically every moment of every day. He wasn't as normal or as uninteresting as the average man... He

was a genius in several aspects of character, rather than purely as a poet.

I never saw Dylan slightly drunk. You see, he'd first be getting "a pint for Dylan Thomas!" And an hour later, if would be "a half a pint for Dylan Thomas". And hour later, the last half-pint, which he very, very rarely finished. And this went on for over several years. Caitlin drank all the whisky. And became very unfortunate when she did drink it! The first book that was written about him was not the Dylan that I knew, and totally out of character.

That's Brinnin's book?

Yes, it was out of character with the man. Dylan wasn't the type, drunk or sober, to say that "I've drunk sixteen whiskies and that's a record". He couldn't drink sixteen whiskies. I saw him fail on a dozen occasions to drink a pint and a half of beer... he'd throw it up. And he never drank whisky, anyway...

Was Dylan truly a bohemian?

No... playing a part – he was acting the part. Every moment of his life was an act. He dare not look the truth in the face. Because from a financial point of view, he was a failure. And he wouldn't admit failure – couldn't afford to, obviously, his ego wouldn't allow him to.

Some of the things written about him now make him out to be a sponger. Would you say this was true?

Good Lord, quite the opposite... and he would give the shirt off his back. He wasn't a sponger. I've seen him refuse to drink with a dozen people when he was absolutely flat broke. Everybody wanted to buy him a drink, but he wouldn't drink; he drank with people that he liked. And not very much – he would much rather talk and listen. He was a great listener – more so, than a talker. Recalling those days, lots of people said more than Dylan did...

He was drawing things from life, wasn't he, for his work?

Oh, he was. There is no question; he lived very, very close. And the closer that he could get to the good earth... he was happiest when he was with ordinary people. I'll never forget him coming up to the Ivy Bush [in Carmarthen]... there was a young lady and a young fellow there, and this girl came along and she said "You're Dylan Thomas, aren't you?" And he took my wife's hand and he said, "Edna, save me please; I hate to be lionised. Can't we go now?" And we went. He was fundamentally a very shy character. And well, one of the greatest chaps I think there ever lived. Gentle, kind, and the roistering, fighting, drunken picture that he'd taken hours of acting to put that across in the city of London. And they accepted him as the last of the bohemians.

... we'd been duck shooting down in Kidwelly, and my wife and Dylan came down on the bus to pick us up. Dylan had been in town all the afternoon, and he'd met several people and he'd had a few drinks, and he was in a very good humour, tremendously good humour. Well, we get into this pub, and he was the greatest mimic... we get into this little pub and he started to sell nylons off his arm. And you were there, you were in the city of London, there's no question. You were standing by a London-born Cockney, buying nylons and – several people in the pub, they were looking at him. He loved to shock people like that.

We had one beer there, and we went to a pub that Dylan loved to go to, the Black Lion. He said "The only pub I've ever been in where I can look down on the landlord." The landlord serves you from a cellar. He comes up the steps to the hatch, and you can only see the top of his head – and Dylan loved that. Well, we get in there – a very small bar – half a dozen other people came in behind us. He immediately started – he was an American, and you can smell the smoke and grime of Grand Central Station. He took two parts – he was the Limey that had come in off the train, and the American taxi driver was picking him up. Well, you've never heard anything like it in your life.

Dylan wrote a lot of things down on bits of paper that are probably destroyed or completely lost.
Oh, yes, they were usually Woodbine packets. He never carried pencil and paper, just a stub of pencil – I can see it now, a very, very short little red pencil, which he lost and then he'd hunt for it, frantically, through every pocket... he didn't spend his time writing; he was part of the conversation – it was very surreptitious as far as it went.

He didn't flaunt his presence around?
Oh, it wasn't obvious; no, no, no, no. If he heard the word, he may write it down – oh, a quarter of an hour, twenty minutes later. It wasn't obvious at all, he was never obvious.

And he didn't flaunt his poetry, he didn't recite his poetry in pubs.
Not a word, not a word of poetry. Until he died, I didn't know he'd written any poetry.

What do you know what Dylan felt about Wales?.
He was an ardent nationalist. Not to the point that he wanted to blow up the power stations or anything like that, but he was very proud to have been born a Welshman. The only thing that he envied me was my

name. He said "You have a marvellous name – John Morgan Dark. That would look very well at the bottom of an MS."

Was he a very sensitive person?
Very, very sensitive person. Very easily hurt. He was very, very, very shy and practically girlish in his approach to pain. You had to be very, very careful what you spoke about, what you said. You could offend Dylan with a glance, practically.

Phil Richards

With me now at the Cross House Inn, in Laugharne, Mr Phil Richards, the proprietor. Now, you knew Dylan.
Very well. Not as a poet, as a man. He was a great friend, a wonderful fellow… everybody knows Dylan Thomas now, but they didn't know him as a man. Only a few knew him as a friend. He was so nice to everybody, and he was pleasant. I never seen him violent. And I never seen him drinking whisky. Dylan was a timid man… he was not a drunk. He liked a few pints, but he was not a drunk.

Did he come into the pub here?
Oh yes – oh yes, yes. But he didn't drink a lot. I mean, he was working, you see. He didn't have time to drink a lot… we used to go for a little run up the valleys, used to go to clubs… we always took a driver with us… he used to like Glanaman very much. We used to call in the Plough, and the clubs. The clubs were very popular with him… there's one thing that sticks out in the memory. We went to Carreg Cennen castle. And he named the Loughor and the Cennen, and all the rivers, and we seen the castle from a little pub called the Cennen Arms, and had bread and cheese and pickles, and he enjoyed it. You know, he enjoyed it. We come back through the valley then, we called in the club, had a few glasses of beer there. We arrived home late, very, very late. And not very popular – not in the Cross House, nor in the Boat House, mind you!

Did Caitlin come on any of these outings with you?
No – never, no, no. Dylan was like myself – keep the women out.

What was he drinking mostly?
Pints of bitter. And it had to be good bitter at that.

And he stuck to bitter most of the time, did he?
Oh yes, yes, yes. Yes, yes. And not a lot. I think Dylan was a sick man then, you know… I don't think he was a very strong man… I don't think he wanted that last trip to America.

He didn't want to go?
No. "But I'm going, I think I'm a dying man – I don't think I'll see forty," he said.

I just took it with a pinch of salt. Didn't think it anything serious about it

Did you often see him drinking something stronger?
I did see him drinking rum when he had a cold. And not a lot of it...

What about the story of the pigs?
A little feller, a little Irishman, called Bill McAlpine, had a few drinks in the morning here, and he thought he'd have a walk. Not a lot of beer, mind you. What we drunk was very, very small, but felt like a walk, and we got as far as Billy Maelor's place and we seen a pig in the road, and Dylan said "Damn it all," he said, "I'd like to buy that."

... it took us about three hours, bringing the pig – is it three hundred yards? Maybe it's a little more. We had a rope on the back leg, and Bill McAlpine was pushing him, and Dylan pulling as well. Eventually, we arrived home at the Cross House... first thing, Dylan said "We've got to name the thing. What shall we call him? We'll call him Wallace." He used to come down every morning and look over the wall. Old Wallace was doing very, very well.

... anyway, the execution come on a Saturday morning – I'll never forget it. The butcher was here, killing the pig in the garage. Everything ready, we'd been boiling water and the butcher come, and Dylan and I were in the front room. And we were like this – holding our ears, for the last scream, for the last scream like, you see. Had a pint or two again, paid the butcher and the day passed.

Did you ever hear Dylan saying anything about politics?
I think he was staunch Labour. I think he was all for the Labour princi-ples anyway, I know that... he used to admire Jim Griffiths of Llanelli.

Ebie and Ivy Williams, Brown's Hotel, Laugharne

IW: We first met Dylan before he and Caitlin were married... and he came down with Augustus John, and they stayed in the Castle for a while, and then Dylan came up and stayed here with us. And I met his mother and father – they were family friends of ours, you see. And then, the next thing, Caitlin and Dylan they cleared off to Cornwall and got married. They came back here, straight away then, to live.

What was your first impression of Dylan?

EW: Ah, nice fellow. Hail fellow well met.

IW: He was very shy.

EW: And always a pal to everybody – but Mr Brinnin put a nice report in on him, dinn'e? He would always joke with anybody… we'd go along the road now, to drive him to London of a daytime, if we'd see an old roadster, he'd always stop and have a chat with him. And little Woodbine packet always there, write down a word or two, you know. Poor old fellow.

… Mrs Margaret Taylor lived in Park Village East, in Regent's Park. Had a big house there. Well, I stayed there with Dylan and his wife several times. And there was a big pub close by there, the Oak & Albany, and we used to meet a lot of the costers there. And, oh, Dylan was delighted amongst them, you know, to hear them singing and talking and – delighted.

He had a feeling for the ordinary bloke, didn't he?

EW: Oh, absolutely. Anybody that could crack a joke and sing, now, with the costers, Dylan was there. And I can tell you this there was a pub there called the Black Cat we used to go to, and a lot of Irish there, and we used to go there to hear them fellows singing and speaking Irish… he liked to be amongst them, you know. He liked sport and fun.

What about this business of Dylan as a drinker?

EW: Well, ask any of the locals, ask any of the locals you like – Dylan was never an excessive man and I never seen him drink anything else but beer. Unless he went over to the States and them old booze out there, which he didn't like. No.

He never drank whisky here then?

EW: No, never seen him. Very, very, very rare.

IW: But you hear so many stories – you hear about him reciting his poetry in bars. I've never heard him recite.

EW: He might bring out a word or two, you know, a phrase here and there, like.

IW: I've never heard him, in all the years I knew him. I've never heard him recite.

Dylan was, much of the time, in financial trouble.

IW: No, he wasn't… they always kept a maid. Well, if you keep a maid – if you don't pay her one week, she's not there the next.

EW: His money was coming in lumps, now and again, you understand me. He wasn't a regular paid man.

IW: By anybody else's standards, they were quite well off.

What was Dylan's view on religion?
IW: At heart, Dylan was very conventional. Oh yes, he liked a navy blue suit and a black tie and a white shirt. He was very conventional. And all the children were christened and all the children went to church. He really and truly was a Welsh Baptist at heart.

What about Dylan's attitude towards his children?
IW: He had no patience with them, mind you. I don't think many men have. But he was very proud of them.

And Dylan's mother and father?
IW: He was terribly fond of his mother.
EW: Yes. And looked after 'em, fair play to him. Poor old Dyl, he thought the world of them... the house, The Pelican over there, belonged to me, and he took it on a seven year's lease from me when they first went in, poor old feller.

What was the effect on Laugharne when Under Milk Wood *was published?*
IW: I don't know. Because really and truly, it could have been written about any village in any part of the world, couldn't it, whether it was China or anywhere. Of course, it wasn't really written in Laugharne at all. It was written in New Quay, most of it.
EW: I used to stay in the Black Lion in New Quay – we were there several times.

What about Dylan's Welshness?
IW: Dylan's mum told me why Dylan didn't speak Welsh was, when he was small, it wasn't the thing to teach your children Welsh; it wasn't done. So that's why he didn't learn Welsh.

Did he ever speak about being unhappy about not speaking Welsh?
EW: Oh, it were a bit of a handicap to him on times, you know. Poor old feller – bit of a handicap to him... always a big handicap to him.

Was it a handicap in writing stories about Wales or just in contacts with people?
EW: Ah yes, a handicap all round, pretty well. We'd go into different places, and it'd be all Welsh, well I mean, poor old Dylan, he was lost... a Welshman and can't speak your own language, see.

Did he try to speak a few phrases in Welsh?
IW: Oh, yes.
EW: Oh, just a bit of swear words!

What was his most outstanding characteristic, as man?
IW: Generosity.

EW: Yes – ah, yes. Oh – help anybody.

IW: I mean, if he had a shilling in his pocket, and you wanted it, he'd give it to you. Never any question.

EW: Ah – good-hearted fellow.

Billy Williams

We've had many outings in the boat... we used to go to Llansteffan and Ferryside... I had my own boat and we used to go in that, you see, a little cabin cruiser.

Was Dylan much of a sailor?

Oh, he was a good fellow! Ah, he was a good chap. Never seasick, in any case. We used to call at our favourite places...

You went over to Llansteffan. What did you do there?

Well, what do think?

Which were his favourite haunts, then, in those days?

Well, the pub we were in was the Castle... we were there when a raid was on. Police. It was a Sunday... Llansteffan was known for drinks on a Sunday. That's why we went over there.

... we were in there having drinks, and sitting down and all of sudden seven police swooped down and had a raid... the police come in and "We're taking your names." So he asked Dylan "What are you doing with this?" He said "Drinking it – what the hell do you think?" "What are you going to do with it?" "Drink it – what the hell do you think?"

Did it land up in the Courts? I remember there was an account in the papers about it. They picked on Dylan's name, didn't they?

Yes... they didn't appear. They got fined... but they had nothing on Caitlin, because she didn't have a drink.

There were other pubs in Llansteffan that Dylan was fond of...

Edwinsford, yes, but the Castle I was in with him most. And the White Lion, Ferryside.[57]

Did Dylan ever talk about politics with you?

Very seldom, very seldom. And he never talked shop, either. You hear some say that he used to recite in pubs - tripe. If the Swansea boys was in, they'd talk about different things then, in his line, but never to outsiders... he liked a good Welsh singsong... he used to join in - not one of us could sing really!

He had a favourite Welsh song that he sang?

Oh, *Calon Lan* – they used to join in. Dylan didn't know much words than I did.

What impression did you have of Caitlin?

Oh, they're all bohemian type. We went over to Sea View one day for tea. And had cockles, the Laugharne cockles. And it was a table something similar to this – there was no cloth, it was all white, it was nice and clean – and when the cockles were ready, she brought the saucepan and tipped them all on top of the table, you see. Help yourself! Brought 'em out then, with a chicken, and divided it up as well! Everything was spotlessly clean with her. There was no like dirty dishes or anything like that; she always was very clean.

Do you think Dylan and Caitlin had a happy marriage?

Well, they understood each other. Might have had a rough passage on times, but they understood each other – one was as good as the other.

What about Dylan's drinking?

Delyn (*sic*) could drink; but he could always hold it. Could knock back as many beers as you like, but he's always a gentleman, all the time. Yes. Beer was his hobby – bitter. Pints of bitter.

Now I understand that Dylan, if he wanted to work, could cut out the drinking.

He could cut it out. He used to come in the morning, and we used to go home about two o'clock. You wouldn't see him then not till the evening. He used to spend his time over at the hut.

Dylan was quite open about his borrowing of money when he was short…

Dylan always paid back. Always paid back. I found him very honest. If he was in a pub, he always stood his round.

What is your most outstanding memory of Dylan?

His most outstanding quality to me was he was a proper gentleman. That's my definition of Dylan. He'd help anyone, and especially the poor. At heart, I think he was a proper Socialist.

What were his weaknesses?

Well, his weakness was drink! That was all his weakness. Of course, he had the brains as well, see.

Leslie Parsons [58]

When I first knew Dylan, I was a boy in school. Dylan wasn't very old when he came to Laugharne first… I recollect him as a boy, still at school…

How did you come to speak to him the first time?

Well, Dylan was that type of feller, wasn't he? If you met Dylan in a public house, I mean, he'd talk to anybody… he was a very ordinary chap. There was nothing spectacular about Dylan in any way.

He had no airs about him?

Oh, none whatsoever… he was that sort of a fellow. He didn't mix with quarrelsome, argumentative guys but anybody that was sociable, Dylan sat down and had a pint with.

I used to drink a lot in Brown's, and Dylan was there and he'd had quite a few drinks, that particular evening, and he was having a party at the Boat House. He'd bought crates of beer and he'd invited several people over… I had a little van then, and we'd loaded this drink in the back of the van, and I believe it's correct to say that it was the first time a vehicle had gone all the way over to where the little gate walks down to the Boat House. But the point about this is to point out to you that he was not a terrific drinker. Because that evening, Dylan and I had one bottle of beer each, and we sat on the settee something similar to this, and all we did was talk about poetry. We never had another drink in five or six hours.

Did he ever read his poems to his friends at all, in the pubs, or at the Boat House

No – no, no, no, no. Not to my knowledge, anyway… you'd see him casually making little notes on his cigarette packets.

… he said to me "The reason for the party, Les," he said, "is I've just had a cheque for a hundred and fifty pound. I've paid off the grocery bill over in the post office, and we're having a little party, just to celebrate."

One of the stories about Dylan was that he was an awful cadger, and he sponged on his friends.

All I can say is that I've never seen him cadge. And he's never cadged off me.

… Ivy Williams, the landlady of the Brown's Hotel, was one of his very great, great friends… I'd call in on the way back and I'd have a bottle of Guinness myself. Dylan might be there, or he might come in, but – one bottle of Guinness. He'd been and had a coupla sixpenny bets and he'd take a flagon of cider home to work in his little cabin on the cliff. Now, this was Dylan… he came into the village to do a little bit of shopping. He usually had a shopping bag with him. Had his sixpence on the horses and the Guinness and his flagon of cider, and off back.

Do you recall anything about the people they went around with?
No. They were mostly on their own. There was very few people met
Dylan socially in that sort of way. They were loners to a large extent.

How many people were at this party?
They were just local people in the bar, just ordinary working lads… my
experience is that the people that seek out the *crachach*, as we call them,
are the people that are short of a bit of thinking ability… the majority
of decent people that I've come across, I've always met in the public
bar rather than the lounge bar… and Dylan was exactly the same.
Dylan never went in a lounge bar.

This is all wrong about Dylan, completely wrong. I've got into some
fearful arguments about it… I usually went out for a couple of drinks in
the evening and I never heard anything about Dylan being a drunkard
or anything of that nature – and in a small community, whether you meet
the person or not, the gossip goes around. But that was never said of
Dylan. If you said it about Caitlin, that's a different cup of tea altogether.

… he wasn't a drunkard, but I've seen him get four or five pints, or
maybe half-a-dozen pints and just get to the merry stage. But he was
not a rumbustious type, you see. Whereas Caitlin was quite the
opposite… anything could happen. She used to go around with a feller
by the name of Howard Dark. Do you know the Commercial on the
road to Tenby? Apparently they called there one night and it was a little
pub cum farm. They went in there about nine o'clock, Howard and
her, and called a couple of drinks and she brought a drink for a few of
the locals there, and apparently it come time and old Tom called time.
And people there continued drinking, so Caitlin calls another drink,
and he said "What's the matter with you woman," he said. "Haven't
you heard me call time? There's no more sales," he said. So she looks
across at the clock on the wall – one of the old-fashioned wooden
clocks – she goes across, picks it up, through the window. She said
"Now can we have another drink?" He said "No, time's gone now."
That's the type Caitlin was.

… I think in some ways that Caitlin abused him to a certain extent.
Dylan was a placid sort of man. Whereas Caitlin was the opposite.
Turbulent nature. Her temper would rise like a flash.

*But Dylan's mother told me that she admired Caitlin's attention to the
children, keeping them clean and well fed.*
Oh, she kept them well dressed and tidy and under control, there's no
question about that. They were firmly under her control.

191

Dr David and Mrs Phyllis Hughes [59]

You were the doctor for Dylan's family in Laugharne?
... he was a very shy person, and if I were to visit the family professionally it was only occasionally that I saw him... after perhaps I'd examined his wife or one of the children. He was always very polite, almost diffident, almost to the point of self-effacement, in front of the doctor. Rather typical Welsh countryman – natural respect to someone senior in age and certainly as a family doctor, he was always terribly polite... almost deferential... even when he was an established figure. He never adopted a supercilious attitude in talking to the doctor. There was always that deference and politeness. Which I valued and one couldn't help liking him. The contrast, of course, in Caitlin, who was always superbly confident and superbly extrovert in everything... I have no recollection of Dylan ever consulting me about his health.

Dylan had suffered from some complaints as a child. His mother said that he had had chest trouble since a child, and a haemorrhage in his chest...
We can come back to the result of the autopsy. Had there been an active pulmonary lesion, that certainly would have been mentioned, either TB or bronchiectasis or any of these other things. There was no mention of a major TB focus which had been healed – so that nothing emerged from the autopsy. So therefore one is driven to the opinion that he suffered no more from his chest than the average child who, in those days, might have a series of bronchial pneumonias or bronchitis, and it was much more difficult to clear up in those days, before the days of penicillin and the antibiotics, so that it is quite usual for a mother with an only son to say that "My son was delicate and I had a job to rear him" and that sort of thing. So I don't attach an awful lot of importance to that... I'm sure that there were no real physical handicaps. Physically, he was quite firm and well-built. And, I would say, quite strong, and tough; he seemed a tough little chap.

There was comment by someone I was talking to, who nursed Dylan as a child, who recounted fainting spells when he was child, and blackouts, and suggested that this had been evidence of petit mal.
It is the minor form of epilepsy. In contrast to somebody having a major epileptic attack, *petit mal* would mean perhaps several times a day, perhaps a dozen or two dozen, or more occasions, where a person would stop in the middle of an act such as talking, or writing, or reading, or feeding, and they would be quite immobile, quite vacant for

half a minute or a minute. It's classic. But I believe that if Dylan did suffer from *petit mal,* he would need pretty constant medical supervision, and in all the years that he was down in Laugharne, I would think it extremely unlikely that his wife would not have come complaining to or asking me to attend Dylan, but in fact I was never asked to attend Dylan medically. Although I believe that occasionally he did consult a doctor in London.

He was rather careless of his own health, I take it?
I think he must have been. I think he was careless about himself in every way, and I suppose he must have given the impression to Caitlin sometimes that he was careless about his responsibility to his family. He certainly took on a wife on very little money. I can remember when they came to Laugharne first. They lived in one large room in an old house called Sea View... the only furniture they had was a double bed, and large packing cases. Large boxes, soap boxes, which acted as writing desk and dining table, and I can remember the first impression I had as I entered this room, and seeing burnt down candles stuck in the neck of Guinness bottles, and the floor round the box strewn with papers, and foolscaps on the box, showing the classic picture of an impecunious writer, and I felt, rather patronisingly, that this is another ostentatious attempt at greatness, because this is the classical picture of greatness as it begins to evolve.

... I attended them a great deal, but my contribution, if you like, to his posterity was that I sent him many bills, but I was never paid and I'm rather glad that I never attempted to exhort any payment from him. He was so pathetic a figure, a struggling figure in those days that, like many others like him, had their payment by those that could afford it.

... the amount of beer that he drank regularly was moderate, because otherwise he couldn't have done so much work... the drinking of beer was regular. This produced no great harm in him – I'm sure of that – and these odd bouts of drinking of spirits was purely something quite peculiar to him when he went to London or America.

What are the other impressions of Dylan that stick with your mind?
My impression of him is of a simple, child-like, innocent bawd. There was no real wickedness in Dylan... I don't accept that he was as big a Hyde as a Jekyll. I think he was much more of a Jekyll than a Hyde.

What do you recall of Dylan, Mrs Hughes?
Most vividly is the time, or the times, when he'd ring me up, as the doctor's wife. He'd always be most charming, considerate. Before he

mentioned who was speaking on the telephone, I always recognised his voice... just cultured and charming. No affectation whatsoever, but very gracious, I always thought. Most kindly. We get people ringing up here who can be, possibly at times, rather indiscreet and rude, but he was always superbly charming, and grateful and gracious... quite truthfully I can say that. I've always said it, when people have discussed Dylan Thomas and all the rest of it, it's the one outstanding thing I can always remember... he was always so grateful – never demanding, in any sort of way. But always gracious, as I've said before.

Nellie Jenkins (née Keele)

I was a district nurse at Laugharne from 1946 until 1956... and I knew Mr Dylan Thomas very well... the first time I met him was when the baby was arriving [Colm]. She had some slight infection, and they asked me to go up to attend her... Caitlin, yes. When I went up there, she wouldn't let me in the house. So I went back and told the doctor, and he said he'd make arrangements for her to go into hospital, and into hospital she went.

... I didn't see her in the hospital, but I seen her when the baby came home. I was going there for about a week or two... I used to see to Mr Thomas every day. As a matter of fact, he always used to make me a cup of tea. Nurses were very fond of a cup of tea, you know. Oh, he was a great man, very friendly, and when he knew I was from Swansea...

... it was a very easy birth. She wasn't in five minutes. She was bathing – they were right down by the sea. Swimming. They rushed her in and off to hospital and she had the baby in no time.

... I was there for about a fortnight, I used to go every day to bath the baby. And she had beautiful clothes for the baby and everything; lovely bath, and proper nursery and everything. She had it very, very nice, nicely done up.

... well, I thought that she was a kind of an actress, that's what I thought. That's the impression that I had about her... she always used to be entertaining artists and all that sort of thing. And bohemians. I remember telling Dr Hughes, the day I was there with the little boy when he'd burnt himself: "Well, doctor, for goodness sake, take a pair of glasses with you or something, or you'll have a terrible shock," I said. "You'll think you're in with the bohemians."

... she dressed exactly like a gypsy, you know. No care of her clothes or anything... bright colours, exactly like a gypsy. And I remember in the carnival there, she went as a can-can girl... she was banned from all the dances; nobody would have her there... the Pendine establishment... they used to have this big dance, officers' dance and all that sort of thing – well, that's where she was banned from. Because she was terrible. She went in one day and she had a beautiful dress on, and her dress fell off. And all her underclothes were filthy...

16. Nellie Jenkins

... you didn't know what they were doing sometimes. They'd be shouting and bawling and carrying on, and Caitlin would have these friendly bohemians as I call them, when he was there – didn't matter what he said. She would have them there... they were her friends... artists and dancers and all that kind of thing, you know.

... the last time I went to see her... a priest came from Ireland. It is said that Dylan had a lot of beautiful poems about Our Lady – and I don't know where, I've never seen them. But it's quite possible it was true.

But he wasn't a Catholic.

He wasn't a Catholic, but he was very inclined that way... this priest came from Ireland to see him – of course, this was after he died – but he went up to see Caitlin. She was very good to him, and very hospitable, she would make you a meal, you know, awfully kind like that... very good-hearted. She made him a meal, and she told him to come to me... perhaps I would know whether there were any that I knew about. But I've never actually seen them... Father Kelly, his name was.

... that's the one thing she was good with was the old lady... Dylan's mother, yes. Caitlin was very, very, very kind she was – that's the one redeeming feature I had for her... she was wonderful with the old lady. She used to push her about in a wheelchair... it's wonderful how she was so fond of that old lady... she was very, very kind-hearted. If there was anything going on, or if you were selling anything, she'd always give to anything like that, she was very good in that way – and excellent with the old lady.

And you saw Dylan's father – he was very ill then, wasn't he?
He was very ill. I attended him. I used to go three or four times a week to give him injections… the angina, and the severe anaemia he had… it was only in the last week or two of his illness that he took to his bed. He used to be up every day. And go for little walks and that sort of thing… yes, he was a bit aloof, that's quite true. I think it's his temperament, it must have been – but they were devoted to each other, they were.

… he'd do anything for them if they wanted anything. Buy anything for them and I remember his father used to have brandy a lot, because of his condition. He'd always seen that he had that.

Did he ever have the children with him when he was working?
Yes, he did. The little boy. He took the little boy up with him, when he was working on his poems – Colm. That's the one that burnt himself… he was playing in the kitchen I suppose, and pulled out the tray from under the fire, and, of course, put his little legs in them. He was badly burnt… it was one of those grates, Aga stove…

And the tray was for the ashes.
For the ashes. And the child, I suppose, seeing them red pulled them out to play with – and nobody noticed him for a minute or two… he was about two and a half then. Well, when I seen him he was absolutely hysterical. Nobody could do anything with him – and his daddy was wonderful to the children, you know. He said to me "I rang up Dr Davies, I rang up Dr Hughes. We can't get them. Could you do something for my little boy?" So I went in and give him a sedative, and I rung up the doctor and he come up after… he had burnt his leg, and his toes. He stood in the hot ashes. But fortunately, the maid [Dolly Long] had seen him, and picked him up.

… they were well fed, yes, had the best of food and best of everything. The little girl was the one that I used to like… Aeronwy, that's it, yes. She was a dear little… she was pretty – I can see her now, with her lovely long curls.

… oh, he was devoted to his children. Because he'd do anything for me because I was looking after the little boy… he'd take them for walks and all that sort of thing. You'd always see him – if he was home, he'd always have one or two of the children with him.

… Mr Thomas [Dylan] was a real gentleman… never known him to be rude to anybody... I never seen him in a temper, never. He was always very placid. And he seemed to be devoted to his mother and father... oh, he was very humorous. Always a smile on his face, and a proper gentleman, because if I was in the butcher and he was there, even if it was his turn first, because I'd be busy, he'd let me go first. Last time I seen him before he died was in the butcher, buying a big piece of meat - they had visitors there... Gleed the butcher, I think it was the day before he went to America, or a couple of days before, and then within a week of two everything was all over... but it was wrong to make him out that he was an old drunken old devil, you know – because he wasn't.

Sometimes he went on a binge...
I never seen him... I never seen him once, not the worse for drink or anything.

Perhaps you weren't going to Brown's enough!
Perhaps that was it – I'm a teetotaller myself!

Were they obviously worried about money at any time you were there?
... I remember the chemist telling me one time that he'd run up a huge bill there. But he paid everything back, mind... yes, yes – he paid everything. Oh, he had a very good name like that, that if he owed anything, he'd get the money and pay them back.

Sally Brace

I was with Mrs Thomas [Florence] for five years... I was with her the last time he went to America, and I can remember him very well telling me "Sally, I'm off to America. I hope you'll look after my mother until I come back." In which case he didn't come back alive.

... I thought she was a perfect lady, very kind in every way... I'd go up in the morning at nine o'clock, I'd come home at two, and I'd go back up in the night about eight o'clock to give them supper. Of course, Mr Thomas was alive then as well... he was ill all the time. I'd give him his egg and milk, and brandy in it, every night. Come home, lock the door, until I went up the next morning. Lock them in... got the key. For safety.

What do you recall of D.J. Thomas?
Very ill health, all the time. And couldn't get about very well. Very seldom went out... never complained, but to me he always seemed very weak. Struggling to get about... he was very affectionate.

Towards his wife?
Yes. He used to speak to me like he'd speak to Mrs Thomas. 'Sally' – never called me Mrs Brace. Used to treat me like one of their own.

Dylan used to drop in a good deal to see his parents?
Oh yeah, every morning, when he was home, he would go in in the morning, and sometimes in the evening he'd come in... he used to write a lot in The Pelican, you know. I've seen him coming in in the morning now at ten o'clock and stay nearly ten o'clock in the night writing. In the sitting room... all on his own.

What was Dylan's health like in those days?
I wouldn't think there was anything at all wrong with him. Quite a healthy man, I'd say.

Even towards the end? The last visit?
Oh yes... wouldn't think there was anything at all wrong with him.

The popular image of Dylan is a fellow who was drinking constantly.
Well, that's what I don't agree, when they say that Dylan was a drunkard! I get really wild when they say that... I think everybody in Laugharne would say the same – he was not a drunkard.

Aeronwy Thomas

I was born in 1943, March 3, in St Mary Abbot's Hospital – it was during the War and my father had a job in the Ministry of Information. I was the only child with them because poor Llewelyn stayed with my Aunt Brigit and with his Granny Macnamara, down in Hampshire. Because of the bombs. But I think my mother didn't bother with me. Apparently, they had a studio with a glass roof in Manresa Road and years later she told me that she and my father used to go out drinking and meeting friends at night, and they'd leave me without a babysitter under this glass roof, during air raids. Extraordinary, isn't it?

I went to the village school in Laugharne... and I enjoyed the very personal attention you got there. Of course, the classes were no more than eight and it was run by a couple of spinsters. And they were very proprietary, and this sort of treatment I've always responded to very well. A little bit of personal dedication.

... then at one stage my mother tried to take me to Carmarthen – I think I was getting rather old for primary school – she sent me to Carmarthen, which was fourteen miles away, and I had to go there by bus, and I always got very bus sick, every day. And I didn't like the

17. Aeronwy, Flo and Colm

informal atmosphere there, I wasn't doing very well. So my mother
sent me to the Arts Educational School [Hertfordshire], because she
felt that I should be given the chance that she wasn't given. My mother
only had a year's formal schooling, and what she'd really wanted to do
was become a famous dancer. In fact, when my mother married my
father – or this is what she says now – she felt that he took her away
from a promising career, as a dancer. She was dancing at the Palladium
at the time, and she'd gone to Paris to dance for Isadora Duncan as one
of her lead dancers... she wasn't really tall enough for a Bluebell Girl,
but she certainly was a good dancer. But even then, I think before she
knew my father, she had a drinking problem. Because her father,
Francis, had drunk himself to death. Well, hadn't by that time, but was
an alcoholic... and my mother obviously had contracted some of the
drinking habits. It's no good saying that my father made my mother
drink, because I don't think that was true.

At what stage did you go for ballet training?
I went when I was ten. That was the year my father died, in fact... it
was a boarding school.

Your mother encouraged you in this, because of her dancing?
Yes, it wasn't my idea at all. Luckily they had an acting department as
well, which I was much better at. I couldn't co-ordinate my movements

at all, so they just let me concentrate on acting side. I enjoyed that, very much.

And your father more or less didn't resist the plan to send you to ballet school, or acting school?
I think it's rather sad that he didn't – but he didn't. Because then there was more fees to find, and he had a lot of debts anyway. My mother wasn't very good on helping him pay his debts off. She had grand ideas about what she wanted for the children, and there was nothing to deter her. Nothing, no reasonable argument

What is your earliest memory of your father? Is there something that stands out in your mind?
Not an early memory – no, nothing special. He just was a figure that was present in the family... I tended to see him around in the morning. He would sit over the Aga in the kitchen, as the warmest place, and he would toast his feet and always – I think he must have had some sugar deficiency – always had boiled sweets. He was always eating those, and reading letters and writing letters, he'd do that in the kitchen – not so much writing as reading – and he'd read a lot of thrillers, he liked, enjoyed those. Relaxing reading.

You mentioned his love of sweets. I have a particular theory that he may have had hypoglycaemia.
I think the hypoglycaemia we've all inherited.

In the morning, would he come into your bedroom and play with you?
Oh no, no, not at all. My father was not that kind of father at all.

Was rather formal then, was he?
No, he just would talk to our minds, not participate in our physical needs, as far as I can remember, just never helped me do up a shoelace or, nothing physical. He left that part completely to my mother. And if I wanted or needed something practical done, I was always told to go to my mother. But he would, on the other hand, read me stories and buy me books and talk to me about that sort of thing.

Did you read his own poems and stories?
He did quote bits of *Under Milk Wood* all over the house, and he was discouraged from doing this. My mother wasn't very encouraging. She always thought – she says now – that he was a great poet but she didn't like him bringing it home.

... he was fairly amenable to being interrupted in the morning – that wasn't so bad – he'd go off to Brown's Hotel late morning. He'd cross the road and go with his father and do *The Times* crossword puzzle. Yes, at The Pelican, and then he would cross the road and they'd both have their Guinnesses and all this tepid beer they used to consume... and then my father would come home to have his lunch, which was normally a fry-up. My mother's not famous for her cooking, and she really only knew two dishes – tripe and Irish stew. And tended to leave them go on for ever, these things, till they turned green.

... then my mother would boot him out and insist he went and did some work. He usually had things that he had to get ready be a certain time. And he would go to his shed and he would have to stay there until six. On occasion my mother would lock the door so that he didn't get out. But nobody could be sure that he was actually working... I can remember my father always huffing and puffing up the steep path to the cliff walk. Physically, he was a bit like a turtle who'd been stranded.

Six o'clock, he'd come down. And that was time for dinner, was it?
No, he'd go to the pub at six... as children, we were put to bed early... they went as soon as the pub was open. He would start off at about six, and my mother would join him, say, at seven... my mother would go and tuck us down, and leave us – again without a babysitter. We were always left in this house, all on our own, and it's quarter of an hour's walk from the village.

But how did he manage without a meal in the evening? Just that main fried lunch?
I don't know, maybe he went across to his mother? I can remember them coming home and cooking up the odd bit. But, you know, drinkers aren't that bothered about food.

You don't have any memories of your father reciting over your cradle, or over your bed, when you were a child?
Well, he was very fond of the macabre and of the dramatic... he used to read Grimm's Fairytales to me... but I don't remember him reading Dickens or anything.

No poetry?
We used to get the humorous poetry, the Faber collections, and *Possum's Cats*... he would bring marvellous books back from America. Of course, he died when I was ten. So that doesn't give much time, does it, and during those last ten years he was predominantly visiting America. I can remember quite long absences. And always the anticipation of my father's return. I was more aware of my mother's moods and things.

I don't suppose that you recall him talking about any particular works in progress, except you made a reference to Under Milk Wood.

He was always trying out different characters with my mother. We'd be sitting in the kitchen or something and he'd come down and "try a new one". And she would chuck him out if she remembered. She tended to ignore a lot of it, but then she'd get annoyed. She didn't give any obvious support but she did take the accepted the role of being Mother Earth and she said that she had five children... the treasure was Dolly Long [the Thomases' maid]. She had her son, you see. And then there were three of us made four, and then my father was the fifth... my mother considered my father as another child – she treated him as such. She would wash his ears and when he was in the bath, she'd make quite sure he'd washed properly and would wash his hair and then oil it, with olive oil. And cut his nails. Do everything for him... I can remember there was quite a lot of washing and all sort of things to keep him clean and tidy, but once he went up to London, she had no control.

What about his health?

He just looked more and more bloated. It's an unkind thing to say, but that was the impression that I as a child got. Even as a child I noticed that much. And you know how self-centred children are. Ferociously so. But I did notice this bloating...

... one thing I do remember about him is, when you got his attention – after all, he didn't give a lot of his time to us – you'd always felt flattered because he would give you his full attention. He was not somebody who would be thinking of something else when he was talking to you. Or at least he gave that feeling, that you had a special relationship with him. The trouble is, I think everyone's had that feeling. So I don't know in fact whether I did have a special relationship with my father, because I've heard other people say that they did... he was very generous with his faculties, if you like! When you finally got his attention. I used to resent very much people visiting us, because he would then ignore us.

And you had many visitors.

We did – and it got worse. Before he died, there seemed to be troops of Americans coming and staying – not staying actually with us, but coming and gawking, and treating us as if we were rather weird.

Robert Lowell [60]

I met Dylan on his first trip to America in the winter of 1950, and I was teaching at Iowa University, and that was one of his stations on the tour. He came on the train and he arrived from Chicago, and I was looking out for him and suddenly someone bumped into me and said "Lowell, aren't you?" And it was Thomas. And you almost immediately got the impression that remained with you that he looked like nothing at all really, just a little man with a deep voice. And then soon the whole room was listening to him. And the first reading was, as I imagine many others were, rather trying. He'd come from Chicago with some businessman and they'd had a bottle of bourbon on the way, and it looked as though he wouldn't read. And it was rather a genteel English department and they were terrified that this thing they'd prepared for would never come off. And it really seemed as though he wouldn't read. And then he read and everything vanished and he was in the groove. He knew when he had an audience captivated. He played a dirty trick on me. I introduced him and he said "I won't answer any questions." So I said Thomas doesn't want to answer any questions. And then he got up and said "Lowell's trying to muzzle me." And the performance was incredible.

Then afterward, the students gathered around and you had a whole room just listening to his asides, some of them obscene, some rather magical. And I think this gets into the poetry; that he gave a great feeling of health and unhealth, of someone who was ruining himself. His teeth were gone and couldn't eat breakfast, who had awful hangover pains and talked about pain and joy and of health. A marvellous captivating energy. The Brinnin book gives too sombre a picture, though it's perfectly true, I think. It leaves out all the marvellous dialogue that was coming out of him. So it never occurred to one that he was burning himself to pieces.

Tell us a little bit about the themes that run through Dylan's work.
Thomas' themes seem to boil down to very few. One is a sort of love and death or rather an energy that kills, an energy that creates, and those seem closely related. And I remember when I talked to him, he spoke of the incredible joy of life. But then at some other point in the conversation he was talking about the darkness, and he wasn't feeling too well that day. But the joy seemed very real and the darkness seemed very real and neither of them seemed to exist without the other. And

sex is very close to that. Sex, too, is a sort of energy that destroys and creates. And then he always reminds me a great deal of Hart Crane, although the two poets are not alike. That they both wrote very dense, almost unintelligible poetry, perhaps heavily sexual. And then they were both marvellous on very simple poems about childhood, recovery of that almost unearthly time of innocence – innocent in reflection maybe more than in actuality. And I might almost say these were his only themes... there's something else, though that's not exactly a theme but it's very important, that you feel he's a Welsh bard speaking for nature, and often he has that power. As though the trees and the water and the rocks and the people all entered his voice. the birds particularly.

Did he talk about his own poetry?
One might have expected Thomas to have been egocentric and full of himself and unable to take in new experiences... but that wasn't true. That he read a great deal, and his readings were almost entirely other poets, not himself, was a great innovation in America, and a good one, though no one else had been able to carry it off.

Ruth Witt Diamant

The way I contacted Dylan was interesting in itself. Brinnin set him up here in the Palace Hotel [San Francisco, 1950]. Can you imagine Dylan in the Palace Hotel? He came in, he looked at that place, with all the red velvet everywhere, shook his head, left his baggage and left. And never went back... three days later he was found in a bar on Columbus Avenue – The Pup. Some North Beach boys wandered in there, and I got a telephone call saying "Ruth, Dylan Thomas is in town. Do you know him?" I said "I know who he is, by God." And they said "He's got a note in his pocket addressed to you. So I said "Well, read it to me." And it asked me to put him up – and you know, I never have known who wrote that note... I said "Well, bring him out." And they said "Well we can't, we have no car." So I came down in my car and they poured him in... he was absolutely out.

... the people at the bar said he'd been there for three days... he slept there. He ate there... if he ate at all. He was drinking – I think he was only drinking beer. Because when he was alone he never drank anything except beer.

... he was unconscious, it's true, but he came to, and he was very sweet – very sweet indeed. And especially when he felt that nobody was trying to 'make up to his greatness'. Because a lot of people felt impelled to blow themselves up in order to be worthy of him. That kind of thing – he scented that right away, whenever, wherever it occurred, and boy, he slapped it down.

Had he kept an engagement at Berkeley before?
No. He was slated to appear in Berkeley the next day... he was due to appear at CAL, and I took him to CAL and also assured him I could get him engagements all round here. Because there were things that Brinnin didn't know anything about. Small colleges and whatnot.

... the Berkeley thing was in the evening. And that was an amusing affair, because we were assigned a room where there were three hundred seats, and there was another Englishman here, a physicist I guess, who was giving a lecture in the great auditorium – Wheeler Hall – which holds about three thousand, and there were about a dozen people in that Hall, and Dylan's was just overflowing. And so I asked whether somebody could go and find out if we could change places with the physicist, and it took some doing, but they finally managed that, and we came in. After all the seats in Wheeler Hall were filled, there were still people standing along the walls and in the back, and where anybody could stand, and Dylan's first statement was "This is not Henry Miller with demonstrations." And from that minute onward, he had them in his hand... he read some Hardy... maybe MacNeice... he read the birthday poem, 'Thirtieth Year'...

And you could have heard a pin drop it was so, so intense – really. Anyway, it just was a wonderful reading – it was really inspired. And Jimmy Caldwell tried to make a date with him for entertainment, and he didn't want to be entertained that night. So it was a little difficult... he didn't much care for these after-reading parties.

So you brought him back here afterwards?
Yes. He came back in a state – stayed for several days, as long as he was on the west coast, and he went down to Los Angeles, and I told him how to get hold of Isherwood down there.

... when he arrived Isherwood met him at the Biltmore Hotel. Isherwood said "Dylan, this is Hollywood – you can have anything you want, anything you want." And so Dylan said "I'd like to meet Shelley Winters." And almost immediately after he had said "And I would like to meet Charlie Chaplin." And Chaplin said "I'll send a limousine for you." And he sent his limousine from way out Beverley Hills down to the Biltmore Hotel, which is right in the middle of downtown. And they picked him up and drove him out, and Charlie met him with a flourish, a dance, and they both were immediately delighted with each other. And when they went into dinner, guess who was his dinner partner? Shelley Winters. I think that was so charming of Isherwood to have done that. That was a lovely thing – he enjoyed Charlie Chaplin tremendously. And Shelley Winters, after all, is a highly sensitive and social conscious person, and was just the right kind of person to meet Dylan... [he] already knew about her work among the under-privileged, shall we call them, and was very much impressed by that.

What did he do in those extra days he had here, before he left?
Well, a lot people were in town that wanted to see him, who were important. For instance, Kenneth Rexroth and Kenneth Patchen.

Did he meet Rexroth?
Oh yes, he met Rexroth. He liked Rexroth. I don't know how much of a poet he thought he was, but he rather liked him, because Rexroth played up to him. But there was a curious feeling that Rexroth had about him, as though he was over-praised.

Who did Dylan become close to here?
Gavin Arthur.

What was the basis of their closeness? He wasn't a poet, was he?
I think their oddity. Gavin attracted people who were interested in human beings, and he was very warm, and odd human being.

I was never quite clear as to his occupation.
Well, I don't know that he had any. He had various small jobs at various times. He was once a teacher at San Quentin, in the prison. He used to seek out that kind of job. He was an astrologer, and many people sought him to do their horoscopes – their life horoscopes, not daily ones... at one point he was the newsboy with a news stand in the financial district.

He was the grandson of a president, wasn't he?
Grandson of Chester Arthur.

And Dylan would spend a lot of time with Gavin Arthur?
Quite a bit of time... probably more on his second visit than the first one. I don't remember that Dylan mixed much locally in the first visit at all. They kept him busy... The first time he was busy all the time. I mean, Brinnin had sewed up his time with engagements all over the map... we went down to the Big Sur.

Oh, that's right, to Henry Miller!
We didn't really go to Henry Miller, we just went down to the Big Sur.

I took him down to Carmel.

... I came down to Monterey to have lunch with [Noel Sullivan] who supported many of the artists in San Francisco... Sullivan had a model ranch. Everything was model – his sheep were the best possible and his horses were the best possible, and he had nine dogs – dachshunds, beautiful dachshunds... he was a remarkable man and a prince of the Catholic Church, his family brought the Carmelite nuns to California. Set up the first Carmelite nunnery in California. Well, anyway, we came down there for lunch and I think we had brought with us Gavin Arthur and Noel was so delighted that he asked me "Do you think you could bring them back for dinner tonight?"

Dylan?

Yes, with Dylan. He would have a few of the important people in Carmel down for dinner. To meet him. And I said, "Well, ask him – why don't you just ask him?" Which he did, and Dylan said of course he'd be delighted.

So we were going down to the Big Sur, which had a beautiful hot spring down there, and where you could bathe without any walls and just be in the presence of the Pacific Ocean, pounding its way miles below, it seemed, probably two hundred feet below, and that was a delightful experience to have, and I knew Dylan would enjoy it.

Well, on the way down to the Big Sur and the hot spring was Henry Miller's house. And I thought on the way down, it's early (I guess we left Noel's about half-past two or somewhere like that in the afternoon) so I knew there would be time. Henry Miller's place was on a very high hill, a ridge of a very high hill, so I decided to drive up that hill and take Dylan to see Miller.

... Miller was married at that time to a younger, very much younger, woman named Lepska. Apparently, he had given Lepska orders not to wake him when he was sleeping in the afternoons... anyway, we got there and Lepska came out of the house to meet us on the hill right behind their house, and asked us what we wanted, and I said "I'd like to see Mr Miller. This is Dylan Thomas, and he knows Henry Miller and Henry Miller would be very glad, I'm sure, to see him." She said "I can't wake him." And I said, "Well, this is not just some ordinary visit from somebody from San Francisco, this is someone who's come from abroad who I'm sure would be more than welcome to Henry Miller." But she wouldn't wake him. So I stood there for a few minutes wondering what the devil to do. I said "How long will he be asleep?" and she said "I don't know." And that was a puzzle – what would you do? Finally Dylan said "Oh well, let's go."

So I said "I really don't think we should go. I think Henry Miller would blame me if you didn't see him." And either the fuss we were making or maybe Lepska made some kind of a fuss and raised her voice – anyway, Henry suddenly called out "Who's there?" And I said "It's Dylan Thomas, Henry." And so he came out. And then he scolded her dreadfully for having kept Dylan waiting. And so that was all right, and they had a very nice visit. Then we went down to the Big Sur – we asked Henry if he wanted to come to the baths, and Henry said no, he was going later in the week. Anyway, there was a charged atmosphere after that, because I knew that as soon as we departed, Henry was really going to sail into that woman.[61]

So we left and went down to the baths, and the baths were incredible, really incredible... it was just marvellous. There was a wall between the men's and the women's sides, but that was all...

... we had promised to be back by six o'clock to meet Noel Sullivan's guests, who were coming up to see Dylan and I finally made them realise that they had an obligation.

How long had they been in the water then?

Oh, about two hours... I finally got them out and we got dressed, and I think they were lying on the tables on the other side, as I was, in the sun. Stark naked, and just having a heavenly time. Well, we'd gotten back on the road finally – it was not easy – and they began to call me 'Miss Let's Go'. That's because I kept saying "Let's go!" Anyway, we got on the road back, to go back to the Sullivan ranch, and halfway down there I realised it was going to be a dinner party with some formality, because people in Carmel were conventional more or less – not as conventional in the usual sense, that is, they wouldn't put on great banquet or anything stupid like that – but they would all probably be properly dressed. And so I said "I don't know what you two are going to do, because I'm sure that at least you should have a necktie on. I thought we would go into Carmel and buy neckties before we went to the ranch. Then we got very close to the ranch, and I repeated this business about going into Carmel first, and Dylan said "I don't think we'll need to." And he reached into his pocket and pulled out a very rumpled necktie. In as short a time as it takes for me to tell this to you, he ripped it in half, they each made a bow tie of it and stuck it on! It was a delightful thing to see! When we got there – we were late of course – there were quite a number of people there, among them Robinson Jeffers, the poet of Carmel.

... and Jeffers had a kind of curious grin on his face, and he greeted Dylan. It was very clear in a very few minutes that he [Jeffers] was somewhat under the influence of liquor, and he'd been drinking quite a bit apparently, waiting for us. And he and Dylan shook hands and it wasn't more than five minutes after Dylan had been introduced all round before either he or Dylan suggested that they go for a walk in the garden. And so off they went, and I thought that was very sensible thing for them to do, because Dylan wasn't in any mood – if there was a poet there and one that he respected – to engage in the small talk of a dinner party, with people he did not know. And I guess about half an hour later, dinner was just about announced, and they came back in, and one of Jeffers' sons was there to take him home, because I guess Noel himself telephoned to their house and asked one of the boys to come for him, because he was not going to be a guest at that dinner party, wouldn't have been able to talk to anybody other than Dylan. I asked Dylan afterwards if he and Robinson Jeffers had hit it off, and he said "We understood each other perfectly, we were absolutely in accord." And I said "Well, what did you have to say to him?" "We never spoke a word to each other. Not one single word. But we understood each other. Right away," he said. "It was a lovely walk in the garden together."

So you had a big dinner, and then people sat around talking, did they?
Yes. They were very glad to sit around talking, and they would have loved Dylan to burst into poetry at some point, but he wasn't about to do that.

... there was the time when I had to call Jimmy Caldwell of San Francisco, who was the host of Dylan's readings in Berkeley, who was also a poet. And there was actually a party scheduled for that night in Berkeley. A lot of people wanted to meet Dylan and James Caldwell, who was on the Faculty of the English Department in Berkeley, had invited him for a party... Dylan said he was not going to go to Berkeley, he refused to go to a party where there were a lot of people he didn't know. He was asked to do that so much, and, of course, he was obligated to Jim Caldwell, because they were very generous with readings for him... [Dylan] said "Ruth, can't we get this guy on the telephone and tell him that I'm just not up to it, I'm sick." Well, I called Caldwell and said "It's seven o'clock now, and if you're having a group meet at eight o'clock for a reading by Dylan, we're never going to make it. We can't possibly make it." And he said "But if Mr" – very petulant he was, about this – "If Mr Thomas can't make his engagements, we'll have to make other arrangements." And I said "He'll make his reading engagements" – he never missed one of those. And he asked me if he'd been drinking and I said "No, not excessively, no. It's just too much for him, he's being asked to do too much of this kind of thing. "Oh," he said, "but I have a whole host of people coming…"

This was a gathering before the readings?
Yes, before the readings. And Dylan was not up to just meeting a lot of strange people that he didn't know, and trying to be the social lion. And Dylan, I think, would have so much preferred not to be there, if he could have done otherwise. But people expected it of him and almost forced him into that role.

Usually these were after his performances, weren't they – but this one was before?
Yes, because I guess the Caldwell was trying to provide a plum for all the people in Berkeley who might want to…

Did Dylan go to the party?
No. He never did get there. And Caldwell never forgave him for that.

So April 3 1952 he was here with Caitlin. Was there a marked difference in the attendance, between the first appearance at San Francisco State and the second?
It was a different kind, he was already known by that time. He was known all over Mill Valley, all over Marin County, because we used to go to the Two AM Bar in Marin County. And there he could be alone, could be shooting pool or whatever he wanted to do with that. He loved to play those machines and could drink quietly and not be surrounded as he was in every San Francisco place where he could be found. You know, he hadn't been in my house twenty-four hours before he found the only Irish bar within I don't know how many miles around here and that's where he used to drop in every time he was here.

… I brought Dylan for a dinner party… and when we were approaching Carmel, Caitlin was very apprehensive of meeting a lot of people she didn't know. Within ten minutes of the place… Caitlin said "I'm hungry and I want to eat now." I said "Caitlin, there are fifteen or twenty people waiting for us at Marie Short's house for dinner and we're probably late already and I don't think we ought to stop." And then Dylan, in his perverse way, said "If she's hungry now, let's eat now." So it seemed to me I was torn between my role as a hostess – these are my guests – and my obligation to the person to whom we had given an acceptance for a dinner party. Well, anyway, my guests were right round my neck, so there was nothing I could do, but we stopped in a restaurant in Monterey, which is quite close to Carmel. And what did Caitlin order but a dish of spaghetti and a bottle of wine, to get ready for a dinner party! And I said "Thank you, I'm just going to have my dinner and I don't want anything." But I had to have some wine, of course. And so we all sat there... drinking the wine, and Caitlin and Dylan were eating the spaghetti!

... we had this lovely dinner, and after dinner... Caitlin spoke up and said

18. Dylan and Caitlin in America, 1952

"And now we'll have some fucking poetry." So the game had started! I can't tell you how many of those things I went through, but anyway – I'm not writing that down for anybody. So he gave her back an insult, which had to do with her "pea-brain", her pea-sized brain, or something. And she stormed out of there... so he threw something at her, and stormed after her, and they never came back... it was a terrible situation for me.

... anyway, it was very disagreeable and very difficult. Because all those people were mature adults, who were interested in writing... I wondered how they would confront the crowd the next morning, because Marie had arranged for a picnic for all of us for the next morning. And people began to assemble about half past ten or eleven... and Dylan and Caitlin came out of their room like two lovebirds, like nothing you ever saw. Whatever had happened the night before was 'gone with the wind'. They were perfectly happy together. And I had enough of those experiences to know that their quarrels were a kind of backhanded love quarrels, but I would have a suspicion

– and I don't want this to be recorded – that they didn't make love unless they first had some violence.

Do you remember anything of his contacts here with Ferlinghetti?
Not particularly. I remember his contact with Kenneth Patchen... he called and wondered if they could come to dinner. And Dylan said that he would like to meet Patchen. So Patchen lived in North Beach... Caitlin was shopping that day and... Dylan went off to a bar by himself. Dylan found an Irish bar... I thought to myself, if there's any kind of a suggestion that this might be something which he could enjoy, he would immediately try it out to see... I described very precisely to him how to get to Patchen's, which was about three blocks away from that bar... Caitlin had come back from the shopping and had gone to the bar, where she knew Dylan was.

... Dylan called on the telephone at Patchen's and asked for me, and he said he couldn't find the place and he was gonna just stay at the bar... so Patchen said "Tell him to wait there; I'll come and get him." Patchen was not very mobile. He had a very bad back. But anyway, he went down... and in about ten minutes they came to where the dinner party was, where Patchen lived. And Dylan said he wanted to go to the toilet or something, because he didn't want to go into that room with about eight people, and I couldn't blame him... and so he and Patchen disappeared in a back room. And Caitlin and I went into the living room where all these people were, and Caitlin said "Where's the liquor?" So Miriam Patcham, who had hoped against hope that she wouldn't have to start with the liquor this early, before dinner but she did, and she brought it in, and Caitlin then began to drink, and meanwhile Dylan did not come out of the back room with Patchen, and they were there and they were there and, you know, you're in a room with say, six or eight people that you don't know, and you're there for a particular purpose, for an introduction of Dylan to these people, who were the guests of Miriam Patchen. And Miriam came in, tried to make some small talk, but Caitlin was not one to tolerate small talk.

And pretty soon Dylan came out of the back room and wanted to use the phone. He began to call a taxi. So I said "Dylan, you won't need a taxi; wherever you want to go, the car is downstairs; I'll drive you. But," I said, "we haven't had dinner." He said he couldn't because he'd had too much to drink... I looked at Miriam Patchen, but they had nothing to do, and they were not going to stay whatever happened, in that front room... I think he just didn't want to meet those strange people that he didn't know, and nothing to talk about.

Did Patchen come out of that back room?

Yes, Patchen came out, also disturbed – he didn't know what Dylan was trying to do. Dylan obviously didn't want to stay for the dinner party. And didn't. We all went home, to my house – because there was always plenty to eat in my house.

... I had a sabbatical in 1953 and went to Europe... it started in January, and I think I went to Paris first... then London – then I went to Wales... I stopped off at Fortnum & Masons and sent a huge package of food – everything was rationed at the time. Everything. I could buy anything I wanted at Fortnum & Masons, as a foreigner... I really supplied them with liquor, and meat, especially meat, and I remember sending a ham and a great baron of beef. And candy for the kids.

You stayed in the Boat House?

I already knew Caitlin, but I hadn't met the children. Llewelyn was at school, so I just met Colm and Aeron. And it was funny – Colm came into my room the next morning, and he had a book under his arm, and he looked at me for a full five minutes. Do you know how long five minutes is? When nothing is going on. And finally he said "You can read to me." He had been judging me whether, whether I was vulnerable! And then he came in to my bed, and we became friends.

Did you meet Dylan's mother and father?

His father was dead by then. But I met his mother. And the first thing she asked me – are you church or chapel? I don't think she was asking to be inquisitive; she wanted to know which group of people she could introduce me to. Or whom she should ask to come.

... she was warm and very anxious about Dylan and very proud of him and asked me about his success in America. And I remember talking to her about his success, and the adoration he was exciting in everybody. She was very proud of that, and very pleased. And she did take me to a group of women meeting – a tea, I guess it was – but they were disappointed that I wasn't chapel.

What impression, did you have of the relationship between Caitlin and Dylan?

I think they were devoted to each other, and dependent on each other. Perhaps dependent is the best word. They were dependent on each other for what for them was a normal orientation. I think they would both have been diminished without each other.

... I promised I would meet them at the Eisteddfod in Llangollen...

he was for doing that thing for the BBC... he never went near the tent where you saw the Eisteddfod. But you see the people who were performing outside the tent... they come out on the street and do it, too, and then in the next street. And Dylan was at a bar and he knew they were gong to be coming by that way, so we saw them all from the stool of a bar... we were staying in a wonderful thing called the Grapes Hotel. I stayed there, too... we met at the tent – that is, Caitlin and I did. But what happened was that Dylan would come, maybe just deliver them there, and go off on his own, with the newspaper men – there were a lot of newspaper men there – and they all stayed at the Grapes Hotel, and got drunk every night.

What did you think of his sense of humour?
Oh my God, it was ribald, it was marvellous. It was really marvellous. The kinds of things that delighted him had to do with language, really. Especially in the way of his telling the stories. Whether they were bawdy or not, they had a way of evoking the personality of the person in the joke. It was extraordinary; because it just rolled right out to life... he had wonderful way of timing in those stories... I think his best moments, all the way through, wherever he went, were when he was dealing in language, whether he was telling a story or whether he was reading, or whether he was just using that peculiar sort of phraseology that really put everything together so neatly.

Do you think he had a sense of intellectual inferiority when he was with intellectuals?
I don't think that he knew so much that they were intellectuals, but he was afraid they might be. And he didn't like them; he didn't like to be around them. Because he didn't like that kind of literary criticism. They may not have voiced it, but he felt what they would have expressed if they'd dared to... he was apprehensive about that kind of criticism. And anybody that was pretentious in language, he would be very rude to.

I remember an innocent student coming up to him one day and saying "Mr Thomas, could I talk to you a little bit abut some of the problems in poetry?" Dylan said "Problems, in poetry? I don't know of any problems in poetry." And he moved away from the kid. I thought that was hard on the kid.

... that's the kind of the thing he did. I think that evening meeting with the special upper-class society crowd that was at [Marie Short's]... he was apprehensive about going there, the day that Caitlin also said that she wanted spaghetti half an hour before dinner. He understood what she was going through, meeting a roomful of absolute strangers and having to act out some role that she didn't feel stimulated at that moment to perform, and that can be frightening where you're in a social situation where you're expected to come through, to perform...

... he didn't mind the situations after the readings when a whole lot of crazy students were around him, eyes and mouth open and all agog to listen to every jewel that came out of his mouth. I think that amused him no end, and delighted him, too. He didn't mind the silly questions they were asking, but he didn't like to be confronted by intellectuals, and not only that but he was *afraid* of it. Now you might ask yourself what he was afraid of. And I think he felt his lack of that standard education which they all have... I think in some way he felt a little guilty about the fact that he didn't know all that information which they had – even the students. And their information about poetics, I think bored the hell out of him.

What about his attitude to women?
... if he'd felt there were pretensions there, assumptions of either their own or his superiority, he would squelch that without any mercy. And I have seen him being very rude by making some half-comic remark which just brought 'em down flat.

There's all these accounts of him making obscene suggestions to women.
He didn't always do that, and I think he did it to women who obviously needed to have it said.

Women rather threw themselves at him, didn't they?
I don't know whether they really did or not. I'm sure it was exaggerated, and he exaggerated in his discussions, because he wouldn't have had the energy, let alone the time.

What did he drink mostly, when he was here? Was it beer most of the time?
He did here, in this house, he did. He once said somewhere that "fruit juices bred in Ruth Witt Diamant's icebox overnight." Because I always had cans of beer, of orange juice and fruit juices that I thought would bring him back to life.

What was his opinion of Brinnin?
Brinnin came to Laugharne and saw Mrs Thomas, and she thought he was in love with her son, but she didn't mean what that means to us. She didn't know it, and I'm sure she never heard of that! But she was horrified at his book. Her comment to me was "I thought he loved my

son". I was so horrified at that book – were you, did you like that book?

I looked at it and I thought this chap is trying to as honest as he can, but he only saw Dylan at a bad stage of his life.

Well, he also saw Dylan as a possible lover. I'm sure it never erupted into that, and he couldn't take the rejection. I don't think he meant that to come out in that book... it's on every page.

... I think that Dylan felt that Brinnin gave him money grudgingly, just to control him. In other words, that he was trying to manipulate Dylan. And I'm sure if Dylan had, shall we say, serviced him in some way he would have come through with some money of his own.

Where did Dylan meet Pearl Kazin? It's obvious she was completely in love with him.

Oh yes. But I really think there were other people who were, too. But being in love with Dylan and having a night with him here and there is one thing; living with Dylan the way Caitlin had to is an entirely different song and dance.

... in all the troubles that they had, money troubles and so on, Dylan never asked me for a nickel. Never did. And, of course, he could have had anything he wanted in the house, and anything that I had he could have had, but he never did, he never exploited that situation. I loved him, because there was no pretension around, there was no effort to put on a show, he was the sweetest, the most unprotected – and you know how I mean unprotected? He was the most vulnerable person. He was just a dear human being.

Oscar Williams

During the four times that Dylan was in the United States I think I saw him at least twenty-five times, and a great deal of him... I had corresponded with Dylan for ten years before I first met him in 1950... he was ailing in a certain way, although most of the time he was really an extraordinarily healthy person. He rarely ate and never slept, and oddly enough, my opinion is, he never really drank the way we understand it in America. He was not a drunkard. He drank beer, and drank it very slowly, and he drank it only to keep the conversation going. As long there was conversation there was beer, and as long as there was beer there was conversation.

I think he gave people a tremendous sense of existence, and joy in existence. And the reason so many people loved him is that he recognised,

I believe, their human condition as such. It didn't make any difference to him whether a man was rich or poor or could get his poems published or not, or even could get him a drink. These were mundane considerations that never entered Dylan's head. He loved human beings... it's one of the reasons why he became such a fabulous figure. Because whenever he met anybody at all, they loved him for the love that he gave them. And essentially, as you know, the best thing you can ever do for another man is to give him a sense of life. That is the greatest gift of all, and that's what he brought to the people that he was with.

... we talked about life, generally... what he was discussing most of the time was his relationships with life and with people and his childhood. Stories about his childhood, or strange stories that he'd heard that were of great interest. But he was also a great listener. If you could tell a proper story, he would really go for it.

What about Dylan's general topics of conversation? You said he talked a good deal about life.

He always talked about life – that is, his own life or the life of things that he'd read, or had heard, and things that were interesting. He acted as though he was there to entertain the world. And he did it with great force and with great imagination. And a great deal of humour. One day I discussed with him science fiction, and I said "Men think almost incredible things in these science fiction stories." And he said "Yes. Anything that any man thinks is possible. Whatever man can think of, is possible. As a reality. If you think of it at all, it's possible as a reality." And I thought that was a fantastic idea.

... he loved to read thrillers and science fiction and so on. I don't believe he had to write science fiction. I mean, life was marvellous, so wonderful for him in any case that he didn't need to write about other worlds. This world was enough. And *more* than interesting enough for him. But I think one of the things that ought to really be straightened out about people's ideas about Dylan is this. My opinion is that he was not a drinker. Now that seems to be counter to all the facts. He really didn't drink the way people drink in the United States – or what we associate with drinking – which is hard liquor, and you drink and you fall under the table and you are a drunkard and that kind of thing. Dylan had never gotten in that condition. And I think he didn't get into that condition because he really wasn't drinking. Now, what made people think he was a drinker was that he wasn't really eating – and the stomach probably tried to live on the beer, there is some nourishment in beer, after all. On top of that, he didn't sleep. And then, finally and

217

over and above that, he had what I would call the greatest intoxicant in the world, which is adulation. Now you take the combination of not eating and not sleeping and have the whole world adore you, and I ask you whether

19. Dylan and Oscar Williams

you think you need a glass of beer? I don't think you do – because you are already intoxicated. Each of those things is enough to give you a sensation of living out of this world.

... he was having these three wonderful intoxicants of living all the time. He would go to a party or to a bar, and he would stay and keep talking and simply wear the people out who were around him. People would be saying to him "Dylan, I have to go home. I have to go home, I have to get to bed." And he would gaily say goodbye to them. Then along would come some new people who had had their sleep, who would start all over again, but he went along with them. You know, that's telescoping an entire lifetime into a very short time... he was living not eight hours a day, he was living twenty-four hours a day. He was too busy to sleep, and almost too busy to eat. And he was involved. He was involved with the human beings he met; he was talking to them and listening, and things would set him off at all times.

... he drank beer because it was a social thing, and it went along with conversation and a good time and good fellowship and comradeship, and a sense of belonging. In a tavern, he was involved with storytelling, he was listening to other people's troubles and joys and so on, and it was a sense of living with humanity. If he tried to do it for twenty-four hours a day, who can blame him? The fact of the matter remains that Dylan did live a life three times as long as his age. All the time I saw him in the United States, he was living fast, in the sense he was crowding three lives into one... he was enjoying every bit of it. He loved human beings, and he wanted to keep going. He didn't want to give up. He felt essentially it was a waste of time to go home to bed.

People have told me in Britain that 'Americans killed Dylan'. That Americans poured whisky down his throat and that sort of thing. I saw him very rarely order a different kind of a drink than beer, but I noticed he drank it ten times as slowly, and he would tell enormous stories between sips. I didn't at all see him doing any of that kind of drinking. The people who loved him in the United States always had the milder drinks around, in any case... it would take somebody extra-ordinarily thick-skinned and stupid to ask a man to drink hard liquor if he wants a beer, especially if he's a guest. It may have happened to him, but I wasn't there.

Another part of the popular image that exists is that Dylan was something of a wencher.

That I think is another of the canards which has ballooned into shape completely out of reality. Dylan never had either the capacity nor the interest to chase women. But there were a few women who chased him... a poet is always of interest to women. In fact, fame is of great interest to either of the sexes. It's a drawing card. If a man is a great poet, is known as a great poet – or a woman for that matter – he or she are loved by sycophants who are around the place, and from that viewpoint there is no doubt that many women – and men – ran after Dylan. But he was not a Don Juan in any sense of the word, and it's all a great canard.

I think that Dylan was the soul of nobility, he was the soul of honour, and he was the soul of marvellous human relationships. He never took anything from anybody else, that anybody else might have not wanted to give away... I think that people tried to associate themselves with a poet and enlarge their reminiscences completely out of reality. They distort. People claim to be friends of Dylan who only saw him once. And will tell you stories or repeat stories they have heard from others, and there's nobody to stop them, so they just go on and on.

Did Dylan bring out anything about his political attitudes in his conversa-tions with you?

If it's political to be on the side of life, and on the side of brotherly love, I think he was political. But in no other way – no.

But did this take the form of saying something on particular issues of the day – for instance, in the United States it might be the civil rights struggle, although it wasn't really in the headlines.

There was no civil rights struggle in the headlines. The issue was dormant, but it was there.

He said "The war is all over bar the dying", which is his way of putting it. I think that was rather good. Or he said "I'm probably a Socialist – if there is a Socialist Party." Which I think was a fine provision. Of course, if there is no Socialist Party, then he isn't a Socialist.

… I think at all times he was against bureaucracy of any kind. I had heard that he'd been at some enormous party where, I think, President Eisenhower was supposed to be present, too. Also some great owner of hundreds of acres of land – thousands of acres of land – and millions of cattle, and I think Dylan got up in a great rage and said: "What, you own all that? With all these people starving? I will have nothing to do with you!" and stomped out of the room. So the story goes. But I think he was capable of that.

He was always defending the people who were down. If anybody was attacking anybody down, Dylan would always rise to defend and to champion the down-and-out fellow. He really was.

… I don't think he objected to people and their vanity. That's what made Dylan a great man – he was able to bear other people's vanities, small and big. What he really didn't like was any injustice which became apparent. Then he would really rise to quite a bit of rage. I remember that one time – this was in 1952 – and we were at some Village bar, and we were talking about a certain poem by a poet who now is dead. I had brought the poem out and shown it to Dylan. There was a Scotch poet at the table and this poet was shown the poem. And the Scotch poet simply pulled a terrific face – a sneer. And Dylan rose in a towering rage and said to him – I won't mention the name of the Scotch poet – "When you write a poem as good as this, you can afford to sneer!" And so the sneerer made his sneer even more deep, if that's possible, or wider, and then Dylan became more enraged, and gave what I call a kind of a verbal lashing, very much the equivalent of, shall we say, of whipping the money-changers out of the temple, or in this case the sneerer out of the temple of poetry. Well, it got to such a condition where this chap was sneering all the more loudly, and Dylan getting more angry. And Caitlin joined in at the time, too. We finally had to leave, and leave this dissident poet sitting there, licking his own wounds.

You mentioned Caitlin. What did you observe of their relationship, and how much this meant to Dylan in his life?
I think they loved each other very much, they really did. She loved him and he loved her, and it was, well, it was a hot time for both of them, as they say. In the old town.

They were two burning fires, weren't they?
Yes. I think she has a great deal of talent, she really has. She doesn't
have his stature for generosity, or his greatness, but she has a great deal
of talent. And he felt that she could write as well as he, and I think she
can too. I mean prose.

Oh, I must tell you about his *Adventures in the Skin Trade*. Well, one
day I was walking with Dylan and something was sticking out of his
pocket and I said "What's that?" And he said "It's a bit of junk." I said
"What are you doing with that?" And he said "I'm trying to lose it." I
said "I'll take it." I looked at it, and I discovered it was this so-called
part of a novel. So I said "Dylan, do you want me to sell this for you?"
And he said "Well, if you can, but it's junk." And I took it to Victor
Weybright – New American Library. I went up to Victor and I said
"Dylan needs money in a hurry. Could I get a few hundred dollars
right away?" And he said "Yes." And they took part of it right away and
published it. And an issue later they decided to publish all the rest of
it. And finally they put out a book.

… I recall when he sent me that poem of his – this was in 1945 – 'A
Refusal to Mourn the Death, by Fire, of a Child in London'. Dylan
sent it to me and said "Oscar, get me some money right away on it."
Well, you can't get money very fast in a magazine. You mail it, and you
wait, and it's accepted and rejected or whatnot. And I sent it to one of
the weeklies, and believe it or not the editor, who was a very well-
known editress, wrote me saying this was not as good as some of the
others she'd seen, and returned it to me. Imagine saying that about one
of the great poems of the twentieth century! Well, I sent it to the rival
magazine, *New Republic*, there was a chap there by the name of
Mayberry who immediately sent me a cheque for ten dollars. I
airmailed it back to Dylan and I wrote "I'm sorry this is so small, but
I got it fast and you may console yourself with the fact that Milton only
got ten dollars for his *Paradise Lost*, which was considerably longer
than your poem." Well, he wrote back saying "I have received the
money and it burst in a shower of drinks…" He had a terrific time.

What about Under Milk Wood?
My feeling about *Under Milk Wood* is that it is really what I would call
a plastic work. By that I mean, it wasn't really a natural work for Dylan
at all, and it was arranged by some of his friends who were egging him
on to do anything but write poetry, which I think was a mistake
because he was really *the* poet. His feeling about *Adventures in the Skin
Trade, Under Milk Wood* and all the others, including that book he did

for a film script, to him that was just sheer junk. And he was ashamed to even think of it, or even sell it or anything. I think that *Under Milk Wood* was something that a few of his more aggressive friends were sort of getting him to do, and they all joined in – a number of them claimed they were helping him write it, which I thought was a bit of extravagant arrogance. I think that *Under Milk Wood* has a lot of marvellous things in it because they are part of Dylan. His prose is as poetic as his poetry, but it's not a great work in any sense of the word, and it's not even a play. It's a kind of poetic prose...

... when we became very specific about his own poetry, he seemed to shy away from it. For example, you recall his poem 'Vision and Prayer'? It's the poem that's based upon the diamond shape and the hourglass. It begins with a single syllable and it rises to nine syllables and then goes back again to a single syllable – that's all very metaphoric and symbolic. Nine represents the number of birth, and so on... then in reverse, there would be the hourglass, starting with nine, going to one and then branching out to nine again.

... as a result of the rhyme scheme and line scheme, he had seventeen lines to every stanza. The diamond was seventeen lines and the hourglass was seventeen lines. But unfortunately, there was one stanza that had eighteen lines and another stanza that had sixteen, and I knew that something had gone wrong. So I looked up the original copy of the poem, and as it appeared in the book, and as it appeared a bit earlier in some magazine – maybe it was *Horizon*. And I couldn't find any other version than the one I had, which showed these two limp stanzas – or at least, two inadequate stanzas. In a fairly sober moment – and in my opinion, all moments with Dylan were sober and not the reverse – I said "Dylan, do something about this. Can you tell me what's missing here?" And he began to look at it, and looked at it and looked at it, and he says "I can't remember. I just can't remember. There's nothing I can do about it." So there you are – I went to the horse's mouth, and I couldn't get the thing straightened up.

Did he write any poems at all when he was in America?
Dylan was very busy when he was in America; he really didn't have any time to do anything. Dylan's visit either coincided with a change in the poetic scene, or he actually brought on that poetic scene – I think he brought it on. At that time the local scene had been struggling with the reading of poetry, and the reading of poetry aloud, and it was a very tenuous business. The audiences were small; no matter how famous the poets were, the audiences were always small. But when Dylan came,

that first evening at the 'Y', there was a complete turnout of what I would call the entire literary scene, and that, of course, exploded into the great fame of poetry readings. That really launched the reading of poetry aloud in America, so that Dylan was a great innovator, simply by being here and reading so well. And I must say that he had a tremendous modesty because he always read other people's poetry, and he was also shrewd. In America he read only the British poets. And I understand in England he only read the American poets. This prevented him from getting into trouble with the local scenery. And, of course, he read his own poems. But the audience in America was more interested in hearing him read his own poems.

... I knew Dylan's poems, but when I heard Dylan read one of his great poems for the first time, I had a terrific thrill and I saw lights and sights in the poem that I'd never seen before. In other words, he opened visions into his poem which I'd already known. I think the audience, although they may not have been able to verbalise it, always felt that they wanted Dylan to read his own poems, and invariably he read other people's first and then read a few of his own. And I ought to tell you that, at one time, in the Village, I think it was the Cherry Lane Theatre, I arranged a reading for Dylan and the charge was very low – I think it was only a dollar, or even less, and I said "Dylan, you're really surrounded by your friends, because today we want to hear nobody but you, we want to hear nothing but your own poems." And the only reading he ever gave in New York City where he read only his own poems was on this occasion when I was monitoring the show.

In some quarters, Dylan has had the reputation for being a little irresponsible, for not living up to some of his commitments. Was this so here?
That is another canard. Please, I want you to remember these are all actual canards. Dylan always kept his appointments. I think, according to that play, he missed one, and why a fuss was made over one appointment missed I don't understand, because if you have hundreds, something is bound to come up and nullify one arrangement. As a rule, I think he was the soul of honour, as I said. He was not irresponsible, and this reputation is just part of the ill will that people...

What about another allegation that he was a sponger on his friends?
That's ridiculous, isn't it? That's absolutely ridiculous. It's the one thing he didn't do. As a matter of fact, when he was at a bar and he was buying a beer for himself, he always bought the beers for everybody, and you'd have to fight with him to pay his beer for him. It's the one

thing he was not. He was not a sponger; he was the opposite.

... let's recapitulate this: it's not true that he chased women; it's not true that he drank; it's not true that he was a sponger. None of these terrible things are true. It seems to me that any intelligent person could see right away that the kind of character that could produce immortal and great poetry could not possibly have the characteristics of the worst kind of human being. It just is a contradiction in terms.

It's generally understood that Dylan didn't speak Welsh fluently.
Well, let me tell you my experience in relation to that. Dylan and I and three or four other friends were staying in the Village, on 10th Street and 6th Avenue, right opposite the women's jail. A young woman came up to us. She went right over to Dylan and said "Oh, Mr Thomas. Could you kindly say something to me in Welsh?" And so he looked glowingly at her and he said "Of course, by all means." Then he said something which sounded very Welsh indeed. And she smiled and thanked him. And he smiled at her, and she left. And when she was gone, we all turned to him and we said "Dylan, what did you say to her?" And he said "I really can't talk Welsh at all. But I did say an old Welsh swear word that I knew." And so we said to him "What did that mean?" And he said "Well, that meant 'Go and eff your grandmother.'"

Did you ever hear him sing in Welsh?
I heard him sing him all kinds of Welsh songs. Carl Sandberg and I and Dylan all took a taxi from the Academy of Arts and Letters up on 156th Street, that great May Day. The Academy has a great May Day party, the last of every May, and all the poets and painters and musicians show up. Dylan was there; I think that's when he lifted Mrs Katharine Porter off the ground. He gave her a little hug, and it was such a tight hug that it lifted her off the ground (she's been living on it ever since). We all of us went back in a taxi. As you know, Carl Sandberg is a great singer of songs, especially Middle Western songs, so the taxi was full of Welsh and American songs. Carl sang his Middle Western, and Dylan sang his Welsh songs, and we all had a wonderful time. But Carl Sandberg never really understood Dylan's poetry; he just knew that he was a wonderful guy.

It's been claimed that he was religious poet.
All great poets are religious leaders. You can't be a great poet without being deeply religious. The two are one. You can't be a hater, for example, and be great poet, because that would be a contradiction in terms.

Sada Thompson and Nancy Wickwire [62]

NW: Liz Reitell came through one morning looking very distraught and said "Dylan arrives in another week [April 1953] and one of his requests was for five actors because he's going to do a play for voices called *Under Milk Wood...*"

ST: None of us really thought that it was very readable. We liked many parts of it, but we couldn't imagine it as a theatrical piece... those rehearsals were really unique because Dylan had no experience of rehearsing, so his idea of a rehearsal was to read it through, and then he said "That was wonderful, that's wonderful. Now we're through rehearsing." But he would tell us all kinds of marvellous anecdotes about the real people on whom these characters were based, stories that may have enriched our feeling for the work almost more than rehearsing it. And I remember all kinds of silly, funny, little things that happened. One in particular. When I was reading Lily Smalls... she's supposed to be talking in the mirror... she has a secret love, the narrator says "She breathes the name and clouds the shaving glass." So he said "Now I want you to say something passionately into space. Can you think of anything?" And I said "Dwight David Eisenhower", which he insisted that I keep in.

What was your impression of Dylan when you first met him?

ST: That he was an extremely unprepossessing man. But also a sort of mischievous man. And I was always very shy with Dylan. I don't know why that was exactly, because I was as delighted with him as everybody else was. We really all came to love him. He was a man of authentic charm – it's a much overused word, but he was the real article.

NW: I do remember his first walking into the Poetry Office looking as I always thought a poet should look. Perhaps a bit plumper than a poet should look... with a marvellous scarf thrown around his neck, and came in with a wonderful grin on his face and his hair all tousled, and just round and marvellous. He was very shy. You had a feeling that he was as shy with us as we were with him.

ST: But one of the most extraordinary things about him to me was the absolute lack of any side. He was not a snob about actors. There are any number of actors in the city who were far better known than we were, at the time or now, who would have loved to have done it. And he didn't care about that at all. He liked our reading and he liked the fact that we got delight from the work as we read it and he was immediately satisfied... he was always wonderful to us.

... he did not seem concerned at all about our having a Welsh accent. As a matter of fact, that was one of the first things he said to all of us – that it was not written with Welsh rhythms particularly, and he just wanted us to 'Love the Words'. That was really the biggest direction that he gave any of us. But there wasn't to be any rural, ethnic flavour to it.

... I would say he wasn't a director at all. That's really the primary thing that all of us remember, is loving the words, savouring the words the way he did. It was not really to be an acted play. He hoped that we could capture something of the individuality of each of the characters as we read it.

NW: Yes. Dylan wasn't a director, didn't pretend to be... as the narrator, he would set each scene for us so vividly that you just knew somehow what you had to follow in your part of the play. And not by telling us how to do it, but just leading us into the scene.

... Dylan was probably our best audience. I think there are some photographs of Dylan watching us while we're reading parts of the play, and if you ever did glance over at him you could see he was just delighted with it, which of course made us so happy we didn't need anything else... I think he loved actors anyway, and I think he loved watching them work... he would have been a marvellous actor because he just had an instinctive feeling for the stage.

How did Dylan feel at the first performance?

ST: I know that he was nervous. I think he was always nervous performing. But he had a kind of bravado with us all, not about himself, but about jollying us up to go out there and do it. That was very delightful.

NW: I remember the end of the performance... the applause went on and on and on. We couldn't make him take a single bow, and that's what people really wanted. And he wanted it to be for all of us because he was so generous, always so generous to all of us. And we finally had to make him go forward to take a single bow, and that's when you hear the bravos that go on and on. Those are for Dylan at the end. But he had to be prodded into going out to take it.

How did Dylan talk about himself?

ST: I don't remember him talking very much about himself... he certainly had a kind of self-disparaging humour, to which we all responded... always very amusing and in the best of spirits. He wasn't terribly concerned with himself or terribly self-absorbed..

NW: I always felt a great sadness in Dylan... that we all responded to and respected.

ST: Such a vulnerable, open man – I think it would be impossible not to respond to him.

NW: I think he was becoming more and more interested in the theatre... I remember a remark perhaps made at rehearsal or some other time, or he has made it to somebody else, that he felt that as a poet he was beginning to dry up, he was going through an arid creative period, and that he wanted to do something in the theatre.

Did Dylan drink at rehearsals?

NW: Dylan was never drunk at rehearsals – ever. Whether he'd been drinking, we never knew. We always broke from rehearsals and would go across the street to the Clover Leaf bar and there he would tell us marvellous stories while he would have a beer. But we never, never saw him drunk. The only time was after the last performance, and he had come to the party, and whether he was drunk, he was just high, and was having a marvellous time. And that was the only time we ever saw him that way.

ST: I think that Dylan is going to haunt all of us the rest of our lives. I can imagine Nancy and I as old ladies being asked what it was like to read with Dylan Thomas. And we were really quite unappreciative of it at the time. It's like reading with Keats... maybe the most extraordinary person either one of us will ever meet, most creative, bubbling with ideas and images, an exciting person to be with.

Rollie McKenna

What was your first contact with Dylan?

It was on Dylan and Caitlin's trip to America [1952], as I recall... and I was living in the country in a place called Millbrook in Duchess County, and they came and spent a weekend.

... in spite of the fact that I had been commissioned by the Poetry Center of the YMHA to do a series of informal portraits of poets, I really don't know anything about poetry. I felt that to suddenly decide that I was fascinated by it would be false way of going about it. So in photographing poets – of which Dylan was only one – I just let whatever happened happen and didn't attempt to understand the poetry, or like it or not like it. Whatever came was the result of two human beings meeting, not an intellectualisation of their work on my part.

What was Dylan's reaction to being photographed?
I think he rather liked it. He never objected. And there were a few times when, had I been a more aggressive or devoted photographer, I might have photographed him and come up with some more dramatic things even, that he wouldn't have objected to.

Was he sensitive about the way he was photographed?
No, never. Never. He had no vanity in regard to that, as far as I was concerned, or as far as I knew. I think he enjoyed it on the whole, and I think he knew what his own image was, and he really wasn't a bit concerned about what I might do to him.

Did you find him an interesting person to photograph?
I think he was unusually interesting because of his changeability as much as anything, and because you never knew what mood he was going to be in, since he did not object or pose or have any 'side' about him in this respect. I had complete freedom.

The people who knew him well seemed to know a Dylan who was extremely sympathetic as a human being.
Great, great warmth. This was one of his great attractions. He had the ability when he was talking to you, to make you feel as if you were the one he really wanted to talk to. This didn't take the form of flirtatious-ness – with some people it did, perhaps – but this wasn't the real element in it. He seemed to have a genuine interest in whomever he was talking to, at the time that he was doing it.

How did he feel about Under Milk Wood?
I think he was rather pleased with it. It was certainly so much a part of his life at Laugharne, and actually it had been started before in a slightly different form, long ago… I think he was pleased with the reception it had. I was at the first performance at the 'Y', and it was quite fascinating. Everybody sat there with a sort of 'show me' attitude, thinking "Well, we're not going to understand a word of this." And then just gradually the audience relaxed… once they got the drift, and didn't think that they were going to be sat upon by some intellectual poet. The very thing that Dylan was afraid of, the audience thought was going to happen to them, and when they found that *Under Milk Wood* was something completely differ-

ent, they were tremendously relieved! And so was he...

... it was exhausting for him partly because he hadn't finished it, and he wasn't happy with just how to finish it. And he finished the version that was given that particular night at my apartment. He had a dreadful hangover and much too much beer and they were going to perform it that night and he still hadn't written the last two or three pages. We set up a card table for him in a room in the back of the house on the top floor and had two or three typists from the 'Y' in the other room, and he'd get something done and they'd type it and then he'd work over it again.

Summer and Autumn 1953
"The hell with him."

Dylan returns from America in June 1953 and works half-heartedly throughout the summer on *Under Milk Wood*. The play receives its first full British reading in Porthcawl in August, and another in Tenby in October. He makes his first solo television appearance, and begins to write a poem about his father's death, 'Elegy', that he does not finish. He returns to New York in October for two more performances of *Under Milk Wood*. But things go badly – he is a sick man, suffering from bronchitis and pneumonia. He sleeps poorly, smokes and drinks more than is good for him and eats very little. Around midnight on November 4/5, he falls into a coma and is taken to hospital. He dies on November 9. After a memorial service in St Luke's Chapel, Dylan's body is brought back to Southampton. He is buried at St Martin's Church, Laugharne, on November 24 1953.

Billy Williams

I was with him one afternoon in the Brown's; I think we'd had a game of darts. Dylan had his elbow on the mantelpiece. All of a sudden, he dropped, like a log. It was the first time I'd seen him go like that, so I picked him up and put him to sit down on the bench that was there. So, after about a minute and a half, he came round. He asked me how long he was out for. I said about a minute and half to two minutes. "Oh," he said, "that's not so bad."

Bert and Nell Trick

BT: Nell can tell you better than I can… they both had the same experience, they used to get 'big heads', I think you would call them. That when they were lying down just before going to sleep, they had the feeling of their head swelling up like a balloon. Nell had told me about this, but Dylan apparently got exactly the same thing. Do you remember?
NT: Oh yes – we were discussing dreams one night, and Dylan said

that whenever he drank, he always dreamt that he was flying. Used to fly over mountains and trees and huge buildings. So I told him of something that happened to me before I went to sleep. When I was very young, I used to get the most queer sensation of my head swelling to a tremendous size, and almost turning to rubber. Used to worry me dreadfully, although I never told anybody about it, until we were discussing it this night, and Dylan said that he had exactly the same thing. And I have talked about it to a psychiatrist a few months ago, and he said lots of people get it, and it does lead to epileptic fits sometimes. It happens in pre-sleep, and lots of people get it...

Was this something that bothered Dylan a lot?
NT: Oh, no. He hadn't discussed it with anybody, and I hadn't because I thought, when I was very young, they'll say I'm imagining it, and making a fuss about something, so I hadn't told anybody, only Bert...

Thomas Taig

The last time I met him was in the August of 1953. I can point to that date because he went over to America just after, and he died there in that autumn. I was then directing a drama school at Porthcawl for Glamorgan Authority and Dylan came along on a Wednesday afternoon like a sort of visiting VIP, a successful writer, and he chose to read *Milk Wood* – almost all of it... did all the parts himself. Which was a wonderful occasion and, as you can imagine, all the students at the school revelled in it. Well, after this performance in the afternoon, I just had a few words with him before he went back to the Principal's room.

Tom Warner

I only met him twice since the War. Once, quite by accident, in London, and the other time in Swansea, about two months before he died... I met him in Ralph's bookshop, and he was very unhappy... I don't think he was looking forward to going to America, but he had to get the money.

... he hadn't got the sort of bounce and go he'd had. And I remember he was rather sad about his children. He said "We're bohemians and they don't like us. They don't like our way of life."

Guido Heller

In due course Danny Jones and his wife and their two children, and Caitlin and Dylan, all came down here [Worm's Head Hotel, Rhossili], shortly before he went on his last trip to America… we spent the afternoon here, and Dylan asked me if I knew anywhere where there was a house going cheap, because he was being evicted from his place in Laugharne… he wanted somewhere to live and had to find it in a hurry. I said "Dylan, there's the Old Rectory that's empty in the middle of the bay here." And he thought this was a wonderful place. And then suddenly as an afterthought, he turned to me and said "Tell me, where's the nearest pub?" So I said it's either at Llangennith or down at the Ship in Port Eynon. "God," he said, "I could never stick that, that's much too far away."

… but Dylan was quite perturbed over the fact that he was having to get out of his place in Laugharne and had to find somewhere else quickly, but he went on this trip to America and the situation, of course, changed and there was no need for any form of eviction.

Mably Owen

In Laugharne, he drank steadily, but not terribly excessively, and I believe that he drank less towards the end of his life because he really couldn't drink very much without suffering. I remember Phil, the landlord of the Cross Inn, saying that he'd come in and drink no more than a pint or two and make it last the whole evening. I think that the last time I did drink with him, he obviously found it difficult to drink, and he didn't drink very much.

Suffering in which way, Mably?
Well, he very quickly got ill… he was just sick very easily… I didn't know anything about the blackouts. I never knew him to have one.

Ebie and Ivy Williams

IW: I was over in The Pelican talking to his mother, and I was at the back of the room looking at some books, and she said to me "Oh, Ivy, come here." And I went to the window – Dylan was talking to Ebie – and she said "Look at Dylan," she said. "He's like a bull, and Daddy always said he wouldn't live to be forty." And he didn't either. That was about a fortnight before he went to America, when he died.

EW: He didn't want to go... and they wanted him to sign on for five years, the last time. Not the one time he died, the time before that - but he wouldn't do it. He said "I wouldn't live five months out there."

Why was this?

EW: Didn't like the food, didn't like the booze there. He didn't like their way of living, you know. Dylan liked a good old pint of beer – well, you couldn't get that out there. Only this old moonshine and damned dope! Poor old feller.

What about when the news came that he was dead?

EW: Oh – place was dead here, mun... poor Caitlin were shoved in the loony-bin out there, when she seen him first of all – he was out like that, mun! Whoever doped him.

IW: Oh, Ebie, you mustn't say things like that!

EW: Injected him – aawh! And when I seen him in the coffin I didn't believe it was him – that's telling you the truth.

Jane Dark

He had this beautiful hair. When you're cutting it's a skilled art, and if you have curly hair you have to really know what you're doing - when I showed him in the mirror he said "That's the best haircut I've ever had. It's gonna last me a lifetime, it'll last me a lifetime." And it did – he never got another, he never had another haircut... just before he went to America last.

Edna and John Morgan Dark

ED: Before he went to America, we had a kind of a party up in our cottage... with his glass, he said to Jackie "Put it on top of the dresser. I'll have that when I come back." It's still there – I've never touched it. The dust is still...

JMD: He actually went to America to get enough money for the four us – that's Caitlin, my wife Edna, my elder brother [Howard] who was his very, very close friend, and myself – to go to Puck Fair [in Ireland]. My wife was going to look after the money, because he didn't think that he or Caitlin would hold on to it long enough.

   ... I was terribly sorry, because he had a tooth screwed in, which was very, very painful... he had an artificial tooth screwed into the bone, you see. He was tremendously vain about his appearance... he never showed his teeth when he spoke, at any time... and he couldn't go to

America unless he had this tooth put in... and I thought it was such a pity that he went through all that agony for nothing.

... we were over in the Boat House one night, and his custom was to buy cockles, Laugharne cockles, and he had friends that collected the largest and the best of cockles for him. Pick them up in a basket, and then over to the Boat House and boil them immediately. I never ate them, because they were usually full of sand – it was beer and cockles and conversation. I shouted over to him – we were all sitting on the floor – "Dylan, when are you going to make some money?" "After I'm dead, Jack!" And how right it was.

... in the last year I know that he had a dozen blackouts. He'd ask you "How long?" I've seen him out for five minutes; but we never told him that. Only thirty seconds, when he came round. "How long was I out?" "Thirty seconds."

... he was preoccupied with death. There's no question. I think he could feel the draught of angels' wings. There's no doubt about it...

Dr David Hughes

Only on one occasion did his wife complain to me and show any anxiety about his health. And that, strangely enough, was after one of our rare visits to the films - she said that she was very worried about Dylan's blackouts, and persistent headaches. And she was very concerned about it, because he was going to America. And I said "Well look, let me see him, and as soon as you can. Do call in tonight." But they never turned up... so unfortunately I never had the opportunity to examine Dylan at a time which might have revealed something before that disastrous last visit to America.

Robert Pocock

The last occasion I saw Dylan was three days before he went to America for the last time. And this is contrary to the legend which has been created. I was in the Crown and Sceptre, which is in Foley Street by the BBC. It's a rarely-used pub; he rang me up at home and said that he would be in there, he'd like to see me for a final drink. I went there; I met Francis Dillon, John Davenport, and Gerald Hanley and Dylan. And time came up to three o'clock; I suppose we'd had, as between twelve and three, no more than about four pints, and then the others peeled off and Dylan said to me, "Well, what are we going to do now? I suppose return and swallow our own vomit down in Soho." And we went down to the Mandrake, to the downstairs bar there, and we sat there until six o'clock... all that time I should think we had one pint an hour. And if you asked me what we talked about, I do not know. Except that he was extremely quiet, rather depressed, I thought, and in common with a number of people – this is with hindsight – one got the feeling one wasn't going to see him again. I thought that he was going to America and he was going to stay in America. I got the idea that everything was over between him and Caitlin.

... I think he was very much in love with San Francisco and he said that's the one place in the world where he would like to live... he had a letter from a pair of friends there, husband and wife – it was a very curious letter. They'd held a jumble sale for him the week before, and they sent him a cheque as a result of the proceeds there and I thought, "My God, what a bloody thing it is – one of the finest poets of our age has to have a jumble sale held in a foreign country to bring him in funds."

Sean Treacy, the King's Arms (Finches)

I'd seen him in '53, just before he went to America. And that's when I thought he was really looking pretty shaken. And I wondered how the hell he could go on a lecture tour, and how he was going to do it...

... he didn't look very well then, before he went to the States the last time... complexion was gone, and he was blown up. I think that's a good description. You know, puffy face... just downright booze... everybody thought the world of him, you see, and this is the sad thing – he was behaving like a lunatic, really, when you come to think of it... the only thing I can say is that I was very sorry when I'd heard he'd died but I wasn't surprised. Not at all. No, I thought that was well on the cards.

Elizabeth Ruby Milton

The last time I saw him was before he went to America. He was complaining that... the successful intellectual, the sort of recognised intellectual in America, frightened him so much that he used to escape from them the first possible moment and go to his other friends, who were more fun or more human.

... he asked me to go to the movies with him... he loved Westerns. And I couldn't, because I had to collect my children from school. They went to a convent and it would have looked a bit odd if we'd both arrived at the convent with a bottle of gin to collect two little convent children in uniforms…

We were standing outside a costumiers… which had uniforms in the window – theatrical, historical uniforms… we both looking at these uniforms, and he asked me to come to the movies and I wouldn't go with him and he said to me, "You're far too skinny." Sort of suddenly attacked me, and I was furious and I said, "Well, you're too fat!" And we just turned on our heels and left each other – never saw him again.

Constantine FitzGibbon

We met one another in the street. He was going to the George to see the BBC people and we met somewhere outside the BBC and he said, "Oh, let's go to a quiet pub and have a talk. Where we won't see anybody we know." And we went to a pub and talked for a couple of hours over two or three pints of beer, and he started off by being terribly depressed and gloomy and… saying he didn't think he'd live very much longer and so on. I put this down to a mood. I'd heard him talking this way periodically for fifteen years and then after the second beer he began to cheer up a bit… he was looking forward very much to the Stravinsky opera which he regarded as a great thing. He was terribly proud that Stravinsky had chosen him, because Dylan had this tremendous respect for great artists, and to have been chosen by Stravinsky was for him far more important than any honour or any financial reward. Although he was also looking forward to the financial reward – and then he cheered up, and then he wanted to be with people again and we went off to the George and there was the usual crowd of people there, some of whom were extremely dull and I left him there after a while, and I never saw him again.

Philip Burton

He spent his last evening in London with me… to ask me if I would collaborate with him on his first stage play, and he said some extraordinary things that night. He told me that he felt he was coming to the end of his lyrical impulse. He told me that he had written what he thought might be his last poem. Which was about his father; one that they ultimately discovered on scraps of paper in various pockets and that Vernon Watkins edited. He felt more and more the urge to public communication rather than the private page, and he had a fascinating idea for a play. The idea was – which was a Welsh setting – a boy and a girl are born at the beginning of the play in two nearby streets in a south Wales town. And the whole play was to be about the influences that shaped their lives until the final curtain, which was the first moment that they met. And we kept talking about it and gradually we evolved the idea of a great central figure, a kind of Dylanesque, an orator who would represent at various times, a Communist, a cheap-jack seller in the Valleys during the Depression, a religious enthusiast and so on. We began talking about the technique of the play – he was insistent that there should be no intermission. I remember him saying that at least the theatre should achieve the intelligence of the cinema. And I kept saying "You can't do that Dylan, you can't do that, you can't do that, you can't do that." And finally he burst out by saying "For God's sake, let me start with two prodigiously pregnant women!"

... he really wanted to write for the theatre. And he would have been a superb writer for the theatre; absolutely superb, because he had such a wonderful sense of character... I think he's the only man I can think of who would have given us another Falstaff. There was so much Falstaffian in him. Such a richness – such an enjoyment of the gusto of living.

... we agreed that Wordsworth was such an unlucky man to live until he was eighty, since all the Wordsworth poems worth recording had been written by the time he was thirty. But he went on writing until he was eighty. I remember we commented on that that night.

... I said, "Why are you going to America Dylan?" And he said "To make money!" And I said, "How much will you bring back?" And he smiled and said, "Not a cent." He knew what he was doing but couldn't resist doing it.

... something happened that night which in the light of subsequent events was obviously very revealing. He suddenly asked me, after we'd been talking about three hours, I suppose, if he could go and lie down and he asked me to wake him, if he went to sleep, in about half an hour. So he went into my bedroom and lay down and at the end of the half-hour I went in and found it most difficult to wake him. I got really worried. I shook him, I shouted, and finally, from some very deep-down place, he slowly came back. And he took quite a bit of time to focus. He hadn't been drinking – it wasn't that he was drunk at all, not at all. It was an eminently sane night. And he said "Did you find diffi-culty in waking me?" And I said "Yes, I certainly did. I was getting worried." And he said "Yes, it happens these days". And that was all.

... as a matter of fact, after we had news of the death, I had lunch with Louis MacNeice, and we compared notes, and he'd had lunch with Louis that day and apparently he'd had a blackout at lunch. And he asked when he came round how long it had been.

Did he ever explain the source of these blackouts?
No, no – we never discussed it and I don't think he wanted to talk about it, so we just let it go.

Did he complain of his back at all? Because he'd been having injections in his back.[63]
No. No. I knew nothing about that.

Harry Locke

There was this great leave-taking, the great packing-up and all the rest of it, and we went to the BOAC air terminal at Victoria and, as always, allowed a bit of time for a few drinks before the bus left. So we had a few drinks and, oh, the most violent friction was going between Caitlin and Cordy and Dylan.

And so then when the bus came in, Dylan said "Oh, come on let's get away. Let's get on the bus." I said "Well, it won't leave for half an hour." He said "Never mind; let's get away." So we went on to the bus, which was completely empty and Dylan went up on to the upper deck, because "I want to look out – I want to see." And he kept saying to me "Go back. Go back and join the others." And I said, "No, no. I'll wait. I'll wait here." And eventually the driver got on to the bus, started the engine, and I waved to Dylan and Dylan looked at me, and he shook his head and he turned both his thumbs down. He knew he wasn't coming back.

Had he talked to you about his reasons for going to America, for accepting that offer to go?
No, no, not really, no. But I knew. It was to get away from home…

… his last visit to America was because he was going to write the libretto of an opera by Stravinsky, which was gonna be about Space… Stravinsky wrote to Dylan and said, "You must understand that I'm very poor and I live in a small one-roomed apartment in Hollywood, and I shan't be able to support you very well." Dylan said, "Can you imagine it – a man like Stravinsky lives in a one-room apartment in Los Angeles, so I've got to do a lecture tour. I can't go straight to Hollywood and live off this man. I've got to do a series of lectures." And at the same time Stravinsky was having a whole wing [it was just a room] built onto his house for Dylan… it was a joke… and Dylan believed him. He was having a whole wing built... and Dylan believed that Stravinsky was absolutely broke. And lived in one room. That's why he went on the lecture tour.

Nancy Wickwire

The time that it came closest to all of us as to what his genius was as an actor was on the last afternoon [October 25 1953] that we gave *Under Milk Wood*, when he was desperately ill. As a matter of fact, we didn't think that we would be able to do the last performance because he was so ill... Dylan literally couldn't speak he was so ill... his arm was in a sling... he's got to go through this long afternoon with all his speech and he's physically exhausted and so physically ill... we really felt we're going to have to cancel it... the doctor gave him a shot of something and he seemed to recover... I remember him coming out of the dressing-room looking so ill, sounding so ill... he had no voice. We got on stage on our respective stools, and the spotlight came on him, and he was very pale and very ill, and I know whatever nerves we had as actors were completely gone because we were all just so feeling for him. And I think that's probably one of the greatest theatrical moments I've ever known in my life. When that light came on him, sick as he was... it was the most beautiful, inspiring, fantastic performance he ever gave of the play. After it was over he collapsed again.[64]

Rollie McKenna

I saw him about two weeks before he died... he came to my house for a small gathering after a *Milk Wood* performance, and he was drinking beer only... I think he was generally in despair in the last few months... it was a form of severe self-destruction, which started when he was very, very young.

How was he looking?
Ghastly. Very bad. His colour was bad and his spirits were very low.

When he left Britain, his friends told me that he seemed to make a point of going round to see a great number of his friends before his last visit, and that to one or two he expressed the feeling that he would not survive very long. That he would be, in other words, dying very soon.
I think he had considerable foreboding about that. It showed in his face and certainly in his moods, and it shows in pictures I have of him, the last ones particularly. I think that was genuine. They had been warned, of course, by the doctors that he had better slow down or he would

have some real trouble... the last visit he was in particularly bad shape, and there was no question about it. Physically and spiritually.

Do you recall the atmosphere at the hospital?
A crowded waiting room, and everybody asking every second what was going to happen, or had happened. I was there a good part of the four days that he was there. It wasn't very pleasant. It was quite, quite miserable... and the necessity for very important decisions to be made, many of which fell on John [Brinnin]. Important decisions in terms of what to do about him – because when Caitlin arrived she was in no shape to take responsibility – whether to move him or not move him, or something where a relative is usually consulted, and is standing by. But she was just incapable. We all had to rally round and sort things out and pay the nurses – I happened to pay a couple of the nurses' bills myself.

Oscar Williams

The last time I saw Dylan was in Whitehall Spa, two or three days before he went into a coma... for some strange reason, although I'd seen Dylan dozens and dozens of times and now I'd known him it seemed to me as though it were a lifetime, for some strange reason at that time, we shook hands. And that was the oddest thing of all, because I never saw him alive again. At least, I saw him alive but in a coma – I never saw him in his senses. I saw him late on, at the hospital, a few days later.

... the shock was enormous. So many people loved him – even people who had never seen him, they had simply gotten the reflection from other people's love – they felt it was a terrible thing and everybody wanted to find a scapegoat. So first they picked on America, and then they picked on drink, then they picked on this and that. The truth of it is that Dylan really was a sick person when he came to the United States. He wasn't in perfect health.

Ruthven Todd

In New York, I checked all the facts about Dylan having drunk the eighteen whiskies, which is always believed... this eighteen whiskies is absolutely untrue. Dylan was a beer drinker. If Dylan had had eighteen whiskies he would not have been able to get back to the Chelsea. I checked the next day, after Liz Reitell told me about Dylan's remark....
... owing to the ABC, the Alcoholic Board of Control in New York, a

man can tell exactly how many drinks have been used out of a bottle in the previous evening. In the case of Dylan, he had either six or, allowing that two old men who always came in and had a Grandad's nightcap had broke their habit, he might very well have had eight, but that is all he could have had. Six multiplied by three is eighteen – sounds better and I suppose Dylan, like a Welshman, was making a good story better.

… I checked in the Oasis, which was next door to the Chelsea where he was staying. He'd been in there in the morning but they hadn't seen him in the afternoon [or] in the evening, and there's no place between 23rd Street, West 23rd Street and the Hudson, Hudson Street and 11th, where the White Horse is, where Dylan would have taken a drink at all. Because they weren't his kind of pub.

… he wasn't terribly fit but he was not terribly ill – he was very tough. The best story about his toughness was made to a young man who was on the bar the night that Dylan was supposed to be taking the eighteen whiskies, which is one of the reasons why I know. He was a young Irishman called Kevin Rooney. You unfortunately can't get him because he hanged himself in a police cell. He and his wife had a row and somehow or other she got stabbed and he was taken by the police into Charles Street police station where they told him he'd murdered his wife. She recovered all right, but he hanged himself in his shirtsleeves in the cell.

… Kevin Rooney went upstairs to ask how Dylan was… he asked this nurse on duty and she said "It's a good thing your friend Mr Thomas led such a good life and was so healthy. It would have carried most other people off before." Which I'm afraid is rather a macabre story, but it's true.

… the last time I like to remember him was at a party at my house in which Brinnin says "at the gentle insistence of his host he drank only beer". All that happened was that there was plenty of booze around, but I opened a can of beer and said "Dylan, are you ready for another one"? That was all.

… the last time I saw Dylan I helped David Slivka remove the plaster from his face on the death mask… and that was by accident because Ibrahim Lassor, who had done the job professionally, was suddenly called away because there was a very rich American collector who might buy one of his sculptures… and David said "Ruthven, you're neat with your hands. Will you come and help me?" It took two people to take off the plaster – and the floor was cluttered with Colgate's Brushless Shave Cream tubes. You use that to prevent it sticking to the skin… that was the last time I saw Dylan. David and I were very glad when we had it in a carton, tucked in the back of the old station wagon and took it away. Neither of us enjoyed ourselves.

John Griffith and Ralph Wishart

JG: I was possibly... a bit concerned about him and his health, and wanting him to eat something – because I don't remember him eating.
RW: No – indeed, that's right. I've known him go all day...
JG: I think it was before the last visit to America... I had mentioned there was a chance of a programme, and he said he was committed to someone in London... he then said he had worries about his health. I would say that he had premonitions... he'd had one or two very bad attacks and he described them to me.
RW: I think blackouts... one day he came in the shop, with his arm in sling. And a patch over his eye. And I said "By gum, you must have been in the wars last night. What's the other feller looking like?" He said "I fell over going down to the Boat House." About six months before he went to America.

... when Dylan died, Dan come up the shop. "Look Ralph," he said, "we'll have to get something done to get his body back." Because we understood that Caitlin was going to leave the body there. So we got hold of John Ormond... really speaking it's through Dan and John, and perhaps myself, that we got the body in this country. Dan went down to Southampton – he went all that way to get the body, to bury it in Laugharne. But the Americans, I understand, wanted to keep the body there, and she was not desperate... John said to me...
JH: "We'd better have a wreath... you get a wreath from a place I know up in Sketty there." And we had a laurel wreath.
RW: 'Course, I had to pay for that again, see. They tells me to do these things, you know.

Robert Lowell

It would be arrogant to try to place Dylan in English poetry. But he carried something to its extreme and triumphed, and it's a little hard to put my fingers on just what it was. But it has a great deal to do with energy and making a poem radiant... I can't think of any English or American poet of this century who has that quality to such an extreme... they're just so radiant and energetic. No poet bristled with talent and achieved it more than Dylan.

Gwen Watkins

Dylan never in his life cared anything about reviews, or reviewers... he was always his own best critic. He knew exactly what he meant to do, and he knew how far he'd succeeded. He was both modest and certain. He called Swansea "the home of at least two great men", but in the last year of his life he said "My poems are good, but not great. I wish I could have been like Mozart, who was both good and great." I must say, I think personally that this is a failure of his critical sense. I think posterity will find that many of his poems are among the great ones in the English language.

Trevor Hughes [65]

The thought of amending the image of Dylan created by Brinnin and others is always with me... the memory of that bitter, graveside puppet-chant of "I knew Dylan Thomas. He drank", still distresses me; and I cannot understand why so many people, even those whom I had known to worship him, hurried indecently to proclaim their friendship, and to disprove it with one mean story. Only the mean could remember this man in meanness.

Few can have known Dylan, the real Dylan, as I knew him. I knew his genius, his innate wisdom, nobility, his compassion, his utter dedication to his work. I have never claimed to have influenced him – nobody 'influences' such a man... at the news of his illness I went back to the Fitzroy Tavern, where, I felt, I might get near to him. I had some irrational (?) idea that I was contemplating, not the death of a drunk, but the moving of a great man into the mystic night, and that I, helpless, could only love, and question not, and seek to uphold, even after death. I am no hero-worshipper, nor, although it still catches at my throat, do I accept his work uncritically. He was a truly great poet, but I cannot agree that he ever wrote a truly great poem. It is said that, had he lived, he might have written a masterpiece of a play or novel, but there is nothing to support this. Dylan Thomas was a poet, and, I believe, a poet of great significance. but, for me, the remarkable promise of *18 Poems* and *Twenty-five Poems* was never fulfilled.

Inevitably, the tide turned against him. I had been fearful, in his early days, of the danger, not of alcohol, but of adulation. And surely it was the adulation of false friends that destroyed him.

Paul Potts [66]

I always felt shy in his company. As one does in the company of a man one likes deeply but does not fully understand or even agree with altogether. Dylan escapes me a bit. The magic and the mystery and all the Welshness, perhaps. The Welsh are the most foreign of all the peoples in the English speaking world...

He was an exciting elder brother to his children. Loved sweets, bubble and squeak, thrillers, tripe and onions, and T. Thompson the Lancashire writer. Hated good living poets, the upper classes and people who showed off... was the only person I have known who could mercilessly exploit his own personality without believing in his own propaganda and thus become corrupted.

He was a great gentleman, without even ceasing to be a great clown. If he had never written a line of verse, he would still have been one of the most exciting people anyone could meet anywhere... His heart was well bred, his mind legitimate. He never had a single emotion, or one lone thought, that was born outside the wedlock, that always existed, between his love and his equally great talent.

If nowhere in the work of Dylan Thomas you can hear an angry exhortation to end poverty itself, what you will find in his verse, however, is a deep courtesy and true reverence towards the very poor... all true poets loved him and a fair number of football fans as well.

His work when taken into the vicinity of Shakespeare may indeed appear to be very small, but even when viewed from that position it is still very perfect... He was possibly among the greatest minor poets in English literature. Some say he is a Welsh poet, meaning that he doesn't belong in English literature at all. Certainly he doesn't belong to the main stream. He wasn't a radical, never the proud man apart, always one of the boys. He was no kind of traveller – always looked for South Wales wherever he went.

He was a mixture of Puck and Falstaff with a dash of Augustus John thrown in... He was a picnic and his kindnesses were like so many hard-boiled eggshells scattered around his life. He had an enormous range, had friends in many walks of life and layers of temperament. They very often disliked each other intensely, or tried to like each other because of him and failed. When he died one could see men being polite and even reverent to each other, who had never exchanged a word unless it was a sneer, for years. This was the wreath they placed upon his coffin. It was a beautiful thing to behold.

20. Llewelyn, 18 months

21. Dylan, Caitlin and Llewelyn

22. Caitlin and Colm, Laugharne. See page 195

23. D.J. Thomas

24. D.J. Thomas and Ken Owen at Blaencwm, 1940s

25. D.J. Thomas, Florence and Hettie Owen

26. Emyln Williams and Florence

27. Florence and Hettie and Ken Owen

28. Florence at Stratford, 1958

Part Two: Stories and Facts

1: Death by Neglect

with Dr Simon Barton[67]

Alcohol, diabetes and drugs have all been indicted in the death of Dylan Thomas in St Vincent's Hospital, New York, on November 9 1953. But our investigations lead us to conclude that Dylan's death was brought about by a serious chest infection in which chronic bronchitis developed into terminal pneumonia *before* his admission to hospital.

Death was also a consequence of cerebral hypoxia i.e. insufficient oxygen being delivered to the brain cells, causing them to die. This caused cerebral oedema – swelling of the brain tissue and cells. The hypoxia was a result of Dylan's inefficient respiratory system, which had been impaired by the bronchitis and pneumonia, and then by injections of morphine given by his New York doctor, Milton Feltenstein.

Alcohol certainly played a part in Dylan's death but it did not directly kill him. Over the long-term it contributed, together with poor diet, smoking and lack of sleep, to the general debilitation which allowed bronchitis and pneumonia to take hold and flourish.

A critical factor in Dylan's death was medical negligence. Dylan's bronchitis and pneumonia went undiagnosed and untreated in the days before he was admitted to St Vincent's Hospital as an emergency case. There was also a significant delay in getting Dylan to St Vincent's. He was not examined by a specialist or consultant until some thirty-seven hours after his admission.

We begin with an outline of Dylan's medical history. This is followed by a brief note on Dylan's last days in New York. We then describe his admission to St Vincent's Hospital, and examine his medical data. We look at the three causes of death established at the post-mortem – pneumonia, pial oedema and fatty liver – followed by a discussion of how, if at all, drugs and diabetes were implicated in Dylan's death. The post-mortem report is reproduced at the end of the book, along with a chronology of the events in Dylan's final illness and death. Before continuing with this chapter, readers may find it helpful to look at the chronology because it offers useful diagnostic clues.

1. Dylan's Medical History

Dylan's medical history can be assembled from his letters, biographical accounts and the Edwards interviews. From early childhood, it is a chronicle of bronchitis, influenza and colds. Dylan was a 'chesty' boy, teenager and adult, and smoking aggravated his list of bronchial complaints. There were endless, nagging worries about TB, though the closest Dylan ever came to it was visiting his New Quay friend, Griff Jenkins, in the south Wales sanatorium.[68]

Throughout his life, Dylan tried as hard as he could to avoid doctors, and to avoid taking their advice when he did see them. The family doctor at Laugharne, David Hughes, told Colin Edwards that "I have no recollection of Dylan ever consulting me about his health... I was never asked to attend Dylan medically. Although I believe that occasionally he did consult a doctor in London."

Bronchial Woes

In his 1955 book, Brinnin has helpfully documented how Dylan "coughed and flushed" his way through his American tours. Here are two typical examples, taken from Dylan's first visit in 1950:

> Several times already that morning he had fitfully broken into spells of coughing that racked the whole length of his body, brought tears to his eyes, and left him momentarily speechless... These attacks were as a rule brief, did not seem to alarm him, and he recovered always within a few minutes, seemingly undisturbed by a collapse that would have sent almost anyone else to bed (p19).

> ... barely five minutes before he was to go on stage, he was overtaken by a coughing attack so violent I had to hold him to enable him to keep on his feet... As we moved on, he became ill again and began to cough in a spasm so blinding it seemed he would break asunder (pp32, 34).

Caitlin, too, has described Dylan's coughing fits at the Boat House in Laugharne, as have other friends and visitors who talked with Colin Edwards. Dylan's letters from the "bronchial heronry", as he once put it, continue the tale of complaints: at the edge of pleurisy (November 11 1950); gastric influenza (March 20 1951); bronchitis (October 1951); pleurisy (June 28 1952); pneumonia (October 8 1952);

bronchitis, no voice only croaking (November 21 1952); influenza, bronchitis, croaking and snuffling, no voice (February 6 1953). Both Dylan and Caitlin blamed the damp Boat House for these ailments, as well as the rain and wet mists of the Laugharne estuary.[69]

The 'pleurisy' and 'pneumonia' are almost certainly Dylan's exaggerations for bronchitis. All these pulmonary infections are associated with Dylan's breathlessness that was observed in Laugharne by his mother and by some of his friends. Aeronwy Thomas has also recalled her father's condition in her interview with Colin Edwards: "I can remember my father always huffing and puffing up the steep path to the cliff walk. Physically, he was a bit like a turtle who'd been stranded."

There is consensus amongst Dylan's biographers about his "chesty complaints", though sometimes asthma is referred to rather than bronchitis. Nashold and Tremlett also conclude that Dylan's chronic bronchitis and emphysema were all conditions that he suffered from for many years, as he stumbled breathless around Laugharne "on his walking stick, starved of oxygen". They note that Dylan was using an inhaler to help his breathing on his visit to America in the spring of 1953.[70]

Dylan was rejected for war service in 1940 because, it is said, he had "weak lungs". This condition cannot be confirmed because the records of the war service tribunals have been destroyed. When he was examined by a doctor in 1946 at St Stephen's hospital, nothing abnormal was found in his lungs.

Both Dylan's maternal and paternal relations had suffered a range of pulmonary illnesses, described on page 196 of Volume One of *Dylan Remembered*. As death certificates show, Dylan's maternal grandfather, George Williams, died of bronchopneumonia and his paternal grandfather, Evan the Guard, of chronic bronchitis. In 1953, D.J. Thomas, Dylan's father, died of bronchopneumonia, and Dylan's letters describe his father's earlier pneumonia in 1949 and 1950.[71] DJ's two sisters, Jane Ann and Elizabeth, both died in their thirties from pulmonary TB.

Broken Bones and other Woes

There is a record from childhood of falls and broken bones. From at least early manhood, there is a history of poor diet, as well as weight gain leading to obesity, linked presumably to Dylan's fondness for

sweets and beer. His lack of interest in food is described in many interviews in this volume, including those with Fred Janes, Mervyn Levy,
Mably Owen, Edward Evans, Bill Mitchell, Alban Leyshon, Oscar
Williams, Mrs Warfield Darling and Ralph Wishart. Brinnin, too, has
described in his 1955 book Dylan's lack of interest in eating. Dylan's
poor and irregular diet was associated with his alcohol consumption.

There is at least one report, from the late 1930s, of Dylan having a
venereal disease but there is no confirmation.

In his Edwards interview, Bill Green reports an episode of illness
whilst Dylan was living at South Leigh in 1947-48. Dylan visited a
doctor, and pills were prescribed. He gave up drinking for a period
afterwards.

There is a history of vomiting, sometimes without blood (see
Milton, p72) and often with. He was admitted to St Stephen's hospital
in 1946 after vomiting blood. Both Brinnin and the poet Patrick
Boland observed Dylan vomiting blood on his first American trip in
1950, followed immediately by another vomiting attack in the street,
one in the theatre before giving a reading, and another afterwards –
Brinnin does not implicate alcohol or drunkenness in these attacks
(pp31-34). The vomiting seems sometimes to be associated with
anxiety or apprehension, as it was during Dylan's stay in St Stephen's.
Severe nausea and vomiting were a major characteristic of the hours
leading up to Dylan's hospitalisation in St Vincent's. Brinnin's account
also tells us that vomiting and retching sometimes occurred after a
coughing bout – "such shattering fits of coughing, often followed by
frightful retching and vomiting, went on through all the time I was to
know him" (p19). A letter from Dylan in 1943 to Donald Taylor
suggests that the coughing-vomiting condition was of long-standing:

> I've got laryngitis or bronchitis or asthma or something: a
> complaint, whatever it is, that makes your chest like a raw steak,
> prevents breathing, & produces a food-losing cough.

Dylan experienced blackouts and deep sleeps in his later years from
which he could not easily be roused. These are described in several of
the Edwards interviews, and are summarised on page 281. Dylan was
unwell before he left for America – his condition is described by many
of Edwards' interviewees, and in a letter from Vernon Watkins:

> It is a great tragedy that Dylan who had been drinking much less

before he left for America, was allowed to drink so much when he got there. He was not well before he went, and had had several short black-outs, and had even written for a diet-sheet; he was anxious to give up drinking. But I am sure he did not tell anyone he was ill, and I know how difficult it was to stop Dylan. Yet if one did stop him he was grateful, because he really didn't like it, except for beer. [72]

According to Brinnin, Dylan suffered from gout and alcoholic gastritis in America, but there is no medical confirmation of either. Dylan certainly believed that he had gout, and there are numerous reports of his having a very painful toe. Both Brinnin and Dylan report that he was treated for gout with ACTH, a cortisone secretant, whilst on his last two American trips. The ACTH was also used to relieve his breathing and as a general tonic. Dylan received three injections in May, two in October and three in November 1953 – the dosages of all but one are unknown. [73] There seems little to support Nashold and Tremlett's assertion (p124) that Dylan received twice-weekly injections of ACTH in May 1953 – we deal with this in the following Note. [74] There is no information to suggest that Dylan received ACTH or cortisone itself between June and early October 1953 when he was in Laugharne and London. We do not accept that the ACTH or cortisone could have played a part in producing Dylan's puffy demeanour, and we explain the reasons in the following Note. [75]

Nashold and Tremlett have suggested that Dylan had diabetes but this is speculative and is not confirmed by hospital tests either at St. Stephen's in 1946 or St Vincent's in 1953, where on both occasions his test for diabetes was negative.

Hospital Treatment

Lindsay reports that Dylan went to a psychiatrist at a London hospital and asked to be cured of "drinking obsessions". The doctor joked and bantered with him about being a poet. Dylan did not turn up for the next appointment (pp21-22).

Dylan was admitted to St Stephen's Hospital, London, in the early afternoon of March 10 1946. He was taken to Ward 7-B where he gave his address as 39, Markham Square, Chelsea, his religion as non-conformist, and his occupation as writer, poet, journalist and BBC worker. His hospital notes, to be found in the FitzGibbon collection at Texas, are perfunctory and incomplete. The admitting doctor's letter is not with the notes but it appears, from a letter to FitzGibbon from a consultant, that Dylan was admitted to the hospital as a case of haematemesis i.e. vomiting blood. The notes record:

"Urine sugar NIL
Recurrent bouts of depression. Recurrent bouts of alcoholic & smokers [next word unclear]. Recurrent bouts of vomiting & paroxysmal morning cough. Recent attack 3 weeks duration. Apprehensive ++ Pulse high tension BP [blood pressure] 160/98. Tremor. Shaking hands. Obesity. Watery flesh. Dilated pupils. Sympathetictonia[?]. Chest: NAD [Nothing Abnormal Discovered when examined by a doctor]. Heart NAD - Tachycardia [rapid pulse]. CNS [central nervous system] overactive ++. Liver ↓ 2 fingers Tender. Throat Dry granular
= Anxiety."

The liver was not only tender but also enlarged since it was found two fingers down from the ribs. The phrase 'watery flesh' is suggestive of oedema, and on page 270 we note the presence of a generalised oedema found in 1953 at the post-mortem.

A chest X-ray and liver tests were done but the results are not reported in the medical notes. Both the chest and heart were normal when examined by a doctor. Dylan's urine was tested for sugar but none was found. No mention is made in the medical notes of diabetes, nor of any drugs or diet to treat diabetes.

As for medication, Dylan was given only phenobarbitone, as a way of calming him. The notes record that he was put on a normal diet.

By March 12, Dylan's blood pressure had fallen to 132/96. He was also seen that day by a psychiatrist who recorded: "Depression consists mostly of <u>reactive</u> depression with elements of hypercritical attitude. Finds sleep aided by drink - <u>habit</u> +".

Reactive depression is that occasioned directly by events in the external world e.g. the death of a loved one, and is an extension of normal feelings of loss or grief. That the psychiatrist underlined 'reactive' may suggest he had found sufficient reasons in Dylan's external circumstances for a state of depression, though we do not know what these might have been. Neither is it clear whether the phrase 'hypercritical attitude' means that Dylan was hypercritical of himself or of people or circumstances around him.

Dylan was discharged as 'recovered' on March 15 with a final diagnosis of 'gastritis', and was given a prescription for phenobarbitone to be taken three times a day.

We can find nothing in these incomplete notes to support a diagnosis of gastritis, let alone one of alcoholic gastritis as put forward by FitzGibbon (p276). If the hospital had suspected alcoholic gastritis, they would certainly have put Dylan on a special diet and given him appropriate medication.

The vomited blood could have been the result of a Malloy-Weiss tear, i.e. a tear in the lining of the stomach wall that can be caused by vigorous vomiting. Ingestion of excess alcohol and drugs can produce bouts of violent vomiting. Vomited blood could also come from a rupture of an oesophageal vein – there is more on this on page 269 from the post-mortem report – or from a bleeding stomach ulcer.

The collection of signs recorded in the medical notes (apprehension, raised blood pressure, tremor, shaking hands, dilated pupils, fast pulse rate, overactive central nervous system and dry throat) led the doctors to conclude 'anxiety'. They may well have been right but they are suggestive of other factors including the use of amphetamines, such as benzedrine.

We conclude on the facts available to us about this admission that Dylan had

- an enlarged liver probably due to long-term alcohol abuse.
- an anxiety state of unknown cause, possibly induced by amphetamines (which also cause loss of appetite and can cause vomiting).We also note from Edwards' interview with Dosh Murray that when Dylan lived in South Leigh in 1947-49, she found him to be "rather nervy" (p133).
- raised blood pressure, which is not unexpected in an obese, sedentary smoker who drank.
- depression.

We also conclude that Dylan did not have diabetes in 1946.

2. The Last Days

Dylan's friends thought he looked unwell when he left London for New York. He has described how he felt "as sick as death all the way over". He arrived at Idlewild Airport on October 20 1953 to be met by his lover, Liz Reitell. He slept for most of the next few days in his room in the Chelsea Hotel, complaining occasionally that he felt unwell. He became very ill on the 23rd – he was feverish, gasping for breath and exhausted. There was little improvement the next day ("Never this sick, never this much before") and Dr Milton Feltenstein gave him an injection of ACTH. Dylan was "desperately ill" again on October 25 and collapsed at a performance of *Under Milk Wood*, when he was given another injection.

29. The Seton Building

Dylan remained unwell for another two days, including his birthday when he was too sick to stay at the party given for him. After making a temporary recovery, he started drinking heavily on the weekend of October 31. The first few days of November consisted of parties, drinking and hangovers interspersed with bouts of sickness, exhaustion and sleeping. As for much of his adult life, Dylan smoked heavily and ate very little whilst in New York.

Around 2am on November 4, Dylan left Reitell in the hotel room and went to a local bar and drank eight large whiskies before returning to the hotel. When he woke later that morning, he complained of difficulties with his breathing – "suffocating". He went out with Reitell, drank two beers but returned, feeling unwell, to the Chelsea. He stayed in bed for the rest of the day, coughing and retching, with severe attacks of nausea and vomiting, and was looked after by Reitell. She summoned Feltenstein to the hotel on three occasions, and each time he injected Dylan with ACTH and morphine. Within half an hour of the third injection of morphine, Dylan stopped breathing properly and fell into coma around midnight on November 4/5. About an hour later, an ambulance was summoned and it delivered Dylan at 1.58am to the emergency room of St Vincent's Hospital, based in the Seton Building on 11th Street and 7th Avenue.

3. St Vincent's

St Vincent's Hospital had been set up in 1849 by the Sisters of Charity, a religious community of women within the Roman Catholic Church. Its mission had once been to provide free care but by the 1950s most patients were required, as in other private and voluntary hospitals, to meet all or some of their care costs, either by drawing on their own resources or through medical insurance. Patients with enough money or insurance could choose to be in a private room or in a semi-private room with just four or two beds. Those with few or uncertain resources were consigned to the general wards.

After leaving the emergency room, Dylan was taken in the elevator to St Joseph's East, a mens' medical ward on the third floor. In his 1955 book, John Brinnin gives the impression that Dylan was placed in a private room. In fact, there were no private rooms on St Joseph's East. It was a large, general ward divided into sections with eight, six or four beds in each, with some thirty patients overall. It had high ceilings and big windows; it was "well kept, institutional and sterile-looking, not cosy." [76]

We talked with Dave Slivka, who was one of Dylan's visitors. He does not have a clear memory of Dylan's accommodation but recalls "not that large a room, there may have been other beds but there were no other people in the beds." This suggests that Dylan was probably in a four-bed section in the general ward. He had very little privacy. Many friends, as well as strangers who came in off the street, turned up to 'view' him through a glass partition that separated the corridor from the ward. Dylan's wife, Caitlin, has described the scene after Brinnin had escorted her up to the third floor for her first visit:

> I came to a corridor, crowded with people - twenty or thirty of them. I didn't know who they were or where they came from, but I realised that they were all looking through a glass partition down the side of the corridor into the room where Dylan lay...

Caitlin then entered the ward and went up to Dylan's bedside: "I talked to him, but he didn't respond and I felt so embarrassed with all those people gazing at me through the glass; I felt as though I were on a stage." (1986, pp182-83)

Oscar Williams, Dylan's unofficial agent in America, visited Dylan on several occasions and he, too, was extremely critical of Dylan's accommodation, as he explained in 1964 to Colin Edwards:

> They allowed Dylan to be in a public ward; and America's public wards in the hospitals are terrible places... he lay there for three or four days. And he was never really moved to private quarters. And the result was that he was virtually on display and hundreds of people came, all wanting to see him, and there was no defence... I think that was one of the most terrible things that happened to Dylan, the fact that he was not protected at all from the rabble, or from the consequence of being so famous.

John Brinnin was Dylan's sponsor and friend. In Caitlin's absence, he took responsibility for decisions about Dylan's care in St Vincent's, and how it was to be paid for. Discussions certainly did take place about whether to move Dylan out of the general ward, as Rollie McKenna indicates in her interview (p240). The reasons not to move him were probably to do with the cost of doing so (a private room was some $4 per day more than a ward bed), and with weighing the benefits of giving a comatose patient a private room.[77] After all, Dylan was not expected to recover – even on November 5, the day of his admission, his friends were being told by the doctors that he "had a cerebral haemorrhage... with no better than an even chance of life."[78] By the morning of November 7 doctors were advising Brinnin that Dylan "would die within the next few hours", that he was "sinking rapidly" and that his death was not only inevitable but that "it was now also to be desired" because of the extent of brain damage (1955, pp283-84). The next day, Brinnin started fundraising to provide money for Dylan's medical and funeral expenses, and to provide support for Caitlin and the children.

St Vincent's was neither the best nor the worst hospital in New York, lying somewhere between the elite institutions such as New York Hospital and the municipal hospitals such as Bellevue. Its reputation at the time lay partly in the quality of its nursing. St Joseph's East was supervised by Sister Marie Consilio Lillis, a highly experienced nurse who had trained at The London Hospital, before emigrating and entering the Sisters of Charity in 1927. The ward was usually well staffed on the day shift between 8am and 4pm but, as in most hospitals at that time, there were difficulties on the evening and night shifts, for which there were just three staff for each shift. Holidays and sickness could make the situation even worse. In 1954, Priscilla Sassi worked the 4pm to midnight shift in the adjoining St Joseph's West ward, which was also a mens' medical ward with some thirty patients:

> On the evening shift, St Joe's West was usually staffed by a regis-
> tered nurse, a student nurse and an orderly or a nurse's aid. During
> my time at St Joe's West, the registered nurse was on vacation. That
> is why I was there, a senior student nearing graduation. I was
> helped by a first year student. I don't remember any orderly –
> maybe he was also on vacation… there was a nursing supervisor
> who made rounds throughout the hospital to check up on us and
> who was available for any unusual problems.
> Many of the patients were desperately ill. They were the victims
> of strokes, partially paralysed and unable to speak. Others were
> recovering from heart attacks or dying from cancer, cirrhosis or
> other diseases. The work was brutally hard, especially since we had
> no orderly to help lift the heavier patients. We had to prepare them
> for the night, change their sheets if necessary, and clean them up.
> I gave out all the medications, we changed dressings, irrigated
> bladders and colostomies, managed the IVs and on and on. I never
> got to write my charts until the night shift came on at midnight to
> care for the patients. [79]

There was a general shortage of nurses throughout New York hospitals in the early 1950s. Both the numbers of nurses available, as well as
their experience, was a particular problem on general wards. We note
that Dylan was a 'weekend patient', admitted to a general ward on a
Thursday and dead by the Monday. Staff shortages and absences,
including supervisors, technicians, nurses, doctors and specialists,
were a serious worry on weekends – weekend work was unpopular
amongst staff and more expensive for a hospital to fund. Not surprisingly, Brinnin and Rollie McKenna paid for private nurses to come to
St Vincent's to look after Dylan on the weekend of his admission. [80]
The two doctors who admitted Dylan and looked after him
throughout much of his stay were Dr William McVeigh and Dr F.
Gilbertson, second year medicine residents from New York university.
They should have been supervised by a chief medical resident, but no
such doctor appears in the various accounts of Dylan's stay in St
Vincent's. Indeed, McVeigh and Gilbertson were at first supervised
and directed by Milton Feltenstein, who had a private practice in the
fashionable Grammercy Park area of New York. He had no admitting
rights to St Vincent's nor any position of authority in the hospital. His
involvement continued until the evening of November 6 when he was

instructed to take no further part in supervising Dylan's treatment.[81]

Dylan was not examined by a specialist until the afternoon of November 6, when he was seen by Dr C. G. Gutierrez-Mahoney, who had been head of neurosurgery and neurology at St Vincent's since 1945. He had been trained at Harvard Medical School and in Germany and had co-authored the standard text on neurological nursing (1948). Dylan was in good hands, even if they had arrived rather late in the day. The delay, however, was not the fault of the hospital or Gutierrez-Mahoney. When Feltenstein decided in the afternoon of November 5 that Dylan needed to be seen by a brain specialist, he advised Brinnin to hire Dr Leo Davidoff, Chief of Neurosurgery at Beth Israel hospital. It took twenty-four hours for Davidoff to reply, saying that he was unavailable and that he unreservedly recommended none other than Gutierrez-Mahoney, who was immediately contacted and, as Brinnin notes, arrived shortly after at Dylan's bedside.

Dylan's hospital doctors knew virtually nothing of his medical history. Little could be gleaned from Feltenstein because Dylan had told him very little about his previous illnesses. On the night of November 6/7, Daniel Jones gave Gutierrez-Mahoney information about Dylan's blackouts, drinking, possible diabetes and a haematoma (blood clot) on the right temple that, he said, Dylan had experienced two months previously. The absence of a medical history was significant: a few days after Dylan's death, his friend George Reavey talked with the doctors:

> Hospital could not establish how long Dylan had been in coma before being brought. Nor could they get any case history. Doctor said 'everyone was too emotional'. Perhaps they were hiding something. Doctor said Dylan 'had a bad chance in the beginning' because they could get no clear picture. [82]

4. Dylan's Medical Data from St Vincent's

No biographer from John Brinnin in 1955 to Andrew Lycett in 2003 has had access to Dylan's hospital data. We, too, requested the case notes but had no reply from St Vincent's. Nashold and Tremlett were not allowed to see this information, though they were permitted to ask questions which were answered by St Vincent's staff by reference to the case notes. Nashold and Tremlett also interviewed some of the doctors who had looked after Dylan in hospital, but not Milton Feltenstein, who had died in 1974.[83] Neither were they able to interview Sister Consilio Lillis, for she died in 1986.

The only person we have identified who was given access to Dylan's medical notes was Dr William B. Murphy. Having first obtained Caitlin's permission, he visited St Vincent's in the morning of December 3 1964 to read the notes and to discuss Dylan's case with Gutierrez-Mahoney. Murphy then wrote a memorandum about what he had found in Dylan's medical notes, as well as the outcome of his talk with Gutierrez-Mahoney. The following summarises Murphy's memorandum.[84]

When Dylan was admitted in coma to hospital in the early hours of November 5 he was examined by Drs McVeigh and Gilbertson. Murphy refers to their notes as the "intern notes" and we shall follow him in this. The Intern Notes record that prior to admission Dylan

- had delirium tremens before falling into a coma, and that he had had delirium tremens "several times in the past."
- had been given half a grain of morphine and eight units of ACTH approximately half an hour before lapsing into coma [i.e. sometime between 11pm and midnight on November 4.]

The Intern Notes then went on to say that on admission Dylan

- had seizures and was placed on Dilantin. [This is the brand name of phenytoin, an anti-epileptic drug. It was given to calm seizures, which in Dylan's case were induced by hypoxia.]
- was "profoundly comatose", in that "he had extensor plantar response bilaterally." [This is a sign that both sides of Dylan's brain were malfunctioning – see the following Note for more detail.[85]]
- had coarse crepitant rales audible in all areas of his chest. [These are noises associated with bronchitis.]
- had bronchial pneumonia as shown by a chest film.
- had a red blood cell count of 5,100,000 and a white cell count of 21,050. [The red cell count was normal but the white cell count is raised, which is associated with an infection, in this case, bronchopneumonia.]
- tested negative for diabetes. Tests also ruled out poisoning by barbiturates or other drugs.

Finally, the admitting doctors noted "in their rather scanty history", as Murphy described it, that Dylan

- suffered from a stomach ulcer three years prior to admission.
- attempted suicide with Siconal in 1951 (Sicanol is the trade
  name for chemicals, made by a Belgium company, that are used
  in the beverages industry. We believe that it is a typing error, and
  that the writer intended Seconal, a barbiturate often used in
  suicides in combination with alcohol. Murphy records that the
  medical notes give no further information about this incident.
  There is more on Dylan and suicide in the following Note.)[86]
- had old scars, about four, "over the dorsal aspect of both wrists."
- had drunk "smoke", as well as "wood alcohol in the past".
  (Smoke is a cocktail that was once served in some New York bars;
  it mixed alcohol with Sterno, a stove fuel.)[87]

The other main source of data available to us on Dylan's condition is
the Medical Summary completed on November 9 by Dr McVeigh for
the purposes of the post-mortem. It described the circumstances of
Dylan's admission, diagnosis and treatment, and is published here for
the first time in its entirety:

> Pt. brought into Hosp in coma at 1.58am 11/5/53. Remained in
> coma during Hosp stay. History of heavy alcoholic intake.
> Received gn.1/2 of M.S. [morphine sulphate] shortly before
> admission. CSF [cerebrospinal fluid] clear on 2 occasions, press
> 260mm/H$_2$O, Protein 34 mg %. Urine neg for barbiturates. Serum
> Amylase normal.
>
> No history of injury.
>
> LUMBAR PUNCTURE 11/5/53 11/8/53
>
> Impression on admission was Acute Alcoholic Encephalopathy –
> for which patient was treated without response. Expired after 4+
> days in coma.

What does all this mean, particularly for an understanding of the
cause of Dylan's coma? Dylan was injected with half a grain (30mg)
of morphine shortly before admission. Morphine can cause coma, and
can contribute to it. It can also cause respiratory depression, which can
lead to hypoxia (insufficient oxygen in the blood stream), especially in
someone with a pre-existing lung disease. Hypoxia can lead to coma,
permanent brain damage and death. Morphine is usually metabolised
by the liver, but this would be delayed in a person whose liver was
damaged so that a course of injections in one day, such as Dylan

received, would lead to a build-up of morphine in the body.

The CSF pressure was at the upper limit of normal. The fact that the CSF was clear rules out many other causes of coma, including subarachnoid haemorrhage, major trauma to the head and infection i.e. meningitis. The protein measurement in the CSF of 34 mg % was within the normal range, 18 to 58 mg per dL, but it is also within the range known to occur in acute alcoholism, 13 to 88 mg per dL, so it does not rule in, nor rule out, acute alcoholism, nor most other diagnoses for coma.[88]

Dylan's urine had tested negative for barbiturates, so that an overdose of barbiturates was not the cause of his coma.

Raised serum amalyse is diagnostic of pancreatitis, often a complication of acute and chronic alcohol abuse. But the result was normal.

The lumbar punctures were carried out to extract the cerebro-spinal fluid for diagnostic tests. The second was done on November 8, the day before Dylan died though, curiously, Nashold and Tremlett date it to the 6th.

The hospital treated Dylan for "acute alcoholic encephalopathy" i.e. it suspected that Dylan's brain had been directly damaged by a rapid intake of a large amount of alcohol immediately prior to admission. This 'impression' or diagnosis was based only on information given by Milton Feltenstein and Liz Reitell. The record of delirium tremens could only have come from Feltenstein and Reitell, as probably did the information on drinking 'smoke' and wood alcohol. We can confirm that Reitell and Feltenstein, who persisted throughout with a diagnosis of alcoholic coma, also passed on the false information that Dylan drank "eighteen whiskies" in the early hours of November 4 – Gutierrez-Mahoney has referred to an "acute episode" of drinking "which began in the early morning of 4 November 1953" and this information could have come only from Reitell and Feltenstein.[89]

This drinking 'history' should be treated with caution, and we express our serious doubts about delirium tremens in the following Note.[90] But we can be sure of one consequence of the stories about Dylan's drinking eighteen whiskies, smoke and wood alcohol – they would have deflected attention away from Feltenstein's own treatment of Dylan, and lent authority in the eyes of the two junior doctors to his diagnosis of alcoholic coma.

In modern medical practice, a patient's blood alcohol level would be measured to confirm any diagnosis made simply on the basis of information provided by others, particularly for a patient from overseas whose medical and social history was not known to the hospital. A surprising feature of both the Intern Notes and the Medical Summary is that they contain no information on the amount of alcohol, if any, found in Dylan's body. CSF fluid, urine and blood samples were taken some eighty minutes after Dylan was admitted, as soon as his breathing had been restored to normal. It is conceivable that in 1953 a patient's body fluids were not routinely tested for alcohol. It is also possible that Milton Feltenstein so overawed McVeigh and Gilbertson with his diagnosis of alcoholic coma that they felt it unnecessary to measure Dylan's alcohol level.

We have gleaned further data from other sources which we draw upon in this chapter. Nashold and Tremlett discovered from the questions they put to hospital staff that on admission Dylan was severely dehydrated (p172) and that blood sugar tests on November 5 "showed a level of over 500 milligrammes against a norm of between 100 and 120 milligrammes" (p159). They were also told that Dylan's heartbeat was faint; his pulse weak but steady; his face "dry and clammy with blue lips and a splotchy, red and white, bloated face"; and the pupils of his eyes were small, not dilated (p155). Nashold and Tremlett report that Dylan was found to have anaemia (p115), but this is not borne out by the blood cell count described in the Intern Notes.[91]

We know little about Dylan's treatment in hospital. He was given artificial respiration on admission but after some fifteen minutes he was still not breathing spontaneously. After about an hour's compression and pumping, he began to breathe shallowly, and was given an oxygen mask. These difficulties in restoring Dylan to spontaneous breathing indicate how seriously ill he was at this early stage.

A blood transfusion was given on the morning of November 5, noted by Brinnin (p279), and a tracheotomy late on November 6. Dylan was then placed in an oxygen tent. He was put on a saline and dextrose drip which, according to Nashold and Tremlett, was changed to insulin on the 6th because the hospital suspected, for a while, that Dylan may have had diabetes. However, this information is not in the Medical Summary or the Intern Notes. We also note that both dextrose and insulin were used at the time in the treatment of delirium tremens.

We do not know what drugs, if any, Dylan was given to fight the pneumonia. In 1953, most common forms of pneumonia could be treated with penicillin which was being strongly marketed by Pfizer – presumably a sick patient in a hospital would have received it. However, we have no bacteriologic data to establish whether penicillin would have been the correct drug. We have to consider, too, whether Dylan's friends and doctors might even have thought it merciful, given the extent of Dylan's brain damage, to withhold drugs to allow the pneumonia to run its course.

5. The Causes of Death

Mortuary attendants collected Dylan's body from St Vincent's and took it and the Medical Summary to the City Morgue at Bellevue hospital for the post-mortem. The examination was carried out on the afternoon of Tuesday November 10 by Dr Milton Helpern, New York's Deputy Chief Medical Examiner and an Associate Professor of Forensic Medicine. He became America's leading forensic expert, known as the 'World's Greatest Medical Detective'. His biography became an international bestseller, though it said nothing about Dylan's post-mortem.

Milton Helpern would have first read the Medical Summary noting that Dylan was described as a patient with a "history of heavy alcoholic intake" who had been diagnosed as having acute alcoholic encephalopathy. He would have seen there were no body alcohol measurements on the form, nor other test results which offered positive confirmation of this diagnosis. Dylan's file is still in the Office of the Chief Medical Examiner in New York and we have established that it neither contains nor records any other medical data sent by the hospital to the post-mortem.

Helpern first examined the head. He found "considerable" pial oedema over the vertex (the crown). The brain was heavy and congested (cerebral oedema) but there were "no areas of softening or haemorrhage made out anywhere", nor blood clots (haematomata) nor tumours. The pons, cerebellum and brain stem were grossly i.e. macroscopically, normal. There was no gross pathology observed (as opposed to microscopic pathology) to explain the blackouts Dylan had been experiencing in Laugharne and London. The damage that was undoubtedly done to Dylan's brain cells by the hypoxia was not noted in the report because Helpern did not carry out a microscopic examination of cellular tissue.

As for the lungs, Helpern found that bronchopneumonia was "very evident" and "extensive" with "markedly diminished aeration" with "All of the lobes [appearing] to be involved in this bronchopneumonic process." Both lungs were affected, a condition commonly known as double pneumonia. The position of the diaphragm at the level of the fourth rib and fourth rib space was much higher than normal, suggesting that the lungs were contracted by the disease process.

Dylan's lungs were also "slightly emphysematous", hardly surprising given Dylan's history of smoking, and were "posteriorly somewhat atelectatic" i.e. collapsed, brought about by the pneumonia and also by immobility in coma. Helpern then considered the bronchi – the main air passages to the lungs – and found they were "deeply congested", indicating that Dylan had bronchitis. The bronchi were also covered with a patchy fibrin-and-pus membrane. Then Helpern noted another respiratory disorder – Dylan had "acute tracheobronchitis", described as a reddening and irritation of the upper part of the trachea (windpipe). The condition of the bronchi, taken together with the reddened and irritated trachea, add up to tracheo-bronchitis – inflammation of the trachea and bronchi. This inflammation would almost certainly have been caused by the same infection present in Dylan's lungs. It would also have been aggravated by his smoking. In short, Dylan had a badly impaired respiratory system.

Helpern's findings in Dylan's heart are typical of a 39 year old who led a sedentary life and who drank and smoked a good deal. The insides (lumen) of the coronary arteries had been narrowed by fatty deposit, in one case by fifty percent, with "considerable sclerosis with calcification". This means that Dylan was heading for angina and a possible heart attack as one or both of the arteries became completely blocked.[92]

Helpern then found several fine varices (dilated veins) at the lower end of Dylan's oesophagus. These varices are most common in patients with alcoholic liver disease. They can burst, especially as they get larger, leading to the vomiting of fresh red blood, and even causing a life-threatening haemorrhage.

Helpern did not note any signs of alcoholic hepatitis or cirrhosis in the liver but it was "firmer than normal [with] fairly evident fatty infiltration" and weighed 2,400 grams. This was much in excess of normal which is about 1,500g. There are many causes for fatty infiltration of the liver including long term alcohol ingestion and poor diet. It is not possible to tell from the post-mortem findings how well Dylan's liver was functioning, though the possibility of some liver damage cannot be ruled out.

Dylan's kidneys were fatty, as was the pancreas, which showed "considerable fatty infiltration, surrounded and concealed by fat... no evidence of fat necrosis or old pancreatitis but considerable fat between the lobules." Helpern also noted that the spleen was "moderately enlarged", a condition which is suggestive of liver damage.

Dylan's stomach showed no sign of ulceration, despite the history of vomiting blood in the past. It contained a litre of fluid, even though a tube had been inserted through Dylan's nose on November 6 to drain the stomach contents (noted by Brinnin, p236). Draining is important because vomiting or regurgitation of stomach contents is a risk in a comatose patient.

There are several references to oedema in Helpern's report (pial and cerebral oedema, oedematous foreskin, puffy face). Some oedema is to be expected as a consequence of the coma but we suggest it is also possible that this generalised oedema could have been contributed to, over the long-term, by hypoproteinaemia (low blood protein levels) caused by poor diet and/or a malfunctioning liver, with low protein levels in the blood leading to fluid 'leaking' out of the blood vessels into the tissues. Hypoproteinaemia is consistent with Dylan's fatty and enlarged liver, and both in turn are consistent with his alcohol consumption and poor diet. Hypoproteinaemia is consistent with Dylan's flesh being described as "watery" when he was admitted to St Stephen's hospital in 1946. It is also consistent with his puffy demeanour being apparent to Olive Suratgar as early as 1951: "an unpleasant pallor and puffy, extremely puffy, for a young man" (Colin Edwards interview). We stress, however, that we have no blood test results available to confirm or refute a diagnosis of hypoproteinaemia.

Helpern concluded that the causes of death were "Pial Edema: Fatty Liver: Hypostatic Bronchopneumonia." He noted that Dylan had been "In too long for alcohol studies." The last entry on Helpern's report is a hand written note which says "Classify as Acute & Chronic Ethylism [alcoholism]. Hypostatic bronchopneumonia." Helpern would have seen from the Medical Summary that Dylan had been injected with a half grain of morphine just before going into coma, but he made no comment about its likely effects on Dylan's respiratory system.

After the post-mortem, Dylan's brain and liver was sent for chemical analysis. This was done the following day by Alexander Gettler, the City's Principal Chemist, who is acknowledged today as one of the founders of modern toxicology. He found no sign of ethyl or methyl alcohol, barbiturates, other volatile poisons or morphine. This is hardly surprising since all these would have been metabolised in the days since Dylan's admission to hospital on November 5.

i. Hypostatic Bronchopneumonia

'Hypostatic' refers to pneumonia which develops as a result of a lack of movement. This occurs in patients who are not active because, for example, they are in coma. Helpern was wrong about this, but through no fault of his own. The Medical Summary he had been given failed to mention that Dylan had pneumonia on admission to hospital. His immobility in hospital will have exacerbated the pneumonia but it did not cause it.

Helpern's finding of bronchopneumonia as a cause of death has been uncontroversial, and most biographers from FitzGibbon to Lycett have followed Helpern and written that the pneumonia was contracted while in coma. Only Ferris has raised the possibility that the pneumonia could have begun earlier, before Dylan's admission to hospital.

Dr William Murphy's examination in 1964 of Dylan's medical records (set out on pp264-65 as the Intern Notes) confirms that Dylan's pneumonia had indeed started before he entered hospital, as the "chest film" taken on admission showed. Murphy included this information in his 1968 paper, noting that there were "physical and radiological signs" of bronchopneumonia on Dylan's admission. Murphy had also sent this data about the pre-hospital pneumonia to FitzGibbon in December 1964, together with his memorandum containing the information he had gathered from the hospital notes. FitzGibbon had also been given the post-mortem report. Yet he did not draw upon any of this material for his 1965 biography, and thus a knowledge vacuum was created which was rapidly filled with myths and falsehoods about Dylan's death.[93]

The confirmation in Dylan's medical notes of pre-hospital pneumonia is consistent with the pervasiveness of the pneumonia identified in the post-mortem report i.e. such severe and extensive pneumonia would have taken longer to develop than the four days Dylan was in hospital. Indeed, it is clear from Brinnin's account (see our chronology on page 358) that Dylan's respiratory system was already in severe crisis by the morning of November 7.

We were unable to see for ourselves the results of Dylan's X-rays, so we asked the distinguished forensic pathologist, Bernard Knight, for a further opinion. Knight is Emeritus Professor of Forensic Pathology at the University of Wales College of Medicine. He was also a friend of Milton Helpern and his biographer. Knight examined the post-mortem report and concluded that:

> death was clearly due to a severe lung infection, with extensive advanced bronchopneumonia. This is often a terminal event to many other underlying causes, but here the pre-existing acute-on-chronic bronchitis could be quite sufficient to flare up into a full-blown pneumonitis... given that Dylan had a history of a cough and chest trouble, confirmed by the autopsy finding of some emphysema, he obviously had chronic bronchitis. This often flares up at intervals into acute-on-chronic bronchitis, especially if he persisted in smoking. One would have to go on his history to a large extent, but the severity of the chest infection, with greyish consolidated areas of well-established pneumonia, suggests that it had started before admission to hospital.[94]

The post-mortem report also tells us that in addition to his chronic i.e. long-standing bronchitis, Dylan had acute tracheobronchitis, an infectious disease of the windpipe (trachea). In other words, the infection had taken hold in the whole of his respiratory tract from the windpipe down through the left and right bronchi, and into the lung tissue itself in both lungs (pneumonia). The chronic bronchitis would account for Dylan's longstanding cough and sputum, but when the sputum became infected (acute bronchitis) it developed into full-blown pneumonia.

The observations of pre-hospital pneumonia and acute-on-chronic bronchitis are consistent with many of the details noted in the chronology: fever and chills, fatigue, paleness, loss of appetite, nausea and vomiting, shortness of breath and excessive sweating. We also note from the chronology that Dylan was seen 'gasping' for breath on October 23, and that in the morning of November 4 he was "suffocating" and that in the afternoon he had "ghastly racking spasms."

Bronchopneumonia is a common outcome for people who are chronically debilitated through, for example, over-indulgence in alcohol, and who also have diet and sleep deficiencies. Throughout his adult life, Dylan neglected to eat regularly and properly, as he himself mentioned to Herb Hanum on October 24: "I guess I just forgot to sleep and eat for too long." Dylan's chronic debilitation would have made it more likely that pneumonia would occur as a complication from bronchitis.[95]

Dylan had always romantically seen himself as "the tubercular poet", but in truth it was his long-standing condition of bronchitis that did for him. His inability to take his health seriously, to stop smoking, to drink less, and to eat and sleep properly ensured that his chronic and acute bronchitis would lead, through pneumonia, to his death.

ii. Pial Oedema

The pia is one of the meninges, the three layers of thin tissue which are wrapped around the brain. We have never heard pial oedema described as a significant finding, nor of it being associated with any specific disease process. Pial oedema is certainly not a diagnosis that would be much used by pathologists today, and it is commonly observed at post-mortem examinations. Much more significant is the swelling or congestion of Dylan's brain tissue which is described as cerebral oedema.

Dylan's cerebral oedema should not be considered in isolation. We have already noted that the post-mortem report indicates that Dylan had a generalised oedema. We have suggested on page 270 that some of this general oedema may have been caused by hypoproteinaemia, which should therefore be considered as something which over a longer period of time may have contributed to Dylan's cerebral oedema.

A more significant factor in causing the cerebral oedema, as well as Dylan's coma, was hypoxia or oxygen starvation. Body cells depend on oxygen to survive. When the brain is deprived of oxygen, cells begin to starve and die. The brain is the largest consumer of oxygen and it is especially sensitive to hypoxia. Brain cells begin to die in large numbers after about five minutes of reducing the oxygen supply, leading to coma, cerebral oedema and even brain death.

It is helpful in diagnosing hypoxia to have laboratory tests on blood oxygen saturation and CO_2 levels but this data is not available. Nevertheless, we can be sure of hypoxia because of other evidence: gross breathing difficulties, cyanosis (blue face and lips, a sign of the low oxygen level in his blood), loss of consciousness and the great difficulty the doctors had in restoring Dylan's breathing.

Dylan's hypoxia was caused by his impaired respiratory system, particularly the pneumonia. Sheldon Cohen, one of America's leading chest specialists, has taken this view. In an article in 2000 co-authored with Philip Rizzo, he summarises Dylan's life-long history of "bronchial woes". Cohen and Rizzo conclude that the primary cause of death was "respiratory tract disease with consequently impaired oxygenation."[96]

Again we turned to Professor Knight to look at the evidence, and he concluded that "there was a mild degree of cerebral oedema terminally, related to the mode of death from a severe chest infection and consequent generalised hypoxia, which can cause cerebral oedema."[97]

We concur that Dylan's bronchitis and pneumonia were a significant contribution to his hypoxia and thus to the onset of coma in his hotel room and the development of cerebral oedema.

A second pertinent factor in causing the hypoxia was morphine. Dylan was given three injections on November 4. About half an hour after receiving the last injection, he stopped breathing normally and his face turned blue. In 1977, Paul Ferris was the first to link the third injection of morphine to hypoxia and cerebral oedema. Twenty years later, James Nashold (a neurosurgeon) and George Tremlett agreed that this third injection had caused hypoxia leading to brain damage. Nashold and Tremlett write that the morphine "was enough not only to send Thomas to sleep but to put him into irreversible coma by totally suppressing his brainstem's ability to control his breathing." (p152) They make the point on two more occasions:

> Thomas was now suffering from cerebral oedema, a swelling of the brain cells directly caused by the hypoxic injury... (p162)

> It was brain swelling that ultimately caused Thomas's death (p168).

An experienced doctor in his late forties, Milton Feltenstein could have been expected to know about the depressing effects of morphine on respiration. Cohen and Rizzo point out that these consequences of morphine have been understood since at least the nineteenth century, most notably described in Salter's medical textbook published in America in 1864. A former colleague of Milton Helpern, forensic pathologist Dr Cyril Wecht, has confirmed for us that the impact of morphine on breathing was known to medical practitioners in America in 1953.

It would be useful to pause here to examine the chain of events that led to Dylan, a sick man with a severe chest infection, being given morphine; and to ask why, when he fell into an hypoxic coma, he was not taken immediately to hospital to be revived.

Dylan woke up in his room at the Chelsea Hotel on the morning of

November 4 complaining of problems with his breathing. His distress was hardly surprising – he had acute and chronic bronchitis, emphysema and pneumonia. Part of his lung would have started to collapse (atelectasis) because of the blockage of smaller airways by infected secretions. If Dylan's liver was damaged, his breathing would also have been depressed by any alcohol that would have accumulated in his system instead of being excreted by the liver.

Reitell called Milton Feltenstein for help. During the day and evening of November 4, he gave Dylan two injections of morphine and ACTH. On both occasions he failed to examine Dylan thoroughly, if at all, but had he done so he would have observed that Dylan's respiratory system was in a parlous state and that he should have been admitted to hospital. Instead, he gave the injections, as well as a lecture about how Dylan should look after himself, and suggested a new diet.

Soon after, Dylan had bouts of incoherence and began "seeing things". Reitell wrongly thought this was delirium tremens, and once more called Feltenstein, who did not realise that the "delirium tremens" were just mild hallucinations brought on by the combined effects of fever, impaired oxygenation and morphine. Even if Dylan did have delirium tremens, Feltenstein would have been wrong to contemplate another injection of morphine - its use in treating delirium tremens was unequivocally contraindicated in leading American texts at the time e.g. Noyes (1953, 4th edition), as well as in medical reference books used by doctors such as the *Merck Manual of Diagnosis and Therapy*. [98]

But Feltenstein took out his needle yet again, and injected Dylan with a further half grain of morphine and eight units of ACTH, sometime between 11pm and midnight. The half-grain was a substantial dose, three times the amount usually given for the relief of pain. It would not normally be lethal but in this case it was given to a man with breathing difficulties. The morphine served to depress Dylan's respiration even further. It was the final insult to a beleaguered respiratory system already close to failure. [99]

Jack Heliker, who was in the hotel room with Dylan and Reitell, has timed Dylan's fall into unconsciousness at around midnight on November 4/5. Brinnin has also said that when Dylan "passed into a comatose condition" it was "a few minutes after midnight." Ruthven Todd, one of Dylan's close friends who had moved from London to New York in 1947, wrote to Louis MacNeice describing what Reitell had observed:

Shortly before midnight, she noticed a sudden change in him. He
was blue in the face and she and Jack [Heliker] could find only the
faintest tremor of a pulse.

Dylan was now in crisis: his chronic chest disease and pneumonia
were affecting his ability to get sufficient oxygen into his blood through
his lungs. His body would have tried to compensate by increasing the
respiratory rate (breathing faster). But the morphine was working in
the other direction, reducing the respiratory rate, further hindering the
body's attempts to maintain an adequate oxygen saturation of the
blood. If Dylan's liver was damaged, then the effects on respiration of
the third injection of morphine would have been compounded by the
liver having not fully metabolised the two previous injections. Dylan
thus drifted into an hypoxic coma, the most significant causes of which
were pneumonia and morphine.

Dylan's life could possibly have been saved if he had been given
immediate medical treatment, but it took almost two hours to get him
to a hospital. The story of this botched emergency is confused but the
main details are clear. Although Dylan went into coma around
midnight on November 4/5, St Vincent's Hospital did not receive a
request for an ambulance to be sent to the Chelsea until about 1am.
What had caused the delay? Reitell and Heliker had probably tried to
revive Dylan themselves. More precious time would have been spent
phoning Feltenstein, who at the beginning of the emergency seems to
have been unavailable. Reitell later confessed that she should have
immediately called the police.[100]

But there was to be yet more delay in getting Dylan to hospital. St
Vincent's was just a few blocks from the Chelsea, some five minutes
drive away for an ambulance at night time. To this must be added the
time it would take ambulance staff to go to a room at the Chelsea,
stretcher the patient down and return to the hospital – the whole
collection and delivery should not have taken more than fifteen
minutes. Yet it took almost an hour, and Dylan arrived at the hospital
at 1.58am on Thursday November 5, as the Medical Summary notes.

Todd's letter to MacNeice mentions that the ambulance personnel
immediately gave Dylan oxygen when they arrived at his hotel room.
If this is true, it may explain some, but not all, of the delay in getting
Dylan to the hospital. Unfortunately, the oxygen would have made
little difference because Dylan had stopped breathing properly.

Drs McVeigh and Gilbertson asked the driver what had caused the hour's delay since the hospital received the request for an ambulance. He blamed Feltenstein, Reitell and Heliker for holding him up: "They insisted on coming with me." This is hardly a convincing explanation, and Nashold and Tremlett wonder if Feltenstein had first tried, but failed, to get Dylan into Beth Israel on East 18th Street, where he had admitting rights.

Some two hours had been lost since Dylan first became unconscious. The delay was probably enough to cause such hypoxic injury that Dylan's brain may have been already damaged when he was brought to St Vincent's in deep coma, his lips blue and his face blotched red and white with fever. For the next hour or so all effort was put into getting him to breathe spontaneously again.[101]

Drs McVeigh and Gilbertson found it difficult to establish how long Dylan had been in coma, and both Reitell and Feltenstein failed to tell them that he had not been breathing properly for some time.

iii. Fatty Liver

Dylan's liver was not only fatty, but its weight of 2,400 grams was very much in excess of normal. The mere presence of excessive fat in a liver is not on its own a serious problem and it rarely causes illness. A fatty liver is usually associated with the consumption of alcohol, though it can also be caused by diabetes, obesity and inadequate diet, particularly one deficient in protein.

We suggest that Dylan's fatty liver was a result of his drinking, poor diet and obesity. Both the fat and the weight of the liver indicate the possibility of liver damage and malfunction. We cannot be certain of the degree of any liver damage, which can only be assessed during life by liver function tests.

In the 1950s, the inclusion of "fatty liver" as a cause of death was a euphemism for "chronic alcoholism" often used by American medical examiners to spare the feelings of grieving relatives. It is likely that today a pathologist would not include Dylan's fatty liver as a cause of death.

iv. Alcohol

The Notice of Death issued by Milton Helpern's office said that the hospital's diagnosis of toxic brain damage was not confirmed:

Comatose upon admission. Never regained consciousness. Hist:
(1) Heavy alcoholism (2) 1/2 grain morphine administered by a
private doctor. Treated in hospital for toxic encephalopathy but
diagnosis unconfirmed."

In other words, there was no confirmation that Dylan's brain had
been directly damaged by alcohol or any other toxic agent. But was
alcohol an *underlying* cause of death, contributing to the primary
causes identified by Milton Helpern? Did alcohol, for example, play
any part in bringing about Dylan's pneumonia? Helpern clearly
thought so. Whilst he did not list alcohol, alcoholism or alcoholic
poisoning as a cause of Dylan's death, he included the euphemism
"fatty liver" as part of the data that would be put on the death certificate. But when he came to classify the death for official statistics there
was no need to pull his punches. He duly wrote "Acute and Chronic
Ethylism [alcoholism]. Hypostatic Bronchopneumonia."

Acute Alcoholism
This means that Helpern believed that Dylan had drunk a large
amount of alcohol in the hours *immediately prior* to going into coma.
What evidence did Helpern have for this? He himself had not been
able to carry out any alcohol studies of the body, as his post-mortem
report declares. The Medical Summary sent to Helpern with the body
did not contain data on Dylan's body alcohol level. Nor does this form
report what other diagnostic steps the doctors took to establish acute
alcoholism e.g. smell of alcohol on the breath, flushed face, dilation of
pupils, low blood pressure and rapid pulse. In fact, the doctors noted
small pupils (which fits with the record of morphine injections), a
steady pulse and a splotchy red-and-white face.

The present history of events for the evening of November 4 does
not support Helpern's classification of acute alcoholism. Dylan drank
moderately on November 3 and went to bed early. In the early hours
of November 4, he drank heavily – eight large whiskies at the White
Horse between 2 and 3-30am. He then had two glasses of beer at
lunchtime. But even with a damaged liver, much of this alcohol would
have been metabolised from his body by late evening on November 4.
According to Brinnin, Dylan did not drink anything alcoholic after the
two lunchtime beers – Reitell was with him all the time, nursing him
whilst he slept fitfully in bed for the rest of the day, and denying him
alcohol.

This history depends wholly on Reitell's account of the evening, as passed onto Brinnin and published in his book. Could Reitell have been mistaken or was she lying as part of a cover-up? As Dylan lay ill in his hotel room in the early and late evening of November 4, did he wheedle any alcohol from her? We accept Reitell's account that he did not. Reitell was a feisty, efficient and determined woman who had been a wartime lieutenant in the Women's Army Corps. Brinnin's book describes other occasions when she had successfully controlled Dylan's drinking and broken up parties to protect him – see the chronology for details. No biographer has yet found any other information to challenge Reitell's account, which has been corroborated by Heliker – he told Ferris that Dylan "wanted a drink very badly, but she wouldn't give him one." When Ruthven Todd went to Dylan's hotel room on November 7 to remove Dylan's possessions, he noticed that the whisky in the bottle of Old Grandad was at exactly the same level as it had been after he, Todd, had opened it on November 3 and poured the very first measure from it for the hotel maid. It had not been touched by Dylan or anyone else on November 3 or 4.[102]

In short, there is at present no evidence from body fluid tests or from the accounts given by Reitell, or any other person, to support Helpern's classification of acute alcoholism. Were such evidence to become available, indicating that Dylan had been drinking on the evening of November 4, then it would confirm that alcohol had played a part, together with pneumonia and morphine, in depressing Dylan's breathing and bringing on hypoxia.

Chronic Alcoholism

In coming to a judgement of chronic i.e. long-term, alcoholism, Milton Helpern presumably drew on the post-mortem evidence of an enlarged and fatty liver, an enlarged spleen and several fine varices (dilated veins) in the lower part of the oesophagus. The condition of the liver alone supported long-term and frequent alcohol use.

Helpern's classification of chronic alcoholism indicates he believed that Dylan's lifetime of drinking played a part in bringing about his death. We broadly agree with this view. We have already described how Dylan's alcohol consumption would have been a factor, along with smoking, inadequate nourishment and sleep deficiency, in the chronic debilitation that allowed his bronchitis and pneumonia to flourish, both of which contributed to the hypoxia that led to cerebral oedema.

Alcohol is also implicated if it had damaged Dylan's liver, perhaps leading to hypoproteinaemia which may have contributed to the cerebral oedema.

There was no evidence, however, that Dylan's alcohol consumption *directly* caused the cerebral oedema or damaged the brain in any other way, as the Notice of Death makes clear. Helpern did not find any signs at the post-mortem of damage or changes to the structure of the brain associated with long-term alcoholism. Whilst chronic alcoholics can suffer from 'wet brain' disease or alcoholic dementia, it is impossible to make such a diagnosis without histology i.e. microscopic examination of the brain tissue. Neither Helpern nor anyone else carried out such an examination.

It is also worth noting here that alcoholic brain damage would not suddenly strike Dylan down in those two weeks in New York. It is a long-term degenerative process, and its range of symptoms, if Dylan was afflicted by it, would have been very apparent back home in Laugharne. In New York, Dylan's mind was functioning perfectly well during his professional and social engagements, including revising *Under Milk Wood*, taking part in two performances of the play, giving a poetry reading and participating in a symposium on film art. He displayed none of the signs of the neurocognitive deficits of alcoholism, not even those associated with mild alcoholism such as impaired memory, a declining capacity for abstract thought, attention deficit and concentration difficulties.[103]

When the post-mortem report and Notice of Death were issued, Gutierrez-Mahoney withdrew his previous diagnosis that Dylan's brain had been directly damaged by alcohol. Later, he went so far as to tell his colleague, George Pappas, that "Dylan Thomas did not have any neurological problems and I doubt whether he was truly alcoholic." (quoted in Nashold and Tremlett, p166)

In summary, alcohol was not a direct or immediate cause of Dylan's cellular brain damage or death, though over the long term it had contributed, together with food and sleep deficits, to such a deterioration in his overall health that bronchitis and pneumonia were able to take hold and kill him. There is one last point to make about alcohol, and that is the intriguing history of the theory that Dylan died of "chronic alcoholic poisoning". This is dealt with in the following Note.[104]

v. Drugs

We know that Dylan took benzedrine and sleeping pills on his last American trip, but these have never been implicated in his death, and there is no record of his having taken them prior to his admission to hospital. Nashold and Tremlett allege that Dylan was also taking barbiturates (p140) and that when he was admitted to St Vincent's "the pupils of his eyes were small, not dilated, which indicated the presence of narcotics." (p155) This allegation is contradicted by the hospital Medical Summary and the Intern Notes which show that Dylan tested negative for barbiturates. In examining Dylan's medical notes, Dr William Murphy also noted that "There was nothing to suggest he had swallowed a fistful of barbiturates, or any other drug."[105] Dylan's small pupils had probably been caused by the morphine.

vi. Diabetes

It is hardly surprising that when Colin Edwards started to talk to his interviewees about Dylan's drinking, many also brought up the matter of his eating habits. It is clear from Edwards' interviews that for much of his adult life Dylan neglected to eat regularly, and went for long periods either without food, or sustained only by sweets and fizzy drinks and, in America, canapés and other party nibbles. Dylan's taste for sweet things (including beer) and the blackouts he experienced, led Edwards to explore with interviewees whether Dylan suffered from hypoglycaemia – low blood sugar levels. A number of interviewees were with Dylan when these blackouts (and deep sleeps) occurred, including Philip Burton, Richard Bell Williams, John Morgan Dark and Billy Williams. Burton also mentions a blackout that happened when Dylan was with Louis MacNeice, and FitzGibbon reports a blackout at the McAlpine's house in London in August 1953 (p342). Dr David Hughes recalls being consulted by Caitlin about the blackouts. Robert Pocock did not witness any blackouts but told Edwards that "I've often thought that the way in which he used to pass out after drinking a certain amount, suggested that he might be a diabetic, or eventually become one."

Brinnin has written that the first lumbar puncture done in the early hours of November 5 had produced "some evidence that Dylan had sustained a diabetic shock", though by late evening, he records, all discussion of diabetes had finished and the doctors were talking of alcoholic poisoning of the brain. Nashold and Tremlett argue that Dylan was an undiagnosed diabetic, writing that the sugar levels in the blood taken from Dylan at around 3am on November 5 were "sky high" (p159). They claim that the levels went even higher as a result of the dextrose that was administered from the early hours of November 5. We note that no sugar levels were recorded either on the Intern Notes or the Medical Summary – neither mentioned raised blood sugar, nor glucose being detected in the urine. And whilst a high sugar level of the kind reported by Nashold and Tremlett would certainly suggest diabetes was a possibility to be investigated, no such single random reading would prove it.

If Dylan's blood sugar levels were "sky high", Ferris has pointed out that these could have occurred as a result of the damage to the brain, something that was not appreciated in 1953. More importantly, the raised levels in the blood taken at 3am would almost certainly have been the result of the three injections of ACTH that Dylan had received on the previous day, November 4. In other words, the high sugar levels reported by Nashold and Tremlett may have been a temporary condition, and in themselves did not mean that Dylan was diabetic or in a state of diabetic shock.

FitzGibbon has pointed out that diabetes was not found in 1940 when Dylan was medically examined for war service (p107). Nor was sugar found in Dylan's urine when it was tested at St Stephen's hospital in 1946. The Intern Notes from St Vincent's record that in 1953 Dylan tested negative for diabetes. Dr William Murphy, writing in December 1964 two weeks after examining Dylan's hospital records, told FitzGibbon that "Laboratory findings prior to death ruled out diabetes... there was nothing to suggest he had... diabetes or other toxic condition."[106]

Nashold and Tremlett, who were not allowed to read Dylan's hospital notes, claim that "details of Thomas's diabetes were sanitised from his medical records", though they do not say what evidence or sources they have for this allegation (p179). In the same December letter to FitzGibbon, Murphy reported: "I saw no evidence that portions of the medical records had been removed or altered."

We conclude that there is no evidence yet available that Dylan had diabetes. There is certainly enough material in both the Edwards interviews to caution us to be open-minded about the possibility that Dylan had problems with his blood sugar levels, though this does not necessarily mean he was an undiagnosed diabetic. Even if he were was, diabetes did not bring about his death. Both Dylan's coma and death were due entirely to respiratory tract disease, morphine and oxygen starvation, as Nashold and Tremlett have themselves conceded at three separate points in their book.

vii. Medical Incompetence and Care Standards

It is inconceivable today that a doctor would inject any morphine, let alone half a grain, to relieve discomfort from gout or to treat delirium tremens. Yet this is what Milton Feltenstein did to Dylan in 1953. And he did this without knowing much about Dylan's medical history, or carrying out any diagnostic tests. He failed to detect that Dylan was a patient with chronic chest disease, suffering from bronchitis and pneumonia. Feltenstein later acknowledged to a colleague that Dylan "had died as a result of his failure to conduct diagnostic tests and his consequent failure to prescribe appropriate treatment."[107]

It is difficult to understand why Feltenstein did not admit Dylan to hospital when he first came to see him at mid-day on November 4. He certainly felt Dylan's condition was serious because he told Reitell that his principal concern was that Dylan might slip into a coma, as Gittins has reported. Gittins also notes that a doctor who had studied Dylan's hospital treatment later said that "Dr Feltenstein's failure to have Dylan admitted to hospital earlier was even more culpable than his controversial course of injections." Dr William Murphy makes the same point in his 1968 paper: "It remains a mystery how so obviously and gravely ill a person, mentally and physically, could have remained outside a hospital." Gutierrez-Mahoney concluded that "Feltenstein's treatment was extraordinarily inadequate on several counts."[108]

Reitell and Heliker failed to call an ambulance immediately, and wasted almost an hour in trying to contact Feltenstein. The fact that the ambulance then took another hour to deliver Dylan to the hospital was a further significant failure of care that contributed to his brain damage and death.

These initial errors were compounded by Feltenstein's failure, and Reitell's, to tell the admitting doctors that Dylan had been unconscious for some two hours before his admission to hospital.

For the first critical day and a half of Dylan's time in hospital, Feltenstein directed Dylan's treatment, overawing and overruling the two house doctors, McVeigh and Gilbertson. These two young doctors appear to have been left during this period without adequate supervision and Feltenstein, who had no position of authority in the hospital, assumed that supervision. This appears to be a serious breakdown in the management system of the hospital.[109]

No specialist or consultant examined Dylan until Gutierrez-Mahoney arrived in the afternoon of November 6, some thirty-seven hours after Dylan's admission.

6. Our Conclusions

Dylan Thomas died from a severe chest infection with extensive and advanced pneumonia, complicated by morphine, leading to oxygen starvation and cerebral oedema. Self-neglect and medical negligence were both implicated. Dylan's smoking, drinking and poor diet, as well as his failure to seek medical help for his various pulmonary ailments, created the circumstances in which bronchitis and pneumonia could flourish in the days before he entered hospital. But Dr Milton Feltenstein took no steps to examine his patient thoroughly or carry out diagnostic tests, and he did not detect Dylan's pulmonary and respiratory problems. In ignorance of these, he injected morphine which depressed Dylan's damaged respiratory system still further.

Reitell and Feltenstein failed to get Dylan to hospital immediately when he went into coma. There was no effective management of Dylan's treatment in the first vital hours of care, nor specialist examination.

The story of the death of Dylan Thomas is one of a chain of neglect. It was an early death that could so easily have been prevented.

2: The Birth of *Under Milk Wood*

"It was written in New Quay, most of it." Ivy Williams, Brown's Hotel, Laugharne

This chapter is a revised and much expanded version of an earlier paper about the writing of *Under Milk Wood*. It contains a good deal more information about the work that was done on the play in New Quay, Elba and New York, as well as a fuller account of the extracts from the play that were read by Dylan in Prague in March 1949.

My original paper, which demonstrated that little of the play was written in Laugharne, appeared in the spring 2001 issue of the *New Welsh Review*. Many found it fascinating, but others rushed to defend Laugharne, pointing out both that Dylan wrote some of his finest poems at the Boat House and that the general public 'loved' Laugharne because it fitted their ideas of where a writer like Dylan *would* live and *would* write a play like *Under Milk Wood*. Who was I to spoil the pretty picture?

Certainly, Laugharne and *Under Milk Wood* are linked in the popular mind as closely as fish and chips or cockles and laverbread. It is widely believed that Llareggub was based on Laugharne and that Dylan wrote the play there. Literary opinion has bolstered the public view, from Ferris in 1977, who wrote that much of the play was written at the Boat House, to Stephens in 2000 who said that the greater part was.[110]

In his 1993 biography, Tremlett was content to claim just the first half for Laugharne but ten years later he would have us believe that all of *Milk Wood* was written there, even though we've known since Brinnin's 1955 book (and Cleverdon's of 1969) that the second half was mostly written in America.[111] Carmarthenshire's tourist office, and the local authority's website, also boast that the whole play was written at the Boat House.

Carmarthenshire, which prides itself on being a "land of myth and legend" where "in certain places, the facts become intertwined with fiction", has turned Dylan's time in Laugharne into a world-wide marketing opportunity to attract the devoted and the curious.

Laugharne, after all, has everything it takes to make a perfect shrine: the poet's grave, his work hut, his favourite pub and a ready-priested shore, all in a magnificent estuary setting. No wonder that within weeks of Dylan's death the *News Chronicle* predicted that "Now will begin the Dylan cult and Laugharne will become a shrine." (November 25, 1953)

The commercial enshrining of Laugharne began with the renaming of the cliff path to the Boat House as 'Dylan's Walk'. This was followed by the opening of the Boat House in 1975, an event consolidated in 1977 by the founding of the Dylan Thomas Society and the publication of Ferris' biography. In 1978, the twenty-fifth anniversary of Dylan's death, three Swansea businessmen enticed Dylan fans to journey on "upmarket pilgrimages" to Laugharne. Chauffeured Bentleys and Mercedes took parties on trips around Dylan's Swansea and Laugharne, stopping for champagne receptions, *cordon bleu* dinners and poetry readings. This promotion was part of a marketing blitz from the Welsh Tourist Board, which believed that "Dylan could soon be one of the biggest attractions to foreign tourists to Wales..."[112] Carmarthenshire Council thought the same and bought the Boat House, spending over half a million pounds to save it from collapse, and refurbishing it as a heritage centre. It has been a wise investment – around 20,000 people annually visit the Boat House, which has become "one of Wales' most popular national monuments".

There are three occasions on which Dylan declared that Laugharne was the setting for the play.[113] But we should not make too much of this because on two of these occasions Dylan was using the play to beg for money. There are also three letters, all written from Laugharne and none asking for money, when Laugharne did not feature in Dylan's thinking at all. In these, he wrote that the play was set "in a small town in a never-never Wales"; "in a Wales that I am sad to say never was"; and in a "Welsh town-that-never-was". When Dylan gave the first reading of the play in America on May 3 1953, he introduced it as a "picture of a small Welsh town-that-never-was". And when John Brinnin came to Laugharne in 1951, Dylan told him only that the play was based on "the life of a Welsh village very much like Laugharne."[114]

Dylan's friend, the author Richard Hughes who lived in Laugharne, told Colin Edwards that when Dylan "came to write *Under Milk Wood*, he didn't use actual Laugharne characters." Hughes had made the same point in his 1954 review of the play. Although Dylan had once intended "to use some of his fellow-townsmen recognisably", reports

Hughes, when he abandoned the plot about a mad town (see below), he also decided on "the total abandonment of particular 'true' portraits." The characters of Llareggub "ought to live in Laugharne, perhaps, but in fact not one of them does".[115]

Hughes is probably right that there are no true or complete portraits of Laugharne residents in the play. But there are certainly some elements of Laugharne that can be found in the text: the name Rosie Probert was that of a former inhabitant of the town; Mog Edwards' boater and butterfly collar came from Laugharne draper, Mr Watts, though his shop was Gwalia not Manchester House; and, as we noted in the Introduction, Duck Lane and Little Willy Wee are from Laugharne. Salt House Farm probably inspired Salt Lake Farm but it is not on top of Sir John's Hill, as some writers claim. Neither does it root *Milk Wood* in the particularity of Laugharne since it was not written into the play until 1953. Denzil Davies MP has claimed Organ Morgan for Laugharne, asserting that he was based on E.V. Williams, the organist at St Martin's Church, who lived a few doors down from Brown's Hotel.[116] Butcher Beynon certainly draws in part on butcher and publican Carl Eynon, though he was in St Clears not Laugharne:

> He [Dylan] used to come in here and sit in the room with the coracle men around an open fire and I'd watch him listening and memorising and writing down. He told me he was writing a play and that I was in it, but he'd put you off if you started fishing him... My fridges are down the lane out the back there and sometimes Dylan would see me walking back up to the shop carrying a cleaver, often with my little dog. It was a dachshund, see, a sausage dog, but in his play he calls it a corgi (Burn, 1972).

And which Laugharne resident was Captain Cat? In his Edwards interview, John Morgan Dark suggests it was a Mr Whitaker Jones, who was not blind, and Jane Dark of Laugharne that it was a sea captain nicknamed Cat, who was. Both agree that, whoever he was, he frequented the Cross House Inn, but neither Phil Richards, who ran the Cross House, nor his daughter Romaine, were at all convinced about this in their Edwards interview, and do not suggest any names of their own. None of these accord with Min Lewis' suggestion (1967) that it was Laugharne resident Johnny Thomas. And most tellingly of all, Billy Williams of Laugharne told Colin Edwards that he thought that the original for Captain Cat was a New Quay sailor.

It is particularly interesting that so few of Laugharne's distinctive

and historic features are reflected in the play. This is hardly surprising
– how could a play about a 'quintessentially' Welsh town peopled with
identifiably Welsh characters be plausibly based on an English-
cultured, English-speaking enclave such as Laugharne? Those who
press Laugharne's claims deal with this problem by advancing two
further arguments. First, that it is not the detail of Llareggub's people,
places and culture that matters but rather the eccentricity of its inhabitants. Only Laugharne, it is claimed, possessed "the play's anarchic
spirit". This is not the strongest of cases as those who know New
Quay's colourful history, or even that of Llansteffan, will appreciate.

Second, there is the default argument: there is no convincing
evidence about Ferryside or the Mumbles (and I agree about that)
and, furthermore, Dylan did not know New Quay well enough because
he lived there for only nine months and never returned. Therefore,
Llareggub must be Laugharne. But Dylan had been visiting New Quay
since the mid 1930s, sometimes to see his aunt and cousin who lived
there. He also came to see Lord Howard de Walden at Plas Llanina,
and worked in its Apple House. Dylan often returned to the town
during the War when he was staying a few miles away in Talsarn, before
ending up in Majoda in 1944/45. He also came back after the War, and
was still writing to Skipper Rymer, who once ran the Dolau pub, as late
as 1953.[117]

Since Dylan took several years to write the play, it is not surprising
that a number of villages and towns would swim in and out of his
consciousness as he sought to create Llareggub's profile – including
Laugharne, Llansteffan and New Quay. When the play is analysed in
detail, New Quay seems to be the most significant of the locations that
Dylan drew upon. Some of the names in *Under Milk Wood* come from
New Quay – Maesgwyn farm, the river Dewi and the Sailor's Home
Arms, for example. Llareggub's Welshness and sea-going history is that
of New Quay, as is its harbour, woods, terraced streets and quarry.
Dylan's sketch of Llareggub is plainly of New Quay and, as Cleverdon,
has pointed out

> The topography of the town of Llareggub… is based not so much
> on Laugharne, which lies on the mouth of an estuary, but rather on
> New Quay, a seaside town… with a steep street running down to
> the harbour (1969, p4).

Cleverdon's description of the "steep street running down to the harbour" helps us to appreciate that the various references in the play to the top of the town, and to its "top and sea-end", refer to toppling, cliff-perched New Quay, not to Laugharne, which has little top and no sea-end at all. *Under Milk Wood* is also full of other words and phrases that root the play in the "particularity and locality" of New Quay. The Fourth Drowned sailor asks about buttermilk and whippets – Jack Patrick Evans of the Black Lion bred whippets and made buttermilk in his dairy next to the hotel. The town's terraced streets viewed from Majoda inspired the phrase "hill of windows". I provide more examples in Thomas 2000 and 2002b.

FitzGibbon has observed that Llareggub "resembles New Quay more closely [than Laugharne], and many of the characters derive from that seaside village in Cardiganshire..." (p237). For example, Dai Fred Davies (one of Dylan's friends – see his letter of August 29 1946) supervised the donkey engine on the *Alpha* and became Tom-Fred the donkeyman in the play. Dan 'Cherry' Jones inspired the name Cherry Owen. Indeed, Dylan inadvertently uses the name "Cherry Jones" in one of his drafts of the play. In an early list of *Milk Wood* characters, Dylan describes Cherry Owen as a plumber and carpenter – Cherry Jones was a general builder in New Quay. One of the town's postal workers, Jack Lloyd (also mentioned in the same August letter), provided the character of Willy Nilly. Lloyd was New Quay's Town Crier. Willy Nilly's penchant for opening letters, and spreading the news from one house to another, is a strong reflection of Lloyd's role as Crier, as Dylan himself noted on one of his worksheets for *Under Milk Wood*.[118]

Llareggub's sailors had travelled the world, and brought back coconuts and parrots for their wives. Captain Cat, who spoke a little French, had been to San Francisco. His drowned companions had visited Nantucket. It is then hardly surprising that Billy Williams of Laugharne, whose little fishing boats seldom went further than Bristol, thought that the inspiration for Captain Cat was a New Quay sailor. In Dylan's day, there were over thirty-five retired, ocean-going captains living in the town, a wonderful gallery of Captain Cats to inspire a writer's imagination. Indeed, one in five of New Quay's men aged twenty and over were master mariners, either retired or serving. One of these was Captain Tom 'Polly' Davies, who lived opposite the Black Lion and drank with Dylan there. Tom Polly had worked as a censor for part of the War, and had been a Government Observer during the Spanish Civil War. Both these roles may have helped to form Dylan's image of Captain Cat as "The Witness", as Dylan described him in a list of the characters of the play, someone privy to the everyday lives and secrets of the people of Llareggub.[119]

And whilst Captain Cat lived in Schooner House, Tom Polly lived in Schooner Town – ninety-nine schooners were built or owned in New Quay between 1848 and 1870. Dylan himself provided a significant clue to New Quay's influence on the play when, in an early draft of *Milk Wood*, he described Llareggub as a "schooner-and-harbour-town".[120]

A few hundred yards to the north of Majoda stood the church of Llanina. Ackerman has rightly pointed out that the story of the drowned village and graveyard of Llanina, "is the literal truth that inspired the imaginative and poetic truth" of *Under Milk Wood* (1998, p127). To the south, between Majoda and New Quay, stood Maesgwyn farm and the little community of Pentre Siswrn but they, two roads and about sixty acres of farmland were lost to the sea over Dylan's lifetime. It is these drowned houses and fields that inspired the "imaginative and poetic truth" of the play, as much as those of Llanina. Not to mention the 150 sailors in local graveyards who died at sea or in foreign ports.

Since Dylan started work on the play at New Quay, it is hardly surprising that the town had a profound influence on the writing of *Under Milk Wood*. I have described elsewhere the many other ways in which New Quay was mother of the play, and I discuss the particular case of Polly Garter in the next chapter. None of this makes Laugharne any less beautiful or attractive to visitors, or less significant as the place that inspired several wonderful poems, but it played a relatively small part in the production of *Under Milk Wood*. I want now to examine the play's growth, and show that most of it was written in New Quay, South Leigh and America.

From Caswell Bay to Prague

According to Bert Trick in his interview with Colin Edwards, an embryonic *Under Milk Wood* was written by Dylan in 1933:

> He read it to Nell and me in our bungalow at Caswell around the old Dover stove, with the paraffin lamps lit at night... the story was then called *Llareggub*, which was a mythical village in South Wales, typical village, with terraced houses with one *ty bach* [lavatory] to

about five cottages, and the various characters coming out and emptying the slops and exchanging greetings and so on; that was the germ of the idea which... developed into *Under Milk Wood*.

It is likely that what Dylan read to the Tricks was a story rather than a play for radio, for at this time Dylan had had no experience of writing for that medium, and did not make his first broadcast until 1937. He also recognised his own limitations for writing something 'long' for the radio. His letter in November 1938 to T. Rowland Hughes, a BBC producer, was a prophetic warning about how difficult the writing of *Under Milk Wood* would prove to be:

> I don't think I'd be able to do one of those long dramatic programmes in verse; I take such a long time writing anything, & the result, dramatically, is too often like a man shouting under the sea. But if you'd let me know a little more about these programmes – length, subjects unsuitable, etc – I'd like to have a try. It sounds full of dramatic possibilities, if only I was.

In 1939, Dylan had a discussion with Richard Hughes about writing a play about Laugharne, in which the villagers would play themselves – see page 75 for Hughes' account of this. Four years later, in 1943, Dylan met again with Richard Hughes, and this time outlined a play about a Welsh village certified as mad by government inspectors. Constantine FitzGibbon has written that "after the revelations of the German concentration camps," Dylan told him the plot about a mad village, and dates this to a "year or so" after 1943 (p237).

In September 1944, Dylan and family arrived in New Quay, Cardiganshire, and moved into a bungalow called Majoda. He wrote *Quite Early One Morning* there, one of the most important precursors of *Under Milk Wood*, commissioned by Aneirin Talfan Davies as *Portrait of a Seaside Town*, and broadcast on December 14 1944. In his Introduction to *Under Milk Wood*, Daniel Jones has noted that, following the success of the broadcast, Dylan contemplated "a more extended work against the same kind of background". Jones also writes that there was much discussion between Dylan and his friends about the form this extended work should take.

In 1945, the BBC producer Philip Burton visited New Quay to prepare a "radio impression of a Welsh village by the sea", broadcast on March 1. Burton's programme may have been another influence on Dylan that secured New Quay as a significant template for *Milk Wood*.

The reminiscing sailors of the play are anticipated at the start of Burton's script (e.g. "I was in Wellington... the night of Pearl Harbour."/ "I'll never forget that dinner in Hong Kong.") And whilst the drowned sailors of Llareggub open *Milk Wood*, Burton's programme ends with the drowned sailors of New Quay, in "cemeteries of empty graves" because "the whole world is the grave-yard of this little village."

Gwen Watkins has noted that the "germ... of the earliest idea" of the play was conceived in New Quay. Theodora FitzGibbon has described how Dylan had told her in 1944 that he was writing a radio play "peopled with what he called 'a good cross-section of Welsh characters.'" Her husband, Constantine FitzGibbon, has also written in his biography that Dylan started to write *Under Milk Wood* in New Quay. This is confirmed by Jack Patrick Evans of the Black Lion, who notes in his Edwards interview that Dylan was working on *Milk Wood* in New Quay. And one of Dylan's closest friends and confidante, Ivy Williams of Brown's Hotel, Laugharne, has said "Of course, it wasn't really written in Laugharne at all. It was written in New Quay, most of it."[121]

Writing in January 1954, just days before the first BBC broadcast of the play, its producer Douglas Cleverdon has also drawn attention to Dylan's work at New Quay: "He wrote the first half within a few months; then his inspiration seemed to fail him when he left New Quay, Cardiganshire, and came to live in London."[122]

The most extended description of the progress of Dylan's work on *Milk Wood* at New Quay comes from the writer and academic, Dan Davin. In the spring or summer of 1945, he went with Dylan to a gathering at a flat in Riding House Street, off Langham Place, in London. There Dylan recited

> some rather bawdy songs and verses he had lately been writing, things he seemed to regard as written for fun rather than in earnest. They were a sort of *vers de société*, except that the society was Welsh and humble, people from a village which Dylan said was called Laugharne but which in the verses he named Llareggub. The verses, quatrains for the most part, were rich in affection, humour, compassion, and vivifying detail, and their effect was somehow medieval in the intimacy of the alliance between the poet and the people he was describing... I remember my admiration and enjoyment being infiltrated and spoilt by a feeling of dismal envy for the remarkable flow of metaphor and fantasy which came so easily to the man – came from him, rather, as water pours from a fountain.[123]

Dylan and Caitlin left New Quay at the end of July 1945 to stay with his parents at Blaencwm in August and September. By early 1946, they were living in Oxford, and there Dylan wrote the other six radio scripts, including *Return Journey*, that are recognised as milestones on the road to Llareggub. In April 1947, Dylan and family went to Italy. He intended to write a radio play there, as his letters home make clear.[124]

Dylan ended his holiday on Elba, staying in Rio Marina, a town, like New Quay, of steep streets, quarries and harbour. It's possible that Rio reminded Dylan of summer in New Quay, packed with South Wales miners, for he arrived at the beginning of the iron miners' holiday. They regarded him with "curiosity and simpatia", the Elba historian Gianfranco Vanagolli told me. Dylan drank with them, and with Pierino the anarchist, the most powerful miners' leader on Elba. Through these friendships, Dylan "perceived the soul of the community... as he was Welsh and the mine was in his blood."

Staying in the same hotel as Dylan was the Florence intellectual, Augusto Livi, who wrote:

> ...in the village of steep houses and stone stairs, the small reddish dogs used to stop at the corners when the poet Dylan Thomas passed by, with his Bacchus head and his two colour clothes, green trousers and pink shirt...[looking] like an archbishop, with his white cap and the long shirt out of his trousers (1949).

Dylan was solitary and introspective, Livi told Colin Edwards in 1969. There were long, silent walks along the coast when Dylan was "preoccupied by poetical activity." Rio had a "very kind and human atmosphere... Dylan loved this atmosphere... I think that he saw in the landscape, the naked landscape, a souvenir of the Galles, of Wales." Both Livi and Luzi describe how Dylan was busy writing during his stay in Rio Marina. Luzi told Edwards:

> On the island of Elba, he managed to get started again, to break his silence, resuming the typical lilt of his poetry but at the same time renewing it. I think it was actually in Elba that he wrote *Under Milk Wood*, if I'm not mistaken. I think that's the composition that he at least started in Elba.

Dylan's letters from Rio mention the "fishers and miners" and "webfooted waterboys" who we later find as the "fishers" and "webfoot cocklewomen" of the first page of *Milk Wood*. The "sunblack" and "fly–black" adjectives of Italy would be re-worked as the "crowblack" and "bible-black" descriptions of Llareggub. Alfred Pomeroy Jones, sea-lawyer, "died of blisters", and so, almost, did Dylan and family as he vividly describes in his letter of August 3 1947. And in time, Rio's "blister-biting blimp-blue bakehouse sea" would appear as Llareggub's "slow, black, crowblack, fishingboat-bobbing sea."[125]

On their return in August 1947, the Thomas family moved to South Leigh outside Oxford, living in the Manor House, a dilapidated cottage, with a caravan provided for Dylan's writing. Phyllis Broome's books describe the village at the time. Rob Brown, who lived near the Manor House, told me that Dylan "worked very hard writing in the caravan." In a 1963 BBC interview, Betty Green of the village shop said that Dylan:

> used to go into the caravan so as to do his poets and he used to be there all day long... he used to write all day long. Dylan was never still, but he must do his poets first, but if he could do his poets, he could go and have a drink. But unless he had done that, he couldn't.[126]

It was here that Dylan continued work on the play, as he told his parents he would in his letter of July 19 1947: "I want very much to write a full-length – hour to hour & a half – broadcast play; & hope to do it, in South Leigh, this autumn." Philip Burton encouraged Dylan to build upon the success of *Return Journey*. He has recalled a meeting in the Café Royal in 1947, when they discussed the play:

> ...he was telling me an idea he had for... *The Village of the Mad*... a coastal town in south Wales which was on trial because they felt it was a disaster to have a community living in that way... For instance, the organist in the choir in the church played with only the dog to listen to him... A man and a woman were in love with each other but they never met....they wrote to each other every day... And he had the idea that the narrator should be like the listener, blind.... (1953 and recorded talk)

Dylan continued with the play in 1948, as he mentioned in his March letter to John Ormond from South Leigh: "A radio play I am writing has Laugharne, though not by name, as its setting." John Davenport has confirmed that Dylan worked on the play at

South Leigh, observing that *Milk Wood* "took six years to make."[127] In his interview with Colin Edwards, Harry Locke, a good friend of Dylan's and a neighbour in the village, comments that Dylan wrote a substantial part of the first half at South Leigh. Talking about Dylan's time in the village, the following exchange occurs:

> Joan Locke: He'd written a great deal of *Under Milk Wood* at that time, hadn't he?
> Harry Locke: Oh yes, he worked on *Under Milk Wood* for about six years but he finished it off at 260 [Kings Street, Hammersmith, Locke's home]... he finished most of it in the pub. In the Ravenscourt Arms.

A few miles from South Leigh was a German POW camp, whose inmates were waiting to be resettled. They chopped wood for Caitlin, looked after the garden and worked on the neighbouring farms. Perhaps the camp was, for Dylan, a daily reminder of the plot about the mad village, which he described to FitzGibbon as having barbed wire "strung about it and patrolled by sentries."[128]

The time at South Leigh was a key period in the writing of *Milk Wood*, building on the work that had been done at New Quay. Distractions were few in early 1948; there were no poems on the go, only a handful of radio broadcasts and the new round of film scripts had only just begun. In one of these South Leigh films (*Three Weird Sisters*), we find the familiar Llareggub names of Daddy Waldo and Polly Probert.

Dylan travelled from South Leigh to Prague in March 1949 to a Congress of the Writers' Union. The visit is often used as an example of Dylan's political naivety. But he had personal reasons for going. In wartime London, he had got to know Jiří Mucha, who had been part of the group in London around John Lehmann, and had translated Czech poets for the periodical *New Writing*. His description of his encounter in Prague with Dylan is given on page 156.

On March 7, Dylan went to a party in the suburb of Horní Krč to meet the leading Czech poet, Vladimír Holan. The host Jan Grossman remembers that

> The evening began with the help of those of us who could speak English... Holan crushed glasses of red wine with sculptor's hands and Thomas... lit cigarette after cigarette to go with the wine; the ash fell on his suit lapels, then onto his lap, and from his lap onto

the parquet floor which he systematically ground in with his shoes. The night came on rapidly, the poets' conversation became more agitated, but the interpreters were no longer necessary. Holan and Thomas began to communicate in a language which was born on the spot, which formed its experience and rules, was built on verbal and mimetic gesture, and insisted on being listened to and reacted to through its intonation and the melody of its sentences... in a moment a world appeared which could be entered into just with a look, with a look of the eye and the soul. And this night lasted until morning. After it there were memories and poems, even those which the master of the house insisted Holan write in his Guest Book: 'Devil take these books,/but he won't take them... /they are immortal, they live on eternally/ and so my name here quickly too!' The night ended late. When we accompanied both poets out an orange sun rose above the frosty morning (Justl, 1988).

In her memoir (see p163 above), Jiřina Hauková, who was Dylan's guide and interpreter, recalls that at the party Dylan "narrated the first version of his radio play *Under Milk Wood*." She describes how she outlined the plot about a town that was declared insane, and then portrayed the predicament of the eccentric organist and the baker with two wives. A government official arrives with evidence of the insanity of the town:

> He said that the document, which had proofs of their insanity, was too voluminous, so he would only read some of the proofs at random. "In this community they play the organ for goats and sheep." The citizens were angered by this and called on the organist. He says: "One evening I went to church to play the organ, I left the gate open and the goats and sheep came into the church and I played for them." "In your city there is also a baker who has two wives." The people protested again. But two women at the assembly stood up and said: "Yes, we both live with the baker and we all like each other."[129]

In their interviews with Colin Edwards, Grossman also said that Dylan "spoke about *Milk Wood*, the radio play, and he quoted some parts of it...." And Josef Nesvadba who, like Grossman, had been educated at the English school in Prague, was another at the party who remembered Dylan referring to the mad town plot, as well as the Voices in the play.[130]

This testimony from Prague, when taken with that of Burton about the meeting in the Café Royal in 1947, indicates that many of the characters of the play were already in place by March 1949: the organist, the two lovers who never met but wrote to each other, the baker with two wives, the blind narrator and the Voices.

Laugharne: dreaming of America

In May 1949, the Thomases moved from South Leigh to the Boat House in Laugharne. Just four months later, on September 23, Dylan met with his agent David Higham, who sent a letter summarising their discussion:

> Your own radio play nearly finished hasn't been taken into account in the above, but I imagine it may finish itself before you go to the USA. We have noted that P.H. Burton of Cardiff knows all about it, and will eventually want to do it.[131]

We know now that 'nearly finished' was an exaggeration, and only the first half was close to completion. Yet it tells us that substantial progress had been made on the play.

Of great interest, too, is an article by the poet Allen Curnow in the *NZ Listener*, in which he writes about visiting Dylan in Laugharne in October 1949. Curnow describes being taken to the writing shed. Dylan "fished out a draft to show me of the unfinished *Under Milk Wood*" that was, says Curnow, titled *The Town That Was Mad*. The draft was fished, not from Dylan's 'littered desk' where he was working on *Vanity Fair*, but from a chest of drawers (1982).

But could this draft, which was undoubtedly the 'nearly finished' play described by Higham a month earlier, have been written at the Boat House between May and September 1949? This is wholly improbable. It conflicts with the evidence from New Quay, South Leigh and Prague. There is nothing in his letters, or in any documentary or biographical source, to suggest that Dylan was working on the play in these first months in Laugharne. Most writers stress the other things on Dylan's mind, including writing *Living in Wales* and 'Over Sir John's hill', and making a start on *Vanity Fair*. There was, too, the birth of Colm, as well as broadcasts, debts, illnesses and a summons to contend with. Curnow has also mentioned that he found Dylan busy preparing himself "very seriously" for the forthcoming American trip, choosing and rehearsing poems for his readings.

Furthermore, the 'nearly finished' script had been discussed with Philip Burton some time before the meeting with Higham. A letter from Jean LeRoy of Highams in March 1950 to Caitlin tells us that Dylan's meeting with Burton had taken place in 1949.[132] They may have met around July 29 when Dylan was in Cardiff for a BBC programme, or even earlier. This further reduces the possibility that Dylan had written the script in the first few months at the Boat House.

Higham had been optimistic in thinking the play might 'finish itself'. Dylan worked on his poetry for the rest of the year, finishing the first draft of 'In the White Giant's Thigh' and starting 'Poem on His Birthday'. But it was hard going; he was "tangled in hack work", Caitlin

30. Dylan at the Boat House, October 1949

was ill, and the Laugharne traders were snapping at his heels for money.[133]

Dylan did not read from the play in Cardiff in October or in Tenby in November 1949, nor is it mentioned in his letters about his forthcoming American trip.[134] At the turn of the year, he was preoccupied with the arrangements for travelling, his father's serious illness and broadcasting in London. It was, he said, "hard to sit down every day in peace... and write..."

It seems unlikely that Dylan did any work on the play in the early part of 1950. His first American visit, a tour of twelve thousand miles and thirty-nine readings, began in February. There is no record that Dylan read from the script or did any writing there. In her March letter to Caitlin, LeRoy asks if Dylan had made any progress in finishing the play. Caitlin replied that she couldn't find the script, but didn't think that Dylan had got very far with it.

Dylan returned in June. The next three months were spent in Laugharne, with trips to London to broadcast. He completed 'In the White Giant's Thigh' and worked on 'In Country Heaven'. He planned a piece on America for *Vogue* and the BBC agreed to take *Letter to America*, but he failed to write either.

September was not a month for writing. The first two weeks were in London with Pearl Kazin and John Malcolm Brinnin, who makes no mention of the play in his account of this time together. Indeed, Brinnin did not hear about 'Llareggub Hill' until 1951. It appears that Kazin, too, did not hear of the play either in America or in London. She told me that she has never heard of the title *The Town that was Mad:* "The only early title I knew of for UMW was Llareggub..."

Caitlin soon found out about Pearl and the marriage was plunged further into crisis. Dylan extricated himself, and in mid-September he went back with Caitlin to London, where she was to have an abortion. He spent a good deal of the next five weeks there, some of it ill with pleurisy. He met with Douglas Cleverdon, who wrote on October 20 1950 to say that the BBC "have agreed to take the Town that was Mad." Later that month, Dylan sent Cleverdon thirty-five handwritten pages of the first half, a script that contained most of the places, people and topography of Llareggub, and which ended with the line "Organ Morgan's at it early..."[135]

I conclude from all this evidence that most of the first half of *Milk Wood* was first written in New Quay and South Leigh, with probably some work done in Rio Marina, as well as later revisions and additions done in America in 1953. The work at South Leigh was completed within three years of Dylan's leaving New Quay, presumably with memories still fresh and Cardiganshire notebooks to hand.

The Chase Begins

The half-script sent to Cleverdon in October 1950 was wholly in the manner of the play as we know it today, and Dylan's plan was to develop the mad town plot in the second half. He did write some pages of mad town script, which are reproduced in Davies and Maud (ppxix-xx), and he then outlined the way in which he would write about the mad town and its trial in the town hall – this is also helpfully reproduced in Davies and Maud. We do not know how much more, if any, of the mad town plot Dylan actually wrote, but the poet John Heath-Stubbs has recalled Dylan one evening in the Wheatsheaf reciting parts of *Under Milk Wood*, which was in the process of composition. This included some scenes which did not find a place in the final version. One of these was set in the town hall where alarming messages were coming through on the ticker tape such as 'The fish have declared war!' and 'Anti-Christ has reached Caernarvon.' (1993, p146)

Cleverdon's job now was to get this second half script from Dylan. In the meantime, he had the first half of the manuscript typed and returned in November: "Let me urge you to press on with it with all speed... June and Angela adored typing it, and are both looking forward eagerly to the next instalment." By December 1950, Cleverdon was sending the first of many letters exhorting Dylan to complete the play: "I am frightfully anxious to get the programme on the air... moreover, I can get the whole thing paid for immediately the script is approved." He advised Dylan to drop the idea of a plot about a mad town, and to write the second half in the same lyrical vein as the first. This, says Cleverdon, "seemed to relieve him considerably; but even so he couldn't get going."[136]

Cleverdon chased Dylan through 1951 but to no avail. Dylan was in Iran in the early part of the year. On his return, the play was 'temporarily shelved', as he put it in his letter of July 18 to Princess Caetani, while he worked hard on poems.

In August 1951, Dylan wrote to Donald Taylor: "I am writing a plotless radio play, first thought of as a film." If he had resumed work on the play, he said nothing to Cleverdon about it who wrote from the BBC in September "I long to see the rest of it. By all that you hold most holy in Wales, do try and finish it." In October, Dylan sent the uncompleted script to *Botteghe Oscure* as "the first half of this piece" – it only went "up to a certain moment of the morning", as Dylan put it in his covering letter to Princess Caetani. It was virtually the same as that given to the BBC a year before, except that he removed some eighty-six lines that had been in the BBC version. These were the exchanges between Mr and Mrs Cherry Owen, and the scene in which Willy Nilly does his rounds. *Botteghe Oscure* published the shortened script the following year.

In an October 1951 notebook, now in Texas, Dylan lists nine new scenes to be written for the play. Between this point and the first cast reading in May 1953, he wrote most, but not all, of the second half. He also re-instated the eighty-six lines from the 1950 BBC script and wrote over a hundred lines of new text for the first half, including the section "In Butcher Beynon's" to "My foxy darling." But when was all this work done?

Dylan's letters indicate that little progress was made in 1952, the year of his second trip to America, although he made two small changes to the *Botteghe* version for the reading at the Institute of Contemporary Arts in May – see page 314. FitzGibbon noted that Dylan was working on the play only

> sporadically and very slowly... *Under Milk Wood* progressed with almost incredible slowness. He was a sick, unhappy man, and very tired.

By late summer 1952, the BBC still had only the first part of the play which, as internal memos suggest, amounted to no more than the script received in 1950.[137] Cleverdon has confirmed this, writing that "nothing more emerged, other than the first half which he had given me earlier." (1954b) Dylan wrote to Cleverdon in August, claiming that "I want, myself, to finish it more than anything else. I'm longing to get to work on it again." He could, he said, finish it in six weeks if he were able to work on it every day ("I write very slowly when I'm very much enjoying it") but hack work to raise money was getting in the way. If the BBC were to pay him a weekly sum, then "I could shove all other small jobs aside & work on 'Llareggub' only".

Rejecting Dylan's request for a weekly wage, the BBC tempted him with five guineas for every thousand words he produced. Dylan accepted but sent nothing. In October, Dylan wrote to Cleverdon promising "to start work on Llareggub today". Cleverdon went to Laugharne a week later but returned empty-handed. Dylan resolved to finish the play in sixteen days of solid work, but nothing came of it.[138]

The same month Dylan met with Brinnin in London. In the back of a taxi en route to Waterloo Station, Brinnin suggested that the title of *Llareggub* "would be too thick and forbidding to attract American audiences. 'What about *Under Milk Wood?*' he said, and I said 'Fine,' and the new work was christened on the spot."[139]

Botteghe Oscure still had only a 'half-play', and in November, Dylan wrote to explain why he hadn't been able to "finish the second half of my piece for you". He had failed shamefully, he said, to add to "my lonely half of a looney maybe-play", but promised the rest of the script by February.

By this point in 1952, Dylan had been at the Boat House for three and a half years, but the half-play had made little progress since his South Leigh days. There is nothing here to support the view that the magic of Laugharne was at the heart of the Llareggub project. The town provided little in the way of inspiration or motivation as Dylan's failure to work effectively on the play clearly shows. Cold and damp Laugharne, which Caitlin grew so much to hate, was less a place of creativity than of burden, as the marriage crashed, debts mounted and the events of the wider world pressed in.

On December 16 1952, Dylan's father died. In the new year, Dylan wrote to Gwyn Jones saying "I've been terribly busy failing to write one word of a more or less play set in a Wales that I'm sad to say never was..." He wrote to Charles Fry in February, complaining that, apart from the 'Prologue' for *Collected Poems*, he had not been able to write anything for a whole year. A memo from Higham's office the same month noted tersely: "He hasn't made any progress on the Llareggub things."[140]

On March 10, Dylan read a 'chunk' of the play in Cardiff. The journalist Alan Road was a student at the time, and turned up in lecture room 103 at the university, gazing down across the steeply raked seating on the diminutive figure of the poet:

> I believe he was wearing a double breasted suit with a polo neck jumper. It was an odd combination in those more conventional times. The neck of the jumper sagged like a horse collar... he said he would give us a preview of a play for radio he was writing called Llareggub and he explained the origin of the name. He said the play's action happened in 24 hours. He had finished the day, he said and added with a stage leer that he was looking forward to the night. I do remember that the applause when he finished was tumultuous. Sufficient, I felt, for an encore, but when the noise had died down Thomas merely said 'Thank You' and vanished from the stage.[141]

Later that evening, Dylan lost the script. It took him seven days to write to his host, Charles Elliott, to ask him to find it: "It's very urgent to me: the only copy in the world of that kind-of-a-play of mine, from which I read bits, is in that battered, strapless briefcase whose handle is tied together with string."

The Show Goes On

It may well be that *Under Milk Wood* – the "infernally eternally unfinished" play – would never have been completed had not Brinnin taken the risk of advertising performances in America for May 1953. This forced Dylan's hand, and he wrote on March 18 promising that the script (at that moment still unfound in Cardiff) would be ready by the date of his sailing. In New York, Brinnin was noting with satisfaction that "hundreds of tickets" had already been sold for the first performance on May 14 at the Poetry Center. Together with his assistant, Liz Reitell, he began assembling a cast, as Nancy Wickwire, one of the young actors, has described:

> I was working in the Poetry Center, working the switchboard...
> and Liz Reitell came through one morning looking very distraught
> and said Dylan arrives in another week and one of his requests was
> for five actors because he's going to do a play for voices called
> *Under Milk Wood*. And she said 'Where do I get actors?' And you're
> looking at one, and I know right in this building you'll find anyone
> you need. I said first of all there's Sada Thompson who's teaching
> speech; that's an actress. Roy Poole who relieved me on the switch-
> board is an actor. Dion Allen who relieved Roy is also an actor. Al
> Collins, who is stage manager of the Kaufman Auditorium, is an
> actor. So there are your actors.[142]

On Dylan's arrival on April 21, Brinnin realised that the play "was still far from finished". If, as it seems, Dylan had arrived with little more than the 1950 BBC text, then some sixty percent of the play that we know today had yet to be written, including some first half material.[143] Brinnin installed Dylan in his Boston apartment and set him to write:

> the unfinished part of his play was no longer merely a matter of
> scenes to be filled in and lines to be brushed up but a problem that
> would demand all of his creative resourcefulness. The making of
> *Milk Wood* had assumed the first proportions of a marathon...

But Dylan had poetry readings to give along the East Coast and, according to Brinnin, Dylan worked on *Milk Wood* on only three days – April 26 and May 1 and 2. On the evening of May 3, Dylan was due to give a solo reading of the play at the Fogg Museum, Harvard. He worked on revisions and additions "from late morning until late afternoon", and then went to a party at the home of the portrait painter, Gardner Cox. The reading of the still unfinished play that evening was, according to Brinnin, "one of his memorable performances" but we do not know how incomplete the play was because no script or recording has ever surfaced. The only records from this event seems to be Gardner Cox's portrait done immediately afterwards – reproduced in Driver (1995) – and the review of the play in *The Boston Herald* the next day.

This review contains details which provide some information on the state of the play at the May 3 reading. The reviewer mentions Mr Pugh's book about the lives of great poisoners, as well as Captain Cat's comments on Mrs Ogmore-Pritchard beeswaxing the lawn to make the birds slip. Both these indicate that Dylan had restored the section about Willy Nilly doing his postal rounds, which he had removed from the *Botteghe Oscure* version of 1951. The review also tells us that Mog Edwards' love letter written to Miss Price on his shop's stationery received its first known public airing at the May 3 reading – it was not in the 1950 BBC script nor in the *Botteghe Oscure* version.

Brinnin describes how the audience's enthusiastic response at the May 3 reading proved a turning point in the making of *Milk Wood*. Dylan's confidence in himself and in the play was boosted and "From that time on his concern for the success of *Under Milk Wood* was deep and constant... he seemed to have come upon a whole new regard for himself as a dramatic writer." (p207)

Rehearsals had already started for the first cast reading to be given on May 14th. Nancy Wickwire has recalled that the script given to the actors ended with First Voice's description of Lord Cut-Glass' clocks. Another of the actors, Sada Thompson, confirmed that "we got about half of the script to begin with, and then we didn't have many rehearsals – there weren't more than half a dozen, if that."[144] The first cast rehearsal with Dylan was on May 8 and it was apparent to the actors that "Dylan had no experience of rehearsing." Wickwire commented that they

> Didn't know how we were going to do it... didn't know who was going to do what or how it was all going to turn out, and we were all reading rather tentatively because we didn't know what the play was about... Dylan, of course, didn't cast the play... there was no casting at all. I read the first woman that came along in the script,

and if that part happened to be repeated then I would read it again; Sada took the next woman that came along… as far as I remember, once we had cast ourselves he made no changes at all.

After the rehearsal, Dylan immediately left for further poetry readings, ending up with Brinnin in Connecticut on the evening of May 13. Dylan was up at dawn the next day, scribbling, says Brinnin, "on the little pieces of scratch-paper that made up a good part of the script of the play." By rehearsal time, he "had completed a whole new series of scenes", most written on the train back to New York. He then wrote until seven in the evening, when he gave up exhausted, with the performance only ninety minutes away. Brinnin is clear that even at this late stage "the final third of the play was still unorganised and but partially written."

Threats to cancel the performance made Dylan buckle down, and he "finished up one scene after another." But the play still had no ending. Liz Reitell locked Dylan in a room in Rollie McKenna's apartment. In her interview with Edwards, McKenna comments: "We set up a card table for him in a room in the back of the house on the top floor and had two or three typists from the 'Y' in the other room, and he'd get something done and they'd type it and then he'd work over it again." Despite Dylan's protests, Reitell squeezed the final part of the play out of him:

> The curtain was going to rise at 8.40. Well, at 8.10 Dylan was locked in the backroom with me. And no end to *Under Milk Wood*. He kept saying "I can't, I simply can't do this." I said "You can, the curtain is going to go up." Strangely enough, he wrote the very end of *Under Milk Wood* then and there, and he wrote the lead-up to it. He would scribble it down, I would copy it, print it so that the secretary could read it, hand it to John Brinnin, and hand it to the secretary, do six copies. We all jumped into a cab finally, and got over to the theatre at half-past eight and handed out the six copies to the actors…[145]

Brinnin's account makes it clear that parts of the play were still being handed to the actors "as they applied their make-up, read their telegrams and tested their new accents on one another. Some lines of dialogue did not actually come into the hands of the readers until they were taking their places on stage." (p213) The reading, nevertheless, was rapturously received by the audience, and at the fifteenth curtain call "squat and boyish in his happily flustered modesty, Dylan stepped out alone".

Dylan added some forty new lines to the second half for the next reading on May 28. The play was now almost complete, and we can safely conclude that most of it had by this point been written in New Quay, South Leigh, Boston and New York.

Dylan came home from America in June, enthusiastic about the play and full of good intentions. He prepared lists of ideas for new passages to write. Work sheets at Texas show that Dylan thought about more songs and poems for the ending section.[146] Dylan also asked "What have I missed out?" and added "Poverty. Jealousy. Idiocy. Incest Greed Hate Envy Spite Malice... Look at the churchyard: remember the early mortalities & fatalities. Quote some epitaphs, briefly... STRESS THE FEAR OF SOME OF THE TOWN AFTER DARK." But his work that summer on the play was 'desultory', as Davies and Maud have described it, and his output failed, as it always did in Laugharne, to match his intentions.[147]

The script was sent to Dent, but the chief editor considered the play pornographic and referred it to Martin Dent, the proprietor. He thought it "a bit broad in places" but decided to publish because "it's too good, too authentic Dylan Thomas to let it go... to turn it down might be to lose the author." (Ferris, 2000)

On August 5, Dylan went to Porthcawl and read 'almost all' of *Milk Wood* at a drama school being run by Thomas Taig, as Taig describes in his interview with Colin Edwards – see page 231. This was the first full British reading. Dylan gave another on October 2 at the Tenby Arts Club. Raymond Garlick has given an extended description of the reading, and written a poem about it.[148]

A few days later, Dylan travelled to London and stayed in Hammersmith with Harry Locke while he waited for his flight to New York. There was, Laurence Gilliam of the BBC told Edwards, a 'frenzy' of writing for the next five days. Locke has recalled that Dylan

> completed the final version of *Under Milk Wood* night after night at my kitchen table. I'd come down in the morning to a bleary-eyed Dylan still writing, the table littered with paper, beer bottles and cigarette ends.

But whether at the Boat House or in Hammersmith, Dylan added only forty-nine lines to the second half, comprising Eli Jenkins' sunset poem, and Waldo's chimney sweep song. He also added some sixty lines to the first half, mostly through rewriting existing passages.

Dylan arranged to have lunch with Cleverdon at Simpson's in the Strand on October 12, when he promised he would hand over the manuscript but neither he, nor the manuscript, turned up. Three days later, on October 15, Dylan arrived at the BBC and gave the much-relieved Cleverdon the 'finished' manuscript but "it was clearly not in its final form." The first part was hand-written as a fair copy, ending at "...and you snored all night like a brewery." It was on this section of the play that Dylan had mainly worked in Laugharne and Hammersmith. The rest was the typed script prepared in America for the May 14 performance, with many corrections added by hand for the May 28 production in New York and the October reading in Tenby. This typed part, says Cleverdon, was in "an extremely disordered state". Eli Jenkins' poem, and Waldo's song were only "working drafts written on leaves torn from an exercise book..." (1969, pp35-38)

It is evident from Cleverdon's description that neither the four months in Laugharne, nor the five days in Hammersmith, had given Dylan the time or inspiration to revise, or even make a fair copy of, the ill-starred second half of the play that had been so hurriedly written in America. Cleverdon took this in hand, and had the script typed onto duplicating stencils at the BBC. He gave the manuscript back to Dylan who promptly lost it. Cleverdon came to the rescue and three copies were made from the BBC stencils and, just before his plane left for America, the copies were delivered to Dylan. A few days later, Cleverdon found the manuscript in the Helvetia pub in Old Compton Street in Soho.

Dylan arrived in New York on October 20, and added another thirty-eight lines to the second half from "Dusk is drowned" to "where the old wizards made themselves a wife out of flowers." Some of these lines had been drafted at Laugharne, and they were incorporated in the script for the two performances of *Milk Wood* given on October 24 and 25.

Dylan continued to work on the script for the version that was to appear in *Mademoiselle*, and for the performance to be given at the 1020 Art Center in Chicago on November 13. In his unpublished memoir, Ruthven Todd has described how Dylan did much of this further work in the basement of his house in Bank Street, on the west side of Greenwich Village. Dylan would invariably turn up with a hangover but Todd describes how a single can of beer would last a whole morning while Dylan and Liz Reitell worked together on the play. With Reitell sitting at Todd's typewriter, Dylan would perch on his captain's chair ("adequate for the tubbiness he had gained around the backside") and

> Glowering at the world in general, and at the dismalness of my basement, he would take some sheets from Liz. Upon these she had marked his tentative suggestions. Growling, he would try out the new words and the revisions. While doing this he would alter, still dispiritedly, from one voice to another. Thus, according to the character, he might be Captain Cat speaking at one moment, or Rosie Probert, and then, quite suddenly, it might be Mrs Organ Morgan or Mrs Ogmore-Pritchard or, sadly, Polly Garter... Each emendation which he had made... had to be considered and weighed in his mouth. If it did not seem right, he would lean forward, his elbows on his knees, the cigarette drooping with the ash falling where it would. He would savour each phrase to the full, speaking slowly and seeming to taste the words. Then he would experiment with a succession of words until he found one which satisfied him, for the moment at least... If I said something was not clear or did not come over properly, he did not want me to make any suggestions for alteration. He, himself, would throw out different words or phrases, twisting them this way or that, until he found something that he wanted.

All this work was almost in vain for Dylan yet again lost the script. Todd received a frantic phone call from Reitell and he set off to search through Dylan's favourite bars. He was on the point of giving up when he decided, somewhat reluctantly, to enter Louie's Bar on Sheridan Square, a gloomy basement joint that Dylan seldom went to. The barman produced a briefcase and from it Todd pulled a dirty shirt, an unopened bottle of Old Grandad and the "rumpled, dogeared, but intact, the much corrected typescript."[149]

There undoubtedly would have been further work done on the play for the Chicago reading but Dylan died on November 9. Later that month in London, Douglas Cleverdon continued work for the broadcasting of the play using the BBC script copies, as well as the revised script sent from New York by Ruthven Todd. Some small cuts were made – the "two tits and a bum" cuts – and the first broadcast of the play, produced by Cleverdon, was made on the BBC Third Programme on January 25 1954, and repeated two days later. But there was a complaint that reception of the Third Programme in Wales was so bad that few people had heard the broadcast… it had been virtually inaudible in Laugharne.

The Welsh Home Service, however, resisted attempts to broadcast the 'lusty, Rabelaisian and uninhibited' play, which it thought unsuitable for

family or home listening… Controller Wales reacts more strongly to it than I do, and his reasoning is only too sound in the context of this region as we know it.[150]

By the end of March, Controller Wales had relented and the sensitive listeners of Wales were allowed to hear their *Milk Wood*, a play about a 'Wales-that-never-was' written almost entirely in England and America. Over the next few years, the play was performed in Edinburgh, New York and Mexico but banned in Cardiff. By 1957, it had already been translated into German, French, Polish, Danish, Norwegian, Finnish, Japanese and Italian.

At most, only some three hundred lines, about seventeen percent, of the play had been written at Laugharne, and some of these could well have been done in London. Claims that all, half, most, or even much, of *Milk Wood* had been written at the Boat House are unfounded.

Post Script

No script has survived that we can positively say is the 'nearly finished' 1949 script mentioned in David Higham's letter. But I have identified a first-half script that predates the one Dylan gave to the BBC in October 1950. The manuscript of the first thirty five pages of this BBC script, provided for Walford Davies and Paul Ferris from the Texas archive, also includes a quantity of additional numbered work sheets. When these are separated out, they form a coherent sequence of pages, a single discrete text with no overlapping material or excess pages. The script has twenty-eight pages, five of which are missing. It is a working draft with many deletions and insertions, and the occasional instruction to improve the text.

The 28-page script, as I shall refer to it, ends with First Voice describing Beynon Butcher's shop, concluding with Mr Beynon's remark "He shd do Bess. It's his brother's." It then peters out with an unassigned sentence: "They grumble at the thought that maybe one day the Govt will make chapel compulsory for all children; will close the pubs; will conduct purges of immorality." This seems to be a note about how the play was to continue. In fact, Dylan changed the Beynons' "everymorning groan and grumble" of the 28-page script to their "everymorning hullabaloo" of the BBC script, and the scene takes the different, cat-eating turn that we know today.

There is no way of telling when the 28-page script was written out. But is it the *text* that Dylan discussed with Higham? It is only seven pages shorter than the 1950 BBC text, so it has sufficient length to correspond with Locke's comment that a 'great deal' of the play had been written in 1947/48, and with the description that it was 'nearly finished' in 1949. If it is not exactly the text discussed with Higham, then it must be very close to it and approximate to the body of work done at South Leigh.

The content of the 28-page script is substantially the same as that part of the play we know today, but without the section, "In Butcher Beynon's" to "My foxy darling". It includes the two Voices, more than three-quarters of the cast list, and nearly all of the place, street and house names of the play, including Coronation Street, Milk Wood, Llareggub and the Dewi. If the first part was 'nearly finished' at South Leigh in 1947/48, the inspiration for these people and names could not have come from Dylan's time at the Boat House. Ackerman's suggestion, for example, that the name *Milk Wood* was inspired by Dylan's view of Sir John's Hill from the Boat House now seems implausible.

In preparing to send the half-script to the BBC in October 1950, Dylan did more work on the play, probably in Laugharne, though some may have been done in London. He deleted a number of lines from the 28-page script, and made other small changes. Only two new characters were added between the 28-page and the BBC scripts – the Old Man and Ocky Sailors. Dylan then wrote out the 28-page script as a fair copy, adding just over a hundred lines to it, which correspond broadly to "Oh, d'you hear that, Lily?" to Captain Cat's lines "Organ Morgan's at it early…" which end the first half (this addition included the section about Willy Nilly doing his rounds, which was not in the 28-page script where Willy Nilly had only one line – "Fishing for puffins.") Dylan also added four pages in which the mad town plot develops. These additions to the 28-page script have the appearance of a working draft, not a fair copy.

Finally, it might to helpful to note the names that were not in the 28-page and BBC scripts, and which first appear in the script for the performance on May 14 1953. They were Salt Lake Farm, Mr and Mrs Utah Watkins, Gossamer Beynon, Mrs Willy Nilly, Mae Rose Cottage, Mrs Organ Morgan, Evans the Death, Bessie Bighead and Ocky Sailors became Sinbad Sailors.

Writing *Under Milk Wood*: A Chronology

1933	Dylan reads an embryonic *UMW* in Bert Trick's Caswell Bay bungalow
1939	Suggests a play about Laugharne to Richard Hughes
1943	Outlines mad town plot to Hughes and later to FitzGibbon
1944/45	New Quay: Dylan writes *Quite Early One Morning*; makes a start on *UMW*.
	Recites extracts from the play at a party in Riding House Street, London
1946/47	Oxford: writes six of the other *UMW* milestones, including *Return Journey*.
	Visits Italy and resolves to write a 'radio play'
1947/48	South Leigh: completes a draft of most of the first half of *UMW*
1949	March 7: reads extracts from the play at a party in Prague
	May: moves to the Boat House, Laugharne
	September: tells David Higham the play is 'nearly finished'
	October: shows incomplete draft of the play to Allen Curnow
1950	October: first half of *UMW* sent to the BBC as *The Town That Was Mad*
1951	July: John Malcolm Brinnin first hears of the play as *Llareggub Hill*
1952	April: *Botteghe Oscure* publishes shortened first half as *Llareggub, A Piece for Radio Perhaps*
	May: Dylan reads part of the play at the Institute of Contemporary Arts, London
1953	March 10: Dylan reads part of the play in Cardiff
	April 21: arrives in America with the first half of the script
	April 26, May 1, 2 and 3: works intermittently on the second half of the script
	May 3: reads an unfinished script, Fogg Museum, Harvard

May 8: first cast rehearsal with Dylan

May 14: completes the second half of the script in time for the first cast performance of the play at the Poetry Center, New York

May 28: second cast performance at the Poetry Center

August 5: Dylan reads 'almost all' the play, Porthcawl

October 2: a reading at the Tenby Arts Club

October 21-23: adds further lines to the script in New York

October 24/25: two more cast performances at the Poetry Center, New York

November 9: Dylan dies

A memorial performance of *UMW* is given in New York with Dylan's roles taken by Walter Abel

1954   January 24: twenty-five minute extract from *UMW* read at the Globe Theatre

January 25: first British cast performance, BBC Third Programme, with Richard Burton. Wins the Italia Prize

February: abridged versions appear in *Mademoiselle* and *The Observer*

February 28: a stage reading at the Old Vic with Richard Burton, Sybil Thorndike and Emlyn Williams

BBC production released as an LP by Argo Record Company

Caedmon LP of the May 14 performance in New York

Dent publish *Under Milk Wood*, as do New Directions in America

September 28: first BBC Welsh Home Service broadcast

1955   Private matinée performance at RADA

1956   August 13: first British stage production at the Theatre Royal, Newcastle

1957   May 9: a BBC television performance

1958   Dent publish the Acting Edition of the play

1968   Translated into Welsh as *Dan Y Wenallt*

1971   Film version with Richard Burton

1988   Musical version produced by George Martin, with Anthony Hopkins

1995   Davies and Maud's definitive edition published

2003   Musical version on CD by Guy Masterson, with music by Matt Clifford

3: Conceiving Polly Garter

The name Polly was familiar to Dylan from early childhood – it was the family name of one his maternal aunts. The name later appeared in some of Dylan's writings, including the film script, *Three Weird Sisters*, and in *Adventures in the Skin Trade*. In the latter, Polly Dacey is "up to no good", as her mother puts it, in an upstairs bathroom, trying to pull a bottle off Samuel Bennet's finger, coaxing him to undress and getting him drunk on eau-de-cologne. Her dead lover, who "was ever so short", prefigures Polly Garter's dearly departed, little Willy Wee.

Colin Edwards was particularly interested in the development of *Under Milk Wood*. Several interviewees shared their opinions about the inspirations for some of the play's characters. It is hardly surprising that Polly Garter attracted special attention, and Jane Dark, for example, told Edwards that in Laugharne we

> had the sort of Polly Garter type... I can quite understand when he wrote this part about "when this person went past, people were quiet" – I mean, they were quiet!

Edwards' search for the 'original Polly', as he once put it, was doomed to failure because, unknown to him, *Under Milk Wood* was a play of two halves, two time periods and two countries. The development of the play's characters was thus exposed to a wide range of inspirations and circumstances. This is reflected in the role of Polly Garter. There are, in fact, two Polly Garters in *Under Milk Wood*: 'mothering Polly' and 'naughty Polly'. Dylan pointed to both in his cast list for the play, when he described her as

> midwife. Loves children, loves loving, is loose and thoughtless, therefore has children.[151]

Dylan's idea of Polly as both a lover of children and a lover of men is also captured in a phrase he uses in the second half of the play, when he describes Polly's "naughty mothering arms". In their search for the original Polly, Edwards and his interviewees focussed only on the 'naughty Polly.' Any search for the original has to look for someone who fits the profile of both Pollys; alternatively, we must consider that there may have been more than one woman who inspired the part.

In the incomplete 28-page and 1950 BBC scripts, there is no sign of the 'naughty Polly'. These two scripts have only the 'mothering Polly', a very small part with just four lines:

> Babies
>
> me, Polly Garter, giving the breast in the garden to my new
> bonny baby and listening to the voices in the voices of
> the blooming birds who seem to say to me: (followed by a children's
> song 'Polly, Love.')[152]

The role of Polly as baby bearer was confirmed by the following exchange between the Pughs:

> Mrs Pugh: He's going to arrest Polly Garter, mark my words
> Mr Pugh: What for, my dear?
> Mrs Pugh: For having babies.

There is nothing explicitly here about the woman who loves loving. However, in his October 1951 letter to Princess Caetani, publisher of the *Botteghe Oscure*, Dylan describes Polly in the following way: "And Polly Garter has many illegitimate babies because she loves babies but does not want only one man's." Even in this description, the emphasis is on Polly as 'the lover of babies', and as someone who could just as easily be seen as rejecting monogamy rather than embracing casual sex – Polly as polyandrous not promiscuous.

When a version of the first half BBC script was published in *Botteghe Oscure* in May 1952, the idea of Polly just as 'mother' had not been changed. In fact, Dylan made only one small alteration to Polly's four lines. The same month, he read the *Botteghe* version at the Institute of Contemporary Arts, with help from Bill McAlpine and Harry Locke. He deleted "and listening to the voices of the blooming birds who seem to say to me" and added "Nothing grows in our garden 'cept washing and babies."[153]

So by mid-1952 the first half Polly still had only four lines, and she was simply a bearer and lover of babies, at ease in her garden, enjoying the singing of the birds. She dreams only of babies, not lovers. It was this maternal Polly who was in the half-script that Dylan had with him when he arrived in America in April 1953. The 'naughty Polly', or the wanton Polly as she is often referred to, emerged as a substantial part in the few weeks after Dylan's arrival. By the May 14 premiere, Polly had become a lover of men as well as of babies. She is a singer and cleaner, a scrubber of floors. She makes love out of doors, and wears garters without stockings. She dreams not of babies but of lovers. She is Saint Polly, martyred in *Milk Wood* by Mr Waldo; she is a woman "that can't say No even to midgets".

When Dylan turned to writing the second half for the May 14 performance, he decided to begin with Polly. Captain Cat's commentary on the women gossiping around the pump that ends the first half had been a mere six lines in the *Botteghe* version. Now Dylan greatly expanded it, bringing in Polly towards its conclusion ("giving her belly an airing, there should be a law,"). After a few words about Ocky Milkman, Dylan starts the second half with Polly approaching the pump, and clearly establishes the idea of the 'naughty Polly'. The women fall silent and Captain Cat wonders "Who cuddled you when? Which of their gandering hubbies moaned in *Milk Wood* for your naughty mothering arms and body like a wardrobe, love?"

This portrayal is quickly followed by the first of Polly's songs about her lovers Tom, Dick, Harry, and little Willy Wee. In case we are left in any doubt, Dylan includes the couplet "Now men from every parish round / Run after me and roll me on the ground" Not long after, we have Polly birdnesting in *Milk Wood* with Mr Waldo, with her dress over her head, and then lying in the arms of the *"good* bad boys from the lonely farms".

Dylan gave only one line ("Me, love.") to Polly in the second half of the play. Yet the part of Polly in the May 14 and subsequent versions of the script was far more prominent, not least because Dylan used Polly to begin and end the second half. He also gave her thirty-five lines of song, and enhanced her role as the object of comments made by other characters, including the two Voices.

The emergence of Polly in the May 14 script as a major role was due in large part to the way in which Dylan responded to the American actors who were rehearsing the parts. In an interview in 1967, two of the actors, Sada Thompson and Nancy Wickwire, make clear that the development of the Polly Garter role took place between May 8, the date of the first rehearsal, and the first performance on May 14. The role was expanded largely because of the way Wickwire played it during the rehearsals. Thompson recalls that:

He seemed to respond so excitedly to us – it was really wonderful for all of us... he told us that he was going to develop a number of the characters further as he went along, but he claimed at any rate that he developed a number of them because of hearing them read... I think he thought of Polly Garter as a relatively minor role, a charming role, but he really fell in love with Nancy's version of Polly and expanded it. And there were some other characters, too, that were fulfilled in the latter part of the play in perhaps quite a different way than if he'd just gone at it as a literary work entirely and hadn't heard it read by actors... certain choices were made to expand certain characters because he enjoyed the way actors were reading them.[154]

Dylan did not provide Polly with so many lines of song because he admired Wickwire's voice. On the contrary:

When we got to the part of the script where it says "Polly scrubs," I think it says, "and sings." there was a long thing written and I said "Do you want me to sing?" and he said "Yes." And I said "Well, what's the tune?" And he said "Make something up." So I said "Right now?" He said "No, next rehearsal." So I guess it was the next day or whenever it was. I don't write songs; I don't know *how* to write songs, but I made something up which is rather reminiscent, I think, of "Mary had a little lamb"... and he loved it. So he said "Keep it."

After the May 14 performance, Dylan made one final revision of Polly Garter. This was to expand the "Me, Polly Garter..." first half monologue, which had consisted of only three lines. Now that Polly had an established position in the second half, Dylan seems to have felt the need to give her a bigger introduction in the first half, as the interview with Wickwire and Thompson confirms:

... when we did it six months later, there were certain additions; he added certain things of Polly Garter... in the 'Me' section of the very beginning he wanted to introduce her, and so that was added.

Dylan handled this introduction by removing any doubt about the ascendancy of the 'naughty Polly' over the maternal, and this is the passage that we know today:

Me, Polly Garter, under the washing line, giving the

breast in the garden to my bonny new baby. Nothing
grows in our garden, only washing. And babies.
And where's their fathers live, my love? Over the
hills and far away. You're looking up at me now. I
know what you're thinking, you poor little milky
creature. You're thinking, you're no better than you
should be, Polly, and that's good enough for me.
Oh, isn't life a terrible thing, thank God?

Interestingly, the work sheets of this monologue, now in the Texas
archive, suggest that the loss of the maternal Polly was something that
Dylan had struggled with. The drafts contain a number of unused lines
about the 'naughty Polly', but there are even more lines in which Polly
talks lovingly to her children. Moreover, the eight children are given
names – Molly, Mary, Winnie, Flo, Mildred, Millicent, Ernie and
Sidney. Had these lines been used, their overall effect would have been
to strengthen the image of the maternal Polly.

Llareggub and its *Milk Wood* are places of love and loving, of both
sex and fertility. The fecundity of its people are brought home to us
through Polly's children and Mr Waldo's paternity summonses. The
text is also awash with general references to babies, twins and children;
we also find quite specific references to 'babies singing opera', or 'the
snuggeries of babies'. We have, particularly in the second half of the
play, the prominence of the children's voices and their singing.

The details and imagery of fertility are re-enforced by further references to milk, buttermilk, milking cows, milk churns, milk cans, milk
pails, dew-adulterated milk and even milk stout. The Third Boy runs
home "howling for his milky mum", Polly describes her baby as a
"milky creature", and Mae Rose Cottage goes "young and milking".
Nature, too, gets its share of milky references, including "that milkmaid
whispering water" and Spring "with its breasts full of rivering May-
milk". And who, asks the Fourth Drowned, "milks the cows in
Maesgwyn?"[155]

Maesgwyn Farm: A Fertile Snuggery

New Quay's Maesgwyn stood on Brongwyn Lane, on the left-hand
side in the descent to the beach. At one time, the lane went most of the
way to Majoda, and it was one of Dylan's routes into the Black Lion.

'Maesgwyn' means 'white or blessed field'. The white, two-storied
farmhouse faced north towards Majoda. Its stone outbuildings were

also whitewashed, and for most of the year white geraniums grew in pots along the window-sills and in the yard. There was also a large and distinctive white stone marking the entrance to the farm, with a white wall surrounding the front garden, which was, as we shall see, usually full of washing and babies.

Sometime in the early 1900s, a woman called Sarah Evans moved into Maesgwyn. She had come to New Quay from the Rhondda, travelling in a horse and cart with her furniture piled in behind her. For the first few years, Sarah ran the Sailor's Home Arms (later, the Commercial) and then went to Maesgwyn with her husband, Evan.

The farm sold milk to the residents of upper New Quay, who also used its seafields to air and beat their rugs, and to play football in. Secluded and leafy Brongwyn Lane was a favourite walk both for locals and visitors alike. One of Evan and Sarah's great-grandchildren remembers being told about one particular visitor calling for milk:

> … my great-grandmother sold milk because she had a drawer in a chest - in an old family chest of drawers - that my mother called the Milk Drawer and the milk money used to go in there, and it stood in the hallway of Maesgwyn… my mother said that Dylan Thomas had a mug of milk at Maesgwyn but when that was I don't know as Dylan visited New Quay before 1945.

Maesgwyn also had babies galore, a veritable seaside snuggery. Two of Sarah's children came with her from the Rhondda: Thomas John Evans (b.1877) and Hannah Jane Thomas (b.1890). Hannah lived in Maesgwyn and had eight children. Thomas and his wife, also a Sarah, lived on the slope behind Maesgwyn in a house called Tanyfron, and they had six children. Another of Evan and Sarah's children, Mary Ann (b. 1876) married William Dare and had ten children. Although Mary Ann and William lived in Port Talbot, some of the children were born in Maesgwyn, and at least one, Blodwen, came to live there as a child.

As the Maesgwyn families grew larger, the parents and children moved out into other parts of New Quay. When Evan died in 1932, Sarah went to live in Rock Street, with her grand-daughter, Blodwen Dare. She died there in 1937, and a newspaper report of her funeral notes that she had five children, twenty-nine grandchildren and sixteen great-grandchildren.[156]

Thomas and Sarah moved into Maesgwyn in 1934, and carried on the farming. They were there in 1939, as the Register of Electors confirms. A grand-daughter remembers going there for tea in the early years of the War. Then Thomas and Sarah went to Llanarth in 1941 where they both died within a year. It is not clear if anyone moved into Maesgwyn after them, but it is unlikely because the sea was getting closer and closer.

By the time that Dylan first came to New Quay in the 1930s, most of Evan and Sarah's many grandchildren were young adults, and having babies themselves. Maesgwyn itself had become embedded in local folklore, partly because of its babies, and partly because of the threat posed by the encroaching sea.

Some of the six children of Thomas and Sarah Evans also helped to establish Maesgwyn in the folk culture of New Quay. Their eldest son was famously named Oliver Cromwell, two other sons went to Australia and one of them was murdered there by a fellow lumberjack. But it was Thomas and Sarah's eldest daughter, Phoebe, who was one of the town's real characters, and is still remembered affectionately in New Quay today. She was well-known to locals and visitors alike:

> She was quite chuffed to have known Dylan, she was always talking about him. She was adamant she was Polly Garter.

> Mam was proud of being Polly Garter. She said Dylan always had his little notebook, and he was writing all the time when he was having a drink.

> Phoebe was great friends with Caitlin.

> She used to babysit for them.

Phoebe is mentioned in the *Botteghe Oscure* draft of *Under Milk Wood*, giving her name to one of the boats that tilt and ride in the dab-filled sea: "the Arethusa, the Curlew and the Skylark, Phoebe and Sally and Mary Ann, Zanzibar, Rhiannon, the Rover, the Cormorant, and the Star of Wales..." She also appears in *Quite Early One Morning*, Dylan's radio broadcast about New Quay:

> Do you hear that whistling? – It's me, I am Phoebe,
> The maid at the King's Head, and I am whistling like a bird.
> Someone spilt a tin of pepper in the tea.
> There's twenty for breakfast and I'm not going to say a word.

There was no King's Head in New Quay, but Phoebe helped out as a general maid in the Penwig Hotel. Polly was a cleaner and scrubbed the steps of Llareggub's Welfare Hall; Phoebe, too, was a cleaner, 'doing' for the sea captains and summer visitors, as well as cleaning Lloyds Bank and Towyn Chapel. Dylan's cast list describes Polly as a midwife; Phoebe Evans had considerable experience of pregnancy and birth and she was often called upon to act as an unofficial midwife, her advice valued on difficult births and, later, difficult children. Like Polly, she brought praise for the Lord that the Welsh are a musical nation: "Oh, she could sing beautifully. She sang in the Hall at concerts, and in Towyn. At parties and functions, hymns often, duets with

31. Phoebe Evans as a young woman

her son... people were always asking her to sing." Above all, Phoebe, like Polly, loved children and she may well have contributed to Dylan's conception of the mothering Polly Garter, written well before the naughty Polly appeared in the script in 1953.

After her marriage to Stanley Evans in 1922, Phoebe followed on in the Maesgwyn tradition and had nine children between 1923 and 1943, as well as bringing up two of their grandchildren. She also looked after other children in the wider Evans family in New Quay, and earned extra money by babysitting:

> Phoebe was a motherly figure, very, very child-orientated. She always had children around her. Always.

> She just loved feeding children, and they didn't have two pennies to rub together. How the hell they managed to feed everyone –

320

three cooked meals a day."

She was like a honey pot – the children were always coming home to her. A wonderful mother.

She really was well-loved, and really well-loved by her family... full of fun, always happy, always smiling, sparkling.

I don't think she could have had a life without kids.

If there'd been enough room, Mam would have filled the house with kids.

A motherly figure, always in her apron, always doing something and then you'd see her out, and I can hear her walking – she went

32. Phoebe in the 1970s: "Oh, isn't life a terrible thing, thank God?"

trit-trot, trit-trot, trit-trot. She was a small, dainty sort of person and I could hear the little footsteps coming.

My mother was the most sacrificing, loving person I have ever known. I would never betray her trust, I know what they sacrificed. As a young adult, home was a special thing. I couldn't wait to get there. I never wanted to be anywhere else.

And when Phoebe went out with Stanley, "she dressed like a Queen, all bangles and rings. She really believed in dressing up." They preferred New Quay's quiet pubs and the Star of Wales in Aberaeron:

Up until the day she died, she was always wanting to go out. She loved people around her, she loved talking.

She was a very strong character. She always attracted a crowd, she was never on her own. Funny thing, she attracted young men. I don't know how she did it! She had this magic. They used to listen to her, she always had a story to tell. She'd mix with the young and old. She could mix with anybody.

> Everybody was enthralled by her because she had that wonderful
> social personality that would come out. She was quite captivating.
> There was something about her that was different, and Dylan
> would have noticed that and liked it.

During the War years, Phoebe and Stanley lived within nappy throwing distance of Maesgwyn, in a small cottage called Gwynfa behind the
police station. Stanley was away for much of the War, but returned on
leave and sometimes had a pint with Dylan in the Black Lion. Like
Dylan he had a passion for Westerns, and also wrote poetry, later having
his verses published in the *Cambrian News*. Phoebe drank with Caitlin
in the Dolau and with Dylan in the Commercial. She also knew
Augustus John, who asked if he could paint her eldest daughter, Ray:

> He had had his eye on Ray for a while. She was just fifteen, and he
> asked if he could paint her. But Phoebe knew Augustus socially
> and she wouldn't have anything to do with it because she knew his
> reputation.

Phoebe continued throughout her life to befriend visiting celebrities
such as the actors Rex Harrison and Paul Schofield – "She always
wanted to be an actress, but in those days it wasn't the done thing." In
New Quay, Phoebe became a legend in her own lifetime. She was a
popular figure about the town, always willing to help out, despite the
great demands on her time from her own family:

> She was a lovely person, always smiling and laughing, great fun.
> She was so loveable - and loyal.

> If anybody wanted any help, she'd give it. She wouldn't say 'No'.
> She *couldn't* say 'No.'

> She never looked for the bad in people, she was one of the kinder
> people.

Phoebe was a devout chapel-goer, and played a full part in the life
of the community. In her later years, she joined the Women's Institute
and the British Legion and worked hard to raise money for the New
Quay lifeboat. Just before her death in 1980, one of her children gave
her a copy of *Under Milk Wood* inscribed "To Mam (The Polly
Garter)", an affectionate acknowledgement of the part she surely
played in Dylan's conception of the maternal, child-loving Polly.

4: At Ease Among Painters

"I am in the path of Blake," wrote the teenage Dylan to Pamela Hansford Johnson in October 1933, "but so far behind him that only the wings on his heels are in sight." He was talking about Blake's poetry not his painting, for Dylan Thomas had no aspirations to be a painter. He did, however, have a great interest in art from an early age, and friendships with painters and sculptors – mostly men – throughout his life. Dylan's poetry and prose reflected this interest in art, particularly painting, and in turn influenced the work of several artists, most notably Ceri Richards.

By the time Dylan had started grammar school, he was already "amazingly good at line drawings – all very abstract and fascinating", recalled school friend Vera Phillips. Fred Janes spoke to Colin Edwards both of Dylan's interest in art and the influence of Daniel Jones:

> Dan had this sort of universal outlook... he was very well-informed about painting and the history of painting... I don't think Dan ever actually tried painting. I'm not aware that he did, he might have done... whereas, of course, Dylan tried to draw – he did quite a number of drawings and little paintings and was very actively interested in this...

In his book about Dylan, Jones has written about early experiments at his home with sculpture and painting. Early in his correspondence with Hansford Johnson, Dylan wrote that he couldn't draw but "I paint a good deal". In another letter, he describes the room in Cwmdonkin Drive where he sits and writes:

> On the wall immediately in front of me hangs my pastel drawing of the Two Brothers of Death; one is a syphilitic Christ, and the other a green-bearded Moses. Both have skin the colour of figs, and walk, for want of a better place, on a horizontal ladder of moons (November 11 1933).

Not long after, in April 1934, he wrote to her that "I have just finished an incompetent drawing in pastels of a negro riding on a leopard down the clouds..." A few days later he was describing the

323

drawings he had done for the set of Noel Coward's *Hay Fever*, being performed at the Little Theatre. Dylan continued to draw and doodle throughout his life, as his letters reveal. Geoffrey Grigson had seen drawings that Dylan had made in his early twenties: "people having their throats cut, bad dreams, a 'world-devouring ghost creature' biting out genitals..." Glyn Jones, himself once a painter, recalled "women with milk coming from them, a half-wit running through a wood..." Most of these London paintings appear to have been destroyed when Grigson's house was bombed during the blitz.

Dylan's 1937 drawings and cartoons done for Veronica Sibthorp are now in the National Library of Wales. In December 1941, Dylan went to visit his friend Freddy Hurdis-Jones in Magdalen College, Oxford. Hurdis-Jones asked Dylan to autograph his copy of *Twenty-five Poems*. Dylan went one better, sketching on the covers, end-papers and margins. The drawings included a self-portrait and portraits of various friends including the Sitwells. A few years later, he amused John Davenport's children with a surrealist painting of a man balanced on a ladder balanced on a bicycle handing a petition to a giraffe. In the 1950s, Dylan would sketch for his drinking companions in the White House Tavern in New York. He also did a series of drawings for Elizabeth Reitell, and at least two pen and ink drawings for Oscar Williams, 'Little Girl Observes a Fish on Land' and 'English hostess looks with scorn at unusual family'.[157]

The Arty Provincial

Vernon Watkins has pointed to the importance of the discussions in the Kardomah about artists and paintings, a venue for artistic exploration that Dylan himself refers to in *Return Journey*. Equally formative were the twice-weekly evening discussions with Bert Trick and others, as well as Dylan's friendships with Fred Janes, Ronald Cour and Mervyn Levy, respectively representing three major facets of art – painting, sculpture and criticism. Dylan was also friendly with Kenneth Hancock, who was born in Swansea, went to the Art School there and later became its Principal in 1946. The sculptor Denis Mitchell, who attended the School in 1930 and later became Barbara Hepworth's assistant, was another friend.

Dylan also knew Leo Solomon, Dannie Abse's cousin. Solomon was on good terms with Janes and was a life long friend of Levy, with whom he taught for a while at the Army College in Swindon. Solomon had been a student at Swansea College of Art, developed his talent as a portrait painter and in 1954 was appointed Principal of Rochdale College of Art. Leo's uncle, Sam Clompus, was an antique dealer in Swansea whom the *Evening Post* once described as "one of the few patrons of the Swansea school of young artists between the two wars" – he encouraged artists such as Levy and Janes by buying "their student efforts".[158]

33. Leo Solomon

In his Edwards interview, Ron Cour remembers Dylan's keen interest in the modern movement and abstract art. Indeed, when Dylan was about fifteen, he was confident enough to tell the school art teacher "that there was more in the newer, modern art than there was in the old", suggesting he should start painting abstractly himself.[159]

In January 1933, when he was just eighteen, Dylan wrote an article for the *Evening Post* on 'Genius and Madness Akin in World of Art'. Not surprisingly, his letters of that year to Hansford Johnson reveal a young man who appears to move easily between the realms of poetry, music and art. He quotes Herbert Read and Geoffrey Grigson on modern art. Writing on October 15 1933, he discusses the differences between a poet and an artist, and writes of Reuben Mednikoff, a painter and a friend of Hansford Johnson – "as a poet he's a bloody good painter". A month later, he accepted Hansford Johnson's offer to show his poems to Mednikoff, asking which 'circle' he moved in – "The squared circle of the Geometrists? The fleshy circle of the Academicians?" In fact, Mednikoff was a surrealist painter and poet, a friend of David Gascoyne, and someone whose poems were, like Dylan's, published by Victor Neuberg in the *Sunday Referee*.

Bert Trick has told Colin Edwards (see Volume One) that the teenage Dylan was reading *transition*, an avant-garde magazine published mostly in Paris that did much to make the links between French and

British surrealism.[160] Dylan was also reading and sending poems to *New Verse*, started by Geoffrey Grigson in January 1933. In October that year, *New Verse* had published David Gascoyne's 'And the Seventh Dream is the Dream of Isis', the first surrealist poem written in English. The very same month, Dylan was making fun of it in a letter to Hansford Johnson, a telling indication of how close the teenage Dylan was in touch with events in London. Two months later, *New Verse* published Charles Madge's essay on 'Surrealism for the English', followed in later issues by a spate of translations of surrealist works and book reviews.

By now, Dylan was part of a cultural network whose own experiments in poetry, music and art were influenced by a resurgence of interest in the arts in Swansea. William Grant Murray had become Principal of the School of Art and Crafts in 1909 with a determination

> to encourage the development of the arts in Swansea, to make the town aware of its artistic talent and to win over the people of the town with exhibitions at the Glynn Vivian.[161]

Murray was soon putting the artistic talent on display: Evan Walters had his one-man show in the Glynn Vivian Gallery in 1920. In 1926, the National Eisteddfod was held in Swansea, and Grant Murray organised the art and craft section 'on a vast scale'. Evan Walters won first prize. Mumbles-born painter James Tarr won the painting prize in the 1930 National Eisteddfod in Llanelli. Ceri Richards had his first one-man show in the Glynn Vivian the same year. Such was the success of Swansea's art school that in 1935 the Glynn Vivian put on an exhibition of the school's past students.

Some of the harbingers of surrealism also came to Swansea – in January and February 1935, Paul Nash's Unit One exhibited at the Glynn Vivian Gallery, showing works by Nash himself, as well as work by John Armstrong, Ben Nicholson, Barbara Hepworth, Edward Burra and Henry Moore. The exhibition helped to reinforce the influence of George Cooper Mason, recruited to the School of Art from the Royal College of Art in London, who brought with him 'new' modernist thinking. His students designed Art Deco murals and posters that soon caught the eye of the Swansea public.

Other Swansea painters were beginning to make their mark both in Wales and London: for example, Archie Rhys Griffiths, Vincent Evans and Cedric Morris. Dylan considered using Morris to provide sketches for a book he proposed in 1937 about a journey through Wales visiting various writers and painters. In his Edwards interview, Eric Hughes mentions: "it was always a tremendous experience to get into the centre of a discussion between [Augustus] John, Dylan and Cedric Morris..." Dylan and Morris was also part of an artistic loop that included Wyn Henderson, a writer, friend of painters and manager of the Guggenheim Jeune gallery. Dylan was soon boasting in a letter to Keidrych Rhys that "I know most of the Welsh artists, in & out of Wales". But there were several important artists in Wales he never knew such as Kyffin Williams, John Elwyn, John Petts, Vera Bassett and Jonah Jones, who executed the plaque for Dylan in Westminster Abbey. Although he had a profound influence on his painting, Dylan met Ceri Richards only once, just before he made his last trip to America in 1953. And David Jones has noted that he met Dylan only "once or twice" (Watkins, 1975).

Stringing along with Surrealism

Dylan went to live in London in December 1934 "in a large room with a bathroom and sort of inferior wash up adjoining." His house mates were all painters – Fred Janes, Mervyn Levy and occasionally Will Evans. When they moved to Coleherne Road they were together with two more painters, William Scott and Robin Pierce. It was at this time that Dylan first met Mervyn Peake – they were introduced to each other by Bill Evans (not Will) a student at the Royal Academy Schools who had already established a 'Welsh Gang' of painters and writers that also included Janes' Swansea friend, Ifor Thomas.[162] Suffolk-born Colin Moss, who was at the Royal College of Art with Levy and living nearby on the Fulham Road, was also assimilated into the gang.[163]

Then there were the sculptors. Founder member of Plaid Cymru, Richard Huws, became a drinking pal about this time. He was a designer and cartoonist, as well as a sculptor, and later competed with Dylan for the attentions of Emily Holmes Coleman. Ron Cour came up to London in 1937 to the Royal College of Art. He seems to have had some teaching from the avant-garde sculptor Frank Dobson, and it was possibly through Cour that Dylan became friendly with Dobson. It is more likely, however, that the friendship was brought about by Edith Sitwell or by the *Daily Telegraph* art critic Tommy Earp, who was one of those closest to Dylan – Earp and Dobson were brothers-in-law.

Both Janes and Levy give accounts in this volume of these early days on the borders of Chelsea, an area that Dylan described as:

> the quarter of the pseudo-artists, of the beards, the naughty
> expressions of an entirely outmoded period of artistic importance,
> and of the most boring Bohemian parties I have ever thought
> possible. Slightly drunk, slightly dirty, slightly wicked, slightly
> crazed, we repeat our platitudes on Gauguin and Van Gogh as
> though they were the most original things in the world... these little
> maggots are my companions for most of the time (December,
> 1934).

But in this letter to Bert Trick, Dylan also boasted that he had also
got to know "scores of better people". Within weeks of his arrival, he
had met Henry Moore and Wyndham Lewis. Dylan could not have
chosen a better time to make contacts in London, for the capital was
beginning to bubble surrealism. Artists, such as Roland Penrose, John
Banting, Eileen Agar and Julian Trevelyan had returned from Paris.
David Gascoyne published his *First Manifesto of English Surrealism* in
1935, and then his translation of Breton's *What is Surrealism?* Dylan
met up with the surrealists at David Archer's bookshop in Parton
Street, and at the Arts Café opposite, where Roger Roughton edited
Contemporary Poetry and Prose – Dylan regularly met here with
Gascoyne, George Reavey, and Trevelyan, who describes the meetings
in his *Indigo Days*.

Through his friendship with Norman Cameron, Dylan met surrealists involved in advertising, such as painter, sculptor and film-maker
Len Lye. The meetings often took place in Henekey's bar, near
Cameron's office on the Strand, as the novelist William Sansom has
described:

> When the office closed, we would often walk along to a wineshop
> where goodish cheap hock was served on heavy wooden tables, and
> there I met a number of Norman's friends - an astounded cherub
> called Thomas, a clerkly-looking fellow called Gasgoyne,
> eggdomed Len Lye like an ascetic coster in his raffish cap... unlike
> certain other writers *manqués* back in the office, they did not
> discuss literary theory or whine about their souls and sensitivities -
> they made up things there and then, grabbed down extraordinary
> stories and myths from the air, wrote down doggerel and verse.

Dylan was on good terms with a number of other experimental filmmakers who later found themselves in surrealism or on its edges – Basil Wright, Alberto Cavalcanti and, in particular, Humphrey Jennings, who was also making his mark as a surrealist painter, collagist and photographer. He also talked on the radio about poetry, and presented a series on *The Poet and the Public*. Dylan became friendly with the painter and poet Max Chapman, and with his partner Oswell Blakeston, once a conjuror's assistant and cinema organist but now a painter, poet, novelist, film-maker, columnist for *Film Art* and, as Paris correspondent for *Close-Up*, an early reporter on surrealist trends in the cinema. Dylan's letters to him capture the zany fun in their friendship. Blakeston, too, has written about Dylan, describing the evening in a Bloomsbury pub when he held an audience surrealistically enthralled

> with the last adventure of Major Fortescue – the apotheosis of an off-duty story by a poet. Dylan, who had come to London to teach poets there about Welsh magic, had turned himself into a serial story for our amusement, each evening giving a new instalment of the adventures of the Major who had such an independent mind that he collected boomerangs which wouldn't come back and practised topiary until he was attacked by birds in top hats [164]

About this time, Dylan met Eileen Agar, the only person to be a member of the Surrealist Group and the rival London Group. She was at a black-tie party when in walked David Gasgoyne, one of the key people who lay at the interstices of art and literature and who helped writers and artists to meet each other. As Gasgoyne entered the room, Agar noticed someone with him:

> a ruddy-faced cherub with a snub nose and no chin, at home in any scenery... dramatically, as they entered the crowded room, all the lights went out, but Dylan squatted on the floor and in a jiffy was reciting limericks in the dark which made everyone present sit up and take notice (1988, p107).

During the evening, Agar made some "lightning drawings of this ugly suckling" which she used to paint Dylan's portrait in 1960, which was bought by the Tate in 1962.

In the summer of 1935, some of Dylan's London friends decided he needed to get away from the city. Geoffrey Grigson took him to Ireland, to a studio cottage that had been converted by American artist Rockwell Kent. They did nothing more artistic than paint faces on the

Brancusi-headed pebbles on the beach. The same year, Dylan took on the mantle of Art Critic. He had been asked to review Naomi Mitchison's *Beyond This Limit*, the illustrations for which had been done by Wyndham Lewis. Dylan wrote:

> The drawings remind me of Picasso under the influence of Thurber, but not so funny. Every one of them is ugly, pointless, meaningless, careless, affected. Some of them remind me of those designs on toilet paper that are not always done by hand.[165]

Dylan ended the year vigorously refuting Richard Church's comments that his poetry was influenced by surrealism, an experiment in art which Church, in his November 26 letter, described as pernicious, anti-social and destructive. Church was Dent's poetry editor and Dylan was keen to get another collection published. He wrote, with not a little deceit, in the plainest terms:

> I am not, never have been, never will be, or could be for that matter, a surrealist, and for a number of reasons: I have very little idea what surrealism is; until quite recently I had never heard of it; I have never, to my knowledge, read even a paragraph of surrealist literature; my acquaintance with French is still limited to 'the pen of my aunt'; I have not read any French poetry, either in the original or in translation, since I attempted to translate Victor Hugo in a provincial Grammar School examination, and failed (December, 1935).

For the next three years, he would return in his letters to disowning the surrealists, branding them as a 'nasty' school, and a 'highbrow parlour game', proclaiming loftily that "my own sane bee in the bonnet can never be a pal of that French wasp forever stinging itself to a loud and undignified death with a tail of boiled string."

In the spring of 1936, Norman Cameron thought Dylan needed another break, and conspired to have him sent to stay in a cottage owned by Wyn Henderson in Porthcurno. This part of Cornwall was already developing as an artists' colony, and Fred Janes and William Scott were staying in Scott's studio in Mousehole. Dylan was also keen to go to Cornwall to see his old Swansea friends, Endell and Denis Mitchell, who had just returned from a painting trip to Morocco, and had settled in Balnoon, near St Ives. Martin has described the time with the Mitchells, listening to Joyce reading *Finnegans Wake* and reading Djuna Barnes'

Nightwood, which was later, writes Martin, one of Dylan's sources of words for poems, along with the *Thesaurus*, pub conversation and, as a last resort, opening a book at random and experimenting "with any likely word in the top line of each successive page".[166]

Dylan enjoyed Wyn Henderson's company when she was drinking but "when she's drinkless, she's booky". Dylan was particularly uncomfortable with her passion for psychoanalysis, though this probably owed as much to the work of Grace Pailthorpe and Reuben Mednikoff as Freud or Havelock Ellis. In their research, writing and painting, Pailthorpe and Mednikoff, who had been introduced to each other by Neuberg, worked together to achieve a deeper, and more socially useful, integration of surrealism and psychoanalysis. The Welsh painter Merlyn Evans, who had three paintings at the 1936 exhibition, was another surrealist interested in Freudian and Jungian exploration. He knew some of Dylan's friends – Bill Hayter, for example – but we cannot be certain that he ever met up with Dylan.

The following year Dylan went back to Cornwall to marry Caitlin. They stayed in cottages in Lamorna Cove and Mousehole ("you can buy a surrealist in Mousehole... for a couple of whiting") – the interview with Jack Wallis on page 79 gives an idea of how Dylan spent his time. Dylan and Caitlin also stayed in Max Chapman's studio in Newlyn, where they encountered the painter Dod Procter, whose work 'Morning' had been picture of the year at the Royal Academy in 1927 and was purchased for the nation by the *Daily Mail:*

> Newlyn is famous for its fleas and Dod Proctor: I go to bed with the former, and could with the latter. Caitlin was very rude yesterday to the Proctor woman who's thin and red-lipped and shiny. As we were leaving her house, the Proctor said, 'Wait a minute, I must powder my nose'. And Caitlin said, 'Why don't you put it in a bag?'[167]

Dylan was now, as FitzGibbon rightly puts it, a poet among painters, and friendships were made that would continue in various forms throughout his life: Augustus John, of course, but also the artist and art historian Ruthven Todd and Tommy Earp. Dylan was also becoming an accepted figure on the avant-garde art scene in London. His friendships with surrealist painters grew (often at drinking sessions in the Wheatsheaf and Burglar's Rest pubs in Fitrovia), and he became involved a number of important events. In 1936, he had taken part, with his cup of boiled string, in the *International Surrealist Exhibition* held in London in June and July. Many of its organisers – including Roland Penrose, Bill Hayter, David Gascoyne and Roger Roughton – were already known to Dylan, as were some of the British exhibitors such as Lye, Jennings and Peake.

A poetry reading was held on June 26 as part of the surrealist exhibition. Dylan took part ("though I haven't discovered why I am"), along with Paul Eluard, Samuel Beckett, George Reavey and David Gascogyne. Dylan was not at all confident about what to read, and he wrote to Reavey to ask for help:

> I didn't see you (I think) at the Surrealist party to ask you about the Poetry Reading on the 26th. I see my name's down on the little notice. That means I'm definitely invited to read, doesn't it? I'd love to, of course. I don't quite know what stuff to choose, though... Could you spare half-an-hour sometime that day – before the reading – to look through some stuff with me? You'll know what'll go down best (June 17, 1936).

In the event, Dylan read from a postcard. The June 1936 issue of *Contemporary Poetry and Prose* was devoted to surrealism, and Dylan appeared in it with Bunuel, Dali, Eluard and Breton. That autumn, he published a poem and short story in *transition.*

Fellow-travelling with the surrealists brought Dylan a number of diverting opportunities. After the June 26 poetry reading, he met with John Johnson, an editor on *Life and Letters Today*, who was also the editor of the *Group Theatre Paper.* He and Nigel Henderson were keen to get Dylan to write for the Theatre, for which Caitlin had once danced. It had been founded by the painter Robert Medley and his partner Rupert Doone, a distinguished dancer, producer and drama teacher – John Piper was also involved. Doone put on 'political' plays by Isherwood, Auden, Eliot and MacNeice at the Mercury and Old Vic. The Theatre was a revolt against popular realism and was committed to 'total theatre', a synthesis of dance, mime and speech, experimenting with modern sets and fashion.

Dylan considered offering them "a Horrible play, mostly in prose with verse choruses and have got bits of the story mapped out". Johnson later wrote to FitzGibbon to say that Dylan's play "was utterly non-political and dealt with devils and I think was based on some old Welsh legend". But Dylan was reluctant, probably wisely, to write any more until Doone made a promise it would be performed: "I don't feel like devoting a lot of time to it at the moment – I can't as a matter of fact, because I've to review lots of crime stories in order to buy beer and shirts and cigarettes." Some seventeen years later, the Group Theatre's final reprise was to co-sponsor the Globe Theatre homage to Dylan, and Rupert Doone was one of organisers.[168]

1937 was Fred Janes' *annus mirabilis* when he exhibited, alongside Braque, in the Mayor Gallery in London. That November, Dylan was at the *Surrealist Objects and Poems Exhibition*. A drunk insulted him and a fight broke out in which a painting was smashed to pieces. In January 1938, he attended the opening of Guggenheim Jeune, the new gallery in Cork Street run by Peggy Guggenheim, with curatorial help from Marcel Duchamp and decoration by Wyn Henderson. In October that year, Roland Penrose invited Dylan to the unveiling of Picasso's *Guernica* at the New Burlington Galleries, and suggested he read something. A few months later, in March 1938, Penrose asked Dylan to write for the *Gallery Bulletin*, the magazine of the English Surrealists, but Dylan never did, probably because Penrose couldn't promise any payment. Despite this patent lack of enthusiasm on Dylan's part, Penrose nevertheless included him in July that year as one of the thirty-eight members of the English Group of Surrealists.[169]

For many artists and writers, surrealism was not just a way of painting but of living. When the civil war in Spain broke out, a small group of surrealists started to meet in Roland Penrose's house to discuss how to prevent the spread of fascism across Europe. The group, described by Julian Trevelyan in his *Indigo Days*, included Trevelyan himself, Charles Howard, Sam Haile, Roger Roughton and occasionally Dylan and George Reavey.

For the next two years to the start of the war with Germany, London fermented with surrealist exhibitions (eighteen of them) and surrealistic infighting between the various surrealist factions, sometimes about the definition of surrealism, sometimes over political matters such as the fight against fascism, and often in ideological disputes between Stalinists and Trotskyists. London also filled up with painters and sculptors who came as refugees from mainland Europe, many of them Jews or Spanish Republicans or simply 'degenerate' modernists hounded out by the German authorities. The London surrealists, of course, knew how to cock a snook at fascism: wearing masks of Neville Chamberlain, they took a prominent part in the 1938 May Day parade; the London Gallery put on a retrospective Max Ernst exhibition in aid of Czech and Jewish refugees; and the New Burlington Galleries exhibited modern German artists.

Dylan, meanwhile, was planning various collaborative schemes with painters, prominent amongst whom was Mervyn Peake. In February 1937, Dylan proposed writing about a journey through Wales; Augustus John would do a frontispiece portrait of Dylan, and Cedric Morris the illustrations. But Dylan also invited Peake to do some drawings for the book, and Peake went off at Whitsun to the Rhondda, where he spent three days sketching miners and their children. But by March 1938, Dylan had dropped the idea and wrote to Peake apologising but also inviting him to do the drawings for *Portrait of the Artist as a Young Dog*. The letter also mentions that they were planning to work together on a "crazy book... I have no idea what the story will be. Have you?"

Painting in Yiddish

By the beginning of 1939, the Kardomah Boy, though mostly domiciled in Blashford and Laugharne, had well and truly arrived on the London literary and artistic scene, at least that part of it that was modern and anti-establishment. But as war loomed ever closer, he was able to turn to more established figures, pestering Sir Kenneth and Lady Clark about avoiding conscription and exhorting Herbert Read to find him work reviewing books ("preferably not highbrow ones").

Dylan began making films for the Ministry of Information to support the war effort. Some of his surrealist friends left the country (Lye, Roughton and Hayter) but others used their skills in wartime service: some joined Dylan in film making (Banting, Jennings), whilst others became war artists (Moore) or designed, and instructed upon, camouflage (Penrose, Trevelyan and, briefly, Hayter).

Dylan's patrons were by now beginning to provide access to a much broader world of painting and sculpture than the surrealists. In the summer of 1940, Dylan and Caitlin stayed for three months in John Davenport's manor house in Gloucestershire. Davenport was an art collector, his wife Clement a designer. The influential art patron, Peter Watson, did much at his Palace Gate flat to bring together and support the neo-romantic painters such as John Minton, John Craxton and Keith Vaughan, and to open up their friendship with Dylan, to whom he sometimes gave money. Vaughan was also a writer, contributing articles to *Horizon* and *Penguin New Writing*.

Later in the War, Dylan and Caitlin moved into a studio flat at Wentworth Studios which, together with Trafalgar Studios, formed an artist's colony just off Manresa Road in Chelsea. The studio had been vacated by the poet Alun Lewis, as FitzGibbon has described. The books in the flat were

> undoubtedly Alun Lewis's. I am quite sure that neither the Coleridge not the Whitman would have belonged to Dylan, and I would even doubt if they were ever opened by him when he was there. The pictures on the wall, as I remember them, were not Welsh landscapes, *though there may* have been one by Ceri Richards, but violent semi-abstracts by Jankel Adler and one or two by Dylan himself.[170]

The poet Paul Potts has written of Adler that he was "a real artist who was also a real socialist... [he] was the most Jewish person I have known. He was so Jewish, he almost painted in Yiddish" (p213). Dylan and Adler were very close friends, as Potts has described in his essay on Dylan:

> He loved Jankel Adler who on one occasion, with the right amount of lonely dignity, made him an honorary Jew. Dylan not to be outdone in courtesy by a painter, made Jankel Adler an honorary Welshman. Both ceremonies on that occasion were beautiful. Dylan would indeed have been at home beside the wailing wall (p186-187).

Adler was the senior figure in a group of Polish artists that included Josef Herman and Felix Topolski. He had been born in Lodz in Poland, studied painting and printmaking in Germany, and was greatly influenced in the 1930s by his friendships with Paul Klee and Picasso, and had worked in Paris with another of Dylan's friends, Bill Hayter. Adler came to Glasgow, and then settled in London in 1943, in a studio in 77, Bedford Gardens, Kensington. In the studio below were three other friends of Dylan, the Scottish painters Robert Colquhoun and Robert Macbryde, who moved to London from Scotland in 1941. Sharing the studio with them was John Minton, whose love for Colquhoun inevitably led to strained relationships. Minton left the two Roberts in 1946 and set up house with Keith Vaughan.

Adler became an important artistic link between the European avante-garde and several young British painters. He inspired not just Colquhoun and Macbryde (and fellow-Scot William Crosbie), but also other painter friends of Dylan such as Michael Ayrton and Prunella

Clough, as well as Minton and Vaughan. Adler also helped many refugee artists, such as Peter Potworowski, settle into London, securing them their first exhibitions in the capital.

Adler's influence went further than just inspiring the work of the neo-romantics – he was also able to provide Dylan, and the rest of the group, with a personal account of political events abroad. A friend of Martin Buber, Adler had been one of the founders in Lodz of the *Ing Idisz* (Young Yiddish) group, painters and writers dedicated to expressing their Jewish identity. In London, he joined a club for Jewish intellectuals, along with Josef Herman. Adler was never reluctant to tell his friends what the Nazis were doing to the Jews in Europe, or to depict the Holocaust in his paintings. These political discussions must have sometimes been heated – Adler had been in the Polish army, had fought against the Germans and been evacuated from Dunkirk, but Minton and Vaughan had been conscientious objectors and Dylan a self-proclaimed pacifist. In her interview with Colin Edwards, Elizabeth Ruby Milton talks of Dylan's emotional response to the plight of European Jews, as do Mably Owen, Brigit Marnier and Alban Leyshon.

As Spalding describes in her biography (p66), Minton, Colquhoun and Macbryde were at the heart of a group that met from 1943 to1946 on Sundays in the Windsor Castle pub, before returning to continue in the studio in Bedford Gardens. Often with them were Dylan, Ayrton, Vaughan, Clough and John Craxton. Between them, this colourful group of seven mostly-gay painters and one straight writer were later to make a significant contribution to the Festival of Britain.

Elizabeth Ruby Milton talks in her Edwards interview about how Dylan immersed himself in the world of film and art, not least through parties given by friends such as Tambimuttu. Milton remembers the way in which Dylan cared for artists who had fallen on bad times, particularly Nina Hamnett, as she describes on pages 68-69. Milton went with Hamnett to a party at the house of the sculptor Jacob Epstein, and recalls

A little girl with pigtails opened the door and we went into this studio and Epstein and Dylan were there, and some other people... there was a wonderful man called Carol Thompson who was a wonderful painter and he had this disease – a disease that makes you have no control over your limbs at all... I remember Dylan – it must have been about six o'clock one morning – took me to Carol Thompson's studio, which was indescribably squalid... but these beautiful paintings, mostly in greys and wonderful Dufy colours... this man Thompson would never ever let anybody see these paintings, but for some reason he let Dylan come and look at them, and because I was with Dylan he let me come, too. And soon afterwards a bomb fell on them and they were all burnt.

Remy has described the various places in London that throughout the War provided a meeting place or headquarters for poets and painters (pp215-216). These included Anton Zwemmer's bookshop on Charing Cross Road, where Ruthven Todd worked as an assistant. Another important focus was The Modern Gallery, which was opened in 1941 in Charlotte Street by Jankel Adler's close friend, the refugee painter and writer, Jack Bilbo. It was the setting for wild parties but also for talks, poetry readings, and political discussion in the "intellectual fight against Hitlerism and all it stands for". Leftwich (1980) has written about another meeting place, Margaret Waterhouse's bookshop in Swiss Cottage where the poet, Itzik Manger, "first met Arthur Waley and Dylan Thomas. 'He can drink,' Manger told Leftwich, 'but I am the better poet'."[171]

The International Arts Centre in Bayswater, whose patrons included Spender, Lehmann and John Piper, was also a venue for left-wing poets and artists. The surrealist painter and poet, Toni del Renzio, organised poetry readings there during the War, and there were a number of contacts with Dylan:

> I certainly met him on numerous occasions when we agreed on nothing, particularly after the publication of *Arson* which, as far as I remember, Dylan saw as rejecting any claim by him to surrealist status which he had hitherto, somewhat ambiguously, enjoyed along with a certain encouragement from [E.L.T.] Mesens.[172]

As the war progressed, Dylan's circle of painters grew wider still: there were meals with the 'shabby humped elegant' Peter Rose Pulham, parties with Matthew Smith and a three-week visit to Laugharne in 1940 by Rupert Shephard, though he was more Caitlin's friend than Dylan's.[173] In his biography, FitzGibbon has described how he and Dylan would meet writers and painters with 'established reputations' in the Eight Bells pub in Chelsea, including Francis Butterfield who took over Dylan's Manresa Road studio:

> He was the first to acquaint me with the works of William

McGonagall... about whom he never said a derogatory word, and I understand why. McG was an honest man even if he was an incompetent half-wit, and D. liked honesty above many things... One of the most memorable meals I ever had was at Wentworth Studios. Caitlin dug something meaty and luscious from an earthenware pot. Apart from candle-light, the place was in darkness... and nobody said a word... On the bed reposed a baby in glorious oblivion and about two dozen gramophone records (borrowed), two of which I sat on and broke in the darkness. And who shall blame me? I could have squashed the baby in that gloom... I remember in Godfrey Street D.'s reading from the MS he was writing. A novel which seemed to involve a second-hand furniture shop. I thought it amusing. So, I think, did D. – for a time – and then he had second thoughts and flung the pages across the room with a loud grunt of disgust. I never heard more of it.[174]

There were drinking sessions with Dan Davin, Tambimuttu and the abstract expressionist, Gerald Wilde, and pub crawls with Tommy Earp and the painter and writer William Gaunt who, wrote Dylan in 1943, "wants to make a bad day for all three of us... we must have a good bad day." Dylan's painter friends at this time were as diverse as Dick Wyndham, a wealthy amateur painter of country houses, and designer, jazz player and one-time surrealist John Tunnard, who had exhibited in 1939 at the Guggenheim Jeune. Towards the end of 1945, Dylan and Tunnard were considering collaborating on a "literary and artistic venture for the publisher Lund Humphries" (Peat and Whitton, pp77-78).

Magazines provided another point of contact with artists such as Stanley Parker of *John O'London's*, who did a pencil portrait of Dylan in 1946. Dylan also met with painters and illustrators through his work in the film industry and the Ministry of Information. He was close to the painter, John Banting, both a surrealist and a Stalinist, and active with other painters and poets in protests against the war in Spain. He became art director at Strand Films in 1939, and worked with Dylan on two films, *Balloon Site 586* and *This is Colour*. In 1941, he became art director of the left-wing magazine *Our Time*, and regularly contributed scathing satirical drawings about upper class society in wartime Britain. *Our Time* published Dylan's 'Ceremony After a Fire Raid' in May 1944. Banting's unpublished memoir in the Tate archive describes drinking sessions and work assignments with Dylan, including their collaboration on *This is Colour*. Banting thought Dylan was one of the most loveable men whom I had the privilege of knowing – preferring the company of nonentities to that of famous scholars. Essentially kind, he was mercilessly sponged upon by barflies and would occasionally thrust an unsolicited £1 on someone whom he suspected of being in low funds and apologise for doing so... His company was stimulating, sympathetic and free of spite or dogma.

One of Banting's closest friends was Edward Burra, a watercolourist, printmaker and theatre designer who had exhibited with the surrealists in the late 1930s. Whilst Banting presented satirical portraits of English Society, Burra depicted scenes and figures from the urban underworld. He was another patron of the Mandrake Club, and some of his letters in the Tate archive indicate that he knew both Dylan and Caitlin – he tells a confusing story about a Brancusi piece being cracked over Caitlin's head.

The war also brought a renewal of Dylan's friendship with Mervyn Peake, who in 1940 had moved into 3, Trafalgar Studios on Manresa Road. From time to time, Dylan occupied one of the downstairs studios. In another studio lived the painter John Grome, a mutual friend of Peake and Dylan. The same year, Dylan introduced Peake to Kaye Webb, an editor at *Lilliput* who for the next two years kept Peake in funds with commissions for illustrations. Later, Peake moved to 70, Glebe Place, just off the Kings Road. Dylan was staying there in August 1945, writing to Caitlin about finding somewhere to live, and taking Peake's son to the kindergarten and cinema so that Peake had some quiet to get on with *Titus Groan*. Peake did two drawings of Dylan ill in bed which were later published in the July 1954 issue of *Encounter*. Not long after *Titus Groan* was published, Peake and his wife, the painter Maeve Gilmore, found a note though their letterbox:

> Mervyn, dear Maeve,
> Will you please lend me a coat and trousers for a day. Any coat and trousers so long as they aren't my own. I am supposed to speak on a public platform tomorrow, Sunday, just after lunch. May I call early morning –
>
> Love, Dylan[175]

As the last year of the War opened, Dylan proposed a book about the life of the streets of London. Called *Twelve Hours in the Streets*, the book was to have illustrations by his old friend John Banting, though Dylan seems to have been warned that the publisher, Peter Lunn, considered Banting "too gay for such a book." Dylan nevertheless contacted Banting, who was reluctant to take the project on, saying he wished "to do no formalised arty 'picture-arty' work." But he quickly changed his mind when Dylan reassured him that "I would be free to use my own kind of Surrealism. 'Fitzroy Street could be paved with tits and the houses built of bottoms'."[176]

The Great Bard Ennobled

After the War, the surrealists continued to meet on Wednesday evenings at the Barcelona restaurant in Beak Street. Conroy Maddox has noted Dylan's attendance at some of these meetings, when Lucien Freud and George Melly were also present (Levy, p59). In August 1945, the surrealists revived the official name of 'Surrealist Group in England'. Dylan was present in at least one of these meetings, along with Roland Penrose, the chairman, and Conroy Maddox, Henry Moore, Edith Rimmington, Robert and John Melville, John Banting, E.L.T. Mesens and the poet Feyyaz Fergar (Remy, p354).

Dylan's involvement with the surrealists also took on a more public form. In December 1944, the police raided the premises of the anarchist Freedom Press, and took away the proofs of *Free Unions Libres*, a new surrealist review. Three people arrested in the raid, the editors of a bi-monthly political journal called *War Commentary*, were sent to prison. On May 4 1945, Dylan signed a letter in *Tribune*, along with Jankel Adler, Paul Potts, George Barker, George Orwell and Alex Comfort, protesting at the imprisonment. They called for "the whole body of Socialist opinion in this country to identify itself with these editors…"[177]

Only the week before, *Tribune* had published a long review by Charles Hamblett of developments in British poetry. Hamblett was complimentary but Dylan may have felt uncomfortable with being so overtarred with the surrealist's Freudian brush:

> A new force was kicking through the womb of war. A trio of poets, who had emerged during the 30s, but whose influence was not felt at the time, now became significant voices to the poets who filled the early war anthologies. The trio consisted of Dylan Thomas, George Barker and David Gascoyne… Thomas, the most potent in

imagery though the least intellectual, mined the rich ore of the Freudian unconscious, coloured by childhood impressions of biblical hot-gospelling in his native Welsh valleys. It is necessary here to emphasise the unconscious process at work in Thomas. A great craftsman, he nevertheless builds his poems from the jelloid of underconscious logic. There is nothing cerebral in his writing: each word is a painful nerve plucked from his absurdly crucified body. Like Lawrence, he must feel it *there* before he can write it (April 27, 1945).

It would be an exaggeration to say that Dylan had an association with the north-west Essex group of painters who had gathered in Great Bardfield (and in surrounding villages) since the arrival there in 1925 of Edward Bawden and Eric Ravilious, and, in 1933, John Aldridge. But Dylan had an interesting number of connections both to the group and this part of the county.

In 1946, Ruthven Todd invited Dylan to spend a few days at his Essex house, Tilty Mill. It had previously been the home of the painter John Armstrong and Veronica Sibthorp, Dylan's ex-girlfriend. Dylan appears not to have met any painters on his visit. In his unpublished memoir, Todd describes how Dylan charmed the locals, demonstrating again his easy ability to fit into the quiet pace of rural life. He read detective stories, drank pints of fresh milk as he had done at Talsarn during the War, and played darts and shove-halfpenny in the Rising Sun with the locals.

He continued to visit Tilty Mill, and made several trips there between 1950 and 1953 to visit MacBryde and Colquhoun when they were staying with the writers George Barker and Elizabeth Smart. Their son, Christopher Barker, has provided an engaging account of life with Macbryde and Colquhoun, though the visits of friends like Dylan and John Deakin were often so riotous, as Collins has described, that eventually the two Roberts were evicted.[178]

Dylan's friendships within the north-west Essex group were also an expression of his interest in theatre. Besides being painters and printmakers, Colquhoun and Macbryde were both theatre designers. Their work in the theatre brought the two Roberts to London, and it was there, in September 1950, that Brinnin met them at a party he went to with Dylan.[179] Michael Ayrton and Isabel Lambert were also theatre designers as well as painters. Lambert, for long a drinking companion in the George (the 'Gluepot'), moved into Great Sampford, and Ayrton bought a house in Toppesfield in 1951.

Ayrton moved effortlessly through the worlds of art, literature and broadcasting, and was an important figure in bringing people together. Yet Dylan was one of the few to whom he was very close. In early 1947, he and Dylan were planning to work on an opera for William Walton, though nothing came of it. Ayrton wanted to produce a book on Hogarth and asked Dylan to write the introduction. Nothing came of that, either. Then Ayrton was commissioned to illustrate some of Dylan's poems. Dylan 'tearfully begged' him not to. As much as Dylan enjoyed the company of painters, he seems to have found it impossible to collaborate with

34. Oloff de Wet's bust of Dylan

them – not just Ayrton but also Peake, Banting and Tunnard.

Dylan also knew Edward Bawden, though Bawden disliked his 'bohemian' ways.[180] Bawden, who was an illustrator and designer as well as a painter, was the most influential of the north-west Essex group, and had a profound influence, both before and after the War, on the illustration of books. Several of Dylan's friends were also at the heart of the post-War imbrication of painting and poetry. When Frederick Muller published a series of anthologies, William Scott provided the lithographs for *Soldiers' Verse* (1945), and in the same year Michael Ayrton for *Poems of Death*, which included 'And death shall have no dominion'. Two years later, Robert Colquhoun's lithographs for *Poems of Sleep and Dream* revealed the powerful influence of Jankel Adler.

Bohemian and anti-academic, Tambimuttu's *Poetry London* was also an attempt to bring together poetic and pictorial imagery. It published several of Dylan's poems, as well as the illustrations of many of his friends such as Minton, Craxton, Peake and Banting. Dylan's ability to draw prompted Tambimuttu to ask Dylan for some illustrations. Dylan responded enthusiastically but does not seem to have produced anything.[181]

Dylan had long frequented clubs that brought together writers and artists, including the Gargoyle, the Arts and Battledress, the Mandrake, the ML Club and, from 1949, the Savage Club.[182] But in February 1947, Dylan was ennobled as 'the Duke of Gwenno' at the Court of Redonda, a fantasy kingdom of artists and writers that met in various Soho pubs. It may have been at the Court of Redonda that Dylan met the sculptor Hugh Oloff de Wet, who specialised in busts of men of letters. He liked to visit his subjects in their homes to study and sketch them, but in 1951 Dylan sat for de Wet in the London home of their mutual friend Tony van den Bergh. The bust is a remarkable piece of portraiture that to this day remains mostly unknown even to Dylan aficionados, let alone the viewing public.[183]

Dylan and family went to Italy in April 1947. They stayed for a while in Florence and then in a villa in the hills outside the town. Dylan showed little interest in the art and architecture of the city. Neither did he know much about Italy's poets, though he may have seen Toni del Renzio's essay on Italian poetry in the November 1946 issue of *Horizon*.

Dylan's favourite haunt in Florence was the Caffé delle Giubbe Rosse, which since the early 1900s had been the meeting place of the city's writers and painters, especially the Futurists. Here Dylan spent his evenings, as Piero Bigongiari notes in his interview, with the painter Ottone Rosai, whose Futurist-Fascist group had once gathered at the café. As a result of his support for the fascists, Rosai had lost his teaching post in Florence but by the time Dylan met up with him he was being rehabilitated and making his mark anew as a landscape painter with an international reputation – as Parronchi describes in his interview with Edwards (p120). Fascist or not, Dylan borrowed fifty thousand lira from him.

On their return from Italy in August, the family moved to South Leigh, Oxfordshire. This led to opportunities for Dylan to meet two wealthy art patrons, both friends of Mervyn Levy. One was Tony Hubbard who collected Francis Bacon paintings. He had also bought some of Desmond Morris' early paintings and backed his first London exhibition at the London Gallery in 1950, alongside Miro. As for Dylan, Hubbard often kept him afloat in the post-War period, and also helped fund the magazine *Circus*, to which Dylan contributed an article 'How to be a Poet' in 1950.

The other patron was ex-stockbroker Jimmy Bomford, a millionaire art collector and pig-breeder who lived at Laines, a mansion which he had designed overlooking the village of Aldbourne in Wiltshire. The farm manager was Johnny Morris – later of television animal fame. Dylan went to visit Bomford in February 1948 – we do not know what he made of his host's modernist collection which included works by Gauguin, Utrillo, Klee, Cézanne and Manet, though Dylan would probably have been more intrigued by the dance music that came out through Picasso's *Guitar hanging on a wall* – speakers were inlaid in the wall behind the canvas. Sometime after the War, Bomford bought Lee Cottage in the middle of Aldbourne village as a home for Jankel Adler. After Adler's death in 1949, Mervyn Levy moved in.

Not long after the visit to Bomford, Dylan was invited to the Sesame Club by Edith Sitwell to meet Edward James, the wealthy patron and collector of British surrealism, and a critic, poet and novelist in his own right. Dylan wrote to him on April 7 1948 suggesting they meet again in London for a drink. There followed a correspondence into the autumn in which Dylan described the financial worries that deflected him away from poetry into "journalism, third rate scripts, bombastic Third Programme broadcasts and lectures to sandalled girls". They met again in November, and in December Dylan took the plunge and asked for money to clear his overdraft. James sent £20 and suggested that, instead of repaying it, Dylan and he should work together on a translation of a major French, Spanish or Italian classical poem which James would then publish. There was no response from Dylan.[184]

The Colony Room Club opened in 1948, and soon became a haven for writers and artists – Dylan was to become a regular patron. The same year, he received a letter from John Banting, who had gone to Ireland to paint murals for Countess Fitzwilliam. Banting invited him to travel through Ireland, making a film on the way. Dylan replied from South Leigh in November 1948, bemoaning the drabness of the Gargoyle ("empty of all except touts in well-fed suitings") but mentioning that he still saw art critic Tommy Earp. As for Ireland, Dylan told Banting that

> the idea of the Irish film was so good I bled… It is my dream. To dawdle and doodle through Ireland with a cameraman and you and who else, what busy glory, what how-d'you-do's, what a time we'd have! I can feel myself ill after it now (Tate Archive).

But Dylan had to turn down the offer, because he was already under contract to Gainsborough Films for three years "at a wonderful salary which keeps me as insolvent as ever I was". The following month, he met up with Iris Murdoch, a dancing partner from the Gargoyle. They talked about why they preferred the company of artists, as Conradi has described: "Being half-artist and half-intellectual, Iris felt entirely at home nowhere. Talking with Dylan Thomas at a party given by Kay Dick in December 1948, she decided that she best liked the company of artists, or rather Bohemians, not intellectuals." Dylan would certainly have agreed; he enjoyed the company of artists because they were not 'booky', as well as for "their exuberant recreational indulgencies", as Rhys Davies once put it, another writer whose circle of friends included painters.[185]

Dylan's visit to Prague in March 1949 is described in the interviews on pp154-172. He felt more comfortable here than in Florence. He enjoyed the city's northern baroque architecture and he also knew more about Czech poetry and the country's history – he had spent some time in the early part of the War researching for a script the BBC had asked him to do on the Czech army's march across Russia in the 1914-18 war. Dylan's contacts in Prague were as close to the world of painting as of literature. He spent the day with an old friend from wartime London, Jirí Mucha, the son of Europe's leading *art nouveau* painter, Alphonse Mucha. Dylan's guide and interpreter, Jiřina Hauková, had been a member of the surrealist-inspired Skupina 42 (Group 42).

Dylan also met with the painter and poet, Jirí Kolár, and had lunch with Vitezslav Nesval, who had been published by John Lehmann in *New Writing*. Nezval was head of the Film Department in the Czech Ministry of Information. He was a poet, script writer (with a stint in Hollywood), translator and story writer. In the 1920s, he had been one of the founders of the avant-garde group Devetsil, and was influential before the War in promoting surrealism in Czech literature – he had organised the 1935 visit to Prague of André Breton and Paul Eluard.

Even when he was living in his 'vegetable' Wales, Dylan was not without contact with arts and artists. New Quay had a thriving cultural life, including local painters who used the Black Lion as a gallery, as did visitors such as Augustus John and Grant Murray – see Thomas (2002b). Another friend of Dylan's, John Davies, also exhibited in the pub, and his watercolours were featured in the December 1947 issue of *Wales*. At the Boat House in Laugharne, there were encounters with John Piper and Arthur Giardelli, whose wife gave piano lessons to Aeron. Giardelli has described a number of casual meetings with Dylan, including returning with him from the reading Dylan gave at the Tenby Arts Club in November 1949. Caitlin and the children, sometimes with Dylan in tow, also visited Tenby to stay in Little Rock House. This was owned by Geraldine Lawrence, a wealthy amateur painter, whose friends included Caitlin's sister, Nicolette, and her husband, the painter Anthony Devas.

Another good friend of Dylan in Laugharne was Griff Williams, who later became art critic of the *Western Mail* and whose articles in the 1960s helped illuminate Dylan's influence on several Welsh painters, including the poet and artist, John Wright.[186]

Richard Hughes, who had helped to organise the 1935 Contemporary Welsh Art exhibition, was another friend who bought good paintings to Laugharne when he lived in the Castle House – his living room was 'Dufy-hung', as Dylan once put it. When Hughes left after the War, Castle House was taken over by Phyllis Bowen and her husband, David. The daughter of a prosperous Pontypridd baker, Phyllis was sent away to Roedean for schooling. Afterwards, she painted at Benton End with Cedric Morris and Arthur Lett Haines, served in the WRNS during the War and then broadcast and wrote scripts for the BBC Welsh Service. After moving to Laugharne in 1947, she actively encouraged young Welsh artists and built up her own collection at Castle House. She was a pillar of the local community, a JP in St Clears and she provides a resounding testimonial for the often-maligned Dylan:

> I had quite a lot of long talks with him... I often walked across to the post office which was opposite Brown's Hotel, somewhere between half-past eleven and twelve, and by twelve Dylan would probably be sitting in the bay window of Brown's Hotel. The sight of Dylan sitting there was irresistible, one simply had to go in and have a chat... Dylan would be there probably from half-past eleven till one, and I doubt if he'd drink more than two half pints at the very outside. Nobody could call that heavy drinking... There are so many books about him, bringing out his worst weaknesses and his bad behaviour. That may have been so, I don't know. I knew him during these years in Laugharne, and I never saw him drunk; I never saw him being sick on the pavement; I never saw him behave in any obstreperous manner whatever... As far as I was concerned he was a gentle, sweet personality (2002, p152).

There was at least one trip from Laugharne, in 1949, to visit Mervyn Levy in Aldbourne, and to go to another of Bomford's parties.

Levy had always been a source of opportunities to meet artists, and this time it was an up-and-coming surrrealist called Desmond Morris, who had been appointed in 1947 as a lecturer in art at Chiseldon Army College, Swindon, in the department headed up by Levy. Morris was later to make a name for himself as a zoologist and television star, but Levy's encouragement also helped him make his mark as a painter. Levy and Morris exhibited together in Swindon Public Library in 1948, and Morris soon established himself as the only important newcomer to surrealism to emerge in Britain in the late 1940s. And what did the young Desmond Morris make of Dylan? He was

> stunned at the facility with which he could snatch exactly the right word from his memory and insert it precisely where he wanted it. I resolved then and there to spend more time playing with words, juggling with them like a verbal acrobat. It was a good lesson to have learnt and I was grateful to Dylan for it.[187]

Dylan's last public fling with surrealism was in 1950 at a production of Picasso's *Desire Caught by the Tail*. This six-act play had been put on privately in Paris in 1944, produced by Albert Camus, with Jean-Paul Sartre and Simone de Beauvoir in the cast. Roland Penrose then translated the play and it was read, again privately, in London in 1947, with a cast that included several surrealist painters such as John Banting and Julian Trevelyan. In 1950, the first English version was published by Rider and in February that year the play was produced by Eric Capon. He enlisted Dylan as the stage manager, though in a letter to Caitlin, Dylan writes about being 'in' the play, but only if Caitlin could send a clean suit up to London from Laugharne.

Down in Swansea, Dylan's old friends – Fred Janes, Ron Cour, Will Evans and Kenneth Hancock – were teaching in the School of Art. There were parties with Dylan at the Hancock house, and the occasional pint with Janes and George Fairley, another art teacher, in the King's Arms. Cardiganshire painter Aneurin Jones remembers that Dylan modelled for the students in the Thursday evening classes in the early 1950s.

Dylan's later letters continue to reflect his association with artists: there was "tantalising spraygun Michael? Still sculpting away? What a bore for the bronze". Robert Beulah, the portrait painter, is mentioned in the same letter to John Davenport in early 1951. In August that year, Dylan wrote to Donald Taylor about the suicide of the painter Ralph

Banbury – "A tall, languid man, friend & pupil of Cedric Morris, with a Chinese grandmother". Sometime about 1939, Banbury had done a portrait of Dylan and Caitlin, which is reproduced in Lycett's *New Life*.

In April 1953, Dylan appeared on television in a discussion about Alfred Janes' paintings. Two months later, he was sitting in Brown's Hotel when he noticed he was being sketched by a young man sitting in a far corner of the pub. Gordon Stuart was a Canadian travelling the world who had been fetched up by love in

35. Dylan looking rather pleased with himself

Carmarthen. Dylan agreed he would sit for him but had no time to do so until September. Stuart duly turned up at the Boat House. Caitlin opened the door and exclaimed "Another bloody artist". Dylan sat for three afternoons, and Stuart did three oil sketches. As he worked, they talked about George Eliot, Kurosawa's *Rashomon*, R.S. Thomas ("I quite like him", said Dylan) and Cedric Morris ("That bugger").

Painters and sculptors such as Dave Slivka, Loren MacIver and Peter Grippe continued to form part of Dylan's circle of friends on his trips to America. On his first trip in 1950, he broke free from Brinnin's itinerary to give a talk to painters and writers at the Cherry Lane Theatre in New York. Nashold and Tremlett perceptively note that Dylan was always happier in an environment of working craftsmen and women: "He was uncomfortable with the New York literati and chose, instead, to be among those who worked at the coalface" (p87). He discovered the Artists Club in Greenwich Village, where he met up with the painters, sculptors and printmakers of the Atelier 17 studio, of which Grippe was the director. Grippe, who had been a student of Bill

Hayter, was both a sculptor and printmaker with an interest in bringing art and poetry together. In 1960, he published *21 Etchings and Poems*, which included Dylan's 'The hand that signed the paper' illustrated by Grippe himself. Grippe had started the project in 1951 so it is possible that he and Dylan had discussed it.

Dylan also met Max Ernst and Dorothea Tanning on their ranch in Arizona. In San Francisco, he drank with the 'beat' writers and artists who hung around the bars of North Beach, as Ruth Witt Diamant describes (p204), as well as making forays to the Two AM Club in Mill Valley to meet local painters. In Sausalito, Dylan met up with the collagist Jean 'Yanko' Varda and, the story goes, with Salvador Dali in a coffee-house called the Indrawn Breath. Through an interpreter, the two men talked of women, horses and boxing.[188]

Dylan was also able to renew acquaintance with his old London friends from the art world who were now in America – Ruthven Todd, Bill Hayter and Len Lye. Frank Dobson, who had been the Professor of Sculpture at the Royal College of Art since 1946, was also in New York in November 1953. Dylan went to the unveiling of Dobson's statue of Sir Thomas Lipton; the next day, November 3, they met for drinks and planned an outing to the theatre together, but Dylan felt too ill to go.

There were also a number of images made on these American trips: at least three portraits by Gene Derwood and, in 1952, a bust by Grippe. The same year, Peter Evershed did a portrait in charcoal of Dylan in the San Remo on Bleeker Street, New York. In 1953, Evershed filled his sketch-book with drawings of Dylan in the White Horse Tavern. That year, the Boston painter, Gardner Cox, executed a portrait of Dylan, 'painted in a burst of enthusiasm' after hearing him deliver the first public reading of *Under Milk Wood* at the Fogg Museum on May 3. In November, Dave Slivka fashioned Dylan's death mask.

Although Dylan continued to enjoy the company of artists, his interest in art seems to have diminished in later years. Giardelli thought that Dylan "didn't seem interested in painting". Dan Jones noted that though Dylan lived a long time in London, and visited Italy and the USA,

> he made no effort to frequent galleries, and the visual arts did not enter into his conversation, his lectures or, with very few exceptions, his writings. He knew few paintings and few painters; I mean

by this that he could distinguish only a few painters from one another, and only a few styles of painting from one another. Dylan's preferences were influenced by literary considerations; where these were absent or very marginal, he showed little interest...[189]

Yet much of Dylan's later prose and poetry is intensely visual. Vernon Watkins has drawn attention, for instance, to the 'Ballad of the Long-legged Bait':

> The poem is full of visual imagery. It was so much a visual poem that he made a coloured picture for it which he pinned on the wall of his room, a picture of a woman lying at the bottom of the sea.[190]

The notion of Dylan apprehending a poem as if it were a painting was elaborated by Fred Janes in his interview with Colin Edwards:

> ... Dylan's work, where he wrote out the whole poem in a geometric form, obviously was linked with the [poem] as a visual experience, as well as having significance from the structure of the poem point of view and it's interesting to recall that at this time Dylan liked very much to write out the whole poem on the back of a cardboard box or something. I remember one period particularly, he liked to use the laundry packages and write out his entire poems on these, and actually hang them on the wall and enjoy them as a visual experience. I'm referring now to poems like 'Vision and Prayer' and that period.

Watkins has gone further and suggested, in relation to the 1946 collection *Deaths and Entrances*, that Dylan *constructed* poems, rather in the way that a painter assembles a canvas: "... pattern-making and symmetry are strong element in the structure of these poems. The demands of exact pattern are very seldom neglected" (1983). In his interview with Edwards, Janes traces this back to the teenage sessions in Daniel Jones' house where they discussed, and experimented in, poetry, music and painting:

> I think it was this feeling that in all the arts there was this great common sense of design, pattern, structure. Which of course comes through Dylan's work to an enormous degree at that time. Certainly comes through in my work, with very early, very complex patterns... we had this sense of really getting down to constructing our work, with a great deal of dedication, you might say.[191]

This clearly comes out in Dylan's letter of April 15 1934 to Hansford Johnson. He chastises her for thinking that talent alone was enough in itself to produce good poetry:

> the work-woman in your poetess, the intellectual, the thinking craftswoman, has not had half enough to do. You must work at the talent as a sculptor works at stone, chiselling, plotting, rounding, edging & making perfect.

He said much the same to an American student seventeen years later: "What I like to do is to treat words as a craftsman does his wood or stone or what-have-you, to hew, carve, mould, coil, polish and plane them into patterns, sequences, sculptures, fugues of sound..."[192]

As much as Dylan disliked the idea of a poet as a word-painter, he himself was an intensely pictorial writer, laying image upon image as the 'word-painting' was painstakingly built up. "A poem by myself *needs* a host of images," he wrote to Henry Treece in March 1938. And 'a good number' of these images, he told Treece in a later letter, "come from the cinema & the gramaphone and the newspaper, while I use contemporary slang, cliché, and pun." These modern and gaudy constructions were partly why Grigson later dismissed Dylan's work:

> Thomas was a provincial of poetry, smoozing, if with the best hopes and intentions, a masticated old manner with a pop modernism: a Gaudi of South Wales, his poems, one must allow, exhibiting like Gaudi's Barcelona church, Gaudi's punning, plasticine architecture, a certain perversity of attraction (1964).

Dylan attended as much to the aural as the visual elements of a poem's architecture, a word he himself used in a letter to Trevor Hughes in January 1934. The speaking of poetry, he told Hansford Johnson

> should certainly be encouraged. I do hope you read aloud. I myself chant aloud in a sonorous voice every poem I read. The neighbours must know your poems by heart; they certainly know my own, and are bound to be acquainted with many passages of *Macbeth*, *Death's Jester*, and the *Prophetic Books*. I often think that baths were built especially for drowsy poets to lie in and there intone aloud amid the steam and boiling ripples.[193]

351

The attention he gave to sound and image helps to account for Dylan's success as a radio broadcaster in the period after the 1939-45 War. His achievement was to turn listening to the radio into a way of seeing things. He had also once wanted to turn reading into a way of seeing, as Julian Maclaren Ross has described:

> We also shared another ambition, which was to write a film script... a complete scenario ready for shooting which would give the ordinary reader an absolute visual impression of the film in words and could be published as a new form of literature.[194]

Dylan's experience of stage and film productions would have equipped him for writing for the emerging medium of television. He had already appeared in two programmes, and in June 1953 he made a list of letters he had to write, and lectures and talks he had agreed to do, including "Get in touch with Aneirin and D.J. Thomas (suggestions for T.V. 'Butlin Camp' 'Ghost Story')." That Dylan was contemplating writing about Butlin's holiday camp for television suggests he had strayed a long way from the path of Blake.[195]

Appendices

A. Chronology of a Death

A good deal is known about Dylan Thomas' last days in New York because they were keenly observed and recorded by a number of friends, and even by a private detective working for *Time* magazine. Not surprisingly, there is a consensus amongst his biographers about the details of Dylan's comings and goings, and I have used their accounts to compile the following chronology – I have especially drawn on Brinnin's 1955 book and from Ruthven Todd's unpublished memoir. Brinnin's account relies largely on Liz Reitell whose own diary, unfortunately, ends on November 3, 1953. The letters of John Berryman and George Reavey also provide some data. Parts of Nashold and Tremlett's book are also helpful, though one must be constantly alert for the transitions they make between reporting and reconstruction.

I have produced the chronology because I often found myself confused when reading the descriptions of these last days, partly because medical information was mixed up with observations about other matters, particularly the colourful circus of people and events that surrounded Dylan. I believe that important diagnostic evidence has been overlooked and mis-read.

April 21-October 19 1953

Dylan's third visit to America between April and June 1953 was, according to Brinnin and other accounts, one of modest drinking, general sobriety and abstinence for 'whole days at a time'. He arrived in New York 'clear-eyed, hale, sober'. During the visit, he suffered from fatigue, and possibly gout and gastritis. He was treated, from about May 8, with injections of ACTH, a cortisone secretant, by Dr Milton Feltenstein. Brinnin also reports Dylan's continuing indifference to eating. In May, Dylan met with Stravinksy who thought "His face and skin had the colour and swelling of too much drinking... his nose was a red bulb and his eyes were glazed."

Dylan was back in Laugharne by the middle of June. His letters, which for most of his life were full of tales about real and imagined illnesses, tell us nothing about his state of health in this period. As for his drinking, several interviewees in this volume confirm another period of modest consumption. Dylan left Laugharne for America on October 9, breaking his journey in London. Various friends report he was unwell. He drank a good deal of whisky before catching the plane, and "I got on the plane and watched my watch, got drunk, and stayed frightened all the way here... really only a little booze on the plane but mostly frightened and sick with the thought of death. I felt as sick as death all the way here." Dylan arrived at Idlewild airport on October 20, where he was met by Liz Reitell, his lover, secretary, nurse and producer of the New York stage performances of *Under Milk Wood*.

October

Tuesday 20th: Dylan arrives with Reitell at his room at the Chelsea Hotel. Reitell and Dylan have dinner followed by a rehearsal of *Under Milk Wood (UMW)* at which Brinnin finds him "in a sober and serious mood". Then drinks at the White Horse bar until 2am.

Wednesday 21st: Dylan relaxes and walks, with some drinking. He returns to his hotel feeling unwell and sleeps in the afternoon and for much of the evening.

Thursday 22nd: Sleeps late. He goes to an afternoon rehearsal of *UMW*, where Brinnin reports he is "sober and professionally concentrated". This is followed by a few drinks and a dinner at Herdt's restaurant, his last proper meal. Dylan then disappears.

Friday 23rd: Reappears for lunch with Reitell but he is unable to eat food. Reitell observes he is in "an acute state of nervous agitation". Dylan gets very drunk in the afternoon at a party in his hotel room which Reitell breaks up and asks his visitors to leave. Dylan sobers up, and works on the script of *UMW* and goes to an evening rehearsal of the play. He is too ill to take part. He complains the room is too hot, and then freezing cold. He is covered in overcoats but he says he is still "shivering cold". He is given coffee, brandy and hot water-bottles. He is unable to fall asleep or "be rid of his spasmodic restlessness." Sitting upright every few minutes, he asks "What's going on now? What part are they reading now?" He joins the rehearsal for the last twenty minutes but then becomes nauseous and vomits. He is gasping for breath. He tells his friend Herb Hannum: "I'm too tired to do anything.

I can't fuck, I can't eat, I can't drink – I'm even too tired to sleep… I'm too sick too much of the time." Reitell takes Dylan back to the hotel and stays with him much of the night. He sleeps soundly.

Saturday 24th: Dylan has breakfast with Hannum and tells him "Never this sick, never this much before… I've come to the melancholy conclusion that my health is totally gone. I can't drink at all. I always could, before… but now most of the time I can't even swallow beer without being sick. I guess I just forgot to sleep and eat for too long… Without my health I'm frightened. I can't explain it. It's something I don't know about. I never felt this way before and it scares me." Dylan is persuaded to see Feltenstein, who injects ACTH and prescribes benzedrine. Dylan attends an afternoon rehearsal of *UMW*. Brinnin describes him: "His face was lime-white, his lips loose and twisted, his eyes dulled, gelid, and sunk in his head." The actors notice he is sweating, has blotchy skin and unpleasant breath. He is still pale at an evening performance of *UMW*. Refuses drinks at a party afterwards.

Sunday 25th: Dylan has a meeting in the morning with John Malcolm Brinnin, followed by an afternoon performance of *UMW*. He is "desperately ill" before the performance, as Wickwire describes on p239. He is very pale with no voice. Feltenstein is called and injects something, almost certainly ACTH. He collapses again after the performance. Dylan is drinking at a party afterwards and for most of the night, but the quantity is unknown.

Monday 26th: Reitell finds him drunk, and drinking whisky, in the Algonquin hotel in the afternoon. He goes into a 'raving fantasy' about war, blood and death. Reitell takes him to the cinema and he calms down. A few drinks afterwards but Brinnin notes that "Dylan was too distressed and ill to stay for more than a few minutes" in the White Horse.

Tuesday 27th: Dylan's birthday. Drinks in the evening followed by a party when he complains of feeling sick and returns to his hotel.

Wednesday 28-Friday 30th: Speaking engagements, meetings, dinner parties, moderate drinking, mainly beer, sociable, lucid and friendly. According to George Reavey, Dylan looks "very sad and sick looking".

Saturday 31st: Moderate drinking through the day. He has lunch and dinner engagements but eats little. By 9pm he is in the White Horse bar with friends, already drunk, and drinking lager, whisky and beer. Observed taking benzedrine at 2.30am.

November

Sunday 1st: Dylan wakes up with a hangover. Goes with Reitell to the White Horse at noon, drinks beer. Spends the rest of the day in the White Horse with friends, then a party in the evening when he gets drunk. At midnight, he goes to the flat of another friend for a night cap, talk and music, and he recites poetry for an hour. He leaves at 5am. Possibly took benzedrine to keep himself going.

Monday 2nd: Brinnin tells us that Dylan is unable to get up because of a bad hangover, that he is nursed by Reitell through the day and does not leave his hotel. Ruthven Todd, however, tells a different story: he turns up at the Chelsea 'pretty early'. Whilst Dylan 'was not feeling at all bright', they talk, joke and drink beer. Todd notes that a bottle of Old Grandad whisky is unopened. Dylan goes to a gallery in the evening, followed by a restaurant (where he eats little) and a bar. Reavey observes that Dylan is looking sick and depressed.

Tuesday 3rd: Todd comes to the hotel again. Dylan "was still feeling miserable" but they have a beer. At Dylan's insistence, Todd opens the Old Grandad and pours a measure for the hotel maid. Reitell tells Todd that Feltenstein had warned Dylan "to go easy on everything – except food, of which he was to take a great deal more". Dylan has a few late morning drinks with Hannum and David Waggoner, but Reitell breaks up the session and then Dylan sleeps. In the afternoon, he meets with an American agent to discuss and sign a new contract. Sleeps again and goes to an early evening party but drinks moderately. He returns early to his hotel complaining he is exhausted and falls asleep.

Wednesday 4th: He wakes up about 2am and goes, without Reitell, to the White Horse for a drink. Todd describes a photograph taken in the bar in which Dylan appears "so awful and so bloated". Dylan returns after an hour and a half and tells Reitell that he has drunk eighteen whiskies. It is later shown he drank only eight at the most.[196] Todd phones in the morning and Dylan says "he was not feeling at all well. He sounded terrible." Dylan complains to Reitell that he is suffocating, that "he was having trouble breathing, that he must get outside right away". Reitell walks with him to the White Horse where he has two beers. Returns to the hotel feeling sick. He has "ghastly racking spasms". Reitell calls Feltenstein who arrives about mid-day. She tells him of Dylan's boast about drinking eighteen whiskies. Feltenstein injects ACTH and morphine (probably between one-eighth to one sixteenth of a grain). Dylan vomits then sleeps through the afternoon but wakes feeling nauseous and vomits again. Reitell calls Feltenstein who injects more ACTH and morphine, between 5pm and 7pm. Dylan continues to be unwell, with more vomiting and begins to see, he says, "abstractions, triangles and squares and circles". Perspiration breaks out on his face, and he retches. Reitell again summons Feltenstein and incorrectly tells him that Dylan has had delirium tremens. He injects a further eight units of ACTH. He also increases the dosage of morphine to half a grain (30 milligrams), and injects Dylan sometime between 11pm and midnight. The painter Jack Heliker arrives to help Reitell look after Dylan. Reitell remembers "we had sweet calm talks, the three of us..."[197]

Thursday 5th: About midnight on November 4/5, Reitell thinks Dylan is falling asleep and then hears "the terrible sound of this breathing". She also describes hearing "this funny sort of breathing."[198] Both she and Heliker hear "a gasping sound emerging from deep inside Dylan's throat... Reitell has described this 'dreadful gasping sound' as a stoppage of Dylan's normal breathing."[199] She feels his grip stiffen and observes Dylan's face turning blue. He is unconscious. There is a delay of about an hour before an ambulance is called about 1am but it does not deliver Dylan to St Vincent's Hospital until 1.58am. Feltenstein and Reitell arrive at the same time. Feltenstein tells the admitting doctors, McVeigh and Gilbertson, that Dylan has fallen into a coma after a bout of heavy drinking, and also informs them of his injection of morphine. Both Feltenstein and Reitell fail to tell them that Dylan has been unconscious and not breathing properly for about two hours. The doctors observe he is "dry and clammy with blue lips and a splotchy, red and white face" and that the pupils of his eyes are small, not dilated.[200] Dylan is given artificial respiration and oxygen. It takes over an hour before he starts to breathe sponta-neously. Blood samples are taken, and he is attached to a dextrose drip. An oxygen mask is placed over his face. A lumbar puncture is carried out that reveals no cerebral haemorrhage but doctors suspect a diabetic shock. Dylan is given a blood transfusion. Feltenstein argues that Dylan has been poisoned by alcohol and supervises Dylan's treatment in the hospital even though he has no authority there. Brinnin arrives early in the morning at the hospital. He describes Dylan: "his wild hair limp and wet, his face blotched with fever". In the late afternoon, Brinnin sets about hiring a brain special-ist and, on Feltenstein's advice, contacts Dr Leo Davidoff of Beth Israel hospital.

Friday 6th: In the early afternoon, Brinnin is told that Davidoff is unavailable but has recommended St Vincent's own neurosurgeon, Dr C.G. Gutierrez-Mahoney, who arrives at the ward. He examines Dylan but some thirty-seven hours have now elapsed since Dylan's admission. Gutierrez-Mahoney agrees with Feltenstein's diagnosis that Dylan's brain has been damaged by alcohol. According to Nashold and Tremlett, Doctors McVeigh and Gilbertson quarrel with Feltenstein over his diagnosis. They go to see Gutierrez-Mahoney and give him the results of blood and urine tests showing even higher levels of sugar. He issues orders, say Nashold and Tremlett, to switch off Dylan's dextrose supply and to begin giving insulin. Later, a tracheotomy is performed. Gutierrez-Mahoney instructs Feltenstein to play no further part in directing Dylan's care, though he is allowed to remain in attendance.

Saturday 7th: Daniel Jones sends the hospital information on Dylan's health. Brinnin observes that Dylan's "breathing was troubled and irregular; his temperature rose and fell in sudden changes that left his face alternately red and perspiring, blue and pallid... Dylan's now high and constant fever... at times reached 105.5°". Brinnin also describes Dylan's "struggling body as it fought for breath". Dr McVeigh confirms that Dylan is 'sinking rapidly'. Brinnin is advised by Feltenstein that "Dylan's death was not only next to inevitable, but that it was now also to be desired [because] the damage to the brain was so great". Both Brinnin and Rollie McKenna pay for private nurses to look after Dylan at the hospital. When Todd collects Dylan's possessions from the Chelsea, he notes that the level of whisky in the bottle of Old Grandad is the same as it was on November 3.

Sunday 8th: A second lumbar puncture is carried out. Dylan is now in an oxygen tent. Caitlin arrives at the hospital having flown from London. Brinnin starts fundraising to pay for Dylan's medical expenses and funeral care, and together with James Laughlin and Philip Wittenberg they establish the Dylan Thomas Memorial Fund.[201]

Monday 9th: Dylan dies at 12.45pm. Daniel Jones sends a telegram to Gutierrez-Mahoney indicating that it had been Dylan's desire to be buried in Wales.

Tuesday 10th: The post-mortem is carried out. Letters are sent to prospective donors from the Dylan Thomas Memorial Fund Committee, signed by W.H. Auden, e.e. cummings, Arthur Miller, Marianne Moore, Wallace Stevens, Tennessee Williams and Thornton Wilder.

Wednesday 11th: The brain and liver are examined. The Notice of Death reveals that the diagnosis of toxic encephalopathy is unconfirmed. Dylan becomes an official statistic as the City's Department of Health issue permit H24268 to the undertakers, Daniel MacLean and Son, authorising burial. Dylan is embalmed and his cheeks rouged. He is dressed in a blue suit provided by MacLean and a blue-and-white polka dot bow tie bought by Ruthven Todd on Broadway.

Friday 13th: A memorial service, attended by some four hundred people, is held in St Luke's Chapel. The service is Protestant Episcopal, conducted by the Revs. Weed and Leach, who read from chapter 15 of St Paul's Epistle to the Corinthians. Noah Greenberg and his Pro Musica Antiqua sing two motets by Thomas Morley, *Agnus Dei* and *Primavera*. Later, an announcement is made that contributions to the Dylan Thomas Memorial Fund were not yet generous enough "to pay the poet's medical and funeral expenses, and costs of Mrs Thomas' travel." In Chicago, the Modern Poetry Association has cancelled the reading of *Under Milk Wood* due to be given in the evening at the 1020 Art Center.

Dylan's body orifices are sealed with cotton wool ready for transportation. The coffin is placed inside a water-tight wooden box and taken to the SS *United States*, which later sets sail for Southampton. Caitlin is also on board.

St Vincent's waives all its fees for Dylan's care and treatment.

B. Post-Mortem Report

We have faithfully reproduced the post-mortem report, including American spellings and typing errors.

AUTOPSY

Approximate Age	39 years	Approximate Weight 180 lbs.
Height	5'5"	
Identified by		Residence
Stenographer	William J. Burke	Residence (Book #304)

I hereby certify that I **Milton Helpern, M.D.** have performed an autopsy on the body of **DYLAN THOMAS** at **City Mortuary** on the **10th** day of **November** 19 53, **dictation begun @ 2:40 p.m.** hours after the death, and said autopsy revealed

AUTOPSY PERFORMED BY DR. MILTON HELPERN
DEPUTY CHIEF MEDICAL EXAMINER
(In the presence of Drs. DiMaio & Mathus

EXTERNAL INSPECTION:

Adult white male appearing to be about 40 years of age; 5'5" tall; estimated weight 180lb.; obese trunk; puffy face; wavy brown hair on head; moderate frontal baldness; brown eyes; unshaven face; several days growth of brown hair; teeth in upper jaw irregular in alignment, rather widely spaced – in the lower jaw also show some irregularity – all teeth show discoloration – several teeth missing in the left lower jaw; rigor mortis is complete; foreskin short somewhat edematous; purplish post mortem lividity present posteriorly; needle puncture marks with slight ecchymosis of skin over dorsum left hand; lumbar puncture mark posteriorly; mottled purple lividity; skin anteriorly somewhat pale; faint blue lividity of face; slight rosacea of cheeks; small scar 3/4" above outer end of the right eyebrow and also linear scar of the left eyebrow. No other signs of traumatic injury.

360

ON SECTION OF THE HEAD:

On reflecting the scalp no evidence of injury in the galea.

Calvarium 1/8" to 5/16" in thickness. Dura intact.
Brain shows considerable pial edema over vertex with increase in cerebrospinal fluid lifting up piarachnoid. No hemorrhages noted between meninges which are clear. Arteries at the base appear normal. Brain heavy, 1,600 grams; on section shows only congested; no areas of softening or hemorrhage made out anywhere. Lateral ventricles contain clear fluid. Basal ganglions intact. Pons, cerebellum, brain stem grossly normal. No injuries at the base of the skull. Dura strips fairly easily.

ON SECTION OF THE TRUCK:

Panniculus up to 1½" in thickness; recti muscles fairly well developed; considerable excess fat in the mesenteric, omental retroperitoneal fatty depots; fat is rather firm and lobulations are exaggerated. Peritoneum everywhere smooth and shiny. On opening the chest cartilages are slightly calcified. Diaphragm at the level of the 4th rib right, 4th space on the left.

LUNGS: Lie in the posterior portion of pleural cavities which contain no fluid. Anteriorly, lungs slightly emphysematous; posteriorly somewhat atelectatic and also lumpy in consistency with many small punctate hemorrhages in the pleura over the collapsed lumpy portions of the lung posteriorly.

Bronchi deeply congested and also covered with patchy fibrino-purulent membrane. Lungs heavy for their size – left one, 750 grams – right one, 700 grams. On section, parenchyma dark red in color; markedly diminished aeration with a patchy broncho-pneumonia very evidence on the cut surface especially in the depednent portions. Lower lobes – pneumonic areas gray in color somewhat raised. All of the lobes appear to be involved in this bronchopneumonic process.

HEART: Lies free in the pericardial sac; increased fat over anterior surface of pericardium and also in the superior media stinum. Heart weighs 330 grams. Chambers contain dark red fluid and soft clotted blood, also some chicken fat clot. Valves on the right side flexible and natural. Fossa ovalis closed. Some atheroma in the anterior leaflet of mitral valve. Aortic valve cusps normal.

Proximal segment of left anterior descending coronary artery shows considerable sclerosis with calcification and narrowing of the lumen to about 50 per cent of its original size. Right coronary shows only slight atheromatous change. Myocardium flabby, uniformly light brown in color. Aorta throughout its length fairly smooth and elastic.

NECK ORGANS: Larynx removed. Air passages not obstructed. There is considerable reddening with irritation of mucous membrane upper part of trachea extending down from vocal cords. Thyroid dull red in color.

G.I. TRACT: Esophagus – several fine varices in the lower part of the esophagus.
Stomach dilated; mucous membrane bile-stained; contents consist of some green turbid fluid about 1 liter with small particles of food in it; mucous membrane soft and slimy; no evidence of ulceration made out. Duodenum is grossly normal.
Small Intestine contains light yellowish green liquid content, turbid, in considerable amount; farther long more mushy, fecal in character.
Appendix present.
Large Bowel contains mushy greenish brown feces; abundant excess pericolic fat.

LIVER: Smooth, light yellowish brown in color; weighs 2,400 grams; on section, color is similar; markings regular; consistency somewhat firmer than normal; fairly evident fatty infiltration.
Gall Bladder: Contains about 20 c.c. of thin green turbid bile.

SPLEEN: Moderately enlarged; weighs 260 grams; smooth; pulp soft, dark red in color.

PANCREAS: Shows considerable fatty infiltration, surrounded and concealed by fat; on section, lobulations are fairly well preserved; no evidence of fat necrosis or old pancreatitis but considerable fat between the lobules.

ADRENALS: Show well differentiated cortex and medulla.

KIDNEYS: Normal in size; light brown in color; together, 350 grams; marking somewhat indistinct. Pelves and ureters natural.

URINARY BLADDER: Empty; mucosa shows several hemorrhages in the region of fundus evidently associated with catheretization.

PROSTATE, SEMINAL VESICLES, TESTICLES: Grossly normal.

No injuries of SPINE, RIBS, BONES of EXTREMITIES.

Note: There is a transverse tracheotomy – enters the upper part of trachea.

ANATOMICAL DIAGNOSIS: Enlarged fatty liver:

Fatty kidneys:

Pial edema:

Pulmonary congestion, atelectasis: Extensive hypostatic bronchopneumonia, bilaterals

Tracheotomy:

Acute tracheobronchitis:

In too long for alcohol studies: Portion of brain and liver taken for chemical examination (#2396).

CAUSE OF DEATH: PIAL EDEMA:
FATTY LIVER:
HYPOSTATIC BRONCHOPNEUMONIA.

IDENTIFICATION:

Body of deceased identified to Miss L. Hirsch, stenographer, at the City Mortuary, about 4.15pm, Nov. 10, 1953, by:

JAMES LAUGHLIN, FRIEND 20 YEARS, 333 SIXTH AVE., N.Y.C.

*Classify as
Acute + Chronic Ethylism
Hypostatic Bronchopneumonia.
M.H.*

References

J. Ackerman (1998) *Welsh Dylan*, Seren

J. M. Brinnin (1955) *Dylan Thomas in America*, Avon
  (n.d.) *The Making of Under Milk Wood*, mimeo. University of
  Delaware

P. Broome (1997, 1998) *South Leigh Remembered*, Broome

A. Burgess (1988) *Little Wilson and Big God*, Penguin

G. Burn (1972) "Dylan Thomas", *Radio Times*, October 26

P.H. Burton (1953) no title, *Adam International Review*. No. 238. The
  recorded talk is in the Jeff Towns collection

D. Cleverdon (1954) "The Town 'that has fallen over bells in love'"
in the *Radio Times*, January 22
  (1954b) "A talk on *Under Milk Wood*", the *Journal of Design and
  Fine Art*, no.13
  (1957) "The History of a Radio Classic" in the *Radio Times*,
  June 28
  (1966) "*Under Milk Wood*" in the *Weekend Telegraph*, December 16
  (1969) *The Growth of Milk Wood*, Dent
  (1972) Introduction to *Under Milk Wood*, Folio Society

P. Conradi (2002) *Iris Murdoch: A Life*, Harper Collins

A. Curnow (1982) "Images of Dylan" in the *NZ Listener*, December 18

J.A. Davies (2000) *Dylan Thomas's Swansea, Gower and Laugharne*,
  UWP

R. Davies (1998) *Print of a Hare's Foot*, Seren

W. Davies and R. Maud, eds. (1995) *Under Milk Wood: The Definitive
  Edition*, Dent

D. Davin (1985) *Closing Times*, OUP

C. Edwards (1968) *Dylan Remembered* (an unfinished biography,
  National Library of Wales)

P. Ferris (1977 and 1999) *Dylan Thomas*, Dent
  (1995) *Caitlin*, Pimlico
  ed. (2000) *Dylan Thomas: The Collected Letters*, Dent
  (2003) "I was Dylan's Secret Lover" in *The Observer*, August 17
  (2004) "Ink is Wanted by Raving Brother: Dylan Thomas's

Early Years", in *The Paris Review*, Spring.
C. FitzGibbon (1964) "The Posthumous Life of Dylan Thomas", in *The Spectator*, November 27
(1965) *The Life of Dylan Thomas*, Little, Brown
T. FitzGibbon (1982) *With Love*, Pan
P. Fraser (2002) "G.S. Fraser: A Memoir" in *Jacket*, December
R. Fraser (2002) *The Chameleon Poet: A Life of George Barker*, Pimlico
V. Golightly (2003) "'Writing with dreams and blood': Dylan Thomas, Marxism and 1930s Swansea" in *Welsh Writing in English* vol. 8, *NWR*
R. Gittins (1986) *The Last Days of Dylan Thomas*, Macdonald
G. Grigson (1964) "Dylan and the Dragon" in *New Statesman*, December 18
J. Hauková (1996) *Záblesky života*, H & H: Jinočany
T. Hawkes (1965) "Some 'Sources' of *Under Milk Wood*" in *Notes & Queries*, July
J. Heath-Stubbs (1993) *Hindsights*, Hodder and Stoughton
D. Jones (1977) *My Friend Dylan Thomas*, Dent
V. Justl (1988) *Sebrané Spisy Vladimír Holana*, Svazek X1: Bagately, Odeon
M. Lewis (1967) *Laugharne and Dylan Thomas*, Dobson
J. Lindsay (1968) *Meetings with Poets*, Muller
A. Livi (1949) "Sugli Scogli Di Rio" in *Inventario*, II, 3, Autumno
A. Lycett (2003) *Dylan Thomas: A New Life*, Weidenfeld and Nicolson
E. Lutyens (1972) *A Goldfish Bowl*, Cassell
R. McKenna (1982) *Portrait of Dylan*, Dent
J. Nashold and G. Tremlett (1997) *The Death of Dylan Thomas*, Mainstream Publishing
K. Ovenden (1996) *A Fighting Withdrawal: The Life of Dan Davin*, OUP
S. Phillips (1999) *Private Faces*, Sceptre
A. Pini (2000) *Incontri alle Giubbe Rosse*, Edizioni Polistampa
P. Potts (1961) *Dante Called You Beatrice*, Readers Union/Eyre & Spottiswoode
L. Prochnik (1980) "Dylan Thomas" in *Endings*, Crown
B. Read (1964) *The Days of Dylan Thomas*, Weidenfeld and Nicolson
A. Road (1967) "The Ghost of *Under Milk Wood*", *Observer Colour Magazine*, October 1
A. Sinclair (1999) *Dylan the Bard*, Constable
M. Stephens (2000) *The Literary Pilgrim in Wales*, Gwasg Carreg Gwalch

C. Thomas with G. Tremlett (1986) *Caitlin: Life with Dylan Thomas,* Secker and Warburg

D. N. Thomas (2000) *Dylan Thomas: A Farm, Two Mansions and a Bungalow,* Seren
(2001) "*Under Milk Wood's* Birth-in-Exile" in *New Welsh Review,* Spring
(2002a) *The Dylan Thomas Trail,* Y Lolfa
(2002b) "Dylan's New Quay: More Bombay Potato than Boiled Cabbage", in *New Welsh Review,* Summer
(2003) "Severed Heads" in *Planet,* June/July

K. Thompson (1965) *Dylan Thomas in Swansea,* Ph.D, University of Wales

R. Todd (n.d.) *Dylan Thomas,* an unpublished memoir, National Library of Scotland

J. Towns (1995) *Dylan Thomas: Word and Image,* Swansea Leisure

G. Tremlett (1993) *Dylan Thomas: In the Mercy of his Means,* Constable

G. Watkins (1983) *Portrait of a Friend,* Gomer

Medical

C.M. Bell and D.A. Redelmeier (2001) "Mortality among Patients Admitted to Hospitals on Weekends as Compared with Weekdays" in the *New England Journal of Medicine,* August

W.R. Brain (1947) *Diseases of the Nervous System,* OUP, 3rd ed.

R.L. Cecil and R.L. Loeb (1955) *Textbook of Medicine,* Saunders, 9th ed

S.G. Cohen and P.L. Rizzo (2000) "Asthma Among the Famous: Dylan Thomas" in *Allergy and Asthma Proceedings,* May-June

C.G. Gutierrez-Mahoney and E. Carini (1948) *Neurological and Neurosurgical Nursing,* Mosby

M. Helpern (1979) *Autopsy: Memoirs of Milton Helpern,* Harrap

P.A. and B.J. Kalisch (1986) *The Advance of American Nursing,* Little, Brown

S. Kaye and H.B. Haag (1957) "Terminal Blood Alcohol Concentrations in Ninety-Four Fatal Cases of Acute Alcoholism" in *The Journal of the American Medical Association,* October

B.W. Murphy (1968) "Creation and Destruction: Notes on Dylan Thomas" in *British Journal of Medical Psychology,* 41, 149

A. Noyes (1953) *Modern Clinical Psychiatry,* Saunders, 4th ed.

S. Opdycke (1999) *No One Was Turned Away: The Role of Public Hospitals in New York City Since 1900*, OUP

H.H. Salter (1864) *On Asthma: Its Pathology and Treatment*, Blanchard and Lea

D.A. Seehusen et. al. (2003) "Cerebrospinal Fluid Analysis" in the *Journal of the American Academy of Family Physicians*, September 15

G.R. Stuart (1938) *A History of St Vincent's Hospital in New York City 1849-1938*, Stuart

M. Walsh (1965) *With a great heart: the story of St Vincent's Hospital and Medical Center of New York, 1849-1964*

Art

E. Agar (1988) *A Look at My Life*, Methuen

Arts Council (1951) *Jankel Adler 1895-1949*, Memorial Exhibition

J. Banting (n.d.) *An unpublished memoir*, Tate Archives

J. Bilbo (1948) *An Autobiography*, Modern Art Gallery

O. Blakeston (1966) "Bloomsbury, late twenties, early thirties", in *Ambit*, 27

C. Barker (2002) "Life at Tilty Mill" in *Granta* 80, Winter

C. Bennett (1996) *Colin Moss: Life Observed*, Malthouse Press

P. Bowen (2002) *The Baker's Daughter*, Merton Priory Press

W. Chappell (1982) *Edward Burra*, Deutsch

(1985) *The Letters of Edward Burra*, Gordon Fraser

I. Collins (1999) *A Broad Canvas: Art in East Anglia since 1880*, Black Dog Books

P.B. Driver (1995) *Gardner Cox*, Bauhau.

K.B. Dunthorne ed. (2003) *Drawn from Wales: a School of Art in Swansea 1853-2003*, Welsh Academic Press

T.W. Earp (1945) *Dobson*, Tiranti

A. Gill (2002) *Peggy Guggenheim*, Harper Collins

M. Gilmore and S. Peake (1999) *Mervyn Peake: Two Lives*, Vintage

S. Govier (1994) *William Grant Murray: 1877-1950, and the 'Swansea School'* in *Gower*, XLV, 1994

P. Grippe ed. (1960) *21 Etchings and Poems*, Morris Gallery

N. Henderson (2001) *Parallel of Life and Art*, Thames and Hudson

S.W. Hayter (1948) *Jankel Adler*, Nicholson and Watson

J. Hopkins (1994) *Michael Ayrton*, Deutsch

N. Jason and L. Thompson-Pharoah (1994) *The Sculpture of Frank*

Dobson, Lund Humphries

M. Kernan (1994) "One man's fantasy stands tall in a jungle in Mexico" in the *Smithsonian Magazine,* April

J. Leftwich (1980) "Margaret Waterhouse's Role in 'Mangeriade'" in the *Jewish Quarterly,* Summer

S. Levy (2003) *The Scandalous Eye: The Surrealism of Conroy Maddox,* Liverpool University Press

J. Lowe (1991) *Edward James: A Surrealist Life,* Collins

M. Luke (1991) *David Tennant and the Gargoyle Years,* Weidenfeld and Nicolson

C. Mackworth (1987) *Ends of the World,* Carcanet

J. Maclaren-Ross (1991) *Memoirs of the Forties,* Cardinal

R. Medley (1983) *Drawn from Life,* Faber

D. Morris (1979) *Animal Days,* Cape

A. Peat and B.A. Wilson (1997) *John Tunnard: His Life and Works,* Scolar

A. Penrose (2001) *Roland Penrose: The Friendly Surrealist,* Prestel

P. Purser (1978) *Poeted: the final quest of Edward James,* Quartet

P.C. Ray (1971) *The Surrealist Movement in England,* Cornell

M. Remy (1999) *Surrealism in Britain,* Ashgate

M. Salisbury, ed., (2003) *Artists at the Fry: Art and Design in the North West Essex Collection,* Ruskin Press

R. Shephard (1977) *Caitlin and Dylan: An Artist's View of the Macnamara and Thomas Background,* National Museum of Wales

D. Shiel (2002) *Arthur Giardelli,* Seren

F. Spalding (1991) *Dance Till the Stars Come Down: A Biography of John Minton,* Hodder and Stoughton

S. Themerson (1948) *Jankel Adler,* Gaberbocchus Press

C. Thomas (2003) "From School of Art and Crafts to College of Art – inside and out", in *Drawn from Wales,* ed. K.B. Dunthorne

D.M. Thomas (1987) "Wales and the Artist" in *Quite Early One Morning,* Dent

H. Treece (1938) "Dylan Thomas and the Surrealists" in *Seven,* winter

J. Trevelyan (1996) *Indigo Days,* Scolar

G. Watkins (1975) "'An Artful Outsider': Some letters from David Jones to Vernon Watkins" in the *Anglo-Welsh Review,* Spring

G.P. Winnington (2000) *Vast Alchemies: A Life of Mervyn Peake,* Owen

M. Yorke (1990) *Keith Vaughan: His Life and Work,* Constable
(2000) *Mervyn Peake,* John Murray

Acknowledgements

Volume One carried the bulk of acknowledgements to staff at the National Library of Wales, particularly Iestyn Hughes, Dafydd Pritchard, and Scott Wayby, as well as to everyone working in the Reading Room whose help over many years has been outstanding. I am also grateful to Joan Miller for her excellent transcriptions of the Colin Edwards tapes; and to Mary Edwards for her help and support in all aspects of the project.

For contributions throughout the book, I am grateful to John Barber, Charles Burroughs, Edna Dale-Jones, Mary Dark, James A. Davies, Susan Deacon, Janet Dent, Reg and Eileen Evans, Robert Evans, Paul Ferris, Victor Golightly, Gwyn Griffiths, Paul Henderson, John Hughes, Wally Jenkins, Ralph Maud, Ceri Nicholas, Eiluned Rees, Alan Road, Aeronwy Thomas, Gwen Watkins and James Codd at the BBC Written Archives Centre, Reading.

I am grateful to Jonathan Bolton at Harvard for advising on Edwards' Czech tapes, providing valuable additional information, and translating the extract from Jiřina Hauková's memoirs about Dylan's visit to Prague.

Chapter 1 was a partnership: we are particularly grateful to Professor Bernard Knight for his help, advice and encouragement, and to Sandra Opdycke for letting us draw on her knowledge of New York hospitals, as well as her research notes. Likewise, we are indebted to Bernadette McCauley, who drew on her research into St Vincent's Hospital, and generously made available her experience and contacts. Thanks to Sister Rita King, archivist for the Sisters of Charity, New York, who provided information about St Joseph's East and contacted former nurses on our behalf; and to Priscilla Sassi, who was a student nurse at St Vincent's between 1951 and 1954. Brenda Maurer kept us all in touch. We are also grateful for the help of Dr Robert Pitcher and Dr John F. Pickup, consultant histopathologist and principal pharmacist respectively at the Royal Cornwall Hospital. Dr Cyril Wecht, coroner and chief forensic pathologist to Allegheny County, Pittsburgh, advised on a number of points relating to the post-mortem and drug therapies.

Thanks, too, to Dr Sheldon Cohen and Dr Stephen Rowlands. Mary Edwards did research for us in America, Paul Ferris shared material from his files, George Tremlett and Andrew Lycett answered queries, Aeronwy Thomas persevered and Dave Slivka described the ward. We are grateful to Lisa Richter at the Harry Ransom Humanities Research Center at the University of Texas at Austin who provided material relating to Dylan's last days; as did Iris Snyder, Brinnin Special Collection, University of Delaware; Robin Smith, National Library of Scotland; Rebecca Cape, Lilly Library, University of Indiana; and Barbara Bezant at the John Berryman Collection at the University of Minnesota, as well as Mrs Kate Donahue for permission to copy material from the Berryman Collection.

Many people helped with chapter 2: especial thanks to Walford Davies and Paul Ferris for their generous advice and help, and to Jeff Towns and Robert Williams for access to their collections. I am particularly grateful to Kasey Clark for carrying out research in Boston on the reading of *Under Milk Wood* on May 3 1953. Thanks, too, to Tara Wenger at the Harry Ransom Humanities Research Center at the University of Texas at Austin, James Codd, Paul Johnson, Josef Nesvadba, Daniel Thomas, Gianfranco Vanagolli, Liz Welch, Keith Davies, Sue Passmore, Griff Jenkins, James Partridge at Oxford for the Czech translation and Laura Bianconi for the Italian. Archive sources included the Dylan Thomas and David Higham Archives, Texas; the Colin Edwards Archive, the National Library of Wales; and the BBC Written Archives, Caversham. Photocopies of the many drafts and work sheets of *Under Milk Wood*, as well as copies of other material in the Thomas and Higham archives, were provided by the Harry Ransom Humanities Research Center.

Chapter 3 was a family effort: it was a great pleasure to work with some of the children and grandchildren of Phoebe and Stanley Evans – special thanks to Bunny Evans (chair of the Dylan Thomas Society in Ceredigion), and also to Irena, Iris, Pamela and Martin who gave me such a warm welcome and much information. I was also helped by several New Quay families who remembered Phoebe with great affection. I am grateful to Beryl Richards for access to her notes and photographs, and for helping me with details of the family tree and the history of Maesgwyn.

Chapter 4 was a team affair, and I am grateful for everyone's help, particularly Mel Gooding, Robert Meyrick, Desmond Morris and Ellie Dawkins at the Glynn Vivian Gallery, Swansea, but also Dannie

Acknowledgements

Abse, Duffy Ayres, Kate Chapman, Bernard Cheese, Glenys Cour, Tony Curtis, David Caddy, Kirstine Brander Dunthorne, Marion Eames, Arthur Giardelli, Chris Glass, Sonia Gross, Clarissa James, Aneurin Jones, Jonah Jones, Paul Joyner, Ceri Levy, David and Clarissa Lewis, George Little, Osi Osmond, Viviane Overbeeke, Susan Passmore, Kusha Petts, Eric Ratcliffe, Bronwen Roberts, Denys Short, Max and Margaret Solomon, Gordon Stuart, Daniel Thomas, Jeff Towns, Nigel Weaver, G. Peter Winnington, editor of *Peake Studies*, and Kyffin Williams. Thanks also to Pam Lewis at the *Jewish Quarterly*; Sharon Kusunoki, archivist at West Dean College; Marian Syratt Barnes, Middlesex University library; staff at the Hyman Kreitman Research Centre, the Tate Gallery; Sarah Prescott at the Kings College archive; and Terry Tuey at the University of Victoria, Canada. I am indebted to a number of gallery web sites and information services, including the National Portrait Gallery; the Fry Art Gallery, Saffron Walden; Tenby Museum; James Hyman Fine Art; the Gillian Jason Gallery; Modern British Artists; Rex Irwin; Scolar Fine Art; the Knitting Circle; Artnet; and the *Grove Dictionary of Art*.

Thanks also to Mick Felton and Sally Hales at Seren, the Wales Arts Council and the Society of Authors for supporting the project, and Francesca Rhydderch at the *New Welsh Review* for permission to recycle my paper on the writing of *Under Milk Wood*. I am grateful, too, to David Higham Associates for their help and support.

We acknowledge the copyright of Jiřina Hauková in the extract taken from her memoir, *Záblesky života*. Likewise, we acknowledge the copyright of the estate of Paul Potts in the extract taken from his book *Dante Called You Beatrice*. We are grateful to Aeronwy Thomas and the Office of the Chief Medical Examiner, New York, for permission to reproduce the post-mortem report.

This volume required much less archival research, but when it was needed I was again helped unstintingly by Terry Wells of the Carmarthenshire Archive Service and Gaynor Davies at the Carmarthen Register Office.

And once again to Stevie Krayer for the index, and much, much more.

Images

I am grateful to Robert Williams for his kind permission to use Oloff de Wet's sketch of Dylan, 1951, for the cover of the book.

National Library of Wales/Orleans Studios: Dylan as a young man
Colin Edwards archive, NLW: Glyn Jones; Vernon Watkins; Elizabeth
Ruby Milton; Bert Trick; Richard Hughes; Piero Bigongiari; Mario
Luzi; Dorothy Murray; Jiřina Hauková; Alban Leyshon; Jane Dark;
Nellie Jenkins; Jirí Mucha; Dylan and Oscar Williams.
Reg and Eileen Evans: Dylan at Pendine; Caitlin and Colm; Fred Janes
and Florence Thomas; Dylan and Caitlin in America; Dylan looking
pleased with himself; Llewelyn, 18 months; Dylan, Caitlin and
Llewelyn; Aeronwy, Florence and Colm; D.J. Thomas; D.J. Thomas
and Ken Owen; D.J. Thomas, Florence and Hettie Owen; Emlyn
Williams; Florence and Hettie and Ken Owen; Florence at Stratford.
Allen Curnow: Dylan at the Boat House
Irena Berendt: Phoebe Evans
Max Solomon: Leo Solomon
Royal Festival Hall Archive: Oloff de Wet's bust of Dylan
Sisters of Charity: the Seton Building, St Vincent's

Notes

NLW = National Library of Wales.
Texas = Harry Ransom Humanities Research Center at the University of Texas at Austin.

Introduction

1. Letter to Kenneth Patchen, November 27 1939.
2. Presumably the London County Council Institute of Education. Letter to Desmond Hawkins, January 1936
3. Arlott: *Radio Times*, September 27 1973; Arlott's comment on Dylan's profession-alism is echoed by his secretary, Betty Forrester (*Dylan and John*, BBC Radio 4, November 1 2003). Cleverdon is quoted in the *Western Mail* August 12 1971. The same range of comments about Dylan's professionalism appear in Volume One, made by those who worked with Dylan in the Swansea Little Theatre – for example, Thomas Taig and Eileen Llewellyn Jones.
4. NET Festival Series, undated, Colin Edwards Archive, NLW. The interviewer was probably Colin Edwards but we cannot be certain.
5. *Caitlin*: Tremlett 1991, p64; and Caitlin Thomas and Tremlett, 1986, pxi.
6. NET Festival Series, undated. The interview was probably Colin Edwards.
7. Glendower: Ferris, 2003; Meo: Lycett, 2003.
8. Arthur Giardelli also notes that Dylan's drinking in Laugharne was confined to beer (Shiel, 2002, p68)
9. His first novel, *A Smell of Broken Glass*, came out in 1973, and contains descrip-tions of Dylan. He also published *Chez Scally Manny Wagstaff* and *Scallywags*.
10. Lewis (1967) has also made the same point about Rosie Probert.
11. The tragic story of William's death on the day of his grandmother's funeral is told in the *Carmarthen Journal* of August 3 and 10 1917. Gravel Gwyn is part of the beach below Second Steps leading down to Scotts Bay.
12. The information on Dylan and S.B. Williams came from John Hughes, his nephew and son of Dr David Hughes.
13. Lycett has taken Thomas' birth date, and his death date of June 5 1907, from his bank employment record (email to David Thomas). Thomas' full address was Strathmore, Woodside Park Road, North Finchley. I have taken these details and the value of his estate from his Will.
14. The other errors made by Lycett are:
    p6: Florence was not left a share in the Pontypridd shops by her mother – this had been done in 1905 by her father.
    p9: DJ Thomas' grandfather farmed Glan-rhyd-y-gwiail (or gwial) not 'Glanrhyd y Gwinil'.
    p11: Lycett writes that DJ's elder brother, William, died around 1876, when he

was about seven years of age. But William, aged 12, was alive and well at the time of the 1881 census. Moreover, Thompson (1965) says William lived in London and worked in the drapery business. Dylan's letter to his parents of January 12 1947 refers to DJ and his brother Arthur travelling to London to see "about poor Will."

p13: Jim and Annie's farm was Pentowyn not 'Pentrewyn' and it was not "owned by the Williams clan in Llanstephan" – Jim and Annie were tenants of George Mears.

p42: Jim Jones' family did not own Pentrewyman. The 1910 land values survey shows it was owned by Thomas Dowdeswell of Llansteffan.

p44: Bob could not have sold 29, Delhi Street, because he never owned it – various Wills show that it had been left to Polly by her father, who then left it to Florence with a life interest only to Bob. Florence instructed that on Bob's death it should be sold and the proceeds given to Gordon Summersby.

p45: Thomas Williams was not entered on the birth certificate of his grand-daughter, Anne, as her father – no name was given.

p45: Anne's son, William, did not die on the same day as his grandmother, Amy. He died on the day of her funeral.

p117: Florence was not sharing the rental income from 30, Delhi Street – that went to her brothers Thomas and Bob, as Wills show.

p193: Florence was not left 2, Blaencwm by Theodosia – her Will shows it went to Idris Jones.

On page 44, Lycett uncritically quotes Nancy Thomas that Uncle Bob had been gassed in the First World War – this is very unlikely because Bob was 37 at the outbreak of the war, and his job as a coal trimmer would have been a valuable civilian contribution to the war effort.

15. Thanks to Reg and Eileen Evans for establishing through birth certificates that Marjorie Owen was not the mother or grandmother of Ken Owen. Ken Owen's parents were Annie and George John Owen; and his paternal grandparents were Harriet and James John Owen. Florence's letters to Hettie Owen are with Reg and Eileen Evans.

16. William's identity is confirmed in a letter of March 6 1965 from Hettie Owen to John Roberts of Perdita Productions. The letter is in the possession of Reg and Eileen Evans.

Part One: The Memories 1935-1945

17. NET Festival Series. The interviewer was probably Colin Edwards.

18. From Penllegaer, Swansea, lecturer at University College, Cardiff, translator of Dylan Thomas into German e.g. *Der Turm*, June 1946.

19. Poet, writer, critic, broadcaster.

20. The two Thomases seem to have got on well. Siân Phillips describes an encounter with them in the Park Hotel, Cardiff: "Neither inhibited the other and the words cascaded between them, flashing like water... The two Thomases were lordly and careless, profligate with their brilliance." (p111)

21. Dylan's letter to Glyn Jones of March 14 1934 suggests Dylan had some knowl-edge of Rimbaud by that date. In her interview with Edwards, Gwen Watkins says:

"Although Dylan read so widely in English, he knew very little about European poetry, and it was here that Vernon really did help him. He read Rimbaud and Verlaine to him, and translated them, and others of the French symbolists." Vernon Watkins first met Dylan in the spring of 1935. In her Edwards interview, Enid Starkie notes that when Dylan was in Oxford in 1946 he "talked a lot about poetry, and what he was particularly interested in was Rimbaud... I had discovered what I thought was an influence on Rimbaud, an occult dictionary – a *Dictionaire Mytho-Hermétique* – by an eighteenth-century Benedictine, where there were all sorts of images that represented the figures in alchemy... there was in that dictionary what you might call a repertory of ready-made poetic images. I was talking about this to Dylan and he said how wonderful, how he would love to find something English that was the equivalent of that... Dylan was very excited about this... it might be considered cheating on the part of a poet to take someone's images – Dylan did not consider this at all and he thought that, as I personally think, it is the way one uses these images, the way they are put together, and what they are intended to represent, that makes the interest of the poem."

22. *Lifer* 1938, *Jail Journey* 1940, *Turf-Fire Tales* 1947.
23. This was certainly not the writer Oliver Onions who died in 1961.
24. FitzGibbon says that Butterfield took over the flat, which had previously been Alun Lewis', in December 1944/January 1945 (Letter to Ralph Maud, October 1963, Maud Archive, NLW). There are two letters from Dylan to Butterfield in the summer of 1945.
25. Dylan also read swing magazines. See his letter to Henry Treece of June 1 1938.
26. Dylan liked to take people to St David's. Besides the trip mentioned by Trick, he took John Davenport there in 1938 and John Malcolm Brinnin in 1951.
27. Florence told John Marshall: "I remember when he was about five I would read stories to him, and if there was anything about hospitals in them he would cry..." *Daily Mail*, January 31 1956.
28. Dylan did not write to Trick after Trick's move to Wrexham in 1942. After the War, Trick was asked by student Ken Bishop to write to Dylan, to invite him to address students at the teachers' training college in Wrexham, preceded by dinner with the Principal, and other invited guests, and to stay the night at the Tricks'. Dylan replied to Bishop, not Trick, to accept. On the appointed day, April 13 1948, Trick and Bishop went to Wrexham railway station to meet Dylan, but he failed to turn up. Dylan's letter of apology to T.C.H. Parry, the Principal, is in *Collected Letters*. He did not write to Trick. (From Trick's interview with Colin Edwards). Dylan "dropped" Trick in the late 1930s, about the time that he was turning to Vernon Watkins for help with his poetry.
29. Wife of First World War fighter pilot Ira Jones. They lived in New Quay for much of the 1939-45 war.
30. Widow of a general, wife of a doctor and on good terms with the American Rockefellers.

The Memories: 1946-1949

31. Mario Luzi was a poet and Nobel Prize candidate. Edwards carried out two interviews with Luzi, in 1968 and 1969. This extract combines both. The interview was

done in Italian and translated in 2004.

32. Professor Bigongiari was a poet, academic and translator of Dylan's work.
33. For a short history, including Dylan's visits, see the book by Arnaldo Pini, the former owner (2000).
34. Parronchi was a poet, writer and critic. The interview was done in Italian and translated in 2004.
35. The writer Tommaso Landolfi, 1908-1979.
36. André Frenaud: French writer and poet, 1907-1993.
37. Montale was a poet and winner of the 1975 Nobel Prize for Literature. The interview was done in English.
38. Livi was a writer. The interview was done mostly in English.
39. The pub was and is called the Mason Arms – no apostrophe "s".
40. Dylan was at South Leigh from September 1947 to May 1949. In the interview, Mitchell shows Edwards the receipts for the settling of Dylan's paper bills, dated May 19 1950, February 28 1951 and July 12 1951. These bills were settled after Dylan had come into funds: the May 19 receipt seems to have been a payment by Caitlin with the $50 sent by Dylan from America (*Letters*, May 7 1950); the February 28 after Dylan had just returned from Iran; and the July 12 after Dylan had received money from Oscar Williams and Princess Caetani (*Letters*, July 10 and 18, 1951). In other words, Dylan took pains to settle these bills, some considerable time after they had been incurred – he was under no compulsion to do so, as he was living in Laugharne at the time.
41. In the 1963 BBC programme on Dylan, Locke dates this incident to South Leigh.
42. "I can vouch that P.H. Burton wrote the Ralph the books episode." (Aneirin Talfan Davies to Ralph Maud, September 1979, the Ralph Maud Papers, National Library of Wales.)
43. See also the interview with Nellie Jenkins on Dylan and Catholicism.
44. Later a film and television actor, including *Dad's Army*.
45. The participants were Cecil Day-Lewis, T.S. Eliot, Edith Sitwell, Louis MacNeice, John Masefield, Walter de la Mare, Edith Evans and John Gielgud. Dylan also read Lawrence's 'Snake', as well as 'Fern Hill'. Dylan was on the planning committee – see his letters to the Society of Authors in *Collected Letters*, 2000, March 5 1946 and following.
46. NET Festival Series. The interviewer was probably Colin Edwards.
47. Skoumal was Cultural Attaché at the Czech embassy in London between 1947 and 1950. During his stay he visited Ireland twice, and Wales several times. He translated many Irish and English books into Czech.
48. "Brief report on the Proceeding of the Congress", published in the Union's official booklet, *From Words to Deeds*, page 179. Much of it seems to have been written afterwards by Party officials – it is reproduced on pages 304-305 of FitzGibbon. See also Jiřina Hauková's comments on this on page 163.
49. Jiřina Hauková had translated some of Dylan's poetry and was an interpreter and guide on his trip. She had once been a member of Skupina 42 (Group 42). Originally inspired by surrealism, it brought together writers and artists interested in exploring "the reality of the city and its inhabitants and machines." Jiřina Hauková's husband, Jindřich Chalupecký (a literary critic, theorist and editor) was a founding member, and Hauková joined in 1945. It was closed down in 1948. In

her interview, Hauková mentions the Syndicate. This was founded in 1945 (several years before the communist takeover) as a general writers' organisation, open to all regardless of ideology.

50. Besides the people, events, meetings and activities described in Edwards' Czech interviews, Dylan also met with Vitezslav Nezval, who was head of the Film Department of the Czech Ministry of Information. For more details on Nezval, see page 345.

51. Kolár was a painter as well as a poet. He was imprisoned after police discovered his critical manuscript, *Prometheus' Liver.*

52. The party was held on March 7 in the suburb of Horní Krč. Besides Dylan and Holan, those present included Jan Grossman and his wife Viola Zinková, Josef Nesvadba, Jiřina Hauková and her husband Jindřich Chalupecký. A further description by Grossman is given on page 295. Holan's memories of the meeting were recounted to the poet Jan Zábrana in the 1950s. Zábrana's diary notes Holan saying: "Dylan was brilliant, brilliant, brilliant – we met at Grossman's in Krč. A chain smoker, there must still be ash ground into the floor at one place, he rubbed it around with his foot. We showed each other, with our hands: Shelley? Low. Keats? Hands up to his eyes. Big poet." Later in his diaries Zábrana has a short entry: "Dylan's face, the face of Dylan Thomas, was haunting me in a dream last night, so similar to the face of St. Michael by Piero della Francesca." (Thanks to Jonathan Bolton for this information.) Josef Nesvadba has also recalled the meeting: "I was present at the meeting as an interpreter, and so the situation that most impressed me, when both poets spoke in a language of their own, communicating directly. That was the first time I'd ever experienced anything like that in my life and I often recalled it later when Bateson's Communication Theory, extrasensory perception etc, came into fashion. It appears that some artists manage to communicate across the border of language." (Taken from Justl, 1988, translated for me by James Partridge.)

53. Zinková was an actor and the wife of Jan Grossman. Nesvadba graduated in medicine in 1950, specialising in psychiatry. He had translated English poetry into Czech from 1940 onwards. He became the country's foremost writer of science fiction.

The Memories: 1949-1953

54. In her interview, Mrs John Morgan Dark, Jane Dark's sister-in-law, also mentions the friendship with Fred Janes' sister, Kitty, and describes how Fred and Kitty used to come to Laugharne as youngsters.

55. Albert Lewin the director. The film was made in 1951, and the scene about the world land speed record was shot in Pendine. None of the extras, including Dylan, are recognisable. The film starred James Mason and Ava Gardner. Dylan's friend, John Laurie, also took part.

56. John Morgan Dark was the brother of Laugharne draper, Howard Dark, Jane Dark's husband, and Caitlin's lover. Edna Morgan Dark, John's wife, had first met Dylan when he was nineteen through her friendship with Fred Janes' sister, Kitty.

57. Laugharne and Llansteffan were always closely connected until the 1960s, when the ferry across from Laugharne to Pentowyn farm stopped running. Many

chapel-goers used to take the ferry to the other side and walk to services in Llansteffan or Llanybri. And, as Billy Williams describes in his interview, Llansteffan was one of the places that Laugharne people went to on Sundays to drink illicitly. The importance of Llansteffan throughout Dylan's life was described in chapter 6 of Volume One of *Dylan Remembered*. The material in the Billy Williams interview, about his trips with Dylan to Llansteffan by cabin cruiser, provides further confirmation of how closely Dylan kept in touch with Llansteffan during his days after 1949 at the Boat House.

58. Parsons was born in 1913 and lived in Laugharne until 1959. He owned a cockle and shellfish bottling factory.

59. David Mendelssohn Hughes was a man of learning and culture. He was also a gifted painter. His friends included Philip Burton, Richard Burton and Arthur Giardelli.

60. NET Festival Series. The interviewer was probably Colin Edwards.

61. Miller married Janina Martha Lepska in December 1944. They separated in 1951.

62. Interview with Nancy Wickwire and Sada Thompson, 1967. NET Festival Series. The interviewer was probably Colin Edwards.

The Memories: Summer and Autumn 1953

63. Edwards makes the following comments in his interview with Lawrence Gilliam: "I heard that he'd been having injections in his back at Laugharne before, or up in London perhaps it was, but people at Laugharne knew about it... 'cause I was trying to find some reason for, perhaps it might help account for, the injections that he got in America, certain drugs that are said, thought now, to have perhaps contributed to his demise." David Hughes, the family doctor in Laugharne, told Edwards he knew nothing about the injections – indeed, Dylan had never medically consulted him. Edwards comments that the word "pustules" had been mentioned in connection with the injections and Hughes surmises that injections may have been for a form of acne on Dylan's back. Nashold and Tremlett report that when Jane Dark cut Dylan's hair just before his last trip to America she noticed "a profusion of angry red boils across the back of his neck and between his shoulder blades." (1997 p25)

64. NET Festival Series, 1967. The injection mentioned by Wickwire was almost certainly ACTH, a cortisone secretant. Wickwire's account appears at first sight to be very much at odds with Brinnin's, who describes Dylan as "chipper and as full of song as a lark" when travelling from his hotel to the performance on the 25th. But Brinnin did not attend the performance – he describes how he spent the afternoon with Rollie McKenna in her apartment (1955, p261). It is very unlikely that Wickwire has conflated the evening performance on the 24th, when Dylan was also ill, with that in the afternoon of the 25th. If she were conflating, then she would be running together not just two dates, but an evening performance with an afternoon one, an ordinary performance with an outstanding one and an injection given before a rehearsal for the performance on the 24th with one given before the actual performance on the 25th. Furthermore, her fellow actor, Sada Thompson, was also part of the interview and she did not correct Wickwire's account of Dylan's illness and injection on October 25.

65. Letter to Colin Edwards, May 8 1964, in the Edwards archive, NLW.
66. Here I claim an editor's privilege to introduce the only piece in this volume not associated with the Colin Edwards archive. These are extracts from Paul Potts' largely-undiscovered essay on Dylan, "Instead of a Wreath" in his book, *Dante CalledYou Beatrice.* I hope the exercise of the privilege will be an invitation to read the whole essay, which was one of the very first biographical pieces on Dylan to be published in the UK.

Part 2 Stories and Facts

Chapter One: Death by Neglect

67. Formerly GP Principal, Veor Surgery, Camborne, and now Primary Care Advisor (IM&T) for Cornwall.
68. The sanatorium was at Talgarth, Brecon, and Dylan used to visit Jenkins in 1944 and 1945. See a letter from the hospital secretary to FitzGibbon, April 13 1964, in the FitzGibbon collection, Texas. I have written about Dylan's friendship with Jenkins elsewhere – see Thomas, 2000.
69. Caitlin and coughing: 1986, pp174-76. "Bronchial heronry" is in Dylan's letter to Oscar Williams of October 8 1952.
70. Nashold and Tremlett pp85, 114-115 and the inhaler on p19.
71. "...my father is dangerously ill with pneumonia." (to Margaret Taylor, August 5 1949). "My father is off the danger list. He had pneumonia as well, &, though the muck on his lung has not cleared up yet, the Doctors are optimistic." (to Bill McAlpine, February 12 1950).
72. To John Berryman, November 25 1953, in the Berryman Collection, University of Minnesota.
73. Dylan's first injection was just before May 8, and the others were on May 26 and 29, October 24 and 25 and three on November 4. The first four of these injections are detailed by Ferris (1999) and Nashold and Tremlett (1997) and some are referred to by Brinnin. The interview with Nancy Wickwire on page 239 confirms an injection on October 25 – it was almost certainly ACTH. Brinnin did not report this fifth injection but he was absent on the afternoon of the performance of *Under Milk Wood* on October 25 1953, when the injection was given – see Note 64 for further details.
74. Nashold and Tremlett's assertion about twice-weekly injections i.e. about eight in total in May 1953, is based only on Dylan's comment to Stravinsky on May 22: "I prefer the gout to the cure; I'm not going to let a doctor shove a bayonet into me twice a week." This is a highly ambiguous comment, and could just as well mean that Dylan had refused the twice-weekly injections. Feltenstein's bill for his services in May 1953 was "$20... for drugs and medications." Besides ACTH, he prescribed benzedrine, sleeping pills and probably the inhaler that Dylan was having to use. (Taken from Reitell's letter to Brinnin of June 4 1953, reproduced in Nashold and Tremlett, p23.)
75. We do not know the dosages given to Dylan, apart from the eight units of ACTH given before midnight on November 4. Even if we assume high doses, the course of injections was too brief to have produced Cushingoid features such as a puffy

face. Another side-effect that usually appears with a puffy face is striae, or furrows on the skin, which were not noted at the post-mortem. Finally, Dylan's puffy face was observed long before he had been given ACTH – it was apparent to Olive Suratgar in 1951 (p270). It was also noted by Sean Treacy (p235) in October 1953, some four months after Dylan's last injection of ACTH on May 29. We believe Dylan's puffiness may have been caused by hypoproteinaemia – see page 270.

76. Priscilla Sassi. Information on St Joseph's East was provided by nurses who had worked on the ward and remembered Dylan's time as a patient – thanks to Sister Rita King, the archivist of the Sisters of Charity, and Priscilla Sassi.

77. St Vincent's had 686 beds, of which half were in general wards, 13% in private rooms and 36% in semi-private rooms. The cost per patient day was: private $20.88; semi-private $16.71; general ward $16.03. (taken by Sandra Opdycke from *Financial and Statistical Information Relating to Member Hospitals of the United Hospital Fund of New York, and Hospital Statistics for Greater New York,* 1955.)

78. Even chance of life: Jill Berryman to John Berryman, November 5 1953, Berryman Collection, University of Minnesota. Ruthven Todd was also told on the day of admission that "Dylan's condition was so critical that he might die at any moment." (unpublished memoir)

79. Email to David Thomas, March 2004.

80. Brinnin's receipt shows he paid $24 for daytime nursing on Saturday November 7 and McKenna's receipt shows eight hours of nursing for $14.50 on November 9, probably from midnight to 8pm. Brinnin's receipts for private nursing care are in his archive at the University of Delaware; McKenna notes her contribution in her Edwards interview – see page 240 – and there is a photograph of her receipt on page 80 of her book on Dylan. In the early 1950s, there was a national shortage of nurses. *The New York Times* of May 3 1952 ran a front page article called *Shortage of Nurses Found a Peril to Health of Nation.* Even the prestigious and well-heeled New York Hospital had difficulties in recruiting nurses, as its annual reports show. Minutes of its 1951 Board meeting refer to a four-year survey in five Manhattan hospitals showing the average "quit rate" amongst nurses was 64% per year (research by Sandra Opdycke). The book by P.A. and B.J. Kalisch confirms the chronic shortage of nurses at this period; they write that "On a given day from 7.00am to 3.30pm [a patient] would probably see a professional graduate nurse for about six minutes" (1986). In their study (2001) of Ontario hospital admissions, Bell and Redelmeier suggest that not only are hospitals less well staffed on weekends but those who do work are likely to be less experienced; there are also fewer supervisors on duty.

81. The accounts of Brinnin and of Nashold and Tremlett describe Feltenstein's supervision. According to Nashold and Tremlett, it was not until the afternoon of November 6 that McVeigh and Gilbertson were able to snatch a few minutes' discussion with Dr George Pappas, chief resident of neurosurgery at the hospital (pp160-162).

82. Letter to John Davenport November 1953, NLW 14934E. John Berryman was given much the same picture: "There was really nothing they could do except maintain breathing & nutrition, keep him clear of mucous, and administer anticonvulsants... One of his doctors told me immediately after his death that there had

never been the slightest hope... his condition was so extreme that all they could exclude was haemorrhage." (Letter to Vernon Watkins, November 1953, quoted in Watkins, 1983, pp151-52.

83. Telephone conversation with George Tremlett, December 2003.

84. Murphy's memorandum is in the FitzGibbon collection at Texas.

85. This sign is found in patients who are deeply comatose. When a doctor runs a hard object down the sole of the foot, the toes curl downwards – a plantar response. If they curl the other way – an extensor response – it means there is damage in the 'long tracts' of nerves which run up to the brain and back to the foot muscles. Somewhere along that distance is a problem, and when associated with coma, the problem is likely to be in the brain. In Dylan's case, it was bilateral (both feet), so both sides of the brain were malfunctioning.

86. Both Ferris (p278) and Lutyens (pp202-204) give accounts of the incident that took place in the autumn of 1951 when Dylan threatened to kill himself after a row with Caitlin. Ferris also notes other threats from Dylan of suicide, including "nicking himself with a razor blade on one occasion, claiming to have drunk a bottle of Jeyes Fluid on another."

87. In their book on speakeasies, Kahn and Hirshfeld write that O'Leary's on "the Bowery had a recipe for smoke, made with Sterno. I don't know how anybody survived it." The owner of O'Leary's gave them instructions on how to make smoke. The formula ends with the warning, "For God's sake don't drink it." (G. Kahn and A. Hirschfeld (2003) *The Speakeasies of 1932*, Glenn Young Books.)

88. mg%. This nomenclature is no longer used. It would now be written as mg per dL (milligrams per decilitre)

89. Letter to Daniel Jones, January 10 1954, in the FitzGibbon collection, Texas.

90. Since Ferris in 1977, Dylan's biographers have given little credence to Reitell's observation that Dylan experienced delirium tremens, a disorder caused by abruptly stopping the use of alcohol. It most commonly begins between forty-eight and seventy-two hours after the last drink – Dylan's last drink was just some ten hours before the "delirium tremens" incident. People with DTs commonly hallucinate snakes, animals and bugs; Dylan hallucinated not animals, he said, but abstract shapes. Neither did Dylan show other signs associated with DTs: tremors, hallucinating family and friends in the room, picking at the bedclothes, staring wildly and shouting at, and fending off, hallucinated people. Dylan showed no mental confusion, disorientation or terror. DTs is most common in people who have a history of experiencing withdrawal symptoms when alcohol is stopped. But Dylan's own history indicates that he could stop drinking for periods of time without experiencing withdrawal symptoms. We believe that what Reitell described as DTs were mild hallucinations brought on by morphine, fever and poor respiration. The hospital staff may well have considered that Dylan's seizures and dehydration supported a diagnosis of delirium tremens; but the seizures were undoubtedly induced by Dylan's hypoxia, and the dehydration by Dylan's prolonged vomiting.

91. The blood cell count on admission was done on concentrated blood, since Dylan was dehydrated. After the blood volume had been restored by administering fluids, that figure would have dropped because the blood would have been more dilute. This fall in red blood cell concentration could have brought the figure below

normal, which is the definition of anaemia.

92. Dylan's mother, Florence, died of "(a) Coronary Occlusion (b) Coronary arterio sclerosis and Mitral Stenosis". His maternal grandmother, Hannah, died of "Heart failure accelerated by a broken leg result of accidental fall in bedroom." (death certificates)

93. FitzGibbon's biography was published in the autumn of 1965. Murphy's letter to FitzGibbon of January 4 1965 reiterates that he has sent the hospital information to FitzGibbon on the understanding that he would not disclose it in his biography: "I hope you don't intend to make an issue of Feltenstein's efforts, good, bad, or indifferent... I owe Feltenstein nothing but I did promise Dr Mahoney I would not stir up unpleasantness based on access to his hospital records." But in the same letter, Murphy notes that "I know you have other sources of medical data e.g. the autopsy report". It is a puzzle why FitzGibbon did not at least use material from the autopsy in his biography. FitzGibbon certainly had the autopsy report by November 1964, because he refers to it in his article in the *Spectator*, where his comment about the phrase "insult to the brain" being in the autopsy report first appears. Indeed, there is a reference to the autopsy report in correspondence between FitzGibbon and a doctor friend as early as August 4 1964. (Letters to FitzGibbon from Murphy, December 16 1964 and January 4 1965 are at Texas. FitzGibbon had obtained the autopsy report via Ruthven Todd and the Dylan Thomas Estate)

94. Letter to David Thomas, December 17 2003.

95. Bronchitis can also be affected by air quality, which in New York in the early 1950s was comparatively good, but the effects of any pollution could have been aggravated by the weather – it was unseasonably warm when Dylan arrived on October 19. Afternoon temperatures hovered around 20° C until November 4 when it turned much colder.

96. Dr Sheldon Cohen is Scientific Advisor, National Institute of Allergy and Infectious Diseases, and a Scholar at the National Library of Medicine and National Institutes of Health. Philip Rizzo is Emeritus Professor of English at Wilkes University, Pennsylvania.

97. Letter to David Thomas, December 17 2003.

98. Noyes, p190: "Morphine should never be given." Merck Manual, p1098: "Morphine and depressing hypnotics are contraindicated." Other American texts are silent on the matter e.g. neither Brain (1947, third edition) nor Cecil and Loeb (1955, ninth edition) mention morphine in the treatment of delirium tremens.

99. The midday and early evenings injections of morphine were confirmed for Nashold and Tremlett (p152) by Dr Joseph Lehrman – see Note 107 on Lehrman. The Intern Notes indicate that the third injection of half a grain of morphine was approximately half an hour before Dylan lapsed into coma i.e. sometime between 11pm and midnight. Another factor to be considered in relation to hypoxia and Dylan's breathing difficulties are the conditions in Dylan's "small dark" hotel room. It would certainly have been hot and stuffy with the window closed, for the outside temperature dropped on November 4 and hovered around 5° C from late evening to midnight. (Temperature details are taken from the *New York Times*.) Dylan had had trouble with stuffy American hotel rooms, as he made clear in his letter to Caitlin of February 25 1950.

100. "'Oh, John, why didn't I call the *police?*' No one calls the police, I told her, no one calls the police." Brinnin 1955, p278. Lycett's account (p370) that Reitell called the police via the hall porter, and that Dylan reached the hospital "within minutes", is plainly wrong. Reitell continued to feel guilt-ridden by her role in Dylan's death. Many individuals and organisations would have felt fearful of being sued for damages. Reitell certainly was: a 1954 letter from her to Brinnin says "No lawyers after me yet." (The letter is in the Brinnin papers at Delaware; it is quoted by Nashold and Tremlett, p233). George Reavey thought that Feltenstein, Brinnin and Reitell were engaged in a cover-up.

101. The sources for this narrative are: Heliker and midnight: Ferris p122; Brinnin and midnight: letter to John Davenport, November 15 1953 in NLW 14934E; letter from Todd to MacNeice, November 23 1953 – thanks to Andrew Lycett for this information; hospital receives phone call about 1am: Ferris, p322 and Dr Gilbertson in Nashold and Tremlett p154; ambulance driver blames Feltenstein for delay: Nashold and Tremlett, p154 after interviewing Gilbertson; Feltenstein and Beth Israel: Nashold and Tremlett p233.

102. Heliker: Ferris, p322. Todd: unpublished memoir, National Library of Scotland.

103. Lycett suggests (p368) that Dylan was suffering from Korsakoff Syndrome, a psychosis that affects chronic alcoholics, whose many symptoms include a decline in the capacity for thinking and learning, mental confusion, confabulation, impaired vision, eyelid drooping, muscle atrophy, speech impairment, incontinence and memory loss. Lycett produces only one sign, an apparent confabulation about a girl in a taxi. This is problematic for a number of reasons: one sign does not make a syndrome, and this particular sign could just as well be related to other clinical conditions. For example, Nashold and Tremlett (p145) use it and other signs to support their case that it was Dylan's diabetes that was affecting his brain, and cerebellum.

104. On November 6, John Malcolm Brinnin was told by Milton Feltenstein that Dylan had sustained "a severe insult to the brain" and this was due to direct alcoholic poisoning. The next day, Dr Gutierrez-Mahoney saw Brinnin and confirmed a diagnosis of "direct alcoholic toxicity in brain tissue and brain cells". On November 15, the opinion reached British shores in a letter from Brinnin to John Davenport which repeated Gutierrez-Mahoney's statement about direct alcoholic toxicity in the brain which had been confirmed, wrote Brinnin falsely, by the autopsy. (Letter to John Davenport, NLW 14934E.)

When Brinnin published his book in 1955, he simply repeated what he had been told, erroneously, by Gutierrez-Mahoney in the days before the post-mortem. In 1965, FitzGibbon failed to clear the air, writing that "according to his autopsy the cause of death was: 'Insult to the brain'", a phrase never used in the post-mortem report which FitzGibbon had in his possession.

There was no clinical evidence for the statements from Feltenstein and Gutierrez-Mahoney about direct toxicity because they were made, of course, before Dylan's death and therefore before the post-mortem. When Helpern's office issued the Notice of Death that toxic brain damage could not be confirmed, Gutierrez-Mahoney was forced to back-track. When he wrote to Daniel Jones on January 10 1954, he told him that Dylan had died from "chronic alcoholic poisoning" (FitzGibbon collection, Texas). Gutierrez-Mahoney was now choosing his words very carefully. He could no longer report that Dylan had suffered direct or even acute alcoholic poisoning of the brain, because that initial diagnosis had not been confirmed by Helpern or Gettler. Now Gutierrez-Mahoney was suggesting that there had been a chronic poisoning of Dylan's body i.e. Dylan's body had been poisoned by alcohol over a long period of time. It is difficult to know what he meant by this; perhaps he was going along with Helpern in suggesting that long-term alcohol consumption had brought Dylan to a state of chronic debilitation, providing a fertile breeding ground for bronchitis and pneumonia. In any case, Gutierrez-Mahoney's phrase "chronic alcoholic poisoning" fell out of use amongst doctors many decades ago and is now considered archaic.

105. Letter to FitzGibbon, December 16 1964, in the FitzGibbon collection, Texas. There is also a copy in the Edwards archive, NLW.

106. Letter from B.W. Murphy to FitzGibbon December 16 1964, Texas archive with a copy in the NLW Edwards archive.

107. The words are those of Nashold and Tremlett (pp167-68) who had talked to Feltenstein's colleague, Dr Joseph Lehrman (a pseudonym) in 1996. Lehrman was a neurologist and psychiatrist at Beth Israel Hospital, New York. Feltenstein discussed Dylan's case with Lehrman in the spring of 1954.

108. Gittins: pages 154 and 163. Gutierrez-Mahoney: in discussion with William Murphy, December 3 1964, FitzGibbon Collection, Texas.

109. Overawing and overruling: as described by Nashold and Tremlett, pp156-168.

Chapter Two: The Birth of *Under Milk Wood*

110. Ferris, 1977 and 1999 p2. Stephens 2000 p108. Ackerman 1998 Part IV and Davies 2000 p113 both seem to suggest that most of the play was written at the Boat House.

111. Tremlett 1993, pxxv; and "Laugharne and *Under Milk Wood*" in *Dylan Remembered* – Laugharne Festival Programme, 2003. Tremlett is also mistaken in his Chronology (1993, xxv) in dating the writing of the first half to 1951– the first half was sent to the BBC in late 1950.

112. *Daily Express* May 26 1978 and *Western Mail* November 4 1978. It was also the tourism authorities that helped to pay for a memorial plaque (a replica of the one in Westminster Abbey) that was erected in St Martin's Church, Laugharne, in October 1982.

113. Three occasions: London in 1945 – see Davin below on page 292; and letters to John Ormond March 6 1948 and Princess Caetani October 1951.

114. Letters to Pryce-Jones, November 21 1952; Gwyn Jones, January 6 1953; and David Higham, July 6 1953; Brinnin: p132; May 3 introduction: draft on a work sheet at Texas.

115. Review of *Under Milk Wood*, *Sunday Times*, March 7 1954.

116. Denzil Davies, letter in the *New Welsh Review*, 51

117. The Texas archive has a list of people from June 1953 that Dylan intended to write to, including Rymer. And see Thomas 2002 p102 for Dylan's return visits to New Quay after 1945.

118. The work sheet note on Willy Nilly reads: "Nobody minds him opening the letters and acting as [a] kind of town-crier. How else could they know the news?"

– quoted in Davies and Maud, 1999, pxxxvi. It is this note, together with our knowledge that Dylan knew Jack Lloyd, that provides the sure link between Willy Nilly and Jack Lloyd. There may, however, have been another influence at work: the idea of a postman reading people's correspondence also appeared in *Wishing Well*, a play written by Eynon Evans, and published in 1946 i.e. before Dylan wrote Willy Nilly's rounds into the 1950 BBC script. In *Wishing Well*, the postman is Amos Parry: "Two letters for Henry, and one from Portsmouth and the other from Llangynidir. A letter for you John, pension book back I think, and a postcard for you Delith, it's from Sally Jones. She says she likes her new place, her mistress is very good to her, she's met a nice boy working in a bakery, her appendix is worrying her again and she'll have to have it out, and the weather's lovely." There is a further point to make about Jack Lloyd the Post: in his letter to Margaret Taylor of August 29 1946, Dylan describes the scandal of Mrs Lloyd's double bigamy, and the Llareggubian spectacle of all her husbands appearing in court to give evidence of her good character. No doubt this scandal in particular, and New Quay's active and varied sex life in general, inspired some of the bigamous arrangements and lusty couplings of *Under Milk Wood*.

119. Information on the master mariners of New Quay was provided by Griff Jenkins, Keith Davies, Sue Passmore and Kelly's Trade Directories.

120. Quoted in Davies and Maud, 1999, p100.

121. Gwen Watkins: letters to Douglas Cleverdon, February 9 and 18 1968, and quoted in Cleverdon 1969, p5; Theodore FitzGibbon, p156; Constantine FitzGibbon, p267. Ivy Williams: interview with Colin Edwards.

122. January 22 1954 in the *Radio Times*. It has to be said that Cleverdon is not consistent in his dating of work on the play. This reference in January 1954 to New Quay is part of Cleverdon's first article on the subject, and it is closest in time to the events he describes. But in the *Radio Times* on June 28 1957, he noted that Dylan "conceived *Under Milk Wood* in 1947... he wrote the first half within a few months" i.e. Cleverdon here presumably has South Leigh in mind. On December 16 1966, he seems to confirm this in the *Weekend Telegraph* when he writes that "it took seven years to extract *Under Milk Wood*" from Dylan. But by the time of his 1969 book, Cleverdon thought it "unlikely" that Dylan had written much of the play at South Leigh. He then went on to conjecture that the first part "seems" mostly to have been written at the Boat House in Laugharne. By the time of Cleverdon's 1972 Introduction to the play, South Leigh and New Quay had been forgotten.

123. Davin, 1985, p126. Davin writes that after the party he returned to his home in Notting Hill Gate. Davin dates the party as happening before the autumn of 1945. This means before September 30, the day on which he and his family moved from Notting Hill Gate to London. Dylan's letters tell us he made visits to London from New Quay in January, May and June and from Blaencwm in August and September. The use of quatrains, probably much like those that conclude *Quite Early One Morning*, was largely to be abandoned as the play developed.

124. See the letters of May 24, May 29, June 5 and July 19.

125. The webfooted cocklewomen also appear in Dylan's letter to Margaret Taylor written in South Leigh in October 1948.

126. *Dylan Thomas*, a programme transmitted on November 9 1963.

127. Davenport's comment was in his pre-broadcast interview for *Dylan Thomas*, BBC Third Programme, 9/11/1963. He makes the same point in an article amongst his papers in the National Library of Wales.
128. There was also an Italian POW working at Waunfforte farm opposite Blaencwm – see Dylan's letter to Oscar Williams of July 30 1945.
129. Organ Morgan playing for nobody (Burton, in 1947) and playing for sheep (Hauková, in 1949) are both found in a passage at the end of the Davies and Maud definitive version of the play: "Organ Morgan goes to chapel to play the organ. He plays alone at night to anyone who will listen: lovers, revellers, the silent dead, tramps or sheep." (p61)
130. See Nesvadba on p170, and in letters to David Thomas.
131. David Higham archive, Texas.
132. David Higham archive, Texas.
133. The "awful" and "wretched" script of his autumn 1949 letters is now considered to be *Vanity Fair* (Ferris, 2000).
134. Tenby Arts Club; in Cardiff, to the English Society at the university on October, as noted in its Minute Book (letter to David Thomas on June 19 2001 from Charles Elliott, secretary of the Society at the time.)
135. Philip Burton left Cardiff and producing in October 1949 when he was made Chief Instructor at the BBC training school in London. Douglas Cleverdon then took over responsibility of getting *Under Milk Wood* finished and produced.
136. The first two Cleverdon quotes in this paragraph are from the BBC archives, and the third from Cleverdon (1954b).
137. See, in particular, Head of Copyright's memo of September 2 1952 to A/CTP about the "half-written programme" and Cleverdon's memo of August 26 1952 to Mrs Gray in Copyright about having only the first half of the script.(BBC Archives, Caversham.)
138. The resolution was in an engagements book – see the footnote to his October 9 1952 letter to Cleverdon.
139. All quotes from Brinnin are from his book *Dylan in America* (1955) pp186-227.
140. David Higham archive, Texas.
141. Note to David Thomas April 8 2001.
142. Interview, NET series, interviewer not known but was probably Colin Edwards.
143. Notably the section "In Butcher Beynon's" to "My foxy darling" and forty-six lines added to the passage "Oh, d'you hear that, Lily?" to "Organ Morgan's at it early..."
144. Interview, NET series, Colin Edwards archive, interviewer not known but was probably Edwards.
145. BBC 1963 programme on Dylan.
146. For example, a mother-song for Evans the Death, nightmare poem for Lord Cut-Glass, and Eli Jenkins' poem to a swan.
147. Davies and Maud, p82. In his July 6 letter to David Higham, Dylan had written: "Now, however, I am paying as much attention to the evening as, say, to the morning; & I hope to improve 'Milk Wood' very much structurally by this."
148. The article is in *Planet*, February/March 1995, and the poem, "Dylan Thomas in Tenby", is in Raymond Garlick *Collected Poems*.
149. The revised script was given to *Mademoiselle* in the week beginning November

26, as a note at the end of the text in the magazine confirms. A copy of the script with the revisions made in Todd's basement after the readings of October 24 and 25 was sent by Todd to Cleverdon after Dylan's death. See Cleverdon, 1969, p42.

150. BBC archives, Caversham.

Chapter Three: Conceiving Polly Garter

151. Dylan Thomas archive, University of Texas at Austin.

152. The children's song, "Polly, Love", was deleted for the May 14 New York performance, at the insistence of the producer, Elizabeth Reitell. It was never re-instated. The deletion is significant because it diminishes the portrayal of Polly as a mother and lover of babies.

153. I am grateful to Walford Davies for the information about the changes and to Robert Williams for that about Bill McAlpine and Harry Locke.

154. NET Festival series. Edwards was probably the interviewer.

155. Some of these references to babies and milk appear in the script given to the BBC in 1950, but many more, particularly the children's voices and singing, were added between April and October 1953, most when Dylan was in America preparing for the first full reading on May 14th.

156. *Cambrian News,* May 7 1937. Interestingly, the Maesgwyn family were twice related through marriage to Thomas Davies, who was the tenant farmer at Plas Gelli, Talsarn, at the time that Dylan and Caitlin were staying there between 1941 and 1943.

Chapter Four: At Ease Among Painters

157. Vera Phillips: see Thomas, 2000, p34. Grigson and Jones are quoted in Ferris, 1999, p99. FitzGibbon also writes that "...all his life he drew what he called his 'literary pictures' with a pleasant Thurberesque line and often with a caption." Hurdis-Jones: *Western Mail,* undated, Edwards archive, NLW. Surrealist painting of giraffe and the drawings for Reitell: Jeff Towns Collection. Oscar Williams drawings: Oscar Williams, Collection, Indiana.

158. *Evening Post,* November 9 1955

159. School art teacher: see *Dylan Remembered 1914-34,* vol 1 2003, p61.

160. Trick's observation is confirmed by Keidrych Rhys who wrote of *transition* that Dylan "was always fascinated by its published work in back numbers which he borrowed." (Letter to the *Times Literary Supplement,* March 26 1964.)

161. Govier, 1994

162. Ifor Thomas was born in 1911 at Cross Hands. He attended Swansea Art School 1929-1931 and the Royal College of Art from 1933. He was appointed to the staff of the Southampton School of Art in September 1935 as an etching specialist. He exhibited at the Royal Academy in 1934 and 1935.

163. William 'Bill' Evans was a portrait painter, born in Hammersmith in 1911. He showed at the Royal Academy and the London Group. Colin Moss later gained prominence as a painter of working class life. His sketch of the drunken Dylan hanging onto the railings of 415 Fulham Road is reproduced in Bennett's 1996 book.

164. *Ambit,* 1966. The last adventure was the Major's attempt to buy an oval billiard

table.

165. Taken from Daniel Jones 1977, p59.
166. J.H. Martin has described the time with the Mitchells in a letter to the *Times Literary Supplement*, March 19 1964.
167. Letter to Hansford Johnson, August 6 1937.
168. Johnson to FitzGibbon: March 18 1964, FitzGibbon Collection, Texas. Dylan's letters to Johnson and Henderson: June and July 1936. The homage took place on January 24 1954.
169. Remy, 1999, p147.
170. Letter from FitzGibbon to Ralph Maud, October 27 1963, Maud archive, NLW.
171. Waley was a translator of Japanese and Chinese poetry. There is more on Manger and the Waterhouse bookshop in Davin's 1985 book.
172. Email to David Thomas, 2004. *Arson* was a review of surrealism published by del Renzio in 1942. The poetry readings were organised jointly with del Renzio's wife, Ithell Colquhoun, also a surrealist painter and poet, as well as a leading occultist.
173. In his interview, FitzGibbon describes how Dylan introduced Matthew Smith to his father, DJ Thomas. Ebie Williams of Laugharne also mentions he met Matthew Smith at a party given by Margaret Taylor. Shephard made two small oils and a chalk drawing of Dylan.
174. Butterfield in notes to FitzGibbon, Texas.
175. Gilmore and Peake 1999, p57.
176. Book proposal: *Collected Letters*, January 3 1945. Tits and bums: Banting unpublished memoir, Tate Archive.
177. The other signatories were R.E. Waterfield and the poets Nicholas Moore and Lazarus Aarenson.
178. Barker, 2002 and see Collins 1999 on Dylan and the two Roberts in Tilty. Paul Potts has also written of being at Tilty with the two Roberts (1961, p210-211). Interestingly, the north Essex group established a coastal camp in Aberaeron. The Great Bardfield painter George Chapman discovered the Rhondda in 1953, and that year brought Pier Cottage in Aberaeron. His Essex friends followed him for visits and periods of residence, including Bernard Cheese, Michael Rothenstein, Duffy Ayres and John Aldridge, who painted in both Aberaeron and New Quay in 1954. Chapman also attracted other painters such as Denys Short, who later taught with Fred Janes at the Swansea School of Art.
179. Brinnin, p98. The following year, Caitlin was up in London and tried, unsuccessfully to get the poet David Wright to take her to a Colquhoun and Macbryde party – see Ferris, 1995 p118.
180. I am grateful to the late Kate Chapman for this information.
181. Letter from Dylan, June 9 1941
182. Arts and Battledress: Evan Yardley, conversation with David Thomas January 6 1999. Dylan may also have patronised the Arts Club in Dover Street – his letter of August 1940 to Royston Morley at the BBC was written in pencil on Arts Club notepaper (BBC Archives).
183. Van den Burgh was a journalist, author and boxing commentator, who later provided a review of Brinnin's book, *Dylan Thomas in America*, for *Poetry Review*, July-September, 1956. See Thomas, 2003, for more on de Wet's bust.
184. Dylan's letters to James are not in *Collected Letters*, but are referred to in Lowes'

1991 biography of James. The letters were in the James archive at West Dean College, Chichester, but have since been removed without authorisation and their whereabouts are unknown.

185. Conradi on Dylan and Iris Murdoch: p268.

186. Griff Williams (1906-1977) was born in Ton Pentre, Rhondda. He met Dylan after the War whilst he was living in Pendine. Griff married the writer Marion Eames, for whose help I am grateful.

187. Morris, 1979, pp28-29. The other significant surrealist painter to emerge after the War was the hard-drinking Scottie Wilson. We do not know if he knew Dylan but they had many friends in common including William Gaunt and Mervyn Levy.

188. The story of Dylan's meeting with Dali first appeared in the *San Francisco Chronicle* on September 29 1996, authored by Gabriel Neruda. It then appeared in various poetry journals, including the *River King Poetry Supplement, Pudding Magazine, Mandrake Poetry Review* and *Archipelago*, when it appeared under the name David Castleman. To read the article, go to www. archipelago.org/vol1-4/Three Tale.htm

189. Giardelli: conversation with David Thomas and see also Shiel (2002). Daniel Jones 1977, p58.

190. Watkins (1983), p91

191. Ceri Thomas (2003) has taken this point further in relation to the output in the 1930s of Dylan, Janes and Jones. Thomas has studied Janes' painting *Kipper and Pineapple*, and notes that its rhyming motifs of fish and fruit evoke both Dylan's "highly distinctive poetic forms" of this period and Jones' complex-metre musical systems.

192. Quoted in FitzGibbon 1965, p325

193. *Collected Letters*, early November 1933

194. FitzGibbon, 1965, p252

195. Texas archive

Chronology of a Death

196. Soon after Dylan's death, Ruthven Todd showed Dylan's claim was false, and that the most he could have drunk was eight whiskies – see page 240. John CuRoi also saw Dylan in the White Horse with "eight highballs before him" – quoted in Nashold and Tremlett, p151. Biographers concur it was no more than eight whiskies and point out that had Dylan drunk eighteen American whiskies (which would be equivalent to drinking thirty-six British singles) he would have collapsed there and then.

197. Reitell's memory of "sweet calm talks" is taken from notes that Paul Ferris made in his notebook when he interviewed Reitell in May 1975.

198. These descriptions of the breathing are taken from the Ferris notebook.

199. Gittins, p162.

200. This description is taken from Tremlett and Nashold, who interviewed one of the doctors in 1996.

201. Nashold and Tremlett date this second lumbar puncture to November 6, as does Brinnin in his letter to John Davenport of November 15 1953 (NLW 14934E). The hospital record shows it was done on the 8th.

Index

Dylan Thomas' relatives are described by their relationship to his mother, Florence, or to his father, DJ. In order to avoid repetition, both the chronology of *Under Milk Wood* and that of the death of Dylan Thomas have been indexed selectively. The Notes have also been selectively indexed. DMT = Dylan Marlais Thomas *UMW* = *Under Milk Wood*

Index

Mighty Joe Young 138
Miller, Arthur 358
Miller, Henry 205, 206, 207-08
Miller, Joan 210
Milton, Elizabeth Ruby 16, 255, 336
Milton, John 221
Ministry of Information 198, 334, 338
Minton, John 334, 335, 342
Miro, Joan 343
Mitchell, Bill 255
Mitchell, Denis and Endell 324, 330
Mitchison, Naomi 330
Monroe, Marilyn 173
Montale, Eugenio 107, 108, 109, 111, 115
Moore, Henry 326, 328, 334, 340
Moore, Marianne 358
Moore, Nicholas 388
Morgan, Frances 13
Morley, Thomas 359
Morris, Cedric 326, 327, 334, 346, 348
Morris, Desmond 343, 346
Morris, Johnny 344
Moss, Colin 327
Mozart, Wolfgang 243
Mucha, Alphonse 156, 345
Mucha, Jiří 161, 164, 295, 345
Muir, Edwin and Vera 162, 168, 169, 170, 171
Murdoch, Iris 345
Murphy, Dr William B. 264, 271, 281, 282, 283
Murray, Dorothy 'Dosh' 258

Nash, Paul 326
Nashold, James and Tremlett, George, on Dylan's death 353; delay in getting Dylan to hospital 277; diabetes 281-83; Dylan's breathlessness 254; Dylan's condition 267; hypoxia and oedema 274; injections of ACTH 256; role of drugs 281
National and International Eisteddfodau: Colwyn Bay 1947: 154; Llangollen 1953: 213-14; Llanelli 1930: 326; Swansea 1926: 326
National Library of Wales 24, 25, 27, 324
Navrátil, Václav 162
Nesvadba, Josef 164, 166, 296, 377
Neuberg, Victor 325, 331
New American Library 221
Newcastle, Theatre Royal 312

New Quay 11, 18, 31, 84, 98, 101, 321; cultural life 345; painters in 345, 388; sea captains 289; ship building 290; shooting incident 11; see also UMW; and DMT, at New Quay
New Quay, places: 2, Belle Vue 101; Black Lion hotel 18, 99, 101, 102, 187, 289, 292, 317, 322, 345; Brongwyn Lane 317; Dolau Inn 288, 322; Gwynfa 322; Llanina church and village 290; Lloyds Bank 319; Majoda 11, 100-01, 288, 289, 290, 291; Penwig hotel 319; Plas Llanina, Apple House 290; River Dewi 288; Rock Street 318; Sailor's Home Arms/Commercial 288, 318, 322; Tanyfron 318; Towyn chapel 319; see also Maesgwyn farm; and UMW, New Quay, influence of
New Republic 221
New Verse 326
New Welsh Review 285
New Writing 156, 159, 295, 345
New York: Academy of Arts and Letters 224; Alcoholic Board of Control 240-41; Artists Club 348; Atelier 17 studio 348; Bellevue hospital 261, 268; Beth Israel hospital 263, 277; Charles Street police station 241; Chelsea hotel 240, 241, 258, 259, 275, 276; Cherry Lane theatre 223, 348; City Morgue 268; Clover Leaf 227; Grammercy Park 262; Grand Central Station 183; Greenwich Village 220, 348; Hudson Street 241; Louie's Bar, Sheridan Street 308; New York hospital 261; Oasis 241; Office of the Chief Medical Examiner 268; Poetry Center 227; St Luke's chapel 230; St Vincent's Hospital, see separate entry; San Remo, Bleeker Street 349; Whitehall Spa 240; White Horse Tavern 241, 278, 324, 349; women's jail 224; YMHA 223, 227, 228
NZ Listener 297
Nezval, Vitezslav 159, 345
Nicholson, Ben 326
No Room at the Inn 136
News Chronicle 286

Observer, The 19, 312
Onions, Oliver 73
Ormond, John 10, 242, 294

21, 73; friendships with ministers 23, 100, 126; his children christened 24, 187; his children go to church 24, 187; ministers in the family 20-23; no theology 34; praying 73; symbols and images of Christianity 48-49, 146, 158; visit of Irish priest 195

DMT, and the theatre: acting abilities 142, 152-53, 237; writing for 237; *Desire Caught by the Tail* 347; *Hay Fever* 324; *The Devil Among the Skins* 74-75; *see also* Group Theatre

DMT, and Wales: against a society of Welsh writers 54; attitudes to Wales 41, 47, 54, 56, 62-63, 112, 124, 132, 137, 152, 154, 171, 183; attitudes to the Welsh language 112, 168; celebrating St David's Day 127; enjoyment of Welsh humour 41, 174; influences of Welsh literature, *see* DMT, writing, influences; interest in Welsh poems, stories, songs and jokes 40, 44; on being Welsh 36, 41, 44, 58, 112, 132, 153, 158, 174; not taught Welsh 44, 55, 187; singing in Welsh 73, 97, 125, 127, 188, 189, 224; speaking Welsh 44, 63, 73, 127, 139, 153, 160, 174, 187, 224; voice and accent 97, 174

DMT, and war: attitude to 1939-1945 war 43, 71; conscientious objections to 93-94; effect of 1939-1945 war 42-43, 70-71, 89, 94-95, 121; effects of Spanish Civil war 90; 'pacifism' 42-43, 93-94; views on Spanish Civil War 68

DMT, and war, response to Jewish suffering: 42, 43, 70-71, 81, 175; and anti-semitism 35

DMT, and women 70; aggressive towards 15, 16, 69, 215; ambivalence towards 15; boasts about sex 66; canards about 12, 219; 'extra-marital flings' 13, 85; inhibited by guilt 15; lack of interest in 13-14; low libido 12, 14, 15, 219; not a womaniser 12-15, 78, 102-03, 129, 131, 134, 152, 154, 167, 168, 215, 219; physically unattractive 14; prefers company of men 131, 134; prostitutes 69; sexually incompetent 14, 15; teenage friendships 13, 66; wartime girlfriends 13, 70; womaniser 144, 146

DMT, and work: respect for 10, 177; works

hard 10, 11, 33, 61, 66-67, 76, 97, 122, 138, 243; work output 9, 10, 11, 31, 104

DMT, at Blashford 31, 81-82

DMT, at Lampeter 96-99

DMT, at Laugharne 11-12, 31, 73-79, 173, 176-202, 232; behaviour 19, 184, 191, 196-97; drinking 17, 19, 180, 182, 184, 185, 186, 188, 191, 193; health 184, 192, 193, 198, 201, 202; keeps a pig 185; life in the Boat House 176-78, 181, 189, 198-202; not a scrounger 19, 182, 189, 190; produces a play 74-75; writing 11-12, 180, 183, 189, 198, 200, 201, 202; *see also UMW*

DMT, at New Quay 11, 99-103, 291-92; as regarded by locals 100-03; behaviour 101; drinking 101; health 100; life in Majoda 11, 100-01; writing 11, 100, 288-90; *see also UMW*

DMT, at South Leigh 11, 17, 19, 104, 124-140, 294-95, 343; as regarded by locals 130, 131, 132, 133, 134, 135; behaviour 125, 129; drinking 17, 125, 126, 127, 129, 130, 133; health 127, 130, 133; life in the caravan 124, 125, 129, 130; life in the Manor House 125-26, 130, 133, 135; manuscripts burned 126, 133; not a scrounger 19, 129, 130, 134; writing 11, 124, 125, 126, 128, 129, 133, 136, 294-95; *see also UMW*

DMT, drinking 16-18, 63, 84, 85, 122, 140, 152, 177, 214, 234-35, 236, 243; a social drinker 34, 38, 40, 65-66, 76, 96, 171; as a way into the world 167; atmosphere of pubs 18, 39-40, 87-88; behaviour 17, 65, 76, 87, 97, 102, 149, 182-83, 184, 189, 346; caught in police raid 188; choice of pubs 18, 39; drinking cider 65, 190; drinking Guinness 142, 190, 193, 201; drinking eighteen whiskies, false claims of 240-41, 266, 389; drinking 'smoke' and wood alcohol 265, 266; drinking spirits, occasions of 85, 97, 105, 125, 127, 149, 161, 162, 167, 171, 182, 184, 185; drinking spirits, seldom 67, 76, 85, 96, 97, 129, 135, 149, 180, 184, 186, 193, 217, 219; drinking wine 95, 114, 115, 123, 127, 156, 211; effect of alcohol on poetry 61, 105, 115, 116; moderation and abstinence 17, 18,

Index

About the Editor

David N. Thomas was formerly a lecturer and chief executive and is now a freelance writer. He is the author of *Dylan Thomas: A Farm, Two Mansions and a Bungalow, The Dylan Thomas Trail, Dylan Remembered: Volume One 1914-1934* and *The Dylan Thomas Murders*.

David Thomas' other books include: *Organising for Social Change; Skills in Neighbourhood Work* (with Paul Henderson); *The Making of Community Work; White Bolts, Black Locks: Participation in the Inner City,* and *Oil on Troubled Waters: the Gulbenkian Foundation and Social Welfare*.